Great Ideas in Computer Science with Java

Alan W. Biermann and Dietolf Ramm

Great Ideas in Computer Science with Java

The MIT Press
Cambridge, Massachusetts
London, England

This book was set in Times New Roman by Asco Typesetters, Hong Kong, and printed and bound in the United States of America.

Library of Congress Cataloging-in-Publication Data

Biermann, Alan W., 1939–
  Great ideas in computer science with Java / Alan W. Biermann and Dietolf Ramm.
    p. cm.
  Includes index.
  ISBN 0-262-02497-7 (pbk. : alk. paper)
  1. Java (Computer program language) I. Ramm, Dietolf. II. Title.
QA76.73.J38 B52 2001
005.2′762—dc21   2001030635

To our parents,
David J. and Ruth Biermann
Wolfgang and Dora Ramm

To our parents,
David J. and Ruth Biermann
Wolfgang and Dora Ramm

Contents

Preface

A Survival Kit for the Third Millennium

This book is written for people who find themselves on the outside of a high-technology world and who want to find a way in. If you have ever wondered what is meant by a Java class, a file server, an ethernet, the World Wide Web, or Pretty Good Privacy, this book shows you a path to the answers. You have been told you need a compiler, but why do you need it? What does it actually do? Watch out for certain types of problems: they are NP-complete, and you may not be able to compute the answer. You want to have a neat graphics picture jump onto your Web page when you push the button labeled "surprise." Can you make it happen? Your computer runs at 1 gigahertz: that is one billion *what* per second? By the way, what actually *is* a computer?

Most people are beginning to realize that "we are not in Kansas anymore" and that operating a spreadsheet program or clicking onto the Web is not good enough. With millions of people in the world hooking in to the high-tech network and every organization and computer connected to every other one, we need to catch up with what is going on. In our jobs, in our recreation, in our personal lives, we are going to have to live with these machines, and we need some skills and understanding to do it.

More Than a List of Facts

This book presents the story of computer science organized around the theme of the "great ideas" of the field. These are the discoveries, the paradigms, the simplifying equations that attract the attention of everyone who comes near, and they provide the best-known paths to understanding. The book begins with an introduction to the World Wide Web and then moves to programming in Java. The theory is that if you learn to format your own Web pages with HTML, and if you can program your machine to do some interesting tasks, you will truly understand them.

Once you understand programming, you will have a notation and a vocabulary to talk about computing and will be able to dig into the mechanisms behind the facade. This is the second area of study: the hardware and software that deliver the many services to you. What are the operating system, the compiler, the browser, and the applications programs actually doing when you ask for service? Why do they act in the peculiar ways they do? What can we expect in the future? This book has chapters on computer architecture, compilation, operating systems, security mechanisms, and networks, with detailed descriptions of what they do and how they work.

The third area of study examines the limitations and challenges of the field as it exists today. What are the paradigms for understanding the hardest problems that we face? What do we currently not know how to do but have some chance of solving in the years to come? What kinds of problems are probably not solvable by computers, now or in the future?

The book as a whole is designed to give a broad overview of academic computer science with an emphasis on understanding the deep issues of the field.

In Your Bones as well as in Your Intellect

The method of teaching is by doing rather than just by reading and talking. The theory is that if you personally go through the steps of creating a program to do something or if you hand-simulate a process, that mechanism and the related ideas will get built into your body as well as your mind. They will become instinctive as well as intellectually known. You learn about database systems by coding one in Java. You learn about system architecture by reading and writing programs in assembly language. You learn the mechanisms of a compiler by hand-compiling Java statements into assembly language. You learn to understand noncomputability by working with the proof on noncomputability and by learning to classify problems yourself as either computable or noncomputable. This is the problems-oriented approach to teaching that has been so successful in the traditional quantitative sciences.

A Course in Computer Science

This book is unusual in two ways. It covers a very broad set of topics (from HTML text formatting to program complexity and noncomputability), and it covers these topics to a relatively deep level (to the extent that students can solve problems in these domains). As such, it can be used in an introductory computer science course for students who will major in the field. These students will begin their studies with a broad view and will fit each succeeding course into a slot that has been prepared by the earlier studies. But the book can also serve as a text in the only computer science course that some students will ever take. It provides a conceptual structure of computing and information technology that well-informed lay people should have. It supports the model of FITness (Fluency in Information Technology) described in a recent National Research Council study (Snyder et al. 1999) by covering most of the information technology concepts that the study specified for current-day fluency.

A Thousand Heroes

This book is the product of fifteen years of experience in teaching "great ideas in computer science" at Duke University and many other institutions. The list of contributors includes many faculty and student assistants who have taught the "great ideas" approach. (See, for example, a description by Biermann of this type of course at several universities, in "Computer Science for the Many," *Computer* 27 (1994): 62–73.) Our teaching assistants have contributed extensively by helping us develop an approach to introducing Java, by writing many of the notes that eventually evolved into this book, and by developing the laboratory exercises and software for our classes. The primary contributors were Steve Myers, Eric Jewart, Steve Ruby, and Greg Keim. We owe special thanks to our faculty colleagues Owen Astrachan, Robert Duvall, Jeff Forbes, and Gershon Kedem for providing constructive critique, stimulating conversation, and technical advice. Ben Allen prepared some of the Java programs that are presented in the simulation chapter. Carrie Liken created some of the graphics in chapter 5. Matt Evans was the artist for most of the cartoons. Charlene Gordon contributed cartoons for chapters five and eleven. Other contributors have been David and Jennifer Biermann, Alice M. Gordon, Karl, Lenore, and M. K. Ramm, Jeifu Shi, Michael Fulkerson, Elina Kaplan, Denita Thomas, our several thousand students in courses at Duke, long lists of people who helped us with our earlier editions, our manuscript editors Deborah Cantor-Adams and Alice Cheyer, and, as always, our kind executive editor Robert Prior.

Studying Academic Computer Science: An Introduction

Rumors

Computers are the subject of many rumors, and we wonder what to believe. People say that computers in the future will do all clerical jobs and even replace some well-trained experts. They say computers are beginning to simulate the human mind, to create art, to prove theorems, to learn, and to make careful judgments. They say that computers will permeate every aspect of our jobs and private lives by managing communication, manipulating information, and providing entertainment. They say that even our political systems will be altered—that in previously closed societies computers will bring universal communication that will threaten the existing order, and in free societies they will bring increased monitoring and control. On the other hand, there are skeptics who say that computer science has many limitations and that the impact of machines has been overstated.

Some of these rumors are correct and give us fair warning of things to come. Others may be somewhat fanciful, leading us to worry about the future more than is necessary. Still others point out questions that we may argue about for years without finding answers. Whatever the case, we can be sure that there are many important issues related to computers that are of vital importance, and they are worth trying to understand.

We should study computer science and address these concerns. We should get our hands on a machine and try to make it go. We should control the machine; we should play with it; we should harness it; and most important, we should try to understand how it works. We should try to build insights from our limited experiences that will illuminate answers to our questions. We should try to arm ourselves with understanding because the Computer Age is upon us.

This book is designed to help people understand computers and computer science. It begins with a study of programming in the belief that using, controlling, and manipulating machines is an essential avenue to understanding them. Then it takes readers on a guided tour of the internals of a machine, exploring all of its essential functioning from the internal registers and memory to the software that controls them. Finally, the book explores the limitations of computing, the frontiers of the science as they are currently understood.

In short, the book attempts to give a thorough introduction to the field with an emphasis on the fundamental mechanisms that enable computers to work. It presents many of the "great ideas" of computer science, the intellectual paradigms that scientists use to understand the field. These ideas provide the tools to help readers comprehend and live with machines.

Studying Computer Science

Computer science is the study of recipes and ways to carry them out. A recipe is a procedure or method for doing something. The science studies kinds of recipes, the properties of recipes, languages for writing them down, methods for creating them, and the construction of machines that will carry them out. Of course, computer scientists want to distinguish themselves from chefs, so they have their own name for recipes: they call them *algorithms*. But we will save most of the technical jargon for later.

If we wish to understand computer science, then we must study recipes, or algorithms. The first problem relates to how to conceive of them and how to write them down. For example, one might want a recipe for treating a disease, for classifying birds on the basis of their characteristics, or for organizing a financial savings program. We need to study some example recipes to see how they are constructed, and then we need to practice writing our own. We need experience in abstracting the essence of real-world situations and in organizing this knowledge into a sequence of steps for getting our tasks done.

Once we have devised a method for doing something, we wish to *code* it in a computer language in order to communicate our desires to the machine. Thus, it is necessary to learn a computer language and to learn to translate the steps of a recipe into commands that can be carried out by a machine. This book presents a language called *Java*, which is easy to learn and quite satisfactory for our example programs.

The combination of creating the recipe and coding it into a computer language is called *programming*, and this is the subject of the first part of the book (chapters 1–6). These chapters give a variety of examples of problem types, their associated solution methods, and the Java code, the *program*, required to solve them. Chapter 7 discusses problems related to scaling up the lessons learned here to industrial-sized programming projects.

While the completion of the programming chapters leads to an ability to create useful code, the resulting level of understanding will still fall short of our deeper goals. The programmer's view of a computer is that it is a magic box that efficiently executes commands; the internal mechanisms may remain a mystery. However, as scholars of computer science, we must know something of these mechanisms so that we can comprehend why a machine acts as it does, what its limitations are, and what improvements can be expected.

The second part of the book addresses the issue of how and why computers are able to compute.

Chapter 8 describes machine architecture and the organization of typical computers. It presents the basic hardware at the core of a computer system. Chapter 9 addresses the problem of translating a high-level computer language like Java into a lower-level language so that a program written in a high-level language can be run on a given architecture. Chapter 10 introduces concepts related to *operating systems*; these are the programs that bridge the gap between the user and the many hardware and software facilities on the machine. They make it easy for users to obtain the computing services that they want. Chapter 11 examines a topic of great concern in our networked world, computer security. As more and more of our lives become documented on machines and the connectivity of every machine to every other increases, we wonder if our lives will be secure in the new millennium. The final chapter of this section (12) introduces computer networks and the many concepts related to machines' talking to each other.

The final chapters of the book examine the limitations of computers and the frontiers of the science as it currently stands. Chapter 13 discusses problems related to program execution time and computations that require long processing times. Chapter 14 describes an attempt to speed up computers to take on larger problems, the introduction of parallel architectures. Chapter 15 discusses the existence of so-called noncomputable functions, and chapter 16 gives an introduction to the field of artificial intelligence.

A great many programs have been developed to illustrate ideas in this book, and you can obtain them via the Internet. They can be found at Biermann's World Wide Web page at the Department of Computer Science, Duke University (http://www.cs.duke.edu/~awb).

An Approach for Nonmathematical Readers

A problem that arises in the teaching of computer science is that many instructors who know the field tend to speak in technical language and use too much mathematical notation for lay people to understand. Then the difficulty in communication leads them to conclude that ordinary people are not able to understand computer science. Thus, books and university courses often skirt the central issues of computer science and instead teach the operation of software packages or the history and sociology of computing.

This book was written on the assumption that intelligent people can understand every fundamental issue of computer science if preparation and explanation are adequate. No important topics have been omitted because of "difficulty." However, tremendous efforts were made to prune away unnecessary details from the topics covered and to remove special vocabulary except where careful and complete definitions are given.

Because casual readers may not wish to read every part of every chapter, the book is designed to encourage dabbling. Readers are encouraged to jump to any chapter at any time and read as much as is of interest. Of course, most chapters use some concepts gathered from earlier pages, and where this occurs, understanding will be reduced by reading chapters selectively. The programming chapters (1–6) are highly dependent on each other, and the architecture chapter (8) should be read before the translation chapter (9). Also, some of the advanced chapters (13–16) use concepts of programming from earlier chapters (1–5). Except for these restrictions, the topics can probably be covered in any order without much sacrifice.

An overview of what the book contains could be obtained in a single evening by reading the introductory (first) and summary (last) sections of each chapter. The intermediate sections contain the primary material of the book and may require substantial time and effort to read. However, sections with an asterisk before the title could be skipped without loss of understanding of the major lessons: they supplement the main chapter text by treating some points in greater detail.

Great Ideas in Computer Science with Java

1   The World Wide Web

World History and Where We Are

We begin by trying to decide what are the three most important events in human history. Which three occurrences since the beginning of time have had the greatest impact on the human species? Many might deserve this honor: the evolution of spoken language, the first use of tools, the discovery of fire, the discovery of the scientific method, the invention of the printing press, the Industrial Revolution, and so on. One could argue at some length about what the three greatest events have been. But this book suggests that a sure contender for the honor is the evolution of the *World Wide Web*, or more generally, a worldwide electronic communication network that potentially interconnects billions of individuals, businesses, governmental and educational institutions, libraries, and political, social, and religious groups as well as computers, databases, residences, automobiles, bicycles, briefcases, or even home appliances.

We know that the World Wide Web has been growing at an exponential rate. We know that businesses and governmental institutions have been rushing to get connected. We have seen dramatic steps in communication capabilities as fiber optic cables are stretched everywhere and earth satellites are deployed to keep us always in range. Almost every desk in every business has a personal computer, and we can now carry around laptop computers that communicate easily with the Web. We know we can find almost every book title in print, every newspaper being published, every airline flight that is scheduled, every movie title being shown, every university course being taught, and much more by simply clicking onto the Web and searching for the information. We know we can sit at home and do our job (at least in some cases or part of the time), participate in clubs, shop for clothes or a new car, sell specialized products, enter a chat room and share stories with complete strangers, explore a foreign land, or compete in games with people we have never met.

Where all of this will lead we do not know. It is both an exciting time and a frightening time in which to live. Of one thing we can be sure: it is a very good time to try to understand technology and especially networking. What is it, how does it work, what can

it do, what can it not do, how do we use it, and how do we stay safe within its environment? This chapter gets us started on these issues.

Let's Create Some Web Pages

We begin our study with an examination of the World Wide Web (WWW). We want to
know what the World Wide Web is, and we want to utilize its resources to help us learn
the many topics on our agenda. The task for this chapter is to learn to create Web pages
and to connect them to the World Wide Web. Our later studies will build from these
beginnings.

Here is text that we want to be able to view on a computer screen and that we want
others on the World Wide Web to see on their screens also.

Alfred Nobel's Legacy

Alfred Nobel, a nineteenth-century industrialist, died in 1896 and left a will establishing the Nobel
Foundation. This organization has been awarding, since 1901, annual prizes for
outstanding accomplishments to scholars, literary figures, and humanitarian leaders.

The Nobel Prizes are currently given for contributions in six different areas of endeavor.

We give this page the title "The Nobel Prizes."

If we want this text to become a World Wide Web page, we must add formatting
markers called *tags* to tell the computer display system how to present the text. The tags
must be written in a language called Hyper Text Markup Language, or HTML. Here is
the text with all the HTML tags included, to tell a computer system how to format the
page.

```
<HTML>
<HEAD>
<TITLE> The Nobel Prizes </TITLE>
</HEAD>
<BODY>
<H1> Alfred Nobel's Legacy </H1>
<P> Alfred Nobel, a nineteenth-century industrialist, died
in 1896 and left a will establishing the Nobel Foundation.
This organization has been awarding, since 1901, annual
prizes for outstanding accomplishments to scholars,
literary figures, and humanitarian leaders. </P>
<P> The Nobel Prizes are currently given for contributions
in six different areas of endeavor. </P>
</BODY>
</HTML>
```

The markers are easy to understand. There is no deep rocket science here. Each tag is clearly identifiable by the angled brackets that surround it. Thus, if H1 is a tag name, <H1> is the tag. This tag refers to some text that begins at the point where <H1> appears and ends at the tag </H1>. Note that the end tags all have a slant (/) to denote that they mark an end.

Here are some examples of tags. The page title is presented as

```
<TITLE> The Nobel Prizes </TITLE>
```

and the heading of the paragraphs on this page is

```
<H1> Alfred Nobel's Legacy </H1>
```

The first paragraph of the text is typed as

```
<P> Alfred Nobel ... </P>
```

You, the designer of the Web page, are telling the computer display system how you want the page to look. Here is a list of the tags being used and their meanings:

<HTML>   The text surrounded by the tags <HTML> and </HTML> constitutes an HTML-formatted page that is to be displayed.

<HEAD>   The text surrounded by <HEAD> and </HEAD> gives heading information for this page.

<TITLE>   Part of the heading information is the page title. This title will be shown by the computer system near the page when it is displayed. But this title will not be on the page.

<BODY>   This tag defines the material to be on the displayed page.

<H1>   This tells the system to create a heading for the material.

<P>   This tells the system to create a paragraph.

In all these examples, every begin tag <M> has a complementary end tag </M>, indicating both the beginning and ending of the text being formatted. In later examples, some begin tags will not have complementary end tags because the endings will be obvious without them.

Having designed a page and typed the HTML tags to display it, we would now like to see the page displayed on a computer screen. The program that will display it is called a *browser*. The browser is especially designed to obey the HTML commands and to put the material we specify on the computer screen. (Two well-known browsers are Microsoft's Internet Explorer and Netscape Navigator.) We will type the HTML-formatted version into a computer file called nobelinfo.html. You should type this into your own computer using whatever editor that may be provided. It should be in a directory

Alfred Nobel's Legacy

The Nobel Prizes

Figure 1.1

labeled `public_html` so that the browser can find it. Also, your computer must be attached to an Internet server. (You may need to get help from a friend to get started if you are not sure how to use your particular computer or if you do not know how to connect to an Internet server.)

Notice that when you use the browser to display your page, it will be formatted exactly as your HTML commands have stated but not necessarily as you have typed it. Thus if you typed two paragraphs but marked only one of them with the `<P>` and `</P>` tags, only one of them will be properly formatted by HTML. The browser follows the rules of HTML; it does not copy the way you have typed your text.

Thus, we have achieved a great thing. We have created a page and displayed it with a browser. This is the same browser that can reference pages from all over the world and display what other people wanted us to see. Those people have learned HTML and have used it to present their material to us. We are learning HTML so that we can return the favor. You can think of your page as an electronic entity sitting in the computer memory as shown in figure 1.1. Our next job will be to put more entities in that memory.

Now, let's create another page associated with the first, titled "Areas for Nobel Prizes." Here is the text for this page:

Nobel Prizes are given for outstanding contributions in these areas:

- Physics
- Chemistry
- Physiology or Medicine
- Literature
- Peace
- Economic Science

```
┌─────────────────────────────┐
│                             │
│  Nobel Prizes are given ... │
│                             │
│  ─────────────────────      │
│                             │
│  ──────────                 │
│                             │
│  ─────                      │
│                             │
│  ─────                      │
│                             │
│  ─────                      │
│                             │
├─────────────────────────────┤
│  Areas for Nobel Prizes     │
└─────────────────────────────┘
```

Figure 1.2

Here is the HTML version:

```
<HTML>
<HEAD>
<TITLE> Areas for Nobel Prizes </TITLE>
</HEAD>
<BODY>
Nobel Prizes are given for outstanding contributions in these areas:
<UL>
<LI> Physics
<LI> Chemistry
<LI> Physiology or Medicine
<LI> Literature
<LI> Peace
<LI> Economic Science
</UL>
</BODY>
</HTML>
```

This page uses the HTML construct called an *unordered list*, and each entry in the list is called a *list item*. <UL> specifies an unordered list, and <LI> specifies a list item.

Let's put this HTML version into a computer file called nobelareas.html (figure 1.2).

Now things get really interesting. Since we have two pages, we can build links from one page to the other. We will modify the first page so that the words "six different areas" are highlighted. Then if a person reads this page and wonders what the six different areas are, he or she will be able to click on these words and see the other page. We can do this by putting in a special HTML tag <A HREF=?> showing which words to highlight and what to do if someone clicks on those words.

```
<HTML>
<HEAD>
<TITLE> The Nobel Prizes </TITLE>
</HEAD>
<BODY>
<H1> Alfred Nobel's Legacy </H1>
<P> Alfred Nobel, a nineteenth-century industrialist, died
in 1896 and left a will establishing the Nobel Foundation.
This organization has been awarding, since 1901, annual
prizes for outstanding accomplishments to scholars,
literary figures, and humanitarian leaders. </P>
<P> The Nobel Prizes are currently given for contributions
in <A HREF = "nobelareas.html"> six different areas </A> of
endeavor. </P>
</BODY>
</HTML>
```

The displayed page will show the words "six different areas" highlighted.

Figure 1.3 shows a symbolic representation of the two pages and the link between them.

We are still not done, however. We can complete the picture by enabling a person who is looking at the second page to click on the words "Return to main." and transfer back to the previous page.

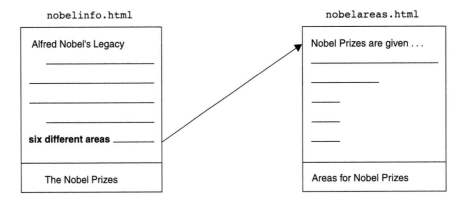

Figure 1.3

```
<HTML>
<HEAD>
<TITLE> Areas for Nobel Prizes </TITLE>
</HEAD>
<BODY>
Nobel Prizes are given for outstanding contributions in these areas:
<UL>
<LI> Physics
<LI> Chemistry
<LI> Physiology or Medicine
<LI> Literature
<LI> Peace
<LI> Economic Science
</UL>
<A HREF = "nobelinfo.html"> Return to main. </A>
</BODY>
</HTML>
```

Figure 1.4 shows how the two pages look with their installed links. You should type them in and make sure the links properly enable you to jump from one page to the other.

This is a nice result. But on more careful thought, it is much more than nice; it is an incredible, astounding, and world-altering discovery. The two pages compose a web—a small web, but still a web. And this is how the World Wide Web got started. Two pages of the kind we have made were linked together some years ago. Then more pages were added by various people and then more. Now there are tens of millions of people and pages all connected by the means we have shown, and they are changing the world in the manner we discussed in the first section.

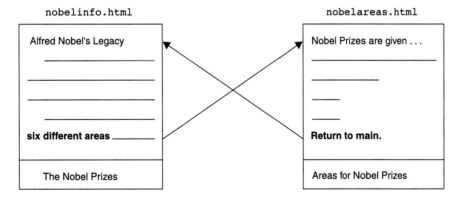

Figure 1.4

We can make still another change to our pages; we can put in an address to a remote site. Why not enable the user to click on the words "Nobel Foundation" and see the entry page (the *home page*) of the Nobel Foundation in Stockholm, Sweden? Not only will the user be able to see our pages but he or she will have a convenient way to jump to the source documents prepared by the originating organization. So here is another HTML version of the first page,

```
<HTML>
<HEAD>
<TITLE> The Nobel Prizes </TITLE>
</HEAD>
<BODY>
<H1> Alfred Nobel's Legacy </H1>
<P> Alfred Nobel, a nineteenth-century industrialist, died
in 1896 and left a will establishing the <A HREF =
"www.nobel.se"> Nobel Foundation </A>. This organization
has been awarding, since 1901, annual prizes for
outstanding accomplishments to scholars, literary figures,
and humanitarian leaders. </P>
<P> The Nobel Prizes are currently given for contributions
in <A HREF = "nobelareas.html"> six different areas </A> of endeavor.
</P>
</BODY>
</HTML>
```

Figure 1.5 shows a symbolic representation of the two pages with installed links.

Suddenly our toy classroom network has jumped to mammoth size because the Nobel Foundation page has numerous additional links for users to follow. A large number of pages that are interlinked in this way compose a *hypertext*; such entities have been studied by scientists for years. One can have arbitrarily many links from any page to any others. It contrasts with the standard notion of a book, which orders all its pages in a simple row. The psychological, artistic, and pedagogic implications of these two forms of organizing pages remain issues for research.

As an additional feature, the pages we have created are reachable by anyone on the Internet if you have placed them in the directory `public_html` and if your computer is connected to an Internet server. All that anyone needs to do is use a browser and go to the address of your *home site* adding `/nobelinfo.html` to the end of the address. For example, Biermann has a Web address of http://www.cs.duke.edu/~awb and The Nobel Prizes information page can be referenced by typing `http://www.cs.duke.edu/~awb/nobelinfo.html` into any Web-connected browser. (Remember that file `nobelinfo.html` was typed into directory `public_html` so that the browser could find it.)

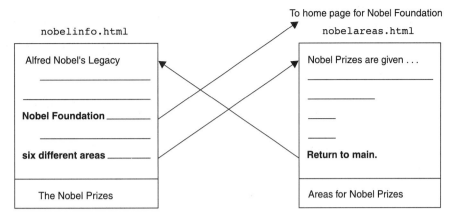

Figure 1.5

In order to make these links to distant pages actually work, the browsers that interpret the HTML and display the text must have a feature not yet discussed. If one has an HREF that points to another page, the browser must be able to follow that address and obtain the HTML document to display. This address-following capability is quite complex because it must send a request across communications networks to foreign computers and do the retrieval. There is an array of features that browsers must have to enable such references to succeed. They will not be discussed further here. We will only acknowledge that they exist, that they are complex, and that the browser must have them.

This concludes an ambitious section of this book. We examined a single page and how to display it with an ordinary browser. We showed how to construct links between pages and build a web or network. Finally, we connected our web to the World Wide Web, thus connecting ourselves to the dragon that is changing the world.

Exercises

1. Identify what, in your opinion, were the three most significant events in the history of humankind. Justify your answer.

2. Name a type of business (if you can) that will *not* be affected by the World Wide Web in the coming years. Justify your answer.

3. Type in the pages shown in this section and view them with a browser.

4. The first HTML page in this section has three different types of titles. Explain each one, its function, and where it appears on the display: The Nobel Prizes, Alfred Nobel's Legacy, and nobelinfo.html.

5. Create a home page for yourself using HTML, telling the major things that you would like the world to know about you. Have a friend view your Web page from a separate computer to be sure that the addressing conventions are working and that your page is truly on the Web.

6. Who won the Nobel Prize in Economics in 1982? What was the first year in which this prize was given? You should be able to answer these questions by following links from The Nobel Prizes page created in this section.

More HTML

This section describes a few more features of HTML. The reader should examine a standard reference for a complete description of this language and its many capabilities. (This section for the most part follows *A Beginner's Guide to HTML* as it appears at http://www.ncsa.uiuc.edu/General/Internet/WWW/HTMLPrimer.html.)

In addition to the unordered list (UL) already described, HTML allows numbering of list items. This is done with the <OL> tag in the expected way:

```
<OL>
<LI> Physics
<LI> Chemistry
<LI> Economics
</OL>
```

which will appear on a Web page as a numbered list

1. Physics
2. Chemistry
3. Economics

Another characteristic of lists is that they can be nested. Thus, one can have a list of lists. We leave the exploration of this idea to the exercises.

One can create a list of definitions with the <DL> tag, as in the following:

```
<DL>
<DT> HTML
<DD> Hyper Text Markup Language
<DT> WWW
<DD> World Wide Web
</DL>
```

This will produce a two-column list on a Web page:

HTML

      Hyper Text Markup Language

WWW

      World Wide Web

    In the previous section, `<H1>` was used to create a heading for a section of text. HTML has additional tags `<H2>`, `<H3>`, ..., `<H6>`, which create sequentially lower levels of headings. Thus, if we wanted to write a section for a Web page about HTML lists that contains subsections on unordered lists and ordered lists, we might type

```
<H1> Lists </H1>
<P> There are two types of lists, unordered lists and
ordered lists. </P>
<H2> Unordered Lists </H2>
<P> Unordered lists have the properties that ... </P>
<H2> Ordered Lists </H2>
<P> Ordered lists are also quite useful ... </P>
```

This would appear on the Web page as

Lists

There are two types of lists, unordered lists and ordered lists.

Unordered Lists

Unordered lists have the properties that . . .

Ordered Lists

Ordered lists are also quite useful . . .

    To make words boldface or italic, use `<B>` or `<I>`.

    Suppose you wish to type something and be guaranteed that the characters and spacing you use will be displayed on a Web page. You can use the tag `<PRE>` to do this. Thus, the HTML

```
<PRE>
     H    H     I
     H    H     I
     HHHHH      I
     H    H     I
     H    H     I
</PRE>
```

will show on a Web page as

```
H   H   |
H   H   |
HHHHH   |
H   H   |
H   H   |
```

If you wish to put in a horizontal line, try <HR>. You can put parameters on this, as in <HR SIZE=4 WIDTH="50%">, which means use a size 4 line and cover only 50 percent of the window width.

The addressing scheme for the World Wide Web uses what are called *Uniform Resource Locators* (URLs). The format for these addresses is

scheme ://*host.domain [: port] / path / filename*

where *scheme* is one of these:

file	a file on your local system
ftp	a file on an anonymous ftp server
http	a file on a World Wide Web server
gopher	a file on a Gopher server
WAIS	a file on a WAIS server
news	a USEnet newsgroup
telnet	a connection to a telnet-based service

The *port* number is usually omitted, and the other parts must be specified as key segments of the address.

You can include an image such as your own picture on a Web page by storing the image at a URL address in a standard format and then using <IMG SRC=ImageName>, where ImageName is the URL of the image file. You will need to check a standard manual for details on how to do this.

HTML provides many other features, such as the ability to create a table. If you format correctly, the system will create a table and put in all the entries as you specify them. You can also ask users to fill in a form and then gather the information that people may enter and send to you.

An interesting exercise for anyone studying HTML is to examine Web pages that others have created and see how they formatted them. You can do this by finding a page of interest on the Web and clicking on the View menu item of the browser to see the actual HTML that created that page. For example, if you go to Biermann's Web page and click on View, you will get this:

```
<HEAD>
<TITLE>Alan W. Biermann</TITLE>
</HEAD>
<BODY><P>
<HR>
<A NAME=tex2html1 HREF=sectionstar3_1.html>
<IMG ALIGN=MIDDLE SRC="next.gif"></A><BR>
<B>Next:</B>
<A NAME=tex2html2 HREF=sectionstar3_1.html>
EDUCATION</A><HR>
```

and much more.

Exercises

1. Create one or several Web pages that use all the features described in this section. Use a standard browser to view your page to make sure your text is formatted as you expected.

2. Find a standard HTML reference manual on the Web and read about formatting tables. Put a table into one of your pages using this feature.

We Love HTML, But ...

We are not going to spend more time on HTML in this book. You may never see very much of it again after reading this chapter. We study HTML not because you will use it a lot but because you cannot understand what the World Wide Web is unless you have studied HTML. But once you understand both, you can move on to the next level of our computer science and networking course. Many people make a lot of money programming in HTML, but that is not our goal here.

In fact, you may be able to create all the HTML you need by using programs designed to do that automatically. If you wish to do a standard job such as creating a personal Web page, you can use a program that will ask you a series of questions and then synthesize the needed HTML. Or you can use an editor such as Microsoft Word to type your document and just select the Save as Web Page option to have your HTML commands created.

Exercises

1. Call up a program that will automatically create HTML code and use it to create a Web page without writing any HTML. Then study the HTML code that it created automatically.

2. Use Microsoft Word to create a document and have it generate your HTML automatically.

Summary

Observing the many changes in lifestyle and capabilities that the World Wide Web is enabling, we suspect that humankind is entering a new era. One cannot predict what wonderful things and what new dangers may present themselves in the coming years. But certainly we are wise to try to understand the World Wide Web so that we will be prepared to profit from its strengths and protect ourselves from its dangers. This chapter has provided a basis for that understanding by showing how to create a simple two-page web and how to make it part of the WWW.

We studied the basics of HTML and the use of a browser for viewing HTML pages. In the next chapter, we will learn that HTML is but a kindergarten-level introduction to what really can be done. Besides simply displaying a page on a screen, we might like to see lots of action on the page. Perhaps we would like the page to ask questions and respond to answers. Or maybe we would like the page to have buttons that can be pushed to activate actions of one kind or another. It is possible that we would like the page to calculate some useful numbers or to display little cartoon figures. All of this and more can be done with the programming language Java, as you will see in the next chapter.

2   Watch Out: Here Comes Java

Let's Put Some Action into Those Web Pages

In chapter 1, we studied how to create Web pages and link them to others on the World Wide Web. Now we want to put some action into these pages. We want them to jump around, flash bright colors, and compute complicated things. Java is a programming language that will enable us to do all these things and more.

As a first example, suppose we wish to modify our Nobel Prizes Web pages so that a user can ask for advice on finding some particularly interesting stories about Nobel prize winners. We assume the user will read the main page, and we place a question at the bottom of that page with buttons the user can push to indicate his answer. The question will be "Would you like to read about a scientist?" The user will be able to push the appropriate button, Yes or No, and then a new question will appear. By answering the series of questions, the user will get the desired advice. Here is a version of The Nobel Prizes page with the needed change:

```
<HTML>
<HEAD>
<TITLE> The Nobel Prizes </TITLE>
</HEAD>
<BODY>
<H1> Alfred Nobel's Legacy <H1/>
<P> Alfred Nobel, a nineteenth-century industrialist, died
in 1896 and left a will establishing the <A REF =
"www.nobel.se"> Nobel Foundation</A>. This organization
has been awarding, since 1901, annual prizes for
outstanding accomplishments to scholars, literary figures,
and humanitarian leaders. </P>
```

```
<P> The Nobel Prizes are currently given for contributions
in <A REF = "nobelareas.html"> six different areas </A> of
endeavor.
</P>
<P> If you would like to read an especially interesting
story about a prize winner, you should answer the questions
below for a suggestion. Then look up the suggested person
on the Nobel Foundation Web pages.
</P>
<APPLET code = "StoryAdvice.class"> </APPLET>
</BODY>
</HTML>
```

When this page is presented by the Web browser, the HTML code will cause it to jump at the step

```
<APPLET code = "StoryAdvice.class">
```

and to execute a program called an *applet*, which will do the work of asking the questions, placing the buttons on the screen, and responding to the button pushes. Here is how the page will appear, assuming the Java applet has been written carefully, placed in the same directory as the HTML file, and given the name StoryAdvice.class.

Alfred Nobel's Legacy

Alfred Nobel, a nineteenth-century industrialist, died in 1896 and left a will establishing the **Nobel Foundation**. This organization has been awarding, since 1901, annual prizes for outstanding accomplishments to scholars, literary figures, and humanitarian leaders.

The Nobel Prizes are currently given for contributions in **six different areas** of endeavor.

If you would like to read an especially interesting story about a prize winner, you should answer the questions below for a suggestion. Then look up the suggested person on the Nobel Foundation Web pages.

Would you like to read about a scientist?

| Yes | | No |

Advice:

Suppose the user pushes the Yes button. Then a new question will be asked: "Would you like to read about Albert Einstein?" and the user will be able to answer again. The questions will continue until the program comes to an appropriate point to present advice. Thus, if the user indicated an interest in a scientist and responded yes to the suggestion of Albert Einstein, the program might respond that Einstein received the Nobel Prize in Physics in 1921 and that a brief biography of him is given on the Nobel Foundation Website.

The point is that HTML code can call a computer program that can be designed to execute almost any process we can imagine. Thus, our energies will now turn to the issue of computer programming—what it is and how you do it. That is the subject of this chapter and of several that follow it.

The Big Deal: Computer Programming

In the old days before computers, if we wanted to do a job, we had to *do* the job. But with computers, we can do many jobs by simply writing down what is to be done. A machine can do the work. If we want to add numbers, search for a fact, flash bright colors on a Web page, format and print a document, distribute messages to colleagues, or do other tasks, we can write a recipe for what is to be done and walk away while a machine obediently and tirelessly carries out our instructions. Our recipe could be distributed to many computers, and they could all work together to carry out our instructions. Even after we retire from this life, computers may still be employed to do the same jobs following the commands that we laid down.

The recipes that we are discussing will, of course, be coded as *programs*. The preparation and writing of them is called *programming*, which implements a kind of "work amplification" that is revolutionizing human society. Programming enables a single person to do a finite amount of work—the preparation of a computer program—and to achieve, with the help of a computer, an unbounded number of results. Thus, productivity is no longer simply a function of the number of people working; it is a function of the number of people and the number of machines working.

There is even more good news: computers are relatively inexpensive, and the cost to buy one is continually decreasing. Machines with 64,000-word memories and 1 microsecond instruction times cost $1 million four decades ago. Now we can buy a machine with roughly one thousand times the memory and speed for about $1,000. For the cost of one month of a laborer's time, we can purchase a machine that can do some tasks faster than a thousand people working together.

Object-Oriented Programming

To cash in on this obvious bonanza, we need to learn to program. But we want not only to program but to program well, and that leads to a long list of concerns that we consider in this book. Specifically, we want to be sure our programs are correct and that we can verify this. Second, they should be easy to modify and upgrade to provide more capabilities. Finally, they should be reusable, either alone, or as components of larger, more ambitious programs. (Recipes for cooking also have such properties. For example, they are usually specified in terms of family-sized meals, not in quantities to feed a crowd. They specify things in units easy to use, for example, cups of flour rather than grams of flour.)

Experience has led us to a way of organizing programs called *object-oriented programming*. In this paradigm, problems and their solutions are packaged in terms of entities called *classes*.

A class contains both information, called *data*, and functionality. Let's use the analogy of an organ that we might find in a home or a church. An organ usually has settings or stops that define the tone quality. These settings are data for that organ. Other data are the volume setting, which keys are being pressed, and so forth. If we have the same model of that particular brand of organ and we duplicate all the data—the settings, keys pressed, and volume—we should get an identical sound. A modern electronic organ might even be able to store music and produce complete pieces automatically. That stored music would be more data.

The functionality of the organ is represented by what it can do. If we press a key, middle C, for example, we expect the organ to emit a tone of that pitch with the tone qualities specified by the various settings. For organs with stored music, "play selection 3" might be a function that plays J. S. Bach's "Toccata and Fugue in D minor."

Our goal, then, is to organize our programs in terms of classes, where each class usually has both data and functionality. Functionality in a class is called a *method*. Thus, in a program to simulate an organ, we would create an `organ` class with several methods. These might include the method `PlayNote()` that would cause a note to be played. A useful program would also need methods to specify chords, duration of the sound, and so on. It would also have methods to play stored selections, acquire new selections, delete old ones (memory is finite), and change the stops and the volume. The names of the methods can be thought of as the verbs in the language. Thus, the action of playing a note on an organ would be specified by the verb `PlayNote`.

Here is a rough idea of how this class would be specified using Java conventions:

```
public class Organ
{
    Data Keys, Stops, Other;

    public void PlayNote(P x)
    {
        Java code
    }
```

```
    public void SetStop(P x)
    {
        Java code
    }
    etc.
}
```

Another analogy might be a lawn mower. Data here consist of `Location`, `Direction`, `IsRunning` (true/false), `FuelLevel`, `OilLevel`, and `ThrottleSetting`. Some methods are `StartEngine`, `StopEngine`, `SetSpeed`, `GoForward`, `GoBackward`, `TurnLeft`, and `TurnRight`. The process of using the mower might involve executing some of these verbs (methods). One could go into more detail, but this is sufficient to illustrate a `LawnMower` class:

```
public class LawnMower
{
    Data Location, Direction, IsRunning, ... ;

    public void StartEngine()
    {
        Java code
    }
    public void StopEngine()
    {
        Java code
    }
    etc.
}
```

Exercises

1. Pick some nontrivial object and design a class for it. Note that it should include both data and functionality.

2. Data and function names may not be unique to a particular class. Think of a data item that might be suitable for both an electronic organ and a lawn mower.

3. Why would a method like `print` or `report` be useful with almost any class you can imagine?

The Java Programming Language

Our programming examples and exercises use the programming language Java. This language is relatively easy to learn and is embedded in a software system that enables students to link to many other programs. Thus, it provides a path into a rich environment for programming within which one can grow and mature for a long time. Since Java is object-oriented, it exemplifies the paradigm that computer scientists currently recommend, and it teaches many of the concepts needed to program in other object-oriented languages. Java is also specially designed to run in networked environments.

We will not study programming in the usual fashion, by learning the voluminous details of a programming language. We will not, for example, mention all rules for placement of semicolons and commas, the most general form of every language construct, the number of characters allowed in variable names, or the maximum allowed sizes of numbers or string lengths. We will have all the pleasure of reading and writing simple programs while suffering as little as possible from syntactic precision and encyclopedic completeness.

We will use only a fraction of the features of Java in order to keep the language-learning task under control. If all of Java were to be learned, there would be no time to study the central theme of this book: the great ideas of computer science. Since only enough details are given here to enable readers to understand sample programs and to write similar programs as exercises, those who want to write more ambitious programs are advised to have a Java manual at hand for reference.

If we are to study programming, we must program something. It would be nice to write programs that embody some useful information-processing structures and that are simultaneously educational and easy to understand. The first domain for programming in this book is thus *decision trees*. Decision trees can be used for classifying objects, for interviewing people, and for many other tasks. An example of a decision-tree-based program is the advice-giving applet at the bottom of The Nobel Prizes page. We will study decision trees and how to write programs for them.

Decision Trees

Suppose we wish to recommend which Nobel winner the user might enjoy reading about. A good way to make the decision of whom to recommend is to ask the user a series of questions. The first question we might ask is whether she wants to read about a scientist. We formulate the question and then indicate with arrows a direction to follow for the next question (figure 2.1). Then we decide what questions should be asked next, depending on the first answer (figure 2.2).

Let's assume that after asking two questions, it is possible to make the appropriate recommendation. Then the decision tree can be completed as in figure 2.3.

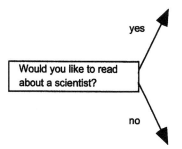

Figure 2.1

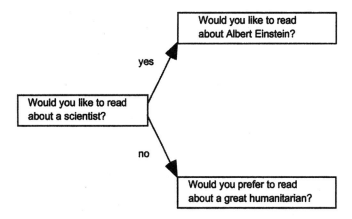

Figure 2.2

Following through the decision tree, we can trace a sample interaction. Assuming the user is interested in humanitarians, the path through the tree proceeds as follows:

Asking for Advice on an Interesting Story
Decision tree question: Would you like to read about a scientist?
Response: No
Decision tree question: Would you prefer to read about a great humanitarian?
Response: Yes
Decision tree advice: You might be interested in Aung San Suu Kyi, who won the Peace Prize in 1991.

This tree asks only two sequential questions before arriving at a decision. But it is easy to envision a large tree that asks many questions and recommends a wide variety of stories at the end of the path. It is also clear that this type of tree can be used to give advice on almost any subject from medical treatment to fortune-telling. Figure 2.4 shows an example of a medical advice decision tree.

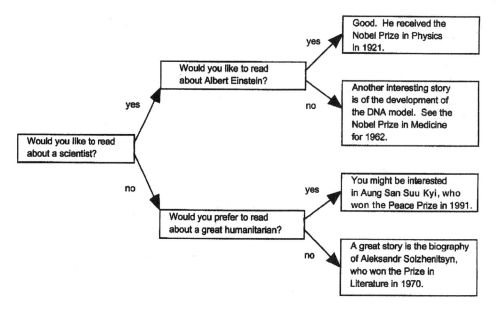

Figure 2.3

Another example is a game-playing tree. This can be illustrated by the simple game Nim, which has the following rules. The first player can place one, two, or three X's at the left end of a horizontal ladder; then the opponent can place one, two, or three O's in the next sequential squares. This chain of moves repeats again and again, filling the ladder from left to right, with the winner being the one to place a mark in the last square. An example for a ladder of seven squares is shown in figure 2.5. The first player might make three X's (fig. 2.5b). Then, suppose the second player makes two O's (fig. 2.5c). The first player could win by placing two more X's (fig. 2.5d).

Figure 2.6 shows a decision tree that will play the role of the second player for a Nim ladder of length 7.

Ordinarily we think of trees as emerging from the ground and spreading their branches toward the sky. The trees in this chapter move from left to right so they will be easier to program. The processing of the tree begins at the leftmost box, or *root node*, and proceeds along a path toward the right. At each decision *node*, the user of the tree is asked a question, and the answer given serves to select the next branch to be followed. The path proceeds toward the right until a final *leaf node* is encountered that has no outward branches. This leaf node will contain a message giving the result of the sequence of decisions, and it will terminate processing.

Such decision trees are applicable to a multitude of information-processing tasks, including advice giving, classification, instruction, and game-playing activities. Our task in this

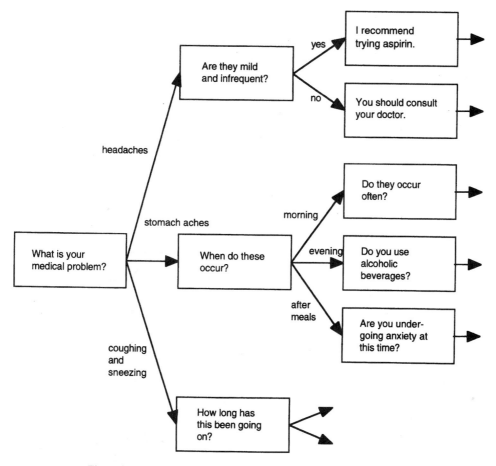

Figure 2.4

chapter is to write programs that contain such trees, lead a user down the correct paths, and print the results. The ability to design and program such trees is a powerful skill with many applications.

Reality Check

The discussion of decision trees showed an important part of the analysis required to program certain kinds of problems. Note that no mention of a computer or of a programming language was required. One implication is that a large part of computer programming is actually problem solving, that is, analyzing a problem and mapping out a

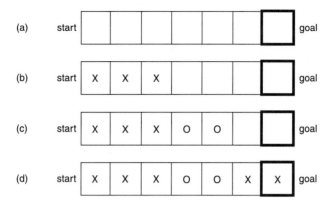

Figure 2.5

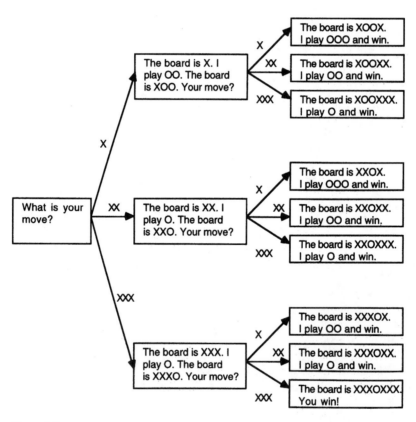

Figure 2.6

methodical solution. The computer becomes involved only after the problem's solution has been understood by the programmer.

Now that we have explained decision trees, we are ready to tackle the actual writing of a program. This takes some knowledge and understanding of the computer language to be used, in this case, Java. We will have to do some serious preparatory work before we are able to implement decision trees with a Java program.

Exercises

1. Design a decision tree that might help someone pick out a new car.

2. For any reasonable decision tree you have seen or can think of, how does the number of leaf nodes compare with the number of other (question) nodes?

3. Design a decision tree that would help an incoming student select courses in your major field or in a field that is of special interest to you.

Getting Started in Programming

A *computer program* is a list of commands that can be carried out by a computer. It is a recipe for actions the machine is to perform, and it must be written in a language that the computer can understand. Most programs in this book are written in Java, an exciting language developed by Sun Microsystems. Sometimes a program or part of a program is called computer *code*. We use both terms in this book.

Here is a sample program written in Java. It is in the applet form: it is meant to be run from a Web page using a Web browser. It could be added to the Web main page (home page) that we wrote in chapter 1 by placing it at the address `HelloWorld.java`, compiling it as described, and placing `<APPLET code = "HelloWorld.class">` in the appropriate place in the HTML text for The Nobel Prizes Web page.

```
import java.awt.*;

public class HelloWorld extends java.applet.Applet
{
    TextField m1,m2;

    public void init()
    {
        m1 = new TextField(60);
        m2 = new TextField(60);
```

```
        m1.setText("H e l l o    W o r l d !");
        m2.setText("This is a simple Java test.");
        add(m1);
        add(m2);
    }
}
```

What does this applet do? It displays the following text on a Web page (the text will be inside rectangular boxes on the screen):

H e l l o   W o r l d !

This is a simple Java test.

Having the computer carry out the instructions in the program is called *running* or *executing* the program. The program will run on your computer only if you first translate the Java into executable form. Such translation is called *compiling*, and it can be done by calling a Java translator called a *compiler*. The usual way to do the translation is to use the command `javac`, but your machine may have a different way of doing this. Thus, for our example code, we must type

```
javac HelloWorld.java
```

The result is a file called `HelloWorld.class`, which will appear automatically in your current directory, presumably your `public_html` directory. This is the file that is executed by the browser from your HTML page. We study compilation in detail in chapter 9.

We use Java version 1.1 here, but later versions of Java should be compatible. However, if your browser processes only earlier versions of Java, the code shown here may not work. In order to properly face up to the issue of versions (or "dialects") and compilers, you may have to get some help in adapting to your specific situation. Computer science, like many disciplines, has an oral tradition, and some of the most important facts are passed on only by word of mouth. You may be able to get along without such help, but learning is usually easier and more fun if you can find it.

To get the maximum benefit from this chapter, you should type in and run some of the programs given here and observe their behaviors. For instance, we have told you how the previous example will print when run. Try out the program and see if you can get things to work the same way.

This program seems very simple, but many details related to its form and execution need to be understood. These include the composition of the program in terms of statements, the order of execution of the statements, and their meaning and structure. We will go through that in detail. However, look at the program and the output it produces. You can probably guess at what changes the program would require to have it print

Good day to you!

My name is Cynthia.

Exercise

1. Put your guesses to work and modify the example program to print a three-line message.

Program Form and Statement Details

The primary parts of the program are a class statement and the declarations of the data and methods that the class contains.

```
public class name of class
{
    declarations of data
    declarations of methods
}
```

The class statement consists of a header including the word `class` followed by an opening brace (`{`) on the next line. This is followed by the declarations of data and method(s), and finally by a matching closing brace (`}`).

The class statement contains a number of important words that will not be explained right now. Simply use them when writing a Java program:

```
public class HelloWorld extends java.applet.Applet
```

One important thing to note is that the class statement includes the name of the class, `HelloWorld`, which we have chosen for this program. This will vary from program to program and is the programmer's choice. The remaining words will be pretty much the same from program to program and simply should be duplicated in the order shown. Another important point is that the header makes this program an applet by saying `extends java.applet.Applet`. As stated before, this makes it suitable for use from a Web browser.

After the opening brace, we find the statement declaring the data items `m1` and `m2`:

```
TextField m1,m2;
```

The statement says that `m1` and `m2` are objects of type `TextField`. `TextField` is itself a class that has been provided to us with the Java language. It displays rectangles on the screen that can contain text. We are saying here that we want two data items of the

`TextField` class and that we have named them `m1` and `m2`. Note that this statement, like most Java statements, ends with a semicolon.

After the data portion of the class, we see the definition of our only method. The method has its own header:

```
public void init()
```

The key point here is that the method is named `init` (every applet must have a method named `init`, for "initialize.") Normally the programmer gets to choose the names for the methods that are to be written, but this method is required. The body of this method is enclosed in opening and closing braces, as was the body of the whole class.

Our method declaration starts with the statements

```
m1 = new TextField(60);
m2 = new TextField(60);
```

This actually creates the `TextField` data objects `m1` and `m2` that we declared. The `new` causes the objects to be created. The `60` in the parentheses says to make the field large enough to hold 60 characters.

The lines

```
m1.setText("H e l l o    W o r l d !");
m2.setText("This is a simple Java test.");
```

use the `setText` method of the `TextField` class to put actual text into the `TextFields`. The text is enclosed in quotation marks and will appear exactly as typed in. Normally in Java the number of spaces is not important. Within quotation marks every space has significance. Note that the `m1.` on the first of these lines shows that `setText` is to be applied to `m1`, not `m2`. Similarly, `m2.` identifies the `TextField` `m2`.

The *object.verb(data)* syntax appears everywhere in Java programs, so you should become comfortable with it. It means do to *object* what *verb* says, using *data*. Returning to the organ example, suppose there are two declared organs, `or1` and `or2`. Suppose the method `PlayNote` needs one piece of data, the note to be played. Here is a sequence of Java commands that will play some notes on the two organs:

```
or1.PlayNote("C");
or1.PlayNote("D");
or1.PlayNote("E");
or2.PlayNote("A");
or1.PlayNote("F");
```

This sequence will play three sequential notes on the first organ `or1`, one note on `or2`, and then a last note on `or1`. Note that the verb must be appropriate for (defined for) the object being addressed. Thus we would not expect anything sensible to result from

```
orl.StartEngine();
```

because the verb `StartEngine` was defined for lawn mowers, not organs.

Our program will be a big disappointment if we do all this work and we never see the `TextFields`. We must tell the system to put them on the screen so we can see them. The last two statements do this. However, these statements do not say where to put the two `TextFields`. They will appear as two long rectangles that can contain text (up to 60 characters each, in this example.) The `add` statements give only minimal instructions as to where to put the `TextFields`. We specify that `m1` should come first, followed by `m2`. Note that this still leaves the browser a lot of freedom, and much depends on how big the display is. All we can specify with `add` is the order of placement, left to right and top to bottom, just as one would write English text on a piece of paper. (Java has more detailed ways of controlling the layout of objects on a screen. These are rather complicated, so most of them are omitted from this book.)

The first line of our example Java program,

```
import java.awt.*;
```

tells the system that we expect to include several optional Java features. For now, just use this as specified.

Exercises

1. The display after the example Java program suggested what the output of the program might look like with a typical browser. What might it look like with an extra-wide browser window?

2. What might it look like if the order of the `add` statements were reversed?

Program Execution

The computer functions by executing statements in order. It first finds the `init` method, and within that, it executes the first statement, the second, and so forth. It always executes statements in order unless special statements require it to do something else. Our example program is finished when it has executed the second `add` statement.

Statement Meaning and Structure

Having just gone through a simple Java program once, we need to go back and look at some things in more detail. The statement

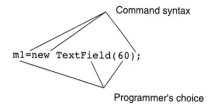

Command syntax

m1=new TextField(60);

Programmer's choice

Figure 2.7

```
m1 = new TextField(60);
```

has two parts (figure 2.7): the command syntax, which specifies exactly what ordering of characters is necessary for the command, and some data or keywords that the programmer has inserted. The command new tells the computer to create a new object named m1. The placement of the object name followed by the equals sign followed by the command new followed by the kind or type of object, with details, followed by a semicolon are all requirements for using the new command. This format is the syntax of the command. Items must be in exactly that order, and everything must be spelled correctly.

Three things are chosen by the programmer. The first is the object name, m1. Once chosen, it must be used consistently. The object type or class, here TextField, was also a choice of the programmer, but it was the only object provided by Java that would do what we required. Finally, the 60 was a choice of the programmer, specifying how big to make TextField. This 60 is essentially data to the statement.

The following version of the init method will not work correctly because of various errors:

```
Public Void Init()                                     // 1
{                                                      // 2
    m1 = new TextField("sixty");                       // 3
    m2 new TextField(60);                              // 4
    m1.setText("H e l l o      W o r l d !);           // 5
    m2.setText("This is a simple Java test.")          // 6
    please add(m1);                                    // 7
    add m2;                                            // 8
}                                                      // 9
```

1. This line is wrong because the words each start with a capital letter rather than the correct form, which here is all lowercase letters.
2. The second line and ninth lines are correct, containing the opening and closing braces, respectively.

3. This line is wrong because it specifies the length of `TextField` with a string `"sixty"` instead of a number as required.
4. This line is missing the equals sign.
5. This line is missing the closing quotation mark between the exclamation point and the closing parenthesis.
6. This line is missing the statement-ending semicolon.
7. `please` seems polite but is syntactically incorrect.
8. This line is missing the parentheses around `m2`.

Most programming languages require perfect syntax, although a few allow some flexibility. Languages of the future may be less demanding.

If the command syntax is correct, the program will carry out the commands regardless of what is included as data. Thus, the following program will run, but maybe not as you hoped:

```java
import java.awt.*;

public class HelloWorld extends java.applet.Applet
{
    TextField m1,m2;

    public void init()
    {
        m1 = new TextField(60);
        m2 = new TextField(60);
        m1.setText("C#7a-%% qwerty 496");
        m2.setText("Please ignore the nonsense above.");
        add(m2);
        add(m1);
    }
}
```

When this is run, we will get:

```
Please ignore the nonsense above.
C#7a-%% qwerty 496
```

Not only will it spew out the nonsense characters we typed in but since we have reversed the order of the `add` statements, the last remaining logic of the program has been destroyed because `above` should now be `below`.

The machine has no basis on which to judge the correctness of the data and will obediently carry out the instructions without regard to what is being manipulated. The computer will do precisely what you say even though that may not be what you want.

One way a correct program can be modified without changing the correctness relates to its spacing. Spaces can be inserted at most places in a program without affecting its behavior. The following program is equivalent to the first sample one. Even though a blank line and many extraneous spaces have been inserted, other blank lines have been removed, and several lines have been combined into one line, it will run perfectly.

```
import java.awt.*;
public class  HelloWorld extends
    java.applet.Applet
{

    TextField       m1,  m2;
    public void init()
  { m1    =     new TextField(60);
                m2 = new TextField(60);
    m1.setText("H e l l o      W o r l d !"    );

    m2.setText("This is a simple Java test."    );
        add(m2); add(m1); } }
```

You would certainly not want to type a program with such random spacing because of its poor readability. But this example does show how complete your freedom is for moving things around on the page, and you may want to use this freedom to format your code in some special way.

Do not insert spaces in the middle of keywords such as new, public, or add, or into the middle of names like m1 or TextField or into the middle of data like 60.

This section has presented a computer program to print two lines and halt. A careful understanding of this simple code is a huge step in the direction of understanding all computer programs. It is important to understand the form of the program and the concept of the programming statement as the fundamental unit of command. Each statement specifies an action; the sequence of statements specifies a sequence of actions and the order of their execution. The formatting of each statement is precise and unforgiving except for the spacing between its parts.

Here is a program that performs another printing task:

```
import java.awt.*;

public class SecondCode extends java.applet.Applet
{
    TextField lineA, lineB, lineC;
    public void init ()
    {
```

```
        lineA = new TextField(70);
        lineB = new TextField(70);
        lineC = new TextField(70);
        lineA.setText("**********************************");
        lineB.setText("Great Ideas in Computer Science");
        lineC.setText("**********************************");
        add(lineA);
        add(lineB);
        add(lineC);
    }
}
```

You should now be able to write a program that will print almost anything.

Exercises

1. If you were to write another applet similar to the HelloWorld applet, which word(s) in the header would you have to change?

2. What would happen to the output of the HelloWorld applet if the add statements were omitted?

3. What syntax errors can you identify in the following statement?

   ```
   m2.setText("My favorite movie is "Star Wars," Episode 4");
   ```

Interactive Programs and Buttons

As you probably know from using a Web browser or other programs or computer games, many programs are *interactive*. That is, the program behavior—exactly what it does—depends on what you do with your mouse or type on your keyboard. In other words, the same program will not always do the same thing. What it does depends on what you do, what data you provide, what you click on, and so forth. An example is the Nobel Prize stories advice-giving program that we described previously.

One of the fundamental actions in operating a Web browser is using the mouse to place the cursor on a button displayed on a screen and pressing the left side of the mouse. This is called "clicking a button". Which button you click affects what the browser does and what it shows you. Since this is so important to most applets (including our example), the next programming example will show you how to create and utilize buttons.

Consider the following short driving instruction module, an applet called TrafficLight.

```java
import java.awt.*;
import java.awt.event.*;
public class TrafficLight extends java.applet.Applet
                    implements ActionListener
{
    TextField m1, m2;
    Button b1, b2, b3;

    public void init ()
    {
        m1 = new TextField(80);
        m1.setText("What are you going to do when the light is");
        b1 = new Button("GREEN");
        b2 = new Button("YELLOW");
        b3 = new Button("RED");
        m2 = new TextField(80);
        add(m1) ;
        add(b1) ;
        add(b2) ;
        add(b3) ;
        add(m2) ;
        b1.addActionListener(this);
        b2.addActionListener(this);
        b3.addActionListener(this);
    }

    public void actionPerformed(ActionEvent event)
    {
        Object cause = event.getSource();

        if (cause == b1)
            {
            m2.setText("Keep on rolling.");
            }
        if (cause == b2)
            {
            m2.setText("Stop if you can!");
            }
```

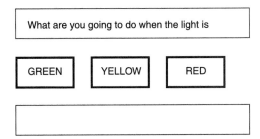

Figure 2.8

```
    if (cause == b3)
        {
        m2.setText("You must stop.");
        }
    }
}
```

Figure 2.8 shows what you should see when this program is first run. Then, if you press the GREEN button, the applet displays

Keep on rolling.

in the lower `TextField`. If you press the YELLOW button, the display is

Stop if you can!

in the `TextField`, and if you press the RED button, you see

You must stop.

With a high-level look at the code, you will see that we now have a second method. Before we had only `init`. For interactive applets, we require a method named `actionPerformed`. This new method is executed whenever an on-screen button is pressed with the mouse.

Before we track down the changes and additions to the rest of the program, let's look at this new method in detail. The method header,

```
public void actionPerformed(ActionEvent event)
```

is required and will be utilized unchanged in future programs. The body of the method is enclosed in braces and starts with

```
Object cause = event.getSource();
```

This statement assigns to the variable `cause` the identity of the object that causes this method to be executed. In this case, it tells which one of the three buttons was pressed. The remaining lines of the method use this information to place the correct message into the `TextField`:

```
if (cause == b1)
{
    m2.setText("Keep on rolling.");
}
if (cause == b2)
{
    m2.setText("Stop if you can!");
}
if (cause == b3)
{
    m2.setText("You must stop.");
}
```

We'll give the details for this kind of statement later, but you should find it plausible, from looking closely at this, that if button `b2`, the YELLOW button, is pressed, the message Stop if you can! is put into the `TextField` `m2`.

Let's move back to the `init` routine and see what changed there. Three `Buttons` and two `TextFields` are set up as in our first program:

```
m1 = new TextField(80);
m1.setText("What are you going to do when the light is");
b1 = new Button("GREEN");
b2 = new Button("YELLOW");
b3 = new Button("RED");
m2 = new TextField(80);
```

These are then positioned on the screen with a series of five `add` statements:

```
add(m1);
add(b1);
add(b2);
add(b3);
add(m2);
```

They tell the browser to first show the `TextField` `m1`, then follow that with the three `Buttons`, `b1`, `b2`, and `b3`. Note that these three buttons were coded to show GREEN, YELLOW, and RED, respectively. Last in the `add` series is the `TextField` `m2`.

What is totally new for the `init` method when writing an interactive applet is the following sequence of lines:

```
b1.addActionListener(this);
b2.addActionListener(this);
b3.addActionListener(this);
```

These use the `addActionListener` method of the `Button` class to register the three buttons so that the executing applet watches to see when they are pressed. If we had other buttons in our program but did not register them like this, then pressing one of those other buttons would have no effect.

There are two other modifications to our original program that need to be mentioned. The class header

```
public class TrafficLight extends java.applet.Applet
                    implements ActionListener
```

now includes `implements ActionListener` at the end. This tells Java that this class will deal with the actions directly. (This could have been dealt with in a separate class. That might be desirable in a much more complicated program.) In addition, we have had to add the line

```
import java.awt.event.*;
```

near the beginning. This tells Java we need to use the interactive features of the language.

Don't Panic

We have now looked at two Java programs in a fair amount of detail without trying to explain everything. Even so, the amount of syntax and detail may feel overwhelming. What is important here is that you understand the broad strokes. Even experienced programmers, when dealing with a new language, copy whole sections of code from a previous program unchanged and then make a few selected changes to "bend" the program to their needs.

When writing your first Java programs, you would do well to start by copying an example that does almost what you want your program to do. Get the example program working without making any of your modifications. Make your modification only when the example is working as was intended. That will ensure that you have copied everything correctly.

Later, we'll explain more of the items that we glossed over, and you will get used to using some of the Java features. Things will become much more comfortable than they are now.

Exercises

1. How would our `TrafficLight` program perform if we omitted the following line?

   ```
   b2.addActionListener(this);
   ```

2. Write a Java program that answers a question about the country you live in. First, it should ask, "What would you like to know about *country name here*?" Then it should have buttons with labels such as "population," "total area," and so forth. When a user pushes one of the buttons, the answer will appear in a `TextField` provided.

Reading and Storing Data

In the previous section we introduced the concept of data—the information being manipulated by the program. We also showed how to set up buttons to select which data we wanted to print. Examples of data so far have been in the form of text strings such as `"Hello World"` and `"Stop if you can!"` You may have wondered if the program could print only data that had been put into the program by the programmer. The answer is no; the programmer does not have to anticipate all possible data a program might want to print and include it in the code. In this section we show how to get your program to collect such data from the keyboard: it will read the keystrokes from typed input and store the data in computer memory. This can be an important part of making a program interactive.

Before introducing the new statement to read data, it is necessary to talk about locations in memory. Such locations are like pigeonholes or containers with names where information can be stored and then retrieved when needed. For example, you might like to have a place in memory where a sequence of characters can be stored, and you might choose to name it `position1`. You could then store data in that location and use the data in various ways. You could instruct the machine to write the data into `position1` or to copy the data from `position1` to some other location.

position1 ┌─────────────────────────┐
          └─────────────────────────┘

The correct way to indicate in the Java language that such a memory location is to be set up is with a *declaration*. To store a collection of characters that we call a *string*, this declaration takes the form

```
String position1;
```

The declaration tells the machine to set up in memory a location named `position1` that can hold a string of characters. The declaration must be included in the program *before* we try to make use of this memory location. The string named `position1` is called a *variable*. (You may recognize the form of this declaration. We have used declarations in previous examples, for example, we declared that we needed some buttons by including the line `Button b1, b2, b3;` in the `TrafficLight` program.)

For strings, once such a memory location is declared, it is set up and ready to use. You can refer to it in other statements as needed.

Reading Strings

We have seen the `TextField` class in every one of our Java examples. It is a versatile class that deals with getting information from the program out to the display screen in a rectangular window, a process often described as "printing" something out. We have looked at the method `setText` for getting information out. The method we use to read information into the program is called, appropriately, `getText`. It captures, or gets, the text that a user of the program types into a particular `TextField` rectangle on the screen. More specifically, the user who is executing the program must use the mouse to place the cursor somewhere into the `TextField` rectangle and click the left side of the mouse. Then the keyboard is used to type in the text. This text is then available for retrieval with an appropriate `getText` statement. So, if our program contained a `TextField` name, say `m1`, then `m1.getText();` could be used to retrieve text from that `TextField`.

If we had declared a `TextField` with

```
TextField message;
```

and then actually created one with

```
message = new TextField(50);
```

then `message.getText();` could be used to retrieve text from that `TextField`.

Now, `getText` has captured the information that was typed on the keyboard. How can we manipulate this text? Java has a kind of statement called an *assignment statement* that allows us to copy information from one object to another. (Chapter 3 gives more details about assignment statements.)

We can write

```
position1 = m1.getText();
```

where the assignment statement is heralded by an equals sign (=). The information held by the object to the right of the equals sign is copied into the object to the left of the equals sign, `position1`, which is the variable that we previously set up as a `String` variable. This is important because we can only make assignments between compatible objects.

position1 is a `String` variable and `getText` gets `String` information. (We have used assignments in our previous examples, to set up `Button` and `TextField`.)

Following is a simple example using the `getText` method and a `String` variable:

```
import java.awt.*;
import java.awt.event.*;
public class DupThree extends java.applet.Applet
                    implements ActionListener
{
    TextField m1, m2, m3, m4, m5;
    Button b1;
    String message;

    public void init ()
    {
        m1 = new TextField(80);
        m2 = new TextField(80);
        m3 = new TextField(80);
        m4 = new TextField(80);
        m5 = new TextField(80);
        b1 = new Button("button");
        m1.setText("Please enter some text below; then press button.");
        add(m1);
        add(m2);
        add(b1);
        add(m3);
        add(m4);
        add(m5);
        b1.addActionListener(this);
    }

    public void actionPerformed(ActionEvent event)
    {
        message = m2.getText();
        m3.setText(message);
        m4.setText(message);
        m5.setText(message);
    }
}
```

Let's look at this in some detail. Our declarations

```
┌──────────────────────────────────────────────┐
│ Please enter some text below; then press button. │
└──────────────────────────────────────────────┘

┌──────────────────────────────────────────────┐
│                                                │
└──────────────────────────────────────────────┘

┌───────────┐
│  Button   │
└───────────┘

┌──────────────────────────────────────────────┐
│                                                │
└──────────────────────────────────────────────┘

┌──────────────────────────────────────────────┐
│                                                │
└──────────────────────────────────────────────┘

┌──────────────────────────────────────────────┐
│                                                │
└──────────────────────────────────────────────┘
```

Figure 2.9

```
TextField m1, m2, m3, m4, m5;
Button b1;
String message;
```

provide for five `TextFields` named `m1` through `m5`, one `Button`, `b1`, and one `String` variable named `message`.

Our `init` method has no surprises. We create the `TextFields` with statements of the form *name* = new `TextField(80);` to create variously named fields, all with a size to hold 80 characters. Similarly, we create a button with `b1 = new Button("button");` and specify that the button be (very cleverly) labeled "button." We then put actual text into the `TextField m1` by writing

```
m1.setText("Please enter some text below; then press button.");
```

This provides the instructions for the user of the program.

Next, our `add` statements specify that we first place `TextFields m1` and `m2`, then `Button`, and then `TextFields m3`, `m4`, and `m5` (figure 2.9).

Finally, the statement

```
b1.addActionListener(this);
```

registers `Button b1` with the system so that it watches for clicks or presses on that button. (We ignore the rest of the code for the moment.)

So, what happens when we run this program? The `init` method sets things up and prompts us with the message

Please enter some text below; then press button.

We then respond to this prompt and type something, say, What a great day! into the next TextField. Then we wait expectantly, but nothing happens. The computer has been told to watch for a press of Button b1. So we must press the button. This activates the actionPerformed method.

We now look at that portion of the program:

```
public void actionPerformed(ActionEvent event)
{
    message = m2.getText();
    m3.setText(message);
    m4.setText(message);
    m5.setText(message);
}
```

This is particularly simple because there is only one button and the program does not have to determine which button was pressed. We go right into the statement

```
message = m2.getText();
```

The getText method reads the message we typed into TextField m2 and makes it available to the program. We assign this to the variable message. This means that whatever was typed into TextField now resides in a memory location named message, that is, the variable message. Now that this information is safely tucked away in the computer's memory, we can make use of it in subsequent statements. The statement

```
m3.setText(message);
```

employs the method setText and puts text into TextField m3, in effect printing it out.

Notice that two different forms of setText are employed. If quotation marks are used, the characters between the quotes are printed. Thus, with m1.setText("Please enter ..."); the characters Please enter ... are printed (without quotation marks). We also specified the String variable message, however, and m3.setText(message); uses no quotation marks. It means treat message as a variable and print its contents. The contents of message are whatever was assigned to it in the previous statement. We had assumed that What a great day! had been typed in. This means TextField m3 now contains What a great day! The next two statements,

```
m4.setText(message);
m5.setText(message);
```

do the same things for TextFields m4 and m5 (figure 2.10). In other words, whatever is typed into the program is duplicated three times; thus the name DupThree was chosen for the applet.

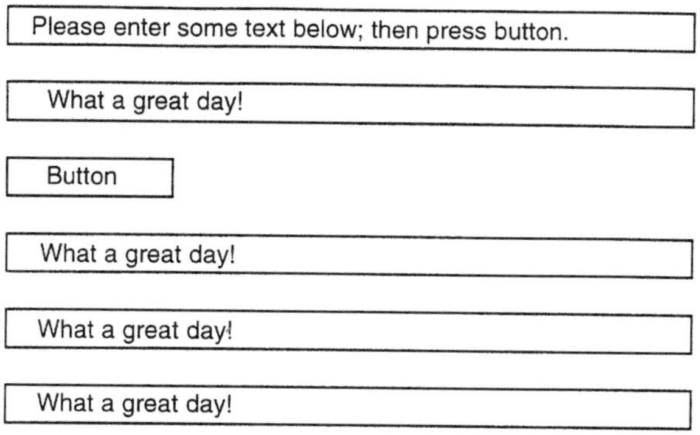

Figure 2.10

A few more points about variables are in order. The names of the places in memory, the variable names, can be almost anything as long as they begin with an alphabetic letter, include only alphabetic and numeric characters, and are properly declared. For example, the names A17 and c8zi could be used, but variable names like taxe$, 4sale, and short-cut are invalid.

Names must follow two additional rules. First, they must not contain spaces. Second, there is a set of *reserved words* for the Java system that may not be used as names. Some examples are if, import, public, class, extends, implements, and void. These are all parts of the Java language, and we would confuse the system if we chose those as names. You might have to consult a Java manual for a complete list of reserved words.

An important point is that storage positions should not be used until something is loaded into them, as is done in the DupThree example by the assignment statements. Then, the variable will continue to hold that information unless it is replaced, possibly by some other assignment statement. If a variable is used at the left side of a subsequent assignment statement, whatever earlier information was contained in it is lost forever, replaced by the new information being assigned.

Exercises

1. Write Java statements to declare variables, using your choice of names, to store your name and address.

2. Design and write a Java program that prompts you for and reads in your first name and then your last name. Then have the program display them in the opposite order.

3. Design and write a Java program that is similar to the previous one but which contains two buttons labeled "First-First" and "Last-First." Design the program so that when the "First-First" button is pressed, the names are displayed in the input order. If the "Last-First" button is pressed, then the last name is displayed before the first name.

A Number-Guessing Game

In order to allow the ideas introduced in the previous section to "settle in," we'll go right to another program, which will enable us to play a game. The basic idea of the game is that one person selects a number between 1 and 100, and the other person tries to guess, as quickly as possible, what the "secret" number is. After each guess, the person with the secret number responds with "The secret is higher than the guess," "The secret is lower than the guess," or "That is the right answer." The program keeps track of everything and implements the details of the game.

The code is as follows:

```
import awb.*; // See Appendix for a discussion of this software.
import java.awt.*;
import java.awt.event.*;

public class AboveBelow extends java.applet.Applet
                   implements ActionListener
{
    TextField m1, m2;
    IntField i1; // This is not standard Java. See Appendix.
    Button b1, b2;
    int secret, guess;

    public void init ()
    {
        m1 = new TextField(80);
        m1.setText("Enter number between 0 and 100; then push
                SECRET.");
        i1 = new IntField(40); // See Appendix.
        m2 = new TextField(80);
        b1 = new Button("SECRET");
        b2 = new Button("GUESS");
        add(m1);
        add(b1);
        add(i1);
        add(b2);
        add(m2);
```

```
        b1.addActionListener(this);
        b2.addActionListener(this);
    }
    public void actionPerformed(ActionEvent event)
    {
        Object cause = event.getSource();

        if (cause == b1)
        {
            secret = i1.getInt();
            i1.setInt(); // extension of awb.*
            m1.setText("Now, enter your guess below; then press GUESS.");
        }
        if (cause == b2)
        {
            guess = i1.getInt();

            if (guess == secret)
            {
                m2.setText("You've got it!");
            }
            if (guess < secret)
            {
                i1.setInt();
                m2.setText("The number is greater than " + guess);
            }
            if (guess > secret)
            {
                i1.setInt();
                m2.setText("The number is less than " + guess);
            }
        }
    }
}
```

First, the big picture. We have a class named AboveBelow with some declarations in
the body, followed by the required init method and then the actionPerformed method,
which is required for any interactive applet. Our declarations include two TextFields,
two Buttons, an IntField, and an int. The latter two are new. An IntField is a refine-
ment of, and looks and behaves very much like, a TextField but is designed to deal with
numeric data rather than strings. This is a special feature introduced by this book and

```
┌─────────────────────────────────────────────────────────────┐
│ Enter number between 0 and 100; then push SECRET.          ·│
└─────────────────────────────────────────────────────────────┘

      ┌──────────┐   ┌──────────────────┐   ┌──────────┐
      │  SECRET  │   │                  │   │  GUESS   │
      └──────────┘   └──────────────────┘   └──────────┘

┌─────────────────────────────────────────────────────────────┐
│                                                             │
└─────────────────────────────────────────────────────────────┘
```

Figure 2.11

is not standard Java. You should study the Appendix to learn more about it and how to get it running on your machine. The `int` declaration sets up memory locations to store numeric data, namely, integers or whole numbers.

The `init` method, as always, is used to set things up at the start of the program. It sets up and names our `Buttons` and creates `TextFields` and `IntFields` and gives some of them initial values. `TextField m1` is set up with the starting message `"Enter number between 0 and 100; then push SECRET."` The two buttons are labeled SECRET and GUESS (figure 2.11) and are set up to be monitored for our use.

Now we are ready to play the game. Assume Sarah and John are playing. While John's back is turned, Sarah enters the number 55 and then presses the SECRET button.

As soon as the button is pressed, the `actionPerformed` method is started up. The following code comes into play:

```
Object cause = event.getSource();
if (cause == b1)
{
    secret = i1.getInt();
    i1.setInt(); // clear Intfield
    m1.setText("Now, enter your guess below; then press GUESS.");
}
```

The variable `cause` is set to give the identity of which button was pushed. That means that in the `if` statement, `cause` will match `b1`, the SECRET button. This means that the statements surrounded by the braces immediately following are carried out. The integer variable `secret` gets a copy of the number Sarah entered into the `IntField`, in this case the number 55. The `setInt` statement clears the IntField `i1` so that the number Sarah entered is no longer showing on the screen. Finally, the `setText` statement places the new message `"Now, enter your guess below; then press GUESS"` into `m1` (figure 2.12). These are instructions to John on how to proceed with the game.

Note that the 55 Sarah entered is gone from the screen. The program, however, has saved the number in the variable `secret`. But John cannot see this when he begins the guessing process. Let's assume that John enters the number 50 and then presses the GUESS button. Again, the method `actionPerformed` is started up and `cause` is set to the iden-

```
┌─────────────────────────────────────────────────────────────────┐
│ Now, enter your guess below; then press  GUESS.                   │
└─────────────────────────────────────────────────────────────────┘

      ┌──────────────┐  ┌──────────────────┐  ┌──────────────┐
      │    SECRET    │  │                  │  │    GUESS     │
      └──────────────┘  └──────────────────┘  └──────────────┘

  ┌─────────────────────────────────────────────────────────────┐
  │                                                               │
  └─────────────────────────────────────────────────────────────┘
```

Figure 2.12

tity of the button. The first `if` will not find a match, since the GUESS button is `b2`. The following `if` statement does find a match:

```
if (cause == b2)
{
    guess = i1.getInt();
```

This causes the assignment statement to get the number 50 that John entered into the `IntField`. So the memory location `guess` contains 50. There are now three logical possibilities.

1. John hit it right on the money. The game is over.
2. John's guess is less than the secret number. The computer should tell him that so he can try again.
3. John's guess is greater than the secret number. The computer should report that and let him try again.

Here are the three `if` statements that accomplish this:

```
if (guess == secret)
{
    m2.setText("You've got it!");
}
if (guess < secret)
{
    i1.setInt();
    m2.setText("The number is greater than " + guess);
}
if (guess > secret)
{
    i1.setInt();
    m2.setText("The number is less than " + guess);
}
```

┌───┐
│ Now, enter your guess below; then press GUESS.   │
└───┘

┌──────────┐ ┌──────────────────┐ ┌──────────┐
│ SECRET   │ │   │ │ GUESS   │
└──────────┘ └──────────────────┘ └──────────┘

┌───┐
│ The number is greater than 50   │
└───┘

Figure 2.13

Except for the winning exact match, notice the `i1.setInt();` statements that clear out the previous answer. Since John entered a 50, which is less than the secret number, 55, the display at this stage will be as shown in figure 2.13.

This calls for some additional explanation.

```
m2.setText("The number is greater than " + guess);
```

includes the explicit text `"The number is greater than "`, which shows up on the screen unaltered. But notice the `+ guess` that follows. `guess` is an integer variable and contains a number. When a string (in quotation marks) is followed by a plus sign and then any variable, Java converts the contents of that variable into a string and appends it to the preceding string. The `50` in `guess` is converted to the string `"50"`, which is then appended to the message. (There are cases where failing to make the distinction between the numeric value `50` and the string `"50"` will cause the program to fail.)

If John proceeds very methodically now, he will have the following series of guesses and resulting messages (including the one shown in figure 2.13):

```
50
The number is greater than 50
75
The number is less than 75
63
The number is less than 63
57
The number is less than 57
54
The number is greater than 54
55
You've got it!
```

This is an example of a binary search, since at each step John uses his guesses to cut the range of values that are still logically possible roughly in half. (With this strategy, it should never take more then seven guesses to nail down the correct secret number.

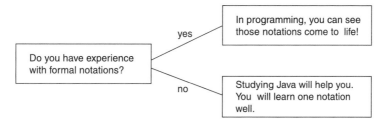

Figure 2.14

Without any strategy, for example, random guessing, it could take up to 100 tries. With a binary search strategy, what is the maximum number of guesses it would take if the secret number were between 1 and 1,000?)

Exercises

1. Come up with another guessing strategy for the number game. Is it better or worse than binary search?

2. Design a similar game program, using words rather than numbers. The secret and the guesses would all be strings. Describe how the program would work, but do not attempt to write a program.

3. What guessing strategy might you use for a word-oriented game?

4. Compare how you use a telephone book to the strategy you came up with in exercise 3.

Programming Decision Trees

Let's begin by programming the simplest possible tree, one with only one branching node (figure 2.14). We studied in the previous sections how to make the machine print these kinds of messages and how to have it read the user's answers. We also introduced, without serious explanation, the `if` statement, which allowed us to do or not do something depending on the answer to the `if` clause. We need to explore the `if` statement and its `if-else` variant more carefully.

In general, the `if-else` statement has the following form:

```
if (some true/false expression)
{
    Java code A
```

```
}
else
{
    Java code B
}
```

In actual code, the true/false expression might be something like `cause == b1`, which we saw in a previous program. It is asking if `cause` is equal to `b1` or, in effect, is the button that was pressed `Button b1`? The answer to that is either true or false (yes or no). The way the `if-else` statement works is that if the outcome of the question is true, then Java code A is executed. If the outcome is false, then Java code B is carried out instead. Here Java code A and Java code B are sequences of Java statements. These sequences with their enclosing braces are called compound statements, which are more carefully defined later.

A simplified variant, called the `if` statement, is just like the `if-else` statement but drops the "else" clause. In this case, if the result of the true/false question is true, the statements right after the `if` are executed. If the result is false, nothing is executed. The form is

```
if (some true/false expression)
{
    Java code A
}
```

We are now able to write the computer program for this simple decision tree:

```
import java.awt.*;
import java.awt.event.*;

public class SimpTree extends java.applet.Applet
                implements ActionListener
{
    TextField mQuery, mAnswer;
    Button bYes, bNo;

    public void init()
    {
        mQuery = new TextField(70);
        mQuery.setText("Do you have experience with formal notations?");
        bYes = new Button("Yes");
        bNo = new Button("No");
```

```
        mAnswer = new TextField(70);
        bYes.addActionListener(this);
        bNo.addActionListener(this);
        add(mQuery);
        add(bYes);
        add(bNo);
        add(mAnswer);
    }

    public void actionPerformed(ActionEvent event)
    {
        Object cause = event.getSource();
        if (cause == bYes)
        {
                mAnswer.setText("In programming, you can see ...");
        }
        else // must have been the No button
        {
                mAnswer.setText("Studying Java will help you ...");
        }
    }
}
```

As you can see, the solution for this ultrasimple case is almost identical to our TrafficLight program except that we only have two buttons. Let's go through this code:

```
import java.awt.*;
import java.awt.event.*;

public class SimpTree extends java.applet.Applet
                implements ActionListener
{
    TextField mQuery, mAnswer;
    Button bYes, bNo;
```

We use the standard import statements and then have a class header that names the class SimpTree, says it is a special case of an applet, and states that the "listener" for any buttons is implemented in this class. Then we declare the TextFields mQuery and mAnswer and the Buttons bYes and bNo.

Next is the `init` method that initializes things, that is, it sets up everything so that it is ready to go. Only the body of `init` is shown in the following:

```
mQuery = new TextField(70);
mQuery.setText("Do you have experience with formal notations?");
bYes = new Button("Yes");
bNo = new Button("No");
mAnswer = new TextField(70);
bYes.addActionListener(this);
bNo.addActionListener(this);
add(mQuery);
add(bYes);
add(bNo);
add(mAnswer);
```

The first two lines create and put text into the `mQuery` `TextField`. The next two statements create buttons labeled Yes and No. Next we create the `TextField` where we will eventually place our "answer." The `addActionListener` statements register the two buttons to be listened for. Finally the four `add` statements place on the screen the query `TextField` first, then the two `Button`s, and then the `TextField` that will contain the answer.

When this applet is run, the `init` method will result in a display such as the one shown in figure 2.15. Pressing one of the two buttons, either Yes or No, will cause the `actionPerformed` method to be started up. Let's look at the body of that routine:

```
Object cause = event.getSource();
if (cause == bYes)
{
    mAnswer.setText
    ("In programming, you can see those notations come to life!");
```

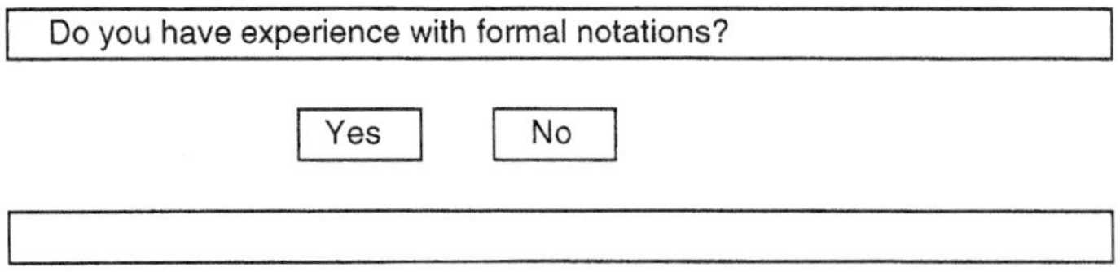

Figure 2.15

```
}
else // must have been the No button
{
    mAnswer.setText
    ("Studying Java will help you learn one notation well.");
}
```

First the variable cause is assigned the identity of the button that was pressed. Then we have an if-else statement that occupies the remaining lines. The cause == bYes is evaluated by the computer to see if it is true or false. If Button bYes was pressed, that will equal what is stored in cause, and the value of cause == bYes will be true. In that case, the TextField mAnswer will be set to "In programming, you can see those notations come to life!" and the lines that come after this, starting with the else, will be skipped. The screen will then show a display such as the one in figure 2.16. If the No button was pressed, if-else would evaluate to false. In the false case, it's the statements immediately after the if through those just before the else that are skipped. The statements after the else are now executed. This will cause the TextField mAnswer to be set to "Studying Java will help you learn one notation well." The display will then look like the one in figure 2.17.

So, there it is, for a very simple tree. If you compare this to the TrafficLight example, you will note that it used three if statements, one for each of the three buttons. Here, since we have only two buttons, we are able to function with only one if-else statement because if it wasn't one button, it had to be the other one.

| Do you have experience with formal notations? |

| Yes | | No |

| In programming, you can see those notations come to life! |

Figure 2.16

| Do you have experience with formal notations? |

| Yes | | No |

| Studying Java will help you learn one notation well. |

Figure 2.17

We'll tackle more complicated decision trees later, but first we need to deal with some points of grammar for Java programming.

Grammar and Style

By now you have probably noticed that (almost) all statements are terminated by a semicolon (;). Let's systematically go through the various kinds of statements we have encountered. Statements invoking methods for various classes end with semicolons. Examples are

```
mQuery.setText("Do you have experience with formal notations?");
```

and

```
add(mQuery);
```

Note also that when invoking a method, parentheses, ( ), are always included after the name of the method. There may or may not be something between the parentheses. Declarations are statements ending with semicolons. For example,

```
Button bYes, bNo;
```

Assignment statements, which always include an equals sign (=) end with a semicolon, as shown in the next example:

```
mAnswer = new TextField(70);
```

The exception, so far, is the `if` statement, which itself is not ended in a semicolon but normally includes one or more statements within the braces that are terminated by semicolons. Method and applet definitions consist of a header and then statements enclosed in braces. The closing brace for such definitions is not followed by a semicolon.

We also spoke earlier of compound statements. These are just collections of one or more statements enclosed in braces. The compound statement itself is not terminated in a semicolon but the statements inside are.

The example programs you have seen so far also follow fairly rigid style rules, that is, the formatting, specifically the indentation, is done carefully and systematically. Just like an outline of a report, indentation reflects the logical structure of a program. As we stated earlier, the distribution of spaces and statements on a line is usually of little consequence to the Java compiler. But it is extremely important to human readers. Since it is very important that programmers fully understand the programs they are working with, any formatting that improves readability is, in practice, a big benefit.

For now, the indentation rules can be summarized by saying that all lines within braces are indented. With every opening brace, the degree of indentation moves one unit to the

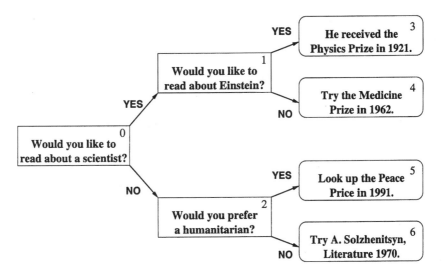

Figure 2.18

right. Every closing brace sets back the degree of indentation one unit. Statements within a pair of braces should all start at the same indentation—they should all line up.

Deeper Decision Trees

More complicated decision trees require more than one `if-else` statement. To arrive at the answer or solution to the problem dealt with by the decision tree, a sequence of questions must be answered. To illustrate this, we implement a variation of the Nobel Prizes decision tree shown earlier in this chapter (figure 2.18). Notice that in addition to making the questions shorter, we have placed a number in a corner of each node. This number is used to help us keep track of how far we have moved along the path toward the desired answer. Imagine that if we presented you with a huge decision tree printed on a wall poster, you might keep a finger on each successive question as you were determining its answer. Thus, your finger would track the path from the root of the tree at the left to the final answer at the right. Since the program has no finger, it will use the number in the node for keeping track of its current location in tree.

Here is a program, `NobelAdvice`, that implements the decision tree in figure 2.18:

```
import java.awt.*;
import java.awt.event.*;

public class NobelAdvice extends java.applet.Applet
                implements ActionListener
```

```
{
    TextField mQuery, mAnswer;
    Button bYes, bNo;
    int myLocation;

    public void init()
    {
        mQuery = new TextField(70);
        mQuery.setText("Would you like to read about a scientist?");
        bYes = new Button("Yes");
        bNo = new Button("No");
        myLocation = 0;
        mAnswer = new TextField(70);
        bYes.addActionListener(this);
        bNo.addActionListener(this);
        add(mQuery);
        add(bYes);
        add(bNo);
        add(mAnswer);
    }

    public void actionPerformed(ActionEvent event)
    {
        Object cause = event.getSource();
        if (myLocation == 0)
        {
            if (cause == bYes)
            {
                myLocation = 1;
                mQuery.setText("Would you like to read about Einstein?");
            }
            if (cause == bNo)
            {
                myLocation = 2;
                mQuery.setText("Would you prefer a humanitarian?");
            }
        }
        else if (myLocation == 1)
        {
```

```
            if (cause == bYes)
            {
                myLocation = 3;
                mAnswer.setText("He received the Physics Prize in 1921.");
            }
            if (cause == bNo)
            {
                myLocation = 4;
                mAnswer.setText("See the Prize in Medicine, 1962.");
            }
        }
        else if (myLocation == 2)
        {
            if (cause == bYes)
            {
                myLocation = 5;
                mAnswer.setText("Look up the Peace Prize, 1991.");
            }
            if (cause == bNo)
            {
                myLocation = 6;
                mAnswer.setText("Try the Literature Prize, 1970.");
            }
        }
    }
}
```

Notice that the class header, declaration, and the `init` method are almost unchanged from our previous decision tree implementation. The additional declaration statement

```
int myLocation;
```

sets up an integer variable that will help us keep track of where in the decision tree we have last been. That variable will utilize the node numbers shown in figure 2.18. The two *different* lines in the `init` method are

```
mQuery.setText("Would you like to read about a scientist?");
```

```
myLocation = 0;
```

Since the question here is different, the `setText` statement contains the new question. We also set the value of `myLocation` to zero to show that we have been at the root node. This

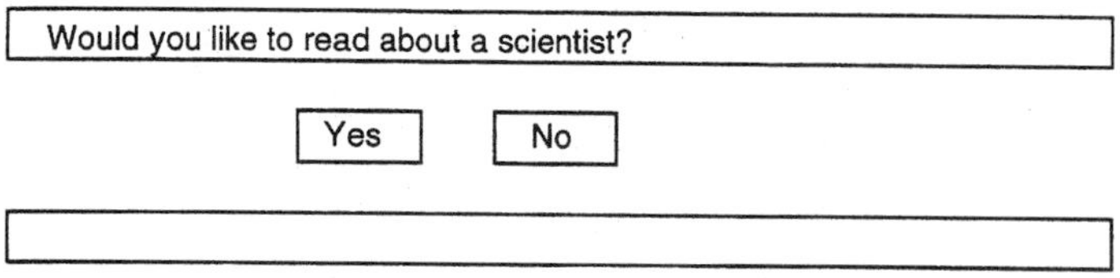

```
Would you like to read about a scientist?
```

```
Yes        No
```

Figure 2.19

means that when we start up the program, we will get the display shown in figure 2.19. Pressing one of the two buttons, Yes or No, will cause the `actionPerformed` method to be started up. Let's look at the "skeleton" of the body of that routine:

```
Object cause = event.getSource();
if (myLocation == 0)
{
    ...
}
else if (myLocation == 1)
{
    ...
}
else if (myLocation == 2)
{
    ...
}
```

The ellipses show where lines of code were omitted. The first line is a normal one where `cause` is given the identity of the button that was pushed to have the program respond. The rest of the lines shown here are designed to have the program decide which part of the tree it's dealing with. What part has already been covered? The number stored in the variable `myLocation` can answer that question. If it contains 0—if the value of `myLocation` is zero—then we've just been at node zero and have responded to the question stored there: `"Would you like to read about scientist?"` If `myLocation` has a value of 1 or 2, this tells the program that we've progressed further. Basically, the previous code excerpt pinpoints where we have just been so that we can understand what question the Yes or No buttons presses are actually responding to.

Grammar Aside

The form of the `if-else` statements may be confusing. There are `if-else` statements within `if-else` statements. Here is a full expansion of the code:

```
Object cause = event.getSource();
if (myLocation == 0)
{
    ...
}
else
{
    if (myLocation == 1)
    {
        ...
    }
    else
    {
        if (myLocation == 2)
        {
            ...
        }
    }
}
```

A rule for compound statements says that when there is only one statement within a compound statement, then the enclosing braces may be omitted. Since each `else` clause contains exactly one `if-else` or `if` statement, those braces can be eliminated. That leaves us with

```
Object cause = event.getSource();
if (myLocation == 0)
{
    ...
}
else
    if (myLocation == 1)
    {
        ...
    }
    else
        if (myLocation == 2)
        {
            ...
        }
```

Now, if we had a larger tree, we would have many more node numbers, and by indenting at each step we would slowly but inevitably run off the page. So, for situations where we distinguish between many mutually exclusive cases (all the node numbers must be unique), we combine the `if` line with the previous `else` line and do not indent at each step:

```
Object cause = event.getSource();
if (myLocation == 0)
{
    ...
}
else if (myLocation == 1)
{
    ...
}
else if (myLocation == 2)
{
    ...
}
```

Decision Trees (Continued)

Now that we've dealt with the skeleton code and understand that its purpose is to keep track of our location in the decision tree, we can focus on the code that was omitted (indicated by the ellipses). The first piece, shown with the enclosing `if` statement, is

```
if (myLocation == 0)
{
    if (cause == bYes)
    {
        myLocation = 1;
        mQuery.setText("Would you like to read about Einstein?");
    }
    if (cause == bNo)
    {
        myLocation = 2;
        mQuery.setText("Would you prefer a humanitarian?");
    }
}
```

On execution, we end up here because we were just at node zero answering the first question with a yes or a no. If the `Yes` button was pushed, we move the question `"Would you like to read about Einstein?"` into the `mQuery` TextField. We also set

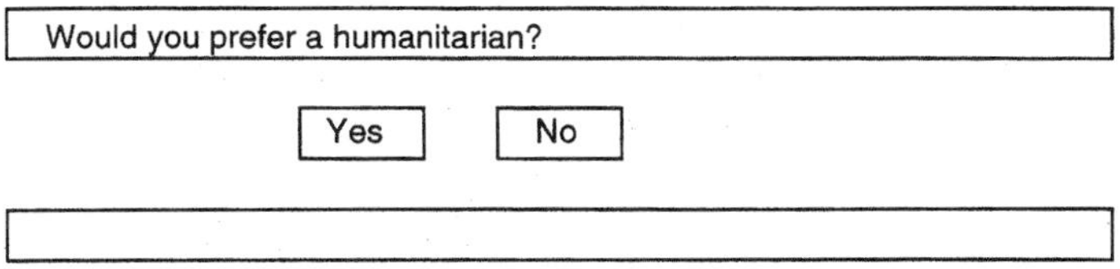

Figure 2.20

`myLocation` to 1 so that when a future button is pushed, the program will know that it is in response to the question in node 1. (The node numbers are arbitrary, but they must uniquely identify a particular node.)

Now, if the No button was pushed, the Would you prefer a humanitarian? message is displayed and `myLocation` is set to 2. Let's continue this discussion with the assumption that No was pressed and `myLocation` now contains 2. The question showing is Would you prefer a humanitarian? (figure 2.20). Let's find out what happens when we now press the Yes button again. The software will again use `myLocation` to find out where in the tree it is working. Since `myLocation` has a value of 2, it will execute the following code:

```
else if (myLocation == 2)
{
    if (cause == bYes)
    {
        myLocation = 5;
        mAnswer.setText("Look up the Peace Prize, 1991.");
    }
    if (cause == bNo)
    {
        myLocation = 6;
        mAnswer.setText("Try the Literature Prize, 1970.");
    }
}
```

Since Yes was pressed, the software will put the message `"Look up the Peace Prize, 1991"` into the `myAnswer TextField`. It also sets `myLocation` to 6 to signify that we have ended up in node 6 even though we will not do anything more with that.

If we were to extend this to a deeper tree with more questions and choices, setting `myLocation` to 6 would be crucial for correct operation. The screen should now look as shown in figure 2.21. Notice that we have only taken one of four possible paths through this tree, namely, the No-Yes path. Make sure you understand how this would work for the paths No-No, Yes-No, and Yes-Yes as well.

Would you prefer a humanitarian?

Yes		No

Look up the Peace Prize, 1991.

Figure 2.21

Exercises

1. Design your own decision tree and write a Java program to go with it.

2. Change all the node numbers in the `NobelAdvice` decision tree in figure 2.18, and change the corresponding numbers in the Java program. Explain why this should not make any difference to the working of the program.

3. You may have noticed that our first decision tree with only one question had three nodes. The `NobelAdvice` decision tree added another level, with three question nodes and seven total nodes. If we added another two levels in the same manner, how many question nodes and how many nodes overall would there be?

*The Arrow Notation and Its Uses

When we discuss a topic and find ourselves saying the same phrases over and over again, a common practice is to invent a notation to enable us to skip over the repetitive words. As an illustration, we find ourselves saying things like "an example of a legal name is X17" or "an example of a legal statement is `myLocation = 6;`." In order to make these statements simpler, we often use the arrow notation, which says the same things:

```
<name> ==> X17
<statement> ==> myLocation = 6;
```

This section introduces the arrow notation and gives the rules that specify all the Java described in this chapter.

The first new notation uses angle brackets around a word: `<name>`. This sequence of symbols, `<name>`, should be read as "an object called a 'name'." The second notation is an arrow, `==>`, which in this context means "can be." Using these notations, we can give a general rule for names:

```
<name> ==> a sequence of alphanumeric characters that begins with a
                        letter
```

Translating this notation into English, we read, "An object called a 'name' can be a sequence of letters and/or digits that begins with a letter." Some examples of names in this chapter are `TrafficLight` and `m2`, and the notation can be used to specify them:

```
<name> ==> TrafficLight
<name> ==> m2
```

That is, a name can be a sequence of characters `TrafficLight` or the sequence `m1`. Conceptually, names are given to objects like classes, variables, and methods.

There are two reasons why this notation is extremely important: (1) It is very useful for talking about and learning the Java language. For example, most of the Java used in this book is summarized in just a few pages at the end of this chapter. Anytime you wish to check on what is legal or how to code a certain construct, a quick reference to this chapter can often yield the answer. (2) This notation provides the basis for the translation mechanism used in chapter 9 and other mechanisms later in the book. If you use the notation regularly along the way, when you get to those chapters you will be comfortable with it.

Another kind of object in Java is called a string. Let's use the arrow notation to define it.

```
<string> ==> <name>
<string> ==> "any sequence of characters"
```

Paraphrasing these rules, a string can be a name or any string of printable characters surrounded by quotation marks. Some strings in this chapter are

```
<string> ==> message
<string> ==> "Do you wish a mathematical approach?"
```

Strings are important because they are the things that can be printed.

Sometimes we want to make distinctions, that is, break things into categories. So we have the rule

```
<expression> ==> <string-expression> | <int-expression> |
                 <oth-expression>
```

The vertical bar (|) is shorthand for "or" and means that you have a choice. It is shorthand in that we could have written

```
<expression> ==> <string-expression>
<expression> ==> <int-expression>
<expression> ==> <oth-expression>
```

This shows three different possible rules for an expression. The vertical bar allows us to state them on one line. We will use either method—the bar or multiple statements—to indicate that we have a choice. Back to our rule:

```
<expression> ==> <string-expression> | <int-expression> |
                  <oth-expression>
```

This says an expression can be a string expression, which can be used for working with text, messages, and the like; or an integer expression, which suggests numbers and arithmetic. We cannot do arithmetic on strings but can perform it on integer expressions. The third choice is some other kind of expression, neither an integer nor a string expression. For now, we continue to deal with strings. We have the rule

```
<string-expression> ==> <string>
```

That's simple: it says that a string expression may be a string. We previously defined `<string>` and know it can be a `<name>` or a sequence of characters surrounded by quotation marks.

We also studied statements in this chapter, and these are represented as `<statement>`. Here are three forms introduced earlier:

```
<statement> ==> <name> = <expression>;
<statement> ==> <name> = new <class>(<arguments>);
<statement> ==> <name>.<method>(<arguments>); | <method>(<arguments>);
```

Summarizing, we have introduced a notation for defining programming entities, and we have shown how to use it to define names, strings, expressions, and statements. We can find the meaning of these terms by starting with a bracketed form, such as `<name>`, and following the arrows. Now we want to do more by using the arrow as a substitution indicator. Specifically, we interpret the arrow, ==>, as saying more than "can be"; we interpret it as saying "can be replaced by."

Generating Java Statements

Here is how the arrow rules can be used to generate a Java statement. Let's start with this statement rule:

```
<statement> ==> <name> = <expression>;
```

Then let's apply the rule that says an `<expression>` can be replaced by a `<string-expression>`. Doing this replacement changes our rule to

```
<statement> ==> <name> = <string-expression>;
```

Next, we apply the rule that says we can replace `<string-expression>` with `<string>`:

```
<statement> ==> <name> = <string>;
```

Then we apply the rule that says `<string>` can be replaced by `<name>`:

```
<statement> ==> <name> = <name>;
```

Finally, we apply the rule that says `<name>` can be replaced by a sequence of characters beginning with a letter.

```
<statement> ==> <name> = address;
```

Or the last step could have been done differently to obtain

```
<statement> ==> <name> = "Hello, my name is Oscar.";
```

This assumes we have a variable named `address` and that someone would be interested in inserting `"Hello, my name is Oscar."` into a program. To complete the process, we need to replace `<name>` in each case using the rule that says a name is a string of alpha-numeric symbols that begins with a letter. So, the following is consistent:

```
<statement> ==> heading = address;
<statement> ==> message = "Hello, my name is Oscar.";
```

Again it assumes that both `heading` and `message` are valid string variable names.

Take a Deep Breath . . .

Let's step back and see what we have accomplished. We have a series of rules that collectively describe (a portion of) the Java language syntax. We started with a syntactical element, in this case a `<statement>` and then by a series of substitutions ended up with two syntactically correct Java statements. We did that with very simple substitutions and by selecting rules that matched our needs. Wherever we had something in angle brackets, `< >`, we looked for a rule that allowed us to replace that item either with a more detailed description using the angle bracket notation or with actual code. When we were done, we had produced actual code for statements.

So, in addition to developing a notation that describes the syntax of Java, we have illustrated a *method* for generating *syntactically correct* Java statements.

If this seems a bit arbitrary and random, it is, because we were just trying to illustrate the process. Normally, you have a Java statement or program for which you want to verify the syntax. That is what the Java compiler does when compiling your programs, and it lets you know when it is unhappy with your syntax.

More Rules

To fully illustrate this technique, we need to spell out a few more rules and then verify some actual code. For now, we will skip much of what pertains to integers and arithmetic. Also, since we have already presented rules that include the items `<class>` and `<string-method>`, we will defer detailed examination of these.

A rule that we need to better resolve some of our previous rules is

```
<arguments> ==> possibly empty list of <expression>s separated by
                commas
```

The argument list, or arguments, is the information placed between parentheses following a method name when using a method in a program. As the rule states, it is a possibly empty list: that is, sometimes there are no arguments and the method name is followed by ( ). There may be only one argument expression. But if there are more than one, they are separated by commas. So far, we have not encountered argument lists longer than 1. Examples of arguments we have used (and their enclosing parentheses) are

```
("H e l l o    W o r l d !")
(70)
(bYes)
```

A previous rule told us that

```
<expression> ==> <string-expression> | <int-expression> |
                 <oth-expression>
```

In other words, arguments may be expressions of strings, numbers, or other objects. Since we are focusing on strings, we can ignore the other options for now. Another useful rule pertaining to strings is

```
<string-expression> ==> <string-expression> + <string-expression>
```

This says that a string may consist of two strings joined together, or concatenated.

Verifying the Correctness of a Statement

Let's use this rule and our previous rules to verify the correctness of the following statement from the guessing program we presented earlier. This will be our target code:

```
m2.setText("The number is less than " + guess);
```

Following is a summary of the rules we have stated so far. The rule numbers are arbitrary but make a rule easy to refer to. (Do not memorize rule numbers; they will change without notice.)

1. `<name> ==> any string of alphanumeric symbols that begins with a
               letter`
2. `<statement> ==> <name> = <expression>;`
3. `<statement> ==> <name> = new <class>(<arguments>);`
4. `<statement> ==> <name>.<method>(<arguments>); |
                   <method>(<arguments>);`

5. `<arguments>` ==> *possibly empty list of* `<expression>`*s separated by commas*
6. `<expression>` ==> `<string-expression>` | `<int-expression>` | `<oth-expression>`
7. `<string-expression>` ==> `<string-expression>` + `<string-expression>`
8. `<string-expression>` ==> `<string>`
9. `<string>` ==> `"any sequence of characters"`
10. `<string>` ==> `<name>`

Since we are dealing with a statement, we need to start with an appropriate rule for statements. There are several rules for statements, so we need to choose the one that fits our target line of code. The one that looks best is

`<statement> ==> <name>.<method>(<arguments>);`

Our strategy is to find rules for replacing items on the right that are enclosed in angle brackets with new items that are either actual code or other items in angle brackets. We will make replacements that make the right side look more and more like the target statement. Let's work on `<name>` first. Rule 1 allows us to replace `<name>` by a string of alphanumeric characters beginning with a letter. More precisely, since we are trying to verify a specific piece of code, we can replace it by m2. That results in

`<statement> ==> m2.<method>(<arguments>);`

It's not much, but we are getting closer to the target,

`m2.setText("The number is less than " + guess);`

Going on to `<method>`, we find we don't have a rule for this yet, so we can state one:

11. `<method>` ==> `setText` | `getText` | `getInt` | `setInt` | `add` | `actionPerformed`

This rule just lists a number of alternative method names we have used so far. Clearly, we want `setText`:

`<statement> ==> m2.setText(<arguments>);`

That leaves `<arguments>`. By rule 5 we can substitute a possibly empty list of `<expression>`s separated by commas. Since there are no commas in our target code, it clearly has only one argument, a single expression. This results in

`<statement> ==> m2.setText(<expression>);`

Now, rule 6 says that `<expression>` can be an `<int-expression>`, a `<string-expression>`, or an `<oth-expression>`. Again, there is no doubt that our target code is dealing with strings because we note the quotation marks reserved for specifying strings. That leads to

```
<statement> ==> m2.setText(<string-expression>);
```

Now we need to decide which of the two rules dealing with string expressions should be used. The clue is the plus sign (+) in the target code. We choose rule 7, which says a string expression can be a string expression followed by a plus sign followed by another string expression. That yields

```
<statement> ==> m2.setText(<string-expression> + <string-expression>);
```

While you may worry that things are getting more complicated rather than simpler, we are on the right track. Dealing with the first <string-expression>, we select rule 8, which says a string expression can be, simply, a <string>. Let's apply this rule to the second string expression as well. We now have

```
<statement> ==> m2.setText(<string> + <string>);
```

Using rule 9, we see that the first <string> is clearly a sequence of characters enclosed in quotation marks:

```
<statement> ==> m2.setText("The number is less than " + <string>);
```

The other <string> can be replaced by <name> using rule 10:

```
<statement> ==> m2.setText("The number is less than " + <name>);
```

The last substitution, using rule 1, can be made because <name> can be any string of alphanumeric symbols that begins with a letter:

```
<statement> ==> m2.setText("The number is less than " + guess);
```

We're done! At the right side of the statement we have our target code. It was a lot of work, yet each individual step was fairly simple, easy enough for even a machine to carry out. We have actually *proven*, in the strongest logical sense, that the code is syntactically correct, consistent with our rules.

Above the Statement Level

We have dealt with rules that allow us to describe single statements. Now we demonstrate that this approach can be applied to larger pieces of a program. We first deal with *control statements*, which affect whether or how often statements are executed. The if-else statement is our only control statement so far.

A *compound statement* is not really a single statement but a way of packaging a number of statements together. However, it can often be used where a single statement is asked for. For our purposes, it will be used only in connection with control statements, but it does have other uses (which are omitted from this book). A compound statement can be described as follows:

```
<compound-statement> ==>
{
    list of <statement>s
}
```

or more compactly,

12. `<compound-statement> ==> {list of <statement>s}`

An example from the NobelAdvice applet is

```
{
    myLocation = 6;
    mAnswer.setText("Try the Literature Prize, 1970");
}
```

We can now specify the rules for the if statements:

```
<statement> ==> if (<bool-expression>)
                    <compound-statement>
<statement> ==> if (<bool-expression>)
                    <compound-statement>
                else
                    <compound-statement>
```

or more compactly,

13. `<statement> ==> if(<bool-expression>)<compound-statement>`
14. `<statement> ==> if(<bool-expression>)<compound-statement>`
    `                    else<compound-statement>`

That leaves `<bool-expression>` undefined. *Boolean expressions* can also be called logical expressions and are naturally used in the English language together with "if" statements. We often say things like, "If your age is less than 21, you may not buy alcohol." The logical expression is "less than 21," which can be either *true* or *false*. Boolean expressions can get extremely complicated, but for now we use a rule that deals with the very simple Boolean expressions we have seen in our code, for example (including the if and the parentheses),

```
if (cause == bYes)
```

Note that the double equals sign (==) is required. A single equals sign is reserved for assignment statements. A simple rule to handle logical expressions is

15. `<bool-expression> ==> <name> == <expression>`

This is consistent with our example because a `<name>` can be `cause` (rule 1), and `<expression>` can be a `<string-expression>` (rule 6), which can be a `<string>` (rule 8), which can be a `<name>` (rule 10), which can be `bYes` (rule 1).

We now have rules to describe a fair portion of the programs we have seen so far. We are missing rules relating to the use of integers as well as rules to describe the declarations that are required in any nontrivial program. At a higher level, we need rules to describe methods and applets.

A declaration can best be described by

16. `<declaration> ==> <type>` *list of* `<name>`*s separated by commas*;

This calls for a rule for types. For now, this is covered by

17. `<type> ==> int | void | <class>`

This is easy to extend. We just need another "or" bar and any additional types. The `<class>` rule just enumerates the Java-provided classes that we have used so far:

18. `<class> ==> String | TextField | IntField | Button | ActionEvent`

With these rules you should have no trouble describing any of the three following declarations from the `NobelAdvice` applet:

```
TextField mQuery, mAnswer;
Button bYes, bNo;
int myLocation;
```

At a higher level, the rule for writing or defining a method can be stated as

19. `<method-def> ==> public <type> <name>(<parameters>)`
    `    {`
    `      ` *possibly empty list of* `<declaration>`*s*
    `      ` *list of* `<statement>`*s*
    `    }`

It describes the header and then specifies that it is followed by a list of declarations and a list of statements, all enclosed in a set of braces. The header includes the type and name, which have been defined, and a parameter list enclosed in parentheses. We leave the discussion of the role of parameters to chapter 4, but we can specify the rule needed for the syntax:

20. `<parameters> ==>` *possibly empty list of* `<type>` `<name>` *pairs separated by commas*

An example of a parameter list is found in the header of the `actionPerformed` method that each of our interactive applets employ:

```
public void actionPerformed(ActionEvent event)
```

Here there is a single parameter specified by the `ActionEvent` event pair. `ActionEvent` is the type (actually, a class) and `event` is the name.

The rule describing an applet is structurally similar to the rule for a method and might alternatively be described as the rule for a class. An applet is just a class with special properties. However, since we are dealing with only a subset of Java, "applet" rather than "class" is appropriate:

21. `<applet> ==> public class <name> extends java.applet.Applet`
    `implements ActionListener`
    ```
    {
      possibly empty list of <declaration>s
      list of <method>s
    }
    ```

Here the rule says we have a header followed by data as represented by a list of declarations, followed by a list of methods.

Checking a Complete (Small) Program

Let's try out our rules on a complete applet, the short `HelloWorld` program, which will be our target code:

```
public class HelloWorld extends java.applet.Applet
{
    TextField m1,m2;

    public void init()
    {
        m1 = new TextField(60);
        m2 = new TextField(60);
        m1.setText("H e l l o    W o r l d !");
        m2.setText("This is a simple Java test.");
        add(m1);
        add(m2);
    }
}
```

We start with the rule for an applet because we are planning to describe or verify a complete applet:

```
<applet> ==> public class <name> extends java.applet.Applet
                    implements ActionListener
{
    possibly empty list of <declaration>s
    list of <method>s
}
```

Starting with the <name>, we use rule 1 to get

```
<applet> ==> public class HelloWorld extends java.applet.Applet
                    implements ActionListener
{
    possibly empty list of <declaration>s
    list of <method>s
}
```

Next, we apply rule 16, dealing with declarations, and since there is only one declaration statement with two names, we get

```
<applet> ==> public class HelloWorld extends java.applet.Applet
                    implements ActionListener
{
    <type> <name>, <name>;
    list of <method>s
}
```

Now rules 17 and 18 allow us to replace <type> with TextField, and rule 1 allows us to replace the two <name>s with m1 and m2:

```
<applet> ==> public class HelloWorld extends java.applet.Applet
                    implements ActionListener
{
    TextField m1, m2;
    list of <method>s
}
```

So, we're inching toward our target code. Now, since we have only one method, we apply rule 19 once:

```
<applet> ==> public class HelloWorld extends java.applet.Applet
                    implements ActionListener
{
    TextField m1, m2;
    public <type> <name>(<parameters>)
    {
        possibly empty list of <declaration>s
        list of <statement>s
    }
}
```

Applying rule 17 for `<type>` to get void and rule 1 for `<name>`, we get

```
<applet> ==> public class HelloWorld extends java.applet.Applet
                    implements ActionListener
{
    TextField m1, m2;
    public void init(<parameters>)
    {
        possibly empty list of <declaration>s
        list of <statement>s
    }
}
```

Since our parameter list is empty in our target code, we can just drop `<parameters>`. Our list of declarations in the `init` method is also empty, so we can drop that. With exactly six statements, we can restate our list of statements by writing an actual list. Thus,

```
<applet> ==> public class HelloWorld extends java.applet.Applet
                    implements ActionListener
{
    TextField m1, m2;
    public void init( )
    {
        <statement>
        <statement>
        <statement>
        <statement>
        <statement>
        <statement>
    }
}
```

Looking at our target code, we see that the first two statements are new statements and need rule 3. The next two statements use the setText method for TextField—rule 4 matches them most closely. The two add statements also fall under rule 4. Making these substitutions yields

```
<applet> ==> public class HelloWorld extends java.applet.Applet
                       implements ActionListener
{
    TextField m1, m2;
    public void init( )
    {

        <name> = new <class>(<arguments>);
        <name> = new <class>(<arguments>);
        <name>.<method>(<arguments>);
        <name>.<method>(<arguments>);
        <method>(<arguments>);
        <method>(<arguments>);

    }

}
```

In the first statement, <name> yields m1 by rule 1; <class> gets us TextField by rule 18; and <arguments> gives us <int-expression> by rules 5 and 6. The second statement uses the same sets of rules. We now have

```
<applet> ==> public class HelloWorld extends java.applet.Applet
                       implements ActionListener
{
    TextField m1, m2;
    public void init( )
    {

        m1 = new TextField(<int-expression>);
        m2 = new TextField(<int-expression>);
        <name>.<method>(<arguments>);
        <name>.<method>(<arguments>);
        <method>(<arguments>);
        <method>(<arguments>);

    }

}
```

The third statement in the `init` method requires rule 1 to get `m1`. Rule 11 converts `<method>` to `setText`, and rules 5 and 6 produce `<string-expression>` from `<arguments>`. The fourth statement follows the same pattern. That yields

```
<applet> ==> public class HelloWorld extends java.applet.Applet
                    implements ActionListener
{
    TextField m1, m2;
    public void init( )
    {
        m1 = new TextField(<int-expression>);
        m2 = new TextField(<int-expression>);
        m1.setText(<string-expression>);
        m2.setText(<string-expression>);
        <method>(<arguments>);
        <method>(<arguments>);
    }
}
```

In a similar manner, we can use rules 11, 5, and 6 to convert the last two statements. That produces

```
<applet> ==> public class HelloWorld extends java.applet.Applet
                    implements ActionListener
{
    TextField m1, m2;
    public void init( )
    {
        m1 = new TextField(<int-expression>);
        m2 = new TextField(<int-expression>);
        m1.setText(<string-expression>);
        m2.setText(<string-expression>);
        add(<oth-expression>);
        add(<oth-expression>);
    }
}
```

It should not be a surprise to find that `<int-expression>` can be `60` for the first two statements. By rules 8 and 9, the third and fourth statements have `<string-expression>` replaced by the actual text strings. Finally, as in the integer case, the other expressions (neither integer nor string but `TextFields`) in the last two statements are replaced by `m1` and `m2`. This gives us back our target code:

```
<applet> ==> public class HelloWorld extends java.applet.Applet
                        implements ActionListener
{
    TextField m1, m2;
    public void init( )
    {
        m1 = new TextField(60);
        m2 = new TextField(60);
        m1.setText("H e l l o   W o r l d !");
        m2.setText("This is a simple Java test.");
        add(m1);
        add(m2);
    }
}
```

You may have noticed one slight difference. This version of the target code includes `implements ActionListener`, which is not required for a noninteractive applet like this one. However, it will not cause any problems and saves us having to have a special rule for this case.

Even though the previous example is quite long, we actually made multiple substitutions at each step. If you are at all uncomfortable with what was done here, you probably should not apply more the one rule per line of code at a time, make the substitutions for each line, and then write out the new state of the code. This will require writing the same code again and again, with the gradual modifications that each rule brings. However, you are more likely to avoid making errors if you only apply one rule at a time. Take it slowly at first. Remember that you are, in effect, doing a mathematical proof. Perhaps you never thought you could even do that, right?

---

*A Set of Rules for Java

We do not study all of Java in this book, but we do study enough to understand the structure of the language. Here is a set of rules that cover most of the Java presented in this book.

1. `<name> ==>` *any string of alphanumeric symbols that begins with a letter*

2. `<statement> ==> <name> = <expression>;`

3. `<statement> ==> <name> = new <class>(<arguments>);`

4. `<statement> ==> <name>.<method>(<arguments>); | <method>`
   `(<arguments>);`

5. `<arguments> ==>` *possibly empty list of* `<expression>`*s separated*
   by commas

6. `<expression> ==> <string-expression> | <int-expression> |`
   `<oth-expression>`

7. `<string-expression> ==> <string-expression> +`
   `<string-expression>`

8. `<string-expression> ==> <string>`

9. `<string> ==> "any sequence of characters"`

10. `<string> ==> <name>`

11. `<method> ==> setText | getText | getInt | setInt | add |`
    `actionPerformed`

12. `<compound-statement> ==> {list of <statement>s}`

13. `<statement> ==> if (<bool-expression>) <compound-statement>`

14. `<statement> ==> if (<bool-expression>) <compound-statement>`
    `                    else<compound-statement>`

15. `<bool-expression> ==> <name> == <expression>`

16. `<declaration> ==> <type>` *list of* `<name>`*s separated by commas;*

17. `<type> ==> int | double | String | void | <class>`

18. `<class> ==> TextField | IntField | Button | ActionEvent`

19. `<method-def> ==> public <type> <name>(<parameters>)`
    `  {`
    `    ` *possibly empty list of* `<declaration>`*s*
    `    ` *list of* `<statement>`*s*
    `  }`

20. `<parameters> ==>` *possibly empty list of* `<type> <name>` *pairs*
    *   separated by commas*

21. `<applet> ==> public class <name> extends java.applet.Applet`
    `implements ActionListener`
    `  {`
    `    ` *possibly empty list of* `<declaration>`*s*
    `    ` *list of* `<method-def>`*s*
    `  }`

22. `<string-method> ==> getText`

23. `<string-expression> ==> <name>.<string-method>(<arguments>)`

24. `<int-method> ==> getInt`

25. `<positive-int> ==>` *any sequence of digits*

26. `<int-expression> ==> <int-expression> <op> <int-expression>`
27. `<int-expression> ==> <name>.<int-method>(<arguments>)`
28. `<int-expression> ==> <name>`
29. `<int-expression> ==> <positive-int> | -<positive-int>`
30. `<op> ==> + |-| * |/| %`
31. `<oth-expression> ==> <name>.<oth-method>(<arguments>)`
32. `<oth-expression> ==> <name> | <oth-method>(<arguments>)`

Summary

This chapter covered the two main stages of writing a program. First, one must have an algorithm for solving the problem at hand. Most of our algorithms in this chapter were specified as decision trees. But we also used some other types of algorithms, such as the button-driven loop for the `TrafficLight` program. The second stage is to write down the Java code to describe the algorithm in terms that the machine can understand. Here we studied a variety of syntactic forms that enable us to express our intentions to the machine. The main constructions examined were the class definition, various type declarations, button-declaring and -actuating code, some applet display features, and the `if-else` branching forms.

The chapter ended with a description of production rules for Java and their use in understanding the language and checking correctness. In the next chapter, we do some numerical computations.

3   Numerical Computation and a Study of Functions

Let's Calculate Some Numbers

How much would a young person save over a lifetime by contributing $2,000 per year to a tax-sheltered stock market fund? (In the United States, this could be an Individual Retirement Account.) More specifically, suppose the person is 20 years old and wishes to make contributions until age 60. Furthermore, suppose the person has an investment plan available that historically has appreciated, on average, at an annual rate of 12 percent. We could make a quick guess by multiplying the number of years by the contribution to obtain $80,000, but this ignores the gains that seem to be achievable with the investment plan.

In order to make a more accurate computation, we must compute the new contribution every year and add it to the investment gains from the previous year. If we repeat the computation 40 times we will obtain the answer. But that is a lot of work. Another way to solve this problem is to write a program and let a machine find the answer.

Another class of interesting tasks is the set of *optimization* problems where we try to find the best value for a parameter in some situation. As an illustration, suppose we wish to construct a cylindrical can made from 1,000 square centimeters of tin, and we want to find the correct dimensions so that the can has the largest possible volume. In our attempts to maximize volume, we might propose to build a very tall cylinder. But since the total amount of material is limited, this could lead to a very narrow shape (figure 3.1a). The cylinder might not hold much. Next, we might propose that the cylinder should be very fat. The material limitation would this time result in a very short container (figure 3.1b). Again, the total volume might not be large. Perhaps some intermediate level would be best, with moderate height and moderate diameter (figure 3.1c). Again, the computer can help us solve the problem by finding the dimensions for the cylinder such that volume is maximized and the total material is exactly 1,000 square centimeters. Simultaneously, we will study a technique for solving optimization problems. (Readers who know calculus will have an analytical solution to this problem. However, our methodology is general and can be applied to problems that do not have such solutions.)

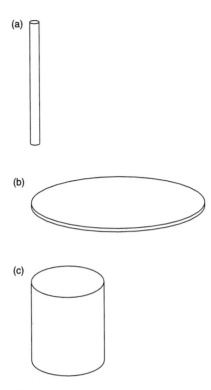

(a)

(b)

(c)

Figure 3.1

Having studied decision trees in chapter 2, we now study numerical computation to round out our experience in computing. We also continue to study new concepts in programming and problem solving.

Simple Calculations

A new type of number is necessary for numerical computing. Earlier, integers were introduced, and they are useful for counting, for referencing nodes in a decision tree, and for other numbering situations. But that type of number has some severe limitations: it cannot take on fractional values like $2\frac{1}{5}$, and the values must not be too large in the positive or negative direction. The Java specification for the int data type gives us, in fact, minimum and maximum values for stored integers. The limitations are that integers may be no lower than $-2,147,483,648$ and no higher than $2,147,483,647$. This means that

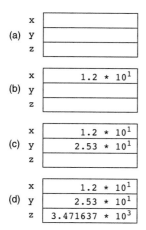

Figure 3.2

you could not do any accurate computations related to the national budget with this data type because the valid numbers are just not large enough. In general computational applications, a type of number is needed that can take on fractional as well as very large and very small values.

The answer is the `double` type, which represents numbers in two parts: the *significant digits* and an *exponent*. The number 177 might be represented as $1.77 * 10^2$, where 1.77 gives the significant digits and 2 is the exponent. The actual value of the number can always be retrieved from the representation ($1.77 * 10^2 = 1.77 * 100 = 177$), and the representation can be efficiently stored in the machine. This type of number solves the two problems of integers and still requires relatively little computer memory. It is used almost universally on modern computers. We will not discuss in detail exactly how the numbers are stored except to say that two storage areas are needed, one to hold the significant digits and one to hold the exponent. The size of these numbers is usually sufficient for most applications. In Java, the specification is that positive or negative numbers may be as large in magnitude as 10 to the power of 308 and as small in magnitude as 10 to the power of -324.

We can get started using this kind of number by making a declaration:

```
double x, y, z;
```

This results in three locations for `double` numbers being set up in memory with the appropriate names (figure 3.2a). Then one can load a number into a location

```
x = 12.0;
```

to obtain the result shown in figure 3.2b, or add two numbers together and put the sum into memory

```
y = 13.3 + x;
```

to obtain the result shown in figure 3.2c. Or one can do a complicated calculation using addition ($+$), multiplication ($*$), subtraction ($-$), and division ($/$)

```
z = (x + 17.2) * (121 - (y / x));
```

and obtain the result shown in figure 3.2d.

As a more practical example, consider the problem of computing the volume of a cylinder using the formula

$$V = \pi r^2 h$$

where V is the volume, π is a constant approximately equal to 3.14159, r is the radius of the cylinder base, and h is the height. In Java, this would be written as

```
V = 3.14159 * r * r * h;
```

A computer program to compute the volume of a cylinder is easy to write.

Algorithm
Find the radius r.
Find the height h.
Calculate $V = \pi r^2 h$.
Print the volume V.

The program is as follows:

```
import awb.*;
import java.awt.*;
import java.awt.event.*;

public class CylinderVolume extends java.applet.Applet
                    implements ActionListener
{
    double r, h, V;
    DoubleField rF, hF, VF;
    Button b1;
    public void init ()
    {
        rF = new DoubleField(20);
        rF.setLabel("Radius");
```

```
        hF = new DoubleField(20);
        hF.setLabel("Height");
        b1 = new Button("Compute");
        b1.addActionListener(this);
        VF = new DoubleField(20);
        VF.setLabel("Volume");
        add(rF);
        add(hF);
        add(b1);
        add(VF);
    }

    public void actionPerformed(ActionEvent event)
    {
        Object cause = event.getSource();
        if (cause == b1)
        {
            r = rF.getDouble();
            h = hF.getDouble();
            V = 3.14159 * r * r * h;
            VF.setDouble(V);
        }
    }
}
```

We note several issues related to this program. First, it follows the format of the programs in chapter 2, so it should be easy to read. But one must be careful to distinguish between the objects that are meant to be seen, `rF`, `hF`, and `VF`, called `DoubleField` variables, and those that are not, `r`, `h`, and `V`, called `double` variables. The user of the program sees the first group of objects and interacts with them. However, calculation is performed with the second group. The programmer must be careful to lift the information (data) from the observable objects to those useful for calculation, then do the calculation, then lift the answers back to the observable objects so that the answers can be seen.

Let's summarize the special features of the two types of objects:

`DoubleField` *Variables*
- Can be seen on the screen; can be output from a program.
- Can have a label that appears on the screen.
- Can be typed into; can be input to a program.
- Cannot be used in computations, as with the operators $+$, $-$, $*$, $/$.
- Their values can be moved to and from a `double` variable using the methods `setDouble` and `getDouble`.

Thus, one can move a value from `r` to `rF` with `rF.setDouble(r)`, and from `rF` to `r` with `r = rF.getDouble()`.

`Double` *Variables*
- Cannot be seen on the screen.
- Cannot receive typed input.
- Can be used in computations and can receive the results of computations. (Example: `V = 3.14159 * r * r * h;`)
- Their values can be moved to and from a `DoubleField` variable using the methods `setDouble` and `getDouble`.

Now let's return to the button action routine and check that it does the correct thing:

User enters value into `rF`, which is labeled `"Radius"`.
User enters value into `hF`, which is labeled `"Height"`.
User pushes `Button b1`.
Computer moves value from `rF`, where it can be seen, to `r`, where it can be used: `r = rF.getDouble();`
Computer moves value from `hF`, where it can be seen, to `h`, where it can be used: `h = hF.getDouble();`
Computer finds the value of volume: `V = 3.14159 * r * r * h;`
Computer moves the result `V` back to `VF`, where it can be seen: `VF.setDouble(V);`

Thus after the button is pushed, we have the following code:

```
r = rF.getDouble();
h = hF.getDouble();
V = 3.14159 * r * r * h;
VF.setDouble(V);
```

Another new feature that is used here is the ability to create a label for each `DoubleField`. This is done with the `setLabel` method for the `DoubleField` type.

As another example of a numerical calculation, let's write a formula for how much money a savings account will hold after receiving interest compounded once. As an example, suppose you put $2,000 into an account that pays 12 percent interest per year. We write 12 percent as a fraction, 0.12. Then at the end of the year, you could expect to have $2,000 plus the interest, which would be $2,000 * 0.12 = $240. You would have exactly $2,240. Thus, at the end of the year, the new savings amount is 2000 + (2000 * 0.12) = 2240, or as a formula,

New Savings = Savings + (Savings * Interest Rate)

In Java, you can perform the calculation on the right and store it back into the same location, `savings`:

```
savings = savings + (savings * interestrate);
```

Again, this can be embedded in a program to find the amount in an account after one interest period.

Algorithm
Find the original amount in the account.
Find the interest rate as a decimal for the time period.
Compute the new amount after one time period using the formula.
Print the result.

The program is the following:

```
import awb.*;
import java.awt.*;
import java.awt.event.*;

public class FindSavings extends java.applet.Applet
                    implements ActionListener
{
    double savings, interestrate;
    DoubleField savingsF, interestrateF;
    Button b1;
    public void init ()
    {
        savingsF = new DoubleField(20);
        savingsF.setLabel("Savings");
        interestrateF = new DoubleField(20);
        interestrateF.setLabel("Interest rate");
        b1 = new Button("Calculate");
        b1.addActionListener(this);
        add(savingsF);
        add(interestrateF);
        add(b1);
        savingsF.setDouble(0);
        interestrate.setDouble(0);
    }

    public void actionPerformed(ActionEvent event)
    {
        Object cause = event.getSource();
        if (cause == b1)
        {
```

```
            savings = savingsF.getDouble();
            interestrate = interestrateF.getDouble();
            savings = savings + (savings * interestrate);
            savingsF.setDouble(savings);
        }
    }
}
```

A demonstration of the program shows the display and the form of the numbers:

Savings 2000.00 Interest rate 0.12 Calculate

The numbers may be typed in ordinary decimal form though they are to be stored in the computer as doubles with a significant-digits part and an exponent. (One point that should be noticed about this program is that one can push the button several times to obtain the total amount in the account after several years. Thus, the program delivers more than we originally promised.)

It is easy to write useful programs of this kind, but two hazards need to be mentioned. The first relates to the problem that the order of the arithmetic operations may be ambiguous. That is, if $x = 2$, $y = 3$, $z = 4$, and we write

```
result = x + y * z;
```

what will be loaded into result? The machine might add x to y (obtaining 5) and multiply by z to get 20. Or it might multiply y times z (obtaining 12) and then add x to get 14. Which will it do? Dramatically different answers occur in the two cases. In fact, Java and most other programming languages employ a precedence mechanism that requires, in ambiguous situations, that multiplication and division be done first, followed by addition and subtraction:

Precedence Order
multiplication, division
addition, subtraction

Thus, the second of the two results is correct, 14.

In a series of computations of equal precedence, the computation moves from left to right. Thus, if $x = 6$, $y = 2$, and $z = 3$, then

```
result = x / y * z;
```

will yield the computation $6/2*3 = 3*3 = 9$. It will not compute the value to be $6/2*3 = 6/6 = 1$.

If precedence is a problem, the programmer should always use parentheses to force the order of actions to achieve his or her goals. Thus,

```
result = (x + y) * z;
```

will force the addition of x to y before multiplication by z.

```
result = x + (y * z);
```

will force the multiplication before the addition in case the programmer has forgotten the precedence order. While the fundamental principles have been given here, many more examples and detailed rules appear in a programming manual, and it should be consulted as necessary.

The second hazard related to calculation with real numbers is that the machine will make errors. The simple numbers 1 and 3 can be stored in a machine precisely, so we can have confidence in their integrity. However, if we divide one by the other, the quotient is

0.33333333333333333333333333333333 . . .

which is an infinite decimal expansion that will not fit in a computer register. So only an approximation to the correct answer is stored—the first dozen or so significant digits. That is, the number

0.333333333333

will be stored because of the limited size of the machine register. For most purposes, this is satisfactory because we need only a few places of accuracy. But in some complicated calculations, these errors can build up and greatly distort answers.

Consider the following program, which should read a number and print the same number:

```
import awb.*;
import java.awt.*;
import java.awt.event.*;

public class ErrorDemo extends java.applet.Applet
                implements ActionListener
{
    double data, extra;
    DoubleField dataF, extraF;
    Button b1;
    public void init ()
    {
        dataF = new DoubleField(20);
        dataF.setLabel("Data");
        extraF = new DoubleField(20);
        extraF.setLabel("Extra");
```

```
                b1 = new Button("Compute");
                b1.addActionListener(this);
                add(dataF);
                add(extraF);
                add(b1);
                dataF.setDouble(0);
                extraF.setDouble(0);
        }

    public void actionPerformed(ActionEvent event)
    {
        Object cause = event.getSource();
        if (cause == b1)
        {
            data = dataF.getDouble();
            extra = extraF.getDouble();
            data = data + extra;
            data = data - extra;
            dataF.setDouble(data);
        }
    }
}
```

The only function of the program is to add a number called extra to data and then subtract it away again. One would hope that this program would read a value for data and then print out the same number. For small values of extra and ordinary data (like 100), the program will work correctly. However, if extra is large, the data will be destroyed. Table 3.1 shows the performance of this program on a standard Java system.

If the values of data and extra are moderate, the program always gives the correct answer. But when extra is increased to a large value requiring more than 16 or 17 digits, the value in data is altered in unpredictable ways. You can see what is happening by actually working through the details associated with the last line of the table. The following sum is computed in the third-to-last line of program ErrorDemo:

```
100000000000000000000
                  100
```
$$\overline{}$$
```
100000000000000000100
```

But the number

```
100000000000000000100
```

Table 3.1

data (Input)	extra (Input)	data (Output)
100	100	100
100	1000	100
100	10000	100
100	100000	100
.	.	.
.	.	.
.	.	.
100	1000000000000000	100
100	10000000000000000	96
100	100000000000000000	128
100	1000000000000000000	0
100	10000000000000000000	0

is approximated by the number

10000000000000000000

because there are not enough significant digits (more than 16) in the real number representation to get the exact value. Then the following computation occurs in the second-to-last line of the program:

10000000000000000000
10000000000000000000
―――――――――――――――――
               0

This shows how the roundoff error results in the incorrect answer.

Clearly, such a computation in the middle of a formula to compute the strength of an aircraft wing or the trajectory of a spaceship could lead to random results, poor decisions, and loss of life. Thus, specialists in numerical analysis must be in charge of large complicated and critical calculations. But for the tasks addressed in this book, the computer will be quite accurate enough, and the issue of numerical error will not be mentioned again. A book on numerical analysis will explain the characteristics of numerical computations.

Exercises

1. The volume of a sphere is $\frac{4}{3}\pi r^3$. Write a program that reads the value of the radius of a sphere and then computes its volume.

2. The temperature f in degrees Fahrenheit can be computed from the temperature c in degrees Celsius by the formula $f = \frac{9}{5}c + 32$. Write a program that reads the temperature in degrees Celsius and returns the temperature in Fahrenheit.

3. Assume that $x = 6.0$, $y = 7.0$, and $z = 3.0$ are real numbers. What will be computed in each case?
   (a) `result = x * y - x * z;`
   (b) `result = x * 20.0 / z + y;`
   (c) `result = (z * x / y) / x + y;`

4. Run the program `ErrorDemo` for the case of `data` = 0.00001. How large must `extra` be before the value of `data` is altered in the computation?

5. Here is a program that uses the Pythagorean formula for right triangles: $a^2 + b^2 = c^2$, where a and b are sides of a triangle and c is its hypotenuse. The program assumes that you know b and c, and it computes the value of a.

```
import awb.*;
import java.awt.*;
import java.awt.event.*;

public class FindSide extends java.applet.Applet
                   implements ActionListener
{
    double a, b, c;
    DoubleField aF, bF, cF;
    Button b1;
    public void init ()
    {
        aF = new DoubleField(20);
        aF.setLabel("A");
        bF = new DoubleField(20);
        bF.setLabel("B");
        cF = new DoubleField(20);
        cF.setLabel("C");
        b1 = new Button("Compute");
        b1.addActionListener(this);
        add(aF);
        add(bF);
        add(cF);
        add(b1);
    }
```

```
public void actionPerformed(ActionEvent event)
{
    Object cause = event.getSource();
    if (cause == b1)
    {
        a = aF.getDouble();
        b = bF.getDouble();
        c = cF.getDouble();
        a = sqrt(c * c - b * b);
        aF.setDouble(a);
    }
}
}
```

We will investigate the accuracy of the program. If the values for *c* and *b* are 1.01 and 1.00, what value should the program compute for *a*? Do the calculation by hand to obtain four significant digits in your answer, and run the program to obtain its answer. How accurate is the program's answer?

Now repeat, holding *b* at 1.00 but allowing *c* to be 1.0001. How accurate is the machine? Try again, allowing *c* to be 1.000001, 1.00000001, 1.0000000001, and so forth. As *c* gets nearer and nearer to *b*, you will see the accuracy degrade until the error becomes 100 percent.

Functions

A *function* is an entity that receives inputs and yields, for each input, a uniquely defined output. An example of a function is one that receives the name of a country and yields the name of its capital. Usually, functions have names. We call this one *F*. If *F* receives the name Egypt, it will return the name of its capital, Cairo. If it receives Japan, it will return Tokyo. Other examples are a function that receives the name of a person and returns that person's mother's name, and a function that receives the dimensions of a cylinder and returns its volume.

Five different methodologies are used in this book to describe functions: English descriptions, mathematical notation, computer programs, tables, and graphs. Any technique that tells how to find the appropriate output for each given input is satisfactory for defining a function. These methodologies are described briefly here.

The usual mathematical notation is to write the input in parentheses following the function name and the output after an equals sign: For the country-capital function *F*, the examples are written

F(   ) =

input   output

$F(\text{Egypt}) = \text{Cairo}$

$F(\text{Japan}) = \text{Tokyo}$

In this chapter, we study numerical functions that accept input and yield numbers. A simple example is the function that doubles its input and returns the answer. If it receives 3, it will output 6. If it receives 17, it will yield 34. Let us call this function *d* and write down these examples:

$d(3) = 6$

$d(17) = 34$

One can say that *d* of anything is twice that anything, or

$d(\text{anything}) = 2 * \text{anything}$

Mathematicians prefer to use the variable name *x* for "anything" and write

$d(x) = 2x$

so this is the usual notation for describing a function that doubles.

Another numerical function is one for computing the volume of a cylinder. This function receives *r* and *h* and computes volume. If the function is named *v*, one would write

$v(r, h) = \pi r^2 h$

A program for computing this function was given previously. Suppose its inputs are $r = 2$ and $h = 3$; then its output will be $3.14159 * 2^2 * 3 = 37.69908$.

Tables provide another way to represent a function. Suppose the doubling function *d* is defined to operate only on positive integers. Then it would be written as follows:

Input *x*	Output *d(x)*
1	2
2	4
3	6
4	8
5	10
6	12
.	.
.	.
.	.

Table 3.2

$v(r,h)$				h			
		1	2	3	4	5	6
	1	3.14	6.28	9.42	12.57	15.71	18.85
	2	12.57	25.13	37.70	50.27	62.83	75.40
	3	28.27	56.55	84.82	113.10	141.37	169.65
r	4	50.26	100.53	150.80	201.06	251.33	301.59
	5	78.54	157.08	235.62	314.16	392.70	471.24
	6	113.10	226.19	339.29	452.39	565.49	678.58

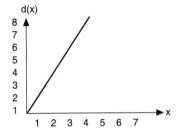

Figure 3.3

The cylinder volume function needs a two-dimensional table to represent its value, since it has two inputs (table 3.2).

Finally, we can graph functions. Figure 3.3 shows the doubling function, and figure 3.4 shows the volume function with one curve for each value of h.

Exercise

1. Consider the function that computes the volume of a sphere from its radius. Show how the five given methodologies (English words, mathematical notation, computer programs, tables, and graphs) can be used to express this function.

Looping and a Study of Functions

We are now able to approach the problem of finding the perfect dimensions for the cylinder described in the introductory section. Its volume is $V = \pi r^2 h$, and its area is $A = 2\pi r^2 + 2\pi r h = 1000$. The second equation can be solved for h and substituted into the first equation to find the volume of the cylinder for each value of r:

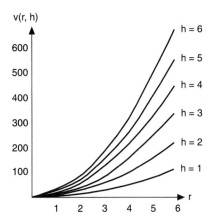

Figure 3.4

$$V = 500r - \pi r^3$$

We are interested in studying the function that computes V as r is varied. A program can be written to compute V for each value of r from 1.0 to 11.0.

Here is what we would like to do. We want to execute the following code:

```
r = 1.0;
V = 500.0 * r - 3.14159 * r * r * r;
rF.setDouble(r);
VF.setDouble(V);

r = 2.0;
V = 500.0 * r - 3.14159 * r * r * r;
rF.setDouble(r);
VF.setDouble(V);

r = 3.0;
V = 500.0 * r - 3.14159 * r * r * r;
rF.setDouble(r);
VF.setDouble(V);
etc.
```

Our coding method will be to set r, compute v, display r and v, increase r, and repeat. Each time we wish to repeat, we will push a Compute button.

```
r = 1.0;
Push Compute Button; // This is not legal Java.
{
    V = 500.0 * r - 3.14159 * r * r * r;
    rF.setDouble(r);
    VF.setDouble(V);
    r = r + 1.0;
}
```

Here is the complete program in legal Java:

```
import awb.*;
import java.awt.*;
import java.awt.event.*;

public class CylinderVolumes extends java.applet.Applet
                  implements ActionListener
{
    double r, V;
    DoubleField rF, VF;
    Button b1;
    public void init ()
    {
        rF = new DoubleField(20);
        rF.setLabel("Radius");
        b1 = new Button("Compute");
        b1.addActionListener(this);
        VF = new DoubleField(20);
        VF.setLabel("Volume");
        add(rF);
        add(b1);
        add(VF);
        r = 1.0;
        rF.setDouble(r);
    }

    public void actionPerformed(ActionEvent event)
    {
        Object cause = event.getSource();
        if (cause == b1)
        {
```

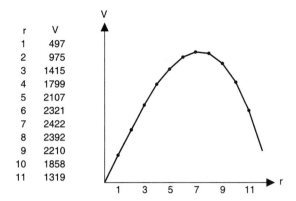

r	V
1	497
2	975
3	1415
4	1799
5	2107
6	2321
7	2422
8	2392
9	2210
10	1858
11	1319

Figure 3.5

```
V = 500.0 * r - 3.14159 * r * r * r;
rF.setDouble(r);
VF.setDouble(V);
r = r + 1.0;
        }
    }
}
```

Running this program produces values for *r* and *V*, which are graphed (figure 3.5) showing how *V* changes for each *r*. This graph makes it possible to confirm the guesses we made at the beginning of this chapter. If the cylinder is extremely tall with a very small radius, the volume will be very small. If the cylinder is very wide with a radius, say, larger than 10, the volume will not be large. In order to get the largest possible *V*, *r* should be set to an intermediate level, about 7. We will find a more exact value later. The cylinder of maximum volume looks approximately like the one shown in figure 3.6.

Let's next consider the savings problem from the introductory section. At the end of every year, the account will have the funds from the previous year (`savings`) plus the year's gain (`savings * rate`) plus the new yearly payment (`payment`):

```
savings = savings + (savings * rate) + payment;
```

This calculation needs to be done on the last day of every year for the forty years:

```
// Initialize the payment and rate of increase
year = 1;
savings = 0;
```

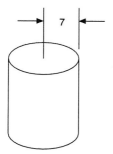

Figure 3.6

```
savings = savings + (savings * rate) + payment;
year = year + 1;
savings = savings + (savings * rate) + payment;
year = year + 1;
savings = savings + (savings * rate) + payment;
year = year + 1;
// until 40 years have been accounted for.
```

But let's try to do this without having to push the button 40 times. Java has a special looping construction that will enable us to do this. It is called `while`, and it is used as follows:

```
// Initialize the payment and rate of increase.
year = 1;
savings = 0;
while (year <= 40)
{
    savings = savings + (savings * rate) + payment;
    year = year + 1;
}
```

The `while` statement says, "While the year is less than or equal to 40, do the statements between the braces { } repeatedly." In order to understand this, study the operation of the `while` here:

```
year = 1;
savings = 0;
Is year <= 40? Yes
{
```

```
    savings = savings + (savings * rate) + payment;
    year = year + 1; // (year = 2)
}
```
Is year <= 40? Yes
```
{
    savings = savings + (savings * rate) + payment;
    year = year + 1; // (year = 3)
}
```
Repeated for many steps. Eventually year = 40.
Is year <= 40? Yes
```
{
    savings = savings + (savings * rate) + payment;
    year = year + 1; // (year = 41)
}
```
Is year <= 40? No
HALT.

Here is the Java program complete with the *while* loop.

```
import awb.*;
import java.awt.*;
import java.awt.event.*;

public class Savings extends java.applet.Applet
                     implements ActionListener
{
    double savings, payment, rate, year, lastyear;
    DoubleField savingsF, paymentF, rateF, lastyearF;
    Button b1;
    public void init ()
    {
        paymentF = new DoubleField(20);
        paymentF.setLabel("Payment");
        rateF = new DoubleField(20);
        rateF.setLabel("Increment rate");
        lastyearF = new DoubleField(20);
        lastyearF.setLabel("Total Years");
        b1 = new Button("Compute");
        b1.addActionListener(this);
        savingsF = new DoubleField(20);
        savingsF.setLabel("Savings");
```

```
        add(paymentF);
        add(rateF);
        add(lastyearF);
        add(b1);
        add(savingsF);
        paymentF.setDouble(0);
        rateF.setDouble(0);
        lastyearF.setDouble(0);
        savingsF.setDouble(0);
    }

    public void actionPerformed(ActionEvent event)
    {
        Object cause = event.getSource();
        if (cause == b1)
        {
            savings = 0;
            year = 1;
            payment = paymentF.getDouble();
            rate = rateF.getDouble();
            lastyear = lastyearF.getDouble();
            while (year <= lastyear)
            {
                savings = savings + (savings * rate) + payment;
                year = year + 1;
            }
            savingsF.setDouble(savings);
        }
    }
}
```

Exercises

1. Type in the Savings program and see how much you will save if your yearly payments are $2,000.

2. Use the methods of this chapter to find the lowest value that the function $f = x^2 - 5x + 4$ can have.

3. Use a program to compute $f = \frac{1}{3}x^3 - 4x^2 + 15x + 3$ for values of x from 1 to 12. Graph the function.

Searching for the Best Value

With some attention to detail, we can find a more accurate solution to the problem of maximizing the volume of the cylinder. Figure 3.5 would seem to indicate that r should be somewhat greater than 6. If r is exactly 6, the volume is

$$V = (500 * 6) - (3.14159 * 6^3) = 2321.42$$

Let us try $r = 6.01$, and see if the volume gets larger:

$$V = (500 * 6.01) - (3.14159 * 6.01^3) = 2323.02$$

So the theory is correct. The volume did increase when r was increased. Perhaps r should be increased again, to 6.02:

$$V = (500 * 6.02) - (3.14159 * 6.02^3) = 2324.61$$

Good! A strategy is to increase r repeatedly and see how many times V will continue to increase. If V ever gets smaller, stop: the previous value was the best. In fact, we can write a program to do this task. We are finding the maximum, just as we did previously, except that we are incrementing by a value other than 1.0 and we are stopping the calculation when the highest value is found.

Algorithm
Set r at some starting value.
Decide how much r should be increased each cycle.
Find V.
Increase r.
Find V.
Increase r.
Find V.
Increase r.
.
.
.

If V has gotten smaller, stop: previous V was the best one found.

Clearly the approach is very repetitive and needs a loop:

Algorithm
Set r at some starting value.
Decide how much r should be increased each cycle.
Find V.

        (1) increase *r*.

        (2) find *V*.

Repeat the previous two steps. If *V* has gotten smaller, stop loop.

Previous *V* was the best one found.

Actually, the computer should be told explicitly to check, on every cycle through the loop, to see whether *V* is smaller than previous *V*:

Algorithm

Set *r* at some starting value.

Decide how much *r* should be increased each cycle.

Find *V*.

        (1) increase *r*.

        (2) find *V*.

        (3) if *V* less than previous *V*, stop loop.

Repeat previous three steps.

Previous *V* was the best one found.

But in anticipation of putting this program into Java using a while loop, it is best to have the loop test at the beginning of the loop:

Algorithm

Set *r* at some starting value.

Decide how much *r* should be increased each cycle.

Find *V*.

Repeat the following:

        (1) if *V* is less than previous *V*, stop loop.

        (2) increase *r*.

        (3) find *V*.

Previous *V* was best found.

This algorithm has a bug in it. The first time the program runs, there is no previous *V*. The test is quite correct each time around the loop, but it makes no sense on the first encounter. The solution is to assume an initial value for previous *V*, which will make the loop work the first time. Assume that *V* will always be positive because it is a volume. Then we initialize previous *V* to be zero so that we can be sure it will be less than *V*.

Algorithm

Set *r* at some starting value.

Decide how much *r* should be increased each cycle.

Initialize previous *V* at zero.

Find *V*.

Repeat the following:

(1) if V is less then previous V, stop loop.

(2) increase r.

(3) find V.

Previous V was best found.

The algorithm is still not complete because previous V is not systematically maintained. When V is computed each time around the loop, the previous value will be lost unless the program stores it. Thus a statement should be inserted just before step 3 of the loop that saves the current V into a place for previous V:

Algorithm

Set r at some starting value.

Decide how much r should be increased each cycle.

Initialize previous V at zero.

Find V.

Repeat the following:

(1) if V is less then previous V, stop loop.

(2) increase r.

(3) save V in a place called "previous V".

(4) find V.

Previous V was best found.

   This completes the design of the algorithm to find the best volume. The development of the loop required much care, as is typical in most programming situations. We can now write the code:

```java
import awb.*;
import java.awt.*;
import java.awt.event.*;

public class CylinderVolumeMax extends java.applet.Applet
                    implements ActionListener
{
    double r, previousV, increase, V;
    DoubleField rF, increaseF, VF;
    Button b1;
    public void init ()
    {
        rF = new DoubleField(20);
        rF.setLabel("Radius");
        increaseF = new DoubleField(20);
        increaseF.setLabel("increase");
```

```
        b1 = new Button("Compute");
        b1.addActionListener(this);
        VF = new DoubleField(20);
        VF.setLabel("Best Volume");
        add(rF);
        add(increaseF);
        add(b1);
        add(VF);
        rF.setDouble(1.0);
        increaseF.setDouble(0.01);
    }

    public void actionPerformed(ActionEvent event)
    {
        Object cause = event.getSource();
        if (cause == b1)
        {
            r = rF.getDouble();
            increase = increaseF.getDouble();
            previousV = 0;
            V = 500 * r - 3.14159 * r * r * r;
            while (V >= previousV)
            {
                r = r + increase;
                previousV = V;
                V = 500 * r - 3.14159 * r * r * r;
            }
            VF.setDouble(previousV);
        }
    }
}
```

You should type this program into a machine and find a better solution to the cylinder maximization problem. Is it possible to find the best possible *r* accurate to three decimal places?

It could happen that this program will not find the best solution if the *V* curve has a strange shape, as shown in figure 3.7. Remember what the program does, and notice how it will work on this problem. If it starts at the left side, which is marked "initial *r*," it will keep increasing *r* and slowly moving to the right while *V* increases. But notice that *V* will start getting smaller where the figure shows "best *V* found." So the program will stop and announce it has found the best *V*. But it will be wrong because a larger *V* exists farther

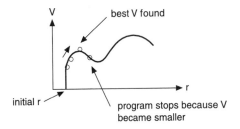

Figure 3.7

toward the right. In the example of finding the best cylinder, this does not occur, but in general one must investigate carefully to be sure the absolute maximum has been found.

This section has demonstrated a method to search for things with a computer. In our example, we were looking for the best possible value of r, but in general one can be looking for almost anything. The search method builds a loop that repeatedly checks for the desired item. The loop computation is continued until the searched-for item is found:

Initialize computation.
While item is not found do:
        (*repetitive portion to get next item*).
Print item found.

Exercises

1. Find the dimensions, r and h, for a cylinder that has 1,000 square centimeters of material and maximum volume. What is the maximum volume that is achieved? Give all answers accurate to three decimal places.

2. Suppose a person deposits $1,000 into a bank account and then puts in monthly payments of $20 regularly for 20 years. Further suppose the bank pays an annual rate of 6 percent, compounded monthly. What will be the total savings at the end of the 20 years?

3. A person has the goal of saving $10,000 in ten years. She can obtain an annual interest rate of 8 percent, compounded monthly. Her plan is to initially deposit $1,000 and then to make monthly payments for the rest of the ten years. How much should her monthly payments be?

4. Suppose we have two functions $f_1 = 2x + 1/(x^3 + x^2)$ and $f_2 = x^2 - 6x$. Write a program that will start x at some low value, say $x = 1$, where f_1 is greater than f_2, and increment x repeatedly while computing the values of f_1 and f_2 each time. The pro-

gram loop should stop when f_1 becomes less than f_2. Find, as well as you can, what value of x is greater than 1 and makes $f_1 = f_2$.

5. Write a program that acts as a desk calculator. The program will have a series of buttons much like some of the programs in chapter 2. It also will have two registers, an x register and a RESULT register. The commands will all operate by manipulating these registers, clearing them, entering values, adding other numbers, and so forth. Following are the commands. Each command results in the indicated action, and then it displays the contents of the register to show its current status.

CR   Clear the RESULT register.
CX   Clear the x register.
C   Copy number x into the register RESULT.
+   Add x to RESULT and leave the answer in RESULT.
*   Multiply x times RESULT and leave the answer in RESULT.
/   Divide x into RESULT and leave the answer in RESULT.
−   Subtract x from RESULT and leave the answer in RESULT.

Storing Information in Arrays

In order to encourage a person to use the savings program, we might like to create an electronic savings table that would show the total amount of the savings at the end of each year. The person would be able to check the amount in the account for any year in the future assuming he or she makes all the payments on time and assuming the market rises at the predicted rate. This record can be constructed by creating an *array* in the computer memory that can hold all of the 40 entries in the proposed plan. In this section, we study the concept of arrays, their utilization, and particularly their usefulness in the savings problem.

The first step in using an array is to create it in memory with a declaration. We do this with a small modification of the usual declaration. If we want one location called table to store a double number, we write

```
double table;
```

and if we want many locations, we write

```
double table[];
```

This tells the Java processor that table will have many values, table[0], table[1], table[2], and so forth. But this processor does not know how many locations to set aside, so in the init routine, we write

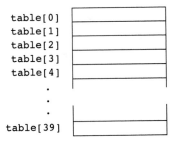

table[0]
table[1]
table[2]
table[3]
table[4]

     .

     .

     .

table[39]

Figure 3.8

```
table = new double[40];
```

to indicate that we want 40 locations. They will be numbered $0, 1, 2, \ldots, 39$.

Each of the individual entries in this array will have its own name. The first is called `table[0]`, the second is `table[1]`, and so forth. Intuitively, the array should be envisioned as shown in figure 3.8.

Before building the electronic savings table, let's study arrays and their manipulation with a few examples. Suppose we wish to write a program whose only function is to (1) create an array called A that can hold four integers, and (2) put the number 10 into each of those four entries. Here is the program:

```
import awb.*;
import java.awt.*;

public class FirstArray extends java.applet.Applet
{
    int A[];
    public void init()
    {
        A = new int[4];
        A[0] = 10;
        A[1] = 10;
        A[2] = 10;
        A[3] = 10;
    }
}
```

Another way to achieve the same result is to use a `while` loop. Notice that the index `i` for the array must be declared to be an integer.

```
import awb.*;
import java.awt.*;

public class SecondArray extends java.applet.Applet
{
    int A[], i;
    public void init()
    {
        A = new int[4];
        i = 0;
        while (i < 4)
        {
            A[i] = 10;
            i = i + 1;
        }
    }
}
```

This program creates the array and then executes this sequence:

```
i = 0;
Is i < 4 ? Yes
A[0] = 10;
i = 1;
Is i < 4 ? Yes
A[1] = 10;
i = 2;
Is i < 4 ? Yes
A[2] = 10;
i = 3;
Is i < 4 ? Yes
A[3] = 10;
i = 4;
Is i < 4 ? No
```

By changing i repeatedly through the loop, the item in the array that is being referenced keeps changing as well.

Once some values exist in the array, we can add a button that will enable us to examine each of those entries:

```
import awb.*;
import java.awt.*;
import java.awt.event.*;
```

```
public class ThirdArray extends java.applet.Applet
                    implements ActionListener
{
    int A[], i;
    IntField iF, valueF;
    Button b1;
    public void init()
    {
        b1 = new Button("Next value");
        b1.addActionListener(this);
        iF = new IntField(20);
        iF.setLabel("i");
        valueF = new IntField(20);
        valueF.setLabel("table value");
        add(b1);
        add(iF);
        add(valueF);
        A = new int[4];
        i = 0;
        while (i < 4)
        {
            A[i] = 10;
            i = i + 1;
        }
        i = 0;
    }

    public void actionPerformed(ActionEvent event)
    {
        Object cause = event.getSource();
        if (cause == b1)
        {
            iF.setInt(i);
            valueF.setInt(A[i]);
            if (i < 3)
                {i = i + 1;}
            else
                {i = 0;}
        }
    }
}
```

This will set up Button b1 and the fields iF and valueF. Then it loads the array with 10s and sets i to 0. If the button is pushed, the action routine will present this:

```
i 0 table value 10
```

If the button is pushed three more times, i will increment and produce

```
i 1 table value 10
i 2 table value 10
i 3 table value 10
```

Here is a program that puts a sequence of integers into an integer array:

```
import awb.*;
import java.awt.*;
import java.awt.event.*;

public class FourthArray extends java.applet.Applet
                    implements ActionListener
{
    int A[], i;
    IntField iF, valueF;
    Button b1;
    public void init()
    {
        b1 = new Button("Next value");
        b1.addActionListener(this);
        iF = new IntField(20);
        iF.setLabel("i");
        valueF = new IntField(20);
        valueF.setLabel("table value");
        add(b1);
        add(iF);
        add(valueF);
        A = new int[4];
        i = 0;
        while (i < 4)
        {
            A[i] = 10 + i;
            i = i + 1;
        }
        i = 0;
```

```
    }
    public void actionPerformed(ActionEvent event)
    {
        Object cause = event.getSource();
        if (cause == b1)
        {
            iF.setInt(i);
            valueF.setInt(A[i]);
            if (i < 3)
                {i = i + 1;}
            else
                {i = 0;}
        }
    }
}
```

This program will set i to 0 and then execute

```
A[0] = 10 + 0
```

on the first loop repetition. So A[0] will receive 10. The other entries in A will be 11, 12, 13, as can be seen by running the program and pushing the button repeatedly.

This understanding of arrays makes it possible to build the electronic savings table. An addition to the first compound interest program, Savings, will create and fill up the needed array.

```
import awb.*;
import java.awt.*;
import java.awt.event.*;

public class SavingsArray extends java.applet.Applet
                   implements ActionListener
{
    double table[], savings, payment, rate;
    int year, lastyear;
    DoubleField savingsF, paymentF, rateF;
    IntField yearF, lastyearF;
    Button b1, b2;
    public void init()
    {
        paymentF = new DoubleField(20);
        paymentF.setLabel("payment");
```

```
        rateF = new DoubleField(20);
        rateF.setLabel("rate");
        lastyearF = new IntField(20);
        lastyearF.setLabel("last year");
        b1 = new Button("Fill table");
        b1.addActionListener(this);
        b2 = new Button("Check entries");
        b2.addActionListener(this);
        yearF = new IntField(20);
        yearF.setLabel("year");
        savingsF = new DoubleField(20);
        savingsF.setLabel("savings");
        add(paymentF); add(rateF); add(lastyearF);
        add(b1); add(b2); add(yearF); add(savingsF);
        table = new double[100];
    }
    public void actionPerformed(ActionEvent event)
    {
        Object cause = event.getSource();
        if (cause == b1)
        {
            payment = paymentF.getDouble();
            rate = rateF.getDouble();
            lastyear = lastyearF.getInt();
            savings = 0;
            year = 0;
            while (year < lastyear)
            {
                savings = savings + (savings * rate) + payment;
                table[year] = savings;
                year = year + 1;
            }
            year = 0;
        }
        if (cause == b2)
        {
            yearF.setInt(year);
            savingsF.setDouble(table[year]);
            if (year < lastyear - 1)
                {year = year + 1;}
```

```
        else
            {year = 0;}
    }
  }
}
```

`Button b1` is the one that computes the savings level for every year and saves the values. It gathers the values of `payment`, `rate`, and `lastyear` from their displayed field values and then enters the loop. The first time around the loop, `year` will have value `0`. So `table[0]` will receive its appropriate entry, the amount of the savings. Each subsequent repetition will increase `year` by 1 and cause the next table entry to be made. The other `Button`, `b2`, is used to look at the values in the table.

Exercises

1. Write a program that has an array capable of holding ten integers. The program should ask the user to type a number and then store it into the array. Then it should ask the user for another number and store it, then another and store it, and so forth, until all ten entries of the array are full. Finally, the program should allow the person to see all the ten entires in the array.

2. Write a program that has an array capable of holding ten integers. The program should ask the user to type in ten integers, and it should store them in the array. Then the program should ask the user to type in another integer. If it finds that last integer in the array, it should type FOUND. If it does not find it in the array it should type NOT FOUND.

3. Suppose a bank gives each of its customers a key number and then requires that users give their numbers before computerized facilites are made available. Then a table must be stored in the computer indicating the key number for each customer so that the appropriate check can be made. Write a program that implements this scheme as follows. It will have two tables, one called `name`, which holds the names of customers, and one called `key`, which holds their key numbers. The key numbers will be positive integers. For example, `name[1]` will hold the name of the first customer and `key[1]` will hold that person's key number. The program will first ask how many customers with their key numbers are to be stored. Then it will enable the bank to input each name and associated key number. After it has stored these, it will enter a loop designed for customers. It will ask the customer for name and key number. If it finds the name in the list and sees that the key number is correct, it will print the message "Welcome to the XYZ Bank Automated Teller." If it does not find the name and key number, it will print "Sorry, your name and key numbers are not approved for entry into this system."

4. A shortcoming with the system of exercise 3 is that a computer expert might be able to find the table of secret key numbers, print them out, and use them in illegal ways. Let's revise the system so that if an expert found the table, he would still have considerable difficulty illegally entering the system. Instead of giving each customer a key number, we will assign two integers that are prime numbers. The table will not store the key numbers because each will be known only to the customer. The computer table will store only the *product* of two numbers in the key array. When the customer is asked for her name, she will be asked to give two key numbers. Then the program will check that they are both positive and greater than 1, multiply them together, and note whether this product is in the table.

From the point of view of the customer, the system will work the same except that two key numbers will be required for entry. From the point of view of the bank, no one will be able to easily enter the customers' accounts even if he has the number in the key table. He will need to find two prime numbers that multiply to produce the number in the key array. If the number in the key array is large, this is not an easy problem.

Finding Sums, Minima, and Maxima

Suppose the bank customer makes a series of deposits. (We ignore for the moment the issue of interest.) We will ask what was the total of the deposits, and what were the smallest and largest deposits. In answering these questions, we will examine general methods for accumulating quantities (sums, in this case) and for finding extreme elements (minima and maxima).

Begin by building a program that can receive the amounts of the deposits and store them into an array. The user simply types the amount of each deposit into the `deposit` location and pushes a button to make the entry. A second button enables one to examine all the entries that have been entered.

```
import awb.*;
import java.awt.*;
import java.awt.event.*;

public class SavingsArray2 extends java.applet.Applet
                    implements ActionListener
{
    double table[], deposit;
    int i, firstempty;
    DoubleField depositF;
    IntField iF, firstemptyF;
```

```
Button b1, b2;
public void init()
{
    depositF = new DoubleField(20);
    depositF.setLabel("deposit");
    iF = new IntField(20);
    iF.setLabel("i");
    firstemptyF = new IntField(20);
    firstemptyF.setLabel("first empty");
    b1 = new Button("Make deposit");
    b1.addActionListener(this);
    b2 = new Button("Check entries");
    b2.addActionListener(this);
    add(depositF); add(iF); add(firstemptyF);
    add(b1); add(b2);
    table = new double[100];
    firstempty = 0;
    i = 0;
    table[0] = 0;
}
public void actionPerformed(ActionEvent event)
{
    Object cause = event.getSource();
    if (cause == b1)
    {
        table[firstempty] = depositF.getDouble();
        firstempty = firstempty + 1;
        firstemptyF.setInt(firstempty);
    }
    if (cause == b2)
    {
        iF.setInt(i);
        depositF.setDouble(table[i]);
        if (i < firstempty - 1)
            {i = i + 1;}
        else
            {i = 0;}
    }
}
}
```

Now let's be sure we know how this program works. Suppose the user starts the program. Then we have from the `init` routine firstempty $= 0$, i $= 0$, and `table[0]` $= 0$. Next, suppose the user types `10.00` and pushes the Make deposit button. Then this code will run

```
table[firstempty] = depositF.getDouble();
firstempty = firstempty + 1;
firstemptyF.setInt(firstempty);
```

and we will have `table[0]` $= 10.00$ and firstempty $= 1$.

Next, the user types `11.00` and pushes the Make deposit button. The same code will run again, and we will have `table[1]` $= 11.00$ and firstempty $= 2$. Now the user types `12.00` and pushes the Make deposit button. This will yield `table[2]` $= 12.00$ and firstempty $= 3$.

Now, the user pushes the Check entries button three times. This means the following code will run three times:

```
iF.setInt(i);
depositF.setDouble(table[i]);
if (i < firstempty - 1)
    {i = i + 1;}
else
    {i = 0;}
```

You can check that this will happen, enabling the user to see that the values were correctly stored:

deposit: 10.00   i: 0   firstempty: 3
deposit: 11.00   i: 1   firstempty: 3
deposit: 12.00   i: 2   firstempty: 3

Next, we wish to make an addition to this program to show how to add up the given numbers.

Algorithm
Initialize sum to 0.
Add `table[0]` to sum.
Add `table[1]` to sum.
Add `table[2]` to sum.

.

.

.

To add `table[0]` to `sum`, add the two quantities together

```
table[0] + sum
```

and put the result back into `sum`:

```
sum = table[0] + sum
```

Algorithm
```
sum = 0
sum = table[0] + sum
sum = table[1] + sum
sum = table[2] + sum
etc.
```

In Java, this is written as

```
sum = 0;
i = 0;
while (i < firstempty)
{
    sum = table[i] + sum;
    i = i + 1;
}
```

Or let us put it into a button push routine:

```
if (cause == b3)
{
    sum = 0;
    i = 0;
    while (i < firstempty)
    {
        sum = table[i] + sum;
        i = i + 1;
    }
    sumF.setDouble(sum);
    i = 0;
}
```

This code assumes that you made some declarations that are not discussed here.

This program illustrates the format of the basic accumulator program:

Initialize accumulator.

Initialize index.

While there are more objects, do:

> (1) let accumulator = object, operation, accumulator;
>
> (2) increment index.

The accumulator can have any name, and the object and operation can have many forms. This basic format can be used to add up deposits as shown previously or to do other similar tasks. Here are several examples of the use of this basic format. The first is a program that adds up the numbers from 1 to *n*:

```
if (cause == b3)
    {
        sum = 0;
        r = 1;
        while (r <= n)
        {
            sum = r + sum;
            r = r + 1;
        }
        sumF.setDouble(sum);
    }
```

Or you could multiply together the numbers from 1 to *n* and obtain *n* factorial. (Remember that *n* factorial means that the numbers $1, 2, 3, \ldots, n$ are to be multiplied together. Thus 4 factorial is $1 * 2 * 3 * 4 = 24$.)

```
if (cause == b3)
    {
        product = 1;
        r = 1;
        while (r <= n)
        {
            product = r * product;
            r = r + 1;
        }
        productF.setDouble(product);
    }
```

Or you could accumulate a string of *n* *A*'s. Again, we assume you made a series of declarations that are not discussed here.

```
if (cause == b3)
    {
        asequence = " ";
        i = 1;
        while (i <= n)
        {
            asequence = asequence + "A";
            i = i + 1;
        }
        asequenceF.setDouble(asequence);
    }
```

Another common task is to find the largest or smallest element in an array. Consider the issue of finding the largest deposit made. Look at the first item, and temporarily store it as the largest seen so far. Then sequentially examine each later item, looking for larger ones. If larger ones are found, they are copied into the "largest-so-far" slot. Here is the code to find the largest deposit:

```
if (cause == b3)
    {
        largestsofar = table[0];
        i = 1;
        while (i < firstempty)
        {
            if (table[i] > largestsofar)
            {
                largestsofar = table[i];
            }
            i = i + 1;
        }
        largestsofarF.setDouble(largestsofar);
    }
```

The general pattern for finding such extremes recurs often in programs:

Let "extremesofar" = first item.
Initialize index.
While there are more objects to examine, do:
        (1) if item is more extreme than "extremesofar", then
                let "extremesofar" = item.
        (2) increment index.

This pattern can be used for finding the largest number, the smallest number, the numbers nearest some value, the longest and shortest strings, and so forth.

Exercises

1. Write a program that reads an integer n and then prints a string of n O's.

2. Add buttons to the savings program described in this section so that a person can enter a series of deposits and then push buttons to find the largest and smallest deposits and the sum of the deposits.

Putting Things in a Row, and a Special Characteristic of Functions

A number of theoretical issues in computer science are addressed in later chapters, and it is important to build the foundations along the way. In this section, we discuss an important concept: mathematicians call it *countability*, and this book calls it "putting things in a row." We use this idea in chapter 15 on noncomputability, but there are so many difficult ideas in that chapter that we had better address this one well beforehand.

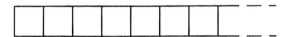

The fundamental idea concerns an unending chain of bins that extends off into infinity and the question of whether there are enough bins to hold all the elements of a set of objects. We assume every bin is arbitrarily large so it can hold any individual object regardless of its size. But the goal for a given set is to put each of its members into some bin in the chain. Two members cannot be in the same bin. If we can succeed with a set, we will say that we have "put this set in a row"; mathematicians would say the set is *countable*.

The first set to consider is the set of positive integers, which can easily be put in a row. Put 1 in the first bin, 2 in the second, and so forth without end:

| 1 | 2 | 3 | 4 | 5 | 6 | 7 | | | |

There are enough bins to hold every positive integer, and regardless of which integer is chosen, it will be somewhere in the chain. The set of positive and negative integers can also be put in a row:

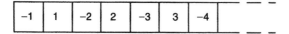

Theoretically, the names of all human beings that have ever been born can also be put in a row by placing the name of the lightest person at birth in bin 1, the second lightest in bin 2, and so forth. Where there are ties, they can be ordered on another dimension, such as by the number of cells in their bodies. The set of all molecules in the universe can be arranged in a row by putting one molecule in bin 1, its closest neighbor in bin 2, its second closest neighbor in bin 3, and so forth. Again, a second dimension can be used to settle ties if necessary.

The main point in each of these examples is that we seek a rule that will show how to place every member of a set into a different bin in the row. If we can find such a rule, we will say the set can be put into a row.

Consider the set of all finite strings of printable characters such as "computers," "#!-7," and "Let us go." This set can also be put in a row by putting the string of length zero in bin 1, and the strings of length one in bins $2, 3, 4, 5, \ldots, n$ because we assume only a finite number of distinct characters. Next, the strings of length two can be placed in bins $n + 1$, $n + 2, \ldots,$. This set of strings would thus contain all the words in any dictionary, all the sentences that could ever be written, all the books that ever have been or will be written, all the books that will *not* be written, and much more. This set can also be put in a row.

At this point, one might decide that some very large sets can be put in a row. Perhaps every set imaginable can be put in a row. It turns out that the functions that input a positive integer and yield a positive integer cannot be put in a row. No matter how one tries to squeeze them all into the bins, there will always be huge numbers more that will not fit. This is an important property with great implications for computer science. A demonstration that this is true appears in the next section, and a discussion of the significance of this fact is given in chapter 15 on noncomputability.

Exercises

1. Imagine a great two-dimensional checkerboard that goes on forever in all directions. Are all the squares on the board countable? That is, can you find a way to put all the squares in a row?

2. Imagine the set of all Java programs. Is it possible to put this set in a row?

x	f(x)	x	f(x)	x	f(x)	x	f(x)
1	2	1	4	1	11	1	17
2	4	2	7	2	11	2	109
3	6	3	10	3	11	3	18
4	8	4	13	4	11.	4	1
5	10	5	16	5	11	5	512
6	12	6	19	6	11	6	62
7	14	7	22	7	11	7	174
⋮	⋮	⋮	⋮	⋮	⋮	⋮	⋮

Figure 3.9

*Putting the Functions in a Row

Let's begin putting the functions in a row and see where this leads us. We will consider only functions that accept positive integers as input and yield positive integers as output, and we will represent each function with its input-output table. Figure 3.9 shows the beginning of the enumeration.

The first function listed is the doubling function; the second calculates a simple polynomial; the third always outputs 11 regardless of the input; and the fourth outputs a rather bizarre and unpredictable array of values. All are perfectly legitimate functions and are completely specified by their infinite tables.

Suppose that an unboundedly patient and speedy being continues the task begun here and puts all the rest of the functions that exist in a row. Then the task will be complete, and we will have shown how to put yet another large set in a row.

However, consider the new function constructed as shown in figure 3.10. Its table is built as indicated. The first entry of the first function is incremented by 1 and put into its first output position. The second entry of the second function is incremented and put into its second output position. And, in general, for each $i = 1, 2, 3, \ldots$, the ith output position in the ith function is incremented and put into the ith output position for the new function.

This new function is clearly as good as any other function. Its table is completely well specified. Therefore our unboundedly patient and speedy being must certainly have included it in one of the bins of a row. Let's try to find it. The new function is not in the first bin because it is different on the first entry. It is not in the second bin because it is different on the second entry. Wait a minute! It is different from the ith function in the ith position for all i. The new function is different from every function in the row and is thus not in any bin. So the speedy being did *not* put every function into a row.

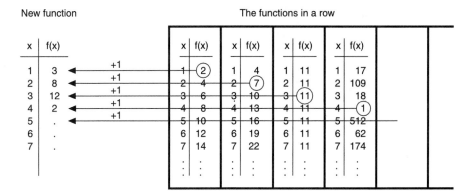

Figure 3.10

It is easy to find millions of functions that were left out. Consider the functions constructed like the preceding new function except that 2 or 3 or something else is added to each entry. Consider the function that is built using the second output of the first function, the third output from the second function, and so forth. This function and all of its similar versions will also not be in the row.

The functions that have positive integers for inputs and outputs cannot be put into a row. Mathematicians say this set of functions is *uncountable*. All the other sets discussed in the previous section are countable, but this one is not. Most other classes of functions are similarly uncountable, but none needs to be considered here. The fact that these functions cannot be put into a row is an extremely important fact for computer scientists (as is discussed in chapter 15 on noncomputability).

Exercises

1. Describe various kinds of functions that will not be in the row of functions built in the preceding construction.

2. The set of infinite strings of printable characters cannot be put into a row. Show how the preceding argument can be modified to prove this fact.

3. Specify which of the following sets can be put in a row and which cannot. Give a full explanation in each case.
   (a) The set of well-formed English sentences.
   (b) The set of functions that input a positive integer and output a positive integer and that each have the following property: for a given function, the output will be the same regardless of what the input is.
   (c) The set of decimal numbers that each have an infinite number of digits.

(d) The set of all living creatures that have existed in the past or will exist in the future.

(e) The set of all paths down an infinite tree constructed as follows: The root node has two branches below it of length 1 inch. At the end of each branch is a node with two more branches below it of length 1 inch. At the end of those branches are nodes with more branches, and so on, without end.

Summary

This chapter has discussed numerical computation and its many aspects.

First, it was noted that integers are not adequate for general numerical computation because they cannot take on fractional or very large or small values. Then the `double` number type was introduced, and many examples were given showing its use.

Next, it was noted that numerical computation with `double` numbers involves two possible hazards: first, the operators have a precedence that may cause an order of computation that is unexpected by the uninitiated and could yield undesired answers. Second, the computer will make mistakes when computing with `double` numbers. These mistakes are the roundoff errors caused by the limited size of the computer's registers. These errors are typically of little importance in textbook computations, but in some calculations they can combine to undermine the integrity of the answer.

A fundamental concept of mathematics and computer science is that of the function. This idea was introduced, and five different methods were given for describing functions. Various programs for computing functions were given. One class of functions was examined and shown to have the property that its members cannot be "put into a row." This is an unusual property of a set and has implications discussed later.

This chapter also examined looping programs and showed how to build them. Such programs can be used for studying the properties of a function by repeatedly evaluating the function on different inputs. For example, you might want to find the minimum or maximum values that a function could have. Looping programs can also be used to calculate complex functions such as the accumulation from a 40-year savings plan. The `while` loop construction can be used for search. The test at the beginning of the `while` loop must be designed to stop the repetitions when the searched-for item is found.

Experienced programmers will point out that there are other ways to code loops in Java. Thus, the form

```
i = 1;
while (i <= n)
{
    code
    i = i + 1;
}
```

can also be written as

```
for (int i = 1; i <= n; i++)
{
    code
}
```

This and many other features of Java are omitted from the current discussion because there are too many of them to include in a book with a far broader purpose. However, anyone who learns and is comfortable with them is encouraged to use them.

This chapter also introduced arrays for storing data and showed their use in various situations. Example programs illustrated ways to read, print, sum, and find the maximum or minimum values in arrays.

4 Top-Down Programming, Subroutines, and a Database Application

Let's Solve a Mystery

As the afternoon sun faded on the village green, Chief Inspector Brown was just lighting his evening pipe when an urgent call came in from Dunsmore Manor. It was from a terrified Miss Secrest, who had found Lord Peter Dunsmore collapsed on the drawing room floor. He was dead. Lady Emily had gone to her chambers in shock, and the chief inspector was implored to hurry to the scene. This he did, and upon examining the body, proclaimed the cause of death: a lethal dose of poison administered within the last few hours.

The family and servants seemed too distraught to be questioned, but a quaint small computer terminal in the corner of the room gave access to some family data. The inspector sat down and began typing:

Who visited the manor today?

The machine responded:

Mr. Mason visited at 3:00 P.M.
The professor visited at 3:00 P.M.
Miss Secrest visited at 5:00 P.M.

Tell me about Mr. Mason.

Mr. Mason has hobby tennis.
Mr. Mason visited at 3:00 P.M.
Mr. Mason is a chemist.

The inspector typed a long series of questions, slowly puffed his pipe, and finally arrived at a suspect. He was able to identify only one person who had all three prerequisites: an apparent motive, access to the poison, and a way of administering it to the victim.

Although we may want to know who committed the crime, as computer scientists we are even more interested in knowing how the computer program works. In this chapter, we study methodologies for creating larger programs than those in previous chapters, and one of them will be the question-answering program the inspector used. In the process, we study the method of top-down programming, the use of subroutines, and techniques for keeping the greater complexity of large programs under control. The final sections of the chapter illustrate the use of these methodologies for other example problems.

Top-Down Programming and the Database Program

The central issue of computer science is the problem of complexity and how to deal with it. There are two important techniques for dealing with great complexity:

1. Represent the problem so that it can be dealt with easily.
2. Decompose the problem into simpler subtasks and then repeatedly decompose those subtasks until at the lowest level each remaining subtask is easy to comprehend (figure 4.1). The solution to the whole problem is the assembly of all the subtask solutions obtained in the decomposition. If each decomposition is simple and clearly correct, and if each lowest-level subtask is easy to code and also clearly correct, the complete program should be correct.

Let's apply these ideas to creating the question-answering program the inspector used. A store of information such as that concerning the Dunsmore family is called a *database*. A program that stores such information and answers questions about it is called a *data-*

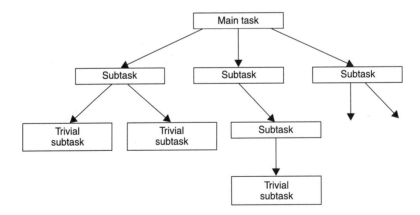

Figure 4.1

base program. Our current task is to build one. However, the specifications implied by the discussion indicate that this program may become an immense undertaking. If we are to achieve success, we must find ways to reduce the problem complexity.

Thus our first task in addressing this problem is to seek a representation that is easy to comprehend and leads to the simplest possible program. As a first simplification, assume that the family information is stored as a set of facts represented by declarative sentences such as

Mr. Mason visited at 3:00 P.M.
Mr. Mason is a chemist.

Once this decision is made, we no longer need to grapple with the vague idea of "information," and the programmer's task is to settle on ways to store and retrieve sentences. We further simplify by assuming that all questions can be answered by simply finding and presenting some of the stored sentences—those that answer the user's question. Thus, if a user asks a question, the machine need only determine whether facts exist in the database to answer it, and if they are found, print them out. We do not consider the case where the program might be asked to infer some new fact that does not already explicitly exist in its database.

Having settled on a representation that clearly specifies what is meant by "information" and the nature of the information, we can begin to see the kinds of processing needed to solve the problem. The second step in dealing with complexity is to decompose the whole task into a set of easily handled subparts.

The program will need two primary abilities: to read in facts and to answer questions related to them. We will construct the program with a command structure employing four commands:

`find`   Receives questions and prints all the relevant facts
`input` Reads facts
`print` Prints all the stored facts
`quit`   Terminates program execution

It is premature to worry too much about the actual code, but given our study of previous chapters, you could imagine a button (as well as various labels and `TextFields`) for each of these four commands. Graphically, the database program has been decomposed into four subtasks (figure 4.2).

Next we examine the three nontrivial subtasks: Input, Find, and Print. Consider the Input routine. First, a new place in memory will be located, and then a fact will be read and placed into that new position:

Input Routine
Find a new place in memory.
Read a new fact into that place.

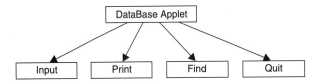

Figure 4.2

The Print routine is also easy:

Print Routine
For a position in memory that has a fact in it, print the contents.
Advance to the next position that contains a fact.

The Find routine will first read the user's question. Then it will check each stored fact and print those facts that help to provide an answer to the question. For example, when the inspector requested general information regarding Mr. Mason, the program printed all the stored facts mentioning Mr. Mason.

Find Routine
Read user's question.
For each position in memory that has a fact in it,
    if that fact helps to answer the question, print it.

The last part of the Find routine seems complicated because we do not know when a fact "helps to answer the question." Let's decompose this process again and create a question-fact comparator. This routine will examine the question and the fact, and report either "answer" or "no" depending on whether the fact partially answers the question or not. Using this routine, the Find routine is now quite simple:

Find Routine
Read user's question.
For each position in memory that has a fact in it,
    call the question-fact comparator.
        If the comparator reports "answer", then
            print the fact.

Of course, the question-fact comparator may be a complex routine, but that is an issue to be examined later.

   The database program has now evolved to the state shown in figure 4.3. Once we have discovered a way to program the question-fact comparator, the program will be reduced to a series of easy subtasks. You should review all the parts and see that the seemingly

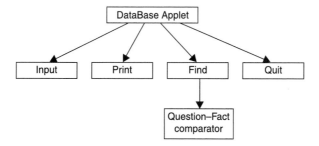

Figure 4.3

complicated database program is effectively reduced to rather easily handled subparts. Before considering these parts further, however, we must consider subroutines to help with the decomposition process.

Exercise

1. Suppose a program is to read the names and backgrounds of a series of men and women and then pair them up, putting people of similar backgrounds together. The program should print out a listing of the couples. How should the data be represented? Show how to decompose this problem into a series of easily programmable subtasks.

Subroutines

A subroutine or subprogram is a sequence of related programming statements. We always associate a name with a subroutine so that we can refer to it. In Java we have seen subroutines before—they are called methods. The terms *subroutine*, *subprogram*, *method*, *function*, and *procedure* are treated as synonyms by most programmers, and some of these are used interchangeably. Following is an example of a method definition for a routine called `Byline`. Assuming that `TextFields` `m1` and `m2` have been set up at the beginning of the applet, the subroutine prints a message with an author's name:

```
void Byline()
{
    m1.setText("This program was written by");
    m2.setText(" Lady Emily Dunsmore");
}
```

This method does the job of printing the two lines shown. A programmer who wants those two lines printed need only include the statement

```
Byline( );
```

to invoke or call this method. Suppose that Lady Emily wrote the database program and decided that, each time it is used, it should begin by printing those two lines and end by printing them again. If her applet was originally as follows

```
public class DataBase extends java.applet.Applet
                    implements ActionListener
{
    declarations

    public void init()
    {
        initialization code
    }
    public void actionPerformed(ActionEvent event)
    {
        Object cause = event.getSource( );

        response code for Input

        response code for Print

        response code for Find

        response code for Quit
    }
}
```

the new version could be packaged this way:

```
public class DataBase extends java.applet.Applet
                    implements ActionListener
{
    TextField m1, m2;
    Button bQuit;

    more declarations
```

```
public void init()
{
    m1 = new TextField(70);
    m2 = new TextField(70);
    bQuit = new Button("Quit");

    more initialization code

    Byline(); // Here Byline is used.

}
public void actionPerformed(ActionEvent event)
{
    Object cause = event.getSource();

    response code for Input

    response code for Print

    response code for Find

    if (cause == bQuit)
    {
        Byline(); // Here Byline is used.
    }
}
}
```

This would invoke `Byline` at the beginning during the initialization of the applet and then again in the `actionPerformed` method, where it would be invoked when the user pressed the Quit button.

In terms of the performance of this program, we have not done anything new. Messages are displayed by the applet on initialization and then again interactively in response to a button press.

What is new is the way it is packaged. By defining the method `Byline` before use, we can call or invoke it at any point by merely typing the statement: `Byline();`.

However, there is a problem with the new version: it does not show the definition of the method. This definition is placed following the other declarations in the applet and before the `init` code:

```
public class DataBase extends java.applet.Applet
                implements ActionListener
```

```
{
    TextField m1, m2;
    Button bQuit;

    more declarations

    void Byline() // Here Byline is defined.
    {
        m1.setText("This program was written by");
        m2.setText(" Lady Emily Dunsmore");
    }

    public void init()
    {
        m1 = new TextField(70);
        m2 = new TextField(70);
        bQuit = new Button("Quit");

        more initialization code

        Byline(); // Here Byline is used.
    }
    public void actionPerformed(ActionEvent event)
    {
        Object cause = event.getSource();

        response code for Input

        response code for Print

        response code for Find

        if (cause == bQuit)
        {
            Byline(); // Here Byline is used.
        }
    }
}
```

The program executes in the following sequence: The computation starts at the beginning of the init method. When most of the init code is executed, we reach the statement Byline();. This causes the lines in the method Byline to be executed one at a time.

After Byline is done, the execution will have finished the first call to Byline and will return to complete the other parts, if any, of the init routine. When it is done with initialization, it will wait for any events like button presses.

When the Quit button is pressed, the computer will go to the actionPerformed routine and execute those statements one at a time. Eventually it will get to the if statement, where it will determine that the Quit button was the cause of the execution. Then it will again execute a Byline(); statement. This causes the lines in the method Byline to be executed one at a time.

These events are graphed in figure 4.4, with the thick lines indicating execution and the thin lines indicating jumps. The path shows the two calls and the consequent jumps to the method body.

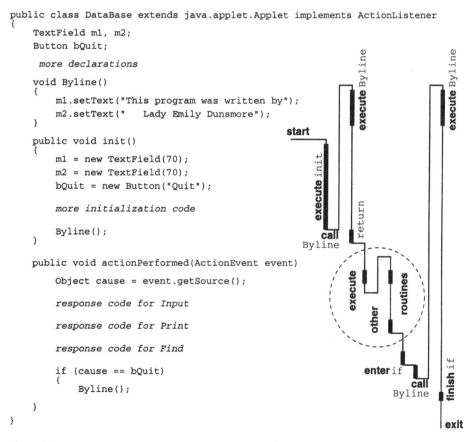

```
public class DataBase extends java.applet.Applet implements ActionListener
{
    TextField m1, m2;
    Button bQuit;

     more declarations

    void Byline()
    {
        m1.setText("This program was written by");
        m2.setText("   Lady Emily Dunsmore");
    }

    public void init()
    {
        m1 = new TextField(70);
        m2 = new TextField(70);
        bQuit = new Button("Quit");

         more initialization code

        Byline();
    }

    public void actionPerformed(ActionEvent event)

        Object cause = event.getSource();

         response code for Input

         response code for Print

         response code for Find

        if (cause == bQuit)
        {
            Byline();
        }
    }
}
```

Figure 4.4

Subroutines are a tremendous help to programmers for two reasons. First, they provide a means for avoiding typing the same lines again and again. If the same task needs to be done twice, as in the DataBase program, or many times, as in other programs, there is no need to type the same lines repeatedly. The code is typed once into a subroutine definition, and in all other instances this code can be invoked by simply typing the name of the subroutine. Since the total program will be shorter, it will use less computer memory and be less wasteful of resources. Because subroutines can be dozens of lines long and may be called often, the savings can be substantial.

The second reason that subroutines are useful is even more important than the first. Subroutines enable the programmer to isolate one task from another and thus simplify his/her problem solving. For example, the programming problem for the Find routine in the DataBase program may seem quite complex. The program is to receive a question from the user and then type all facts that contribute to the answer. But we simplify the problem greatly by isolating part of the job as a subroutine to be written later. We write code that receives the question and then, for each fact, uses a subroutine, the question-fact comparator, to check whether the fact is a part of the answer. If it is, the code will print it out:

Find Routine
Read user's question.
For each position in memory that has a fact in it,
        call the question-fact comparator.
        If the comparator reports "answer", then print the fact.

By pushing part of the task into the question-fact comparator subroutine, we can effectively write part of the code to solve the problem. Later we can concentrate our energies specifically on the subroutine. We have cut the problem into pieces and can hope that each part will be small enough to program easily.

It might be convenient to modify the Byline method so that it will print anyone's name, not simply Lady Emily's. Here is the appropriate change:

```
void Byline2(String name)
{
    m1.setText("This program was written by");
    m2.setText(" " + name);
}
```

The new String variable, name, references the name that we wish to print, which could be any sequence of characters. The variable name is called a *parameter*, and it is identified as such when it is placed between parentheses in the method definition after the routine's name, Byline2. (We have encountered parameters before, such as event in public void actionPerformed(ActionEvent event).)

The variable `name` is different from an ordinary variable in a program because parameters declared as shown here are not assigned their own places in memory. A subroutine parameter such as `name` refers to the place in memory created for some other variable, as is shown next.

Consider the execution of this program:

```java
public class WhoWrote extends java.applet.Applet
                      implements ActionListener
{
    TextField m0, m1, m2;
    Button b1, b2, b3;
    String author1, author2, author3;

    void Byline2(String name)
    {
        m1.setText("This program was written by");
        m2.setText(" " + name);
    }

    public void init()
    {
        m0 = new TextField(70);
        m0.setText("Who wrote the program?");
        m1 = new TextField(70);
        m2 = new TextField(70);
        b1 = new Button("Lady Emily");
        b2 = new Button("Shakespeare");
        b3 = new Button("Mark Twain");
        author1 = "Lady Emily Dunsmore";
        author2 = "William Shakespeare";
        author3 = "Mark Twain";
        add(m0);
        add(b1);
        add(b2);
        add(b3);
        add(m1);
        add(m2);
        b1.addActionListener(this);
        b2.addActionListener(this);
        b3.addActionListener(this);
```

```
    }
    public void actionPerformed(ActionEvent event)
    {
        Object cause = event.getSource();
        if (cause == b1)
        {
            Byline2(author1);
        }
        if (cause == b2)
        {
            Byline2(author2);
        }
        if (cause == b3)
        {
            Byline2(author3);
        }
    }
}
```

As you can see, depending on which of the three buttons is pressed Byline2 prints a different message. If, for example, Button b2, or "Shakespeare", is pressed, the program will display:

This program was written by
  William Shakespeare

The variables author1, author2, and author3 will have their associated locations in memory because they have been declared at the top of the program. But name, which is a parameter, will not. We graphically represent these declared locations in the usual way but indicate a parameter as an arrow that will point to some other entity (figure 4.5).

Just to be sure this new material is understood, let's consider the execution of the program in detail. The init method is run first, and in addition to setting up TextFields and Buttons in the usual manner the String variables are given values when the following statements are executed:

```
author1 = "Lady Emily Dunsmore";
author2 = "William Shakespeare";
author3 = "Mark Twain";
```

After this initialization action, the applet waits for the user to push a button. Assume b1, or "Lady Emily", is pressed. This triggers the execution of the actionPerformed method. The variable cause is assigned the identity of the button pressed, here b1. The

```
public class WhoWrote extends java.applet.Applet implements ActionListener
{
    TextField m0, m1, m2;
    Button b1, b2, b3;
    String author1, author2, author3;                    author1

    void Byline2(String name)          name ──────▶ ?    author2
    {
        m1.setText("This program was written by");        author3
        m2.setText("    " + name);
    }

    public void init()
    {
        m0 = new TextField(70);
        m0.setText("Who wrote the program?");
        m1 = new TextField(70);
        m2 = new TextField(70);
        b1 = new Button("Lady Emily");
        b2 = new Button("Shakespeare");
        b3 = new Button("Mark Twain");
...
```

Figure 4.5

series of if statements follows. We get a match on the first one, so Byline2(author1); is executed. Note the argument author1. This in turn causes the execution of Byline2, which we repeat here. We say that *control is passed* to Byline2:

```
void Byline2(String name)
{
    m1.setText("This program was written by");
    m2.setText(" " + name);
}
```

We know that the argument author1 needs to be related to the parameter name. What happens here, for this specific invocation of Byline2, is that name is effectively replaced by the argument author1. You should mentally replace name by author1. So name and author1 refer to the same memory location at this point in time. The first line of the body of the method is executed in a straightforward manner. The second line is now, in effect:

```
m2.setText(" " + author1);
```

rather than

```
m2.setText(" " + name);
```

Therefore, the output produced is "Lady Emily Dunsmore" (figure 4.6). If another button is pressed, then a different argument is passed to Byline2 and a different parameter substitution takes place.

```
void Byline2(String name)              name
{
    m1.setText("This program was written by");
    m2.setText("    " + name);
}
public void init()
{
        details
}
public void actionPerformed(ActionEvent event)
{
    Object cause = event.getsource();

    if (cause == b1)
    {
        Byline2(author1);
    }
```

author1	Lady Emily Dunsmore
author2	William Shakespeare
author3	Mark Twain

Figure 4.6

To summarize, the parameters of a method do not create new memory locations when they are declared as shown here. Rather, they refer to existing memory locations. These memory locations are linked to the subroutine parameters at the time of the subroutine call.

We reinforce these ideas by changing the program again. We also use this opportunity to introduce the return statement.

Info Out—Using the Return Statement

This time a method is included to read a person's name, and then the Byline2 routine will print that name in the usual format:

```
import java.awt.*;
import java.awt.event.*;

public class WrittenBy extends java.applet.Applet
                   implements ActionListener
{
    TextField m0, g0, m1, m2;
    Button b1;
    String author;

    void Byline2(String name)
    {
```

```
        m1.setText("This program was written by");
        m2.setText(" " + name);
    }
    String GetName()
    {
        String name;
        name = g0.getText();
        return name;
    }
    public void init()
    {
        m0 = new TextField(80);
        m0.setText("Enter author below and press button.");
        g0 = new TextField(80);
        m1 = new TextField(80);
        m2 = new TextField(80);
        b1 = new Button("button");
        add(m0);
        add(g0);
        add(b1);
        add(m1);
        add(m2);
        b1.addActionListener(this);
    }
    public void actionPerformed(ActionEvent event)
    {
        author = GetName();

        Byline2(author);
    }
}
```

The init routine has no surprises and sets up four TextFields and a single Button
(figure 4.7). The user of the program enters a line of text into the second TextField, say
"Lord Dunsmore", and then pushes the button. This activates the actionPerformed
method. Since there is only one button, there is no mystery as to what needs to be done
next. We want to extract the text from the TextField and store it in memory in a
String. However, we invoke the method GetName to carry out this task. Notice the way
it is being invoked. It is to the right of the equals sign in an assignment statement. In fact,
the way we are using it suggests it is a variable and can provide us a value to assign to
author. That is exactly right. We are using the method GetName just like a variable.

```
┌────────────────────────────────────────────────┐
│ Enter author below and press button.           │
└────────────────────────────────────────────────┘

┌────────────────────────────────────────────────┐
│                                                │
└────────────────────────────────────────────────┘

              ┌──────────────┐
              │    button    │
              └──────────────┘

┌────────────────────────────────────────────────┐
│                                                │
└────────────────────────────────────────────────┘

┌────────────────────────────────────────────────┐
│                                                │
└────────────────────────────────────────────────┘
```

Figure 4.7

Let's now jump to GetName and see what code is executed there:

```
String GetName()
{
    String name;
    name = g0.getText();
    return name;
}
```

The method header, instead of starting with void, starts with String. What should go here is the type of information that this method will impart when it is invoked. Here we are saying it will provide us with information of type String.

In the body of the method, we start by creating a new memory location of type String, a variable called name. In the next line, we assign a value to name in an assignment statement. The information comes from the getText method—we are getting the information that the user had typed into the second TextField. Now that the information is preserved in the variable name, how do we get it back to the code that invoked this method in the first place?

For that we have a new statement, called a return statement. It literally returns the information to the method invocation point. However, notice that the type of what is returned (name) must match the type placed at the front of the method's header. In both cases here that is String. Thus, the method GetName can be used as a source of information in the same way as a variable may be used as a source of information. Here, in author = GetName();, it was used on the right side of an assignment statement, and it does in fact provide to author the string that had been entered into the Text-Field.

Now that we have the needed information in name, we can invoke the Byline2 method and complete the job. The result of the program execution is shown in figure 4.8.

```
┌─────────────────────────────────────────────────────┐
│  Enter author below and press button.               │
└─────────────────────────────────────────────────────┘
┌─────────────────────────────────────────────────────┐
│  Lord Dunsmore                                      │
└─────────────────────────────────────────────────────┘
                    ┌──────────┐
                    │  button  │
                    └──────────┘
┌─────────────────────────────────────────────────────┐
│  This program was written by                        │
└─────────────────────────────────────────────────────┘
┌─────────────────────────────────────────────────────┐
│    Lord Dunsmore                                    │
└─────────────────────────────────────────────────────┘
```

Figure 4.8

Exercise

1. Write a method that prints your name. Write a program that calls the method three times and thus prints your name three times.

Subroutines with Internal Variables

Let's write another subroutine in order to study the case where a method may need to have memory locations for its own internal use. (We snuck that in on you in the previous example, where we created the `String` variable `name` in the `GetName` method.)

Suppose a programmer is sketching out a new piece of code and needs to compute factorials on several occasions. (The factorial of positive integer n is the product $1 * 2 * 3 * \cdots * (n - 1) * n$. The factorial of 4 is $1 * 2 * 3 * 4 = 24$.) This sketch might include:

z3 = *the factorial of* x

y = *the factorial of* m

num1 = *the factorial of* y

Then a subroutine can be written that has one parameter: the input. If the name of the routine is `Factorial`, the code can be written as follows:

```
z3 = Factorial(x);
...
y = Factorial(m);
...
num1 = Factorial(y);
```

The subroutine itself is straightforward to define using the accumulation pattern. Notice that the routine needs memory locations: i to be used as a counter in the loop and out to be used to accumulate the product:

```
int Factorial(int n)
{
    int i, out;
    i = 1;
    out = 1;
    while (i <= n)
    {
        out = out * i;
        i = i + 1;
    }
    return out;
}
```

The declaration of i and out follows the method header and has the same form as a declaration after an applet or class header. This declaration tells the machine to set up properly named memory locations to be used by this method only during its execution.

Global Risk

We follow the policy here that all variables be placed internal to a method unless they are needed by more than one method, and even in that case using *parameters* with that method may be better. Variables that are defined outside of a method but used internal to that method are sometimes called *global variables*.

The cause for confusion if this rule is not followed is easy to illustrate. Suppose one executes

```
i = 6;
mX.setInt(i);
```

It seems reasonable to believe that 6 will be printed. If

```
i = 6;
result = Factorial(s);
mX.setInt(i);
```

is executed, one would again expect 6 to be printed because there is no immediately visible reason why it should not be. (The goal should always be to write obviously correct code with no subtle behaviors.) Unfortunately, if Factorial does use i in some way without having its own declaration of i, the following sequence could occur: i = 6; would load 6 into i, the routine Factorial could change i to some new value, say 10, and the setInt statement would print 10. Error! This is a very hard-to-find bug because i was changed in a separate, possibly distant place without any obvious indications. When this occurs, you can spend hours looking for the cause of the error.

Thus, the rule to follow is that every variable in a method should either be specified by parameters or by declarations *in that routine*. When it is, you can be sure that the subroutine can be inserted into a main program without affecting anything in the main program except items specifically listed in the parameter list. An exception is if the enclosing applet or class has defined class variables that are meant to be shared with several methods in the class. Being careful with this will enable you to avoid a kind of programming error that is particularly bothersome to find.

The points made here may not be clear, and they are somewhat subtle. Even experienced programmers may agonize over the best design approach. The decisions to be made are somewhat analogous to political questions regarding local versus federal control. Our suggested programming style recommends local control when reasonable.

Exercises

1. Write a method called Checker that reads an integer and prints Okay if the integer is greater than 0 and less than 100. It should print Not okay otherwise. It should be designed to be called in the following way from a program:

```
applet
{
    ...
    Checker();
    ...
{
```

2. Write a method that has an integer parameter. The routine will check whether the integer is a prime number. If it is, it will return the string "Yes". Otherwise it will return "No". Write a simple applet to invoke your method. It should read the number, call the route, and then take the answer returned by the subroutine and write it to a TextField. (A prime number is an integer greater than 1 that is not evenly divisible by any positive integers except 1 and itself. Thus 2, 3, 5, and 7 are prime numbers, but 4 is not because it is divisible by 2. In Java, we can check whether i divides j by checking whether $(j/i) * i$ is equal to j. If they are equal, then i divides j; otherwise it does not. The subroutine can do its job by having a while loop that checks whether i divides j for every i from 2 to $j - 1$. If none is found, then j is prime.

Subroutines with Array Parameters

Methods can have arrays as parameters using roughly the same methodology as for individual locations. The syntax will be explained in the context of a program to add up a series of integers. The program will have two functionally distinct parts. One part will read data into an array for later processing. This will be done, as in chapter 3, in a interactive manner and will be carried out in the `actionPerformed` routine, collecting one integer value at a time and storing it in an array. We will have a separate method to sum up the values in the array and to report that sum in a `TextField`. This method will be invoked through a button press and will thus need to be triggered through the `actionPerformed` method. Let's look at the code:

```
import awb.*;
import java.awt.*;
import java.awt.event.*;

public class ArraySum extends java.applet.Applet
                  implements ActionListener
{
    TextField mInstruct, mAnswer;
    IntField iCount;
    int B[];
    Button bStore, bTotal, bLargest, bSmallest;
    int count, nextFree;

    int SumArray(int[] data, int firstempty)
    {
        int k, sum;
        k = 0;
        sum = 0;
        while (k < firstempty)
        {
            sum = sum + data[k];
            k = k + 1;
        }
        return sum;
    }
    public void init()
    {
```

```
        B = new int[100];
        mInstruct = new TextField(70);
        mAnswer = new TextField(70);
        mInstruct.setText("Enter Count, then press Store button");
        iCount = new IntField(10);
        bStore = new Button("Store");
        bTotal = new Button("Total");

        bStore.addActionListener(this);
        bTotal.addActionListener(this);
        add(mInstruct);
        add(iCount);
        add(bStore);
        add(bTotal);
        add(mAnswer);
    }

    public void actionPerformed(ActionEvent event)
    {
        int value, total;;
        Object cause = event.getSource();
        if (cause == bStore)
        {
            value = iCount.getInt();
            B[nextFree] = value;
            nextFree = nextFree + 1;
            iCount.setInt(); // clear IntField
        }
        if (cause == bTotal)
        {
            total = SumArray(B, nextFree);
            mAnswer.setText("The total of" + nextFree
                    + " items is " + total);
        }
    }
}
```

Again, the data input part, that is, collecting data in an array one value at a time, should be familiar from chapter 3. The Store button press triggers the collection of a value. What is new is that in response to the Total button press, the method SumArray is invoked. It returns that sum and has the value assigned to the integer variable total. That is then used in the setText invocation:

```
mAnswer.setText("The total of " + nextFree + " items is " + total);
```

Notice that we also display the number of items stored in the array.

The method SumArray is invoked with two arguments. The first is the name of the array, B. The second is the number of useful values stored in that array as stored in the integer variable nextFree.

Let's focus on the method SumArray:

```
int SumArray(int[] data, int firstempty)
{
    int k, sum;
    k = 0;
    sum = 0;
    while (k < firstempty)
    {
        sum = sum + data[k];
        k = k + 1;
    }
    return sum;
}
```

The specification of the array data in the parameter list follows the same format as for other parameters except that the type (or class) is followed by the paired brackets, [ ], indicating that data is an array. In this application the array argument B effectively replaces the parameter data. Using local integer variables k and sum, we sum the elements in a straightforward manner.

It should be clear that one could write other, similar methods to work on the contents of the array. We could easily write a routine to find the *largest* element in the array, or the *index* (or location) of the largest element of the array. The following program extends the capabilities of the previous program and illustrates these two suggested functions.

```
import awb.*;
import java.awt.*;
import java.awt.event.*;

public class ArrayStuff extends java.applet.Applet
                    implements ActionListener
{
```

```
TextField mInstruct, mAnswer;
IntField iCount;
int B[ ];
Button bStore, bTotal, bLargest, bLargeIndex;
int count, nextFree;

int Largest(int[] data, int firstempty)
{
    int k, big;
    big = data[0];
    k = 1;
    while (k < firstempty)
    {
        if (data[k] > big)
        {
            big = data[k];
        }
        k = k + 1;
    }
    return big;
}

int LargeIndex(int[] data, int firstempty)
{
    int k, indexBig;
    indexBig = 0;
    k = 1;
    while (k < firstempty)
    {
        if (data[k] > data[indexBig])
        {
            indexBig = k;
        }
        k = k + 1;
    }
    return indexBig;
}

int SumArray(int[] data, int firstempty)
{
```

```
        int k, sum;
        k = 0;
        sum = 0;
        while (k < firstempty)
        {
            sum = sum + data[k];
            k = k + 1;
        }
        return sum;
    }

    public void init()
    {
        B = new int[100];
        mInstruct = new TextField(70);
        mAnswer = new TextField(70);
        mInstruct.setText("Enter Count, then press Store button");
        iCount = new IntField(10);
        bStore = new Button("Store");
        bTotal = new Button("Total");
        bLargest = new Button("Largest");
        bLargeIndex = new Button("LargeIndex");

        bStore.addActionListener(this);
        bTotal.addActionListener(this);
        bLargest.addActionListener(this);
        bLargeIndex.addActionListener(this);

        add(mInstruct);
        add(iCount);
        add(bStore);
        add(bTotal);
        add(bLargest);
        add(bLargeIndex);
        add(mAnswer);
    }

    public void actionPerformed(ActionEvent event)
    {
        int value, total;;
        Object cause = event.getSource();
```

```
        if (cause == bStore)
        {
            value = iCount.getInt();
            B[nextFree] = value;
            nextFree = nextFree + 1;
            iCount.setInt(); // clear IntField
        }
        if (cause == bTotal)
        {
            total = SumArray(B, nextFree);
            mAnswer.setText("The total of " + nextFree + " items is "
                    + total);
        }
        if (cause == bLargest)
        {
            value = Largest(B, nextFree);
            mAnswer.setText("The largest of " + nextFree +
                    " items is " + value);
        }
        if (cause == bLargeIndex)
        {
            value = LargeIndex(B, nextFree);
            mAnswer.setText("The location of the largest item is "
                    + value);
        }
    }
}
```

There are no real surprises in this code. All the code for ArraySum is there plus the two new methods. In the actionPerformed routine we have the added if statements to identify the activation of the "Largest" and the "LargestIndex" buttons. The heart of the Largest method is a loop over all elements of the array that are in use. In that loop we find

```
if (data[k] > big)
{
    big = data[k];
}
k = k + 1;
```

Before the loop we had initialized the integer variable big to be a copy of the first array element. That is our trial value for big. In the loop, using the if statement, we see if we can find a better element, that is, a larger element than our trial value stored in big. If we find a better value, we replace the number stored in big with the better value by coding big = data[k]; The last thing we do in the loop is increment the index k to point to the next element in the array. When we are done with the loop, big will contain the largest value in the array data, and that is passed back to the calling program by the return big; statement.

The LargeIndex method is really quite similar, structurally. However, what is returned in not the largest value, but the index that shows where that largest value is located in the array.

Exercises

1. Design a way, using two buttons, to display all the elements in an array. Only one value from the array would be seen at any one time.

2. Write a method DoubleArray(n,A) that doubles all the entries in array A.

3. Write a method CopyArray(n,A,B) that copies all the *n* entries in array A into array B.

4. Write an applet that uses the routines DoubleArray and CopyArray from exercise 3 and the methodology you developed in exercise 1 to do the following:

   ■ It reads *n* values into array XX.
   ■ It allows you to display array XX.
   ■ Then it doubles the values in XX and allows you to display them again.
   ■ Then it moves the values in XX to array YY.
   ■ Finally, it doubles the values in YY and allows the array to be displayed.

   Your program should include the necessary buttons and TextFields to carry this out.

Subroutine Communication Examples

Because information flow to and from subroutines can be confusing, several examples of different types of communication are studied here. In each case, the subroutine will be named Triple, and it will triple some number. The interesting point will be how it gets its input and what it does once the number is altered.

The first example is the case where there is no communication at all. The method triples an entry with nothing in it and does nothing with the result (figure 4.9):

Triple

Figure 4.9

```
applet
{
    ...

    void Triple()
    {
        double r1, r2;

        r2 = 3 * r1;
    }
        ...
        Triple();
        ...
}
```

This unsuccessful program can be fixed by putting input and output statements into the method. We have to assume that there are some DoubleFields and TextFields in the containing class, say dR1 and mR2:

```
applet
{
    ...

    void Triple()
    {
        double r1, r2;

        r1 = dR1.getDouble();
        r2 = 3 * r1;
        mR2.setText("Triple the value is " + r2);
    }
```

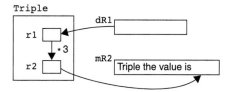

Figure 4.10

```
        ...
        Triple();
        ...
}
```

Figure 4.10 shows the information passing from the keyboard into the subroutine, where it is tripled and then displayed. Next we could pass the information to the subroutine through the parameter list and then have the routine print its answer as before:

```
applet
{
    ...

    DoubleField dR;
    TextField mR2;

    ...
    void Triple(double r1)
    {
        double r2;

        r2 = 3 * r1;
        mR2.setText("Triple the value is " + r2);
    }
        ...

        double r;

        ...
        r = dR.getDouble();
        Triple(r);
        ...
}
```

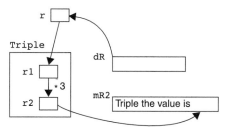

Figure 4.11

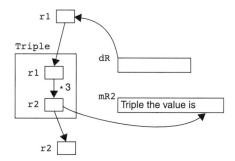

Figure 4.12

In this form information gets *into* the routine but *not out*, except onto the screen (figure 4.11). We could also modify the method to send its output back using a `return` statement (figure 4.12):

```
applet
{
    ...

    DoubleField dR;
    TextField mR2;

    ...

    double Triple(double r1)
    {
        double r2;
```

```
        r2 = 3 * r1;
        return r2;
    }

    ...

    double r1, r2;

    ...
    r1 = dR.getDouble();
    r2 = Triple(r1);
    mR2.setText("Triple the value is " + r2);
    ...
}
```

These four programs summarize four different options (although the first version is useless). Remember that many of the details of the programs were omitted. We were focusing on getting information into and out of a method.

Storing and Printing Facts for the Database

We now must develop a systematic plan for storing database facts of the kind given in the introductory section:

Mr. Mason is a chemist.
The professor visited at 3:00 P.M.

It is important to notice that most of these facts are of the form

(noun phrase) (relationship) (noun phrase)

We will discover later that the question-answering task is made easier if we separate each fact into these three parts:

(Mr. Mason) (is) (a chemist.)
(The professor) (visited at) (3:00 P.M.)

We will call the first part noun1 (for noun phrase 1), the second part relation (for relationship), and the last part noun2 (for noun phrase 2), and declare these as string variables. This strategy would store the first fact with these Java statements:

```
noun1 = "Mr. Mason";
relation = "is";
noun2 = "a chemist.";
```

Figure 4.13

noun1A[0]	Mr. Mason	relationA[0]	is	noun2A[0]	a chemist.
noun1A[1]	The professor	relationA[1]	visited at	noun2A[1]	3.00 P.M.
.			.		
.			.		
.			.		

Figure 4.14

In order to read a fact into these locations, one can use `TextFields` and the statements:

```
noun1 = n1.getText();
relation = r.getText();
noun2 = n2.getText();
```

Thus, the fact should be typed as shown in figure 4.13.

The separation of the statement into three fields enables the program to divide the string of characters into three strings for the three sequential locations.

But the database program needs to store many facts, so the three locations should be expanded into arrays. This can be done with the following declaration, which specifies that each array should hold up to 100 strings,

```
String noun1A[], relationA[], noun2A[];
```

with the following in the `init` method:

```
noun1A = new String[100];
relationA = new String[100];
noun2A = new String[100];
```

The desired result in memory is illustrated in figure 4.14.

Let's create a location called `last` that gives the position of the last fact in the tables. If only two facts are stored, then this location would be

last | 1 |

and if a place is needed for a new fact, we would increase `last` to 2 and put the new fact in position 2. Now it is possible to write rough draft code for the database input routine in English:

Input Routine
Find a new place in memory.
Read a new fact into that place.

The code is

```
void InputFact()
{
    last = last + 1;
    noun1A[last] = gN1.getText();
    gN1.setText(" ");
    relationA[last] = gRel.getText();
    gRel.setText(" ");
    noun2A[last] = gN2.getText();
    gN2.setText(" ");
}
```

This routine does exactly what we need. The variable `last` is incremented to point to the next empty slot in the arrays. Then, for the `TextField` `gN1` we assign the string to the next free slot in the array `noun1A`. Similarly, we get the corresponding information from `gRel` and `gN2`. To make life easier for the person actually entering the data into the applet, we clear each `TextField` after we copy the information. For example, `gN1.setText(" ");` places a null string (i.e., nothing) into the `TextField` `gN1`.

Clearly, we haven't looked at the whole program. In `actionPerformed` we have the code

```
if (cause == bEnter)
{
    InputFact();
}
```

to respond to the user's pressing the Enter button.

After the discussion earlier in this chapter about how information gets into and out of methods, you might have another question: How is the information exchanged here? We are taking advantage of the fact that the methods and data are all in one class, in this case the applet `DataBase`. All member variables that are defined in the class are "known" in all the methods in the class. Therefore, explicit use of parameters and arguments is not required here. This *global* use of data within a class has its risks, but since a larger program is usually implemented by using multiple classes, the risk of everyone's sharing the same data pool is compartmentalized and thus limited.

In summary, then, InputFact places information into three arrays that are known within the class. (This routine assumes the arrays are large enough to store as many facts as the user will ever enter. You might wish to revise the method to print the message "Too many facts" if the user tries to enter more facts than can fit into the arrays.)

A useful next step in developing the database applet is to have a routine that will just dump all data. This is not the way the program will be used, but it is a useful tool in developing the program and ensuring that the facts are getting into the arrays and are available for use. So, the next method, DumpData, is what is sometimes called a *diagnostic routine*. It is there mainly to make our program development easier and to avoid errors. The routine is

```
void DumpData()
{
    mResults.setText("Dump of data\n");
    k = 0;
    while (k <= last)
    {
        mResults.append(k + " " + noun1A[k] + " " + relationA[k] + " "
                    + noun2A[k] + "\n");
        k = k + 1;
    }
}
```

A closer look at the method DumpData should suggest that, again, everything is as usual. Of course, we'll need a button to trigger this dump of information. You should have noticed a new method called append for mResults. It would be natural to assume that mResults is also a TextField because we used the method setText on it at the beginning, but this turns out not to be the case.

This is our first use of a class related to TextField that is called TextArea. It handles multiple lines of text and produces a complete window to display lines of text. We declare it at the beginning of the applet as

```
TextArea mResults;
```

and we create it in the init method with

```
mResults = new TextArea(10, 60);
```

thus specifying that we want it to be able to display up to ten lines of text each up to 60 characters long. Since the display generates a scroll bar, we can actually access many more lines than that.

The fact that both `TextFields` and `TextAreas` can use the method `setText` illustrates another important programming idea of object-oriented programming and its Java instantiation. This is called *inheritance*. Both `TextFields` and `TextAreas` are derived from a parent class called `TextComponent`. It actually implements the `setText` method. Both `TextFields` and `TextAreas` *inherit* the method and can use it.

If you've read the code carefully, you might have noticed that with `TextAreas` we end our strings with the sequence \n. In a string, this is a special control sequence that says "start a new line" and it works very much like the Return key on a typewriter or the Enter key on your keyboard. Since `TextAreas` deal with multiline fields of text, this control sequence is often required.

Following is the whole `DataBase` program as implemented so far. In can only read in data and then confirm that it has all been stored successfully:

```
import awb.*;
import java.awt.*;
import java.awt.event.*;

public class DataBase extends java.applet.Applet
                  implements ActionListener
{
    TextField gN1, gRel, gN2, mInstruct;
    String noun1A[], relationA[], noun2A[];
    TextArea mResults;
    Button bEnter, bAll;
    int last;
    public void init()
    {
        last = -1;
        noun1A = new String[100];
        relationA = new String[100];
        noun2A = new String[100];
        mInstruct = new TextField(70);
        mInstruct.setText
        ("Enter facts in the three fields below and press Enter button.");
        gN1 = new TextField(25);
        gRel = new TextField(25);
        gN2 = new TextField(25);
        mResults = new TextArea(10, 60);
        bEnter = new Button("Enter");
        bAll = new Button("All");
```

```
            bEnter.addActionListener(this);
            bAll.addActionListener(this);
            add(mInstruct);
            add(gN1);
            add(gRel);
            add(gN2);
            add(bEnter);
            add(bAll);
            add(mResults);
    }
    public void actionPerformed(ActionEvent event)
    {
        Object cause = event.getSource();
        if (cause == bEnter)
        {
            InputFact();
        }
        if (cause == bAll) // mainly used for debugging
        {
            DumpData();
        }
    }
    void InputFact()
    {
        last = last + 1;
        noun1A[last] = gN1.getText();
        gN1.setText(" ");
        relationA[last] = gRel.getText();
        gRel.setText(" ");
        noun2A[last] = gN2.getText();
        gN2.setText(" ");
    }
    void DumpData()
    {
        int k;
        mResults.setText("Dump of data\n");
        k = 0;
        while (k <= last)
        {
            mResults.append(k + " " + noun1A[k] + " " + relationA[k] +
                    " " + noun2A[k] + "\n");
```

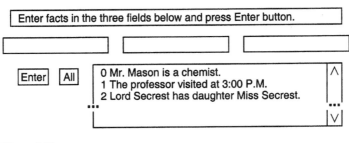

Figure 4.15

```
        k = k + 1;
    }
  }
}
```

Figure 4.15 shows what the screen might look like after three sets of facts had been entered and then dumped by pressing the All button.

Exercise

1. Revise `InputFact` so that if the user attempts to enter more facts than there is room for, the system will refuse to take them and will print the message "Too many facts."

Representing Questions and Finding Their Answers

Suppose a large number of facts are stored in the machine using the method of the previous section. How can someone who does not know those facts access the information? This problem will be approached very conservatively, and then a seemingly narrow technique will be expanded to become a powerful query-handling mechanism.

Let's say a user wants to know, Is it true that Mr. Mason is a chemist? For the purposes of our question-answering program, the query could be recast as, Is the fact that

(Mr. Mason) (is) (a chemist.)

in the database? We will write code so that the system will ask the user for a query, and the user will type in the fact that she wishes to check for. Then the system will respond by displaying that fact again if it is found in the database.

Let's use the model begun in previously to write code to solve this simple problem.

Find Method
Read user's question.
For each position in memory that has a fact in it,
        call the question-fact comparator.
        If the comparator reports a match, then print the fact.

Based on this, we can write the following code:

```
void Find()
{
    String noun1, relation, noun2;
    int k;
    noun1 = gN1.getText();
    relation = gRel.getText();
    noun2 = gN2.getText();
    mResults.setText("THE RELATED FACTS\n");
    k = 0;
    while (k <= last)
    {
        if (QFCompare(noun1, relation, noun2, k) == 1) // 1 means match
        {
            mResults.append(noun1A[k] + " " + relationA[k] + " " +
                    noun2A[k] + "\n");
        }
        k = k + 1;
    }
}
```

This is invoked by the following new lines in the `actionPerformed` method:

```
if (cause == bFind)
{
    Find();
}
```

Note that to enter queries, we used the same `TextFields` that we used to enter facts. However we press the Find button rather than the Enter button. Looking over the Find routine, you see that it prints the header THE RELATED FACTS at the top of the TextArea. Then employing a `while` loop, it steps through every set of facts entered.

Using QFCompare, it checks to see if the query fact is in the database. If so, QFCompare returns a 1, but if the fact is not found, it returns a 0. Whenever we get a 1, we write the corresponding fact to the TextArea.

The job of QFCompare is to return 1 if the query fact is identical to the database fact. That is, it must check whether noun1 = noun1A[k] *and* relation = relationA[k] *and* noun2 = noun2A[k]. All three relations must be true. The code for that follows:

```
int QFCompare(String noun1, String relation, String noun2, int k)
{
    if ( noun1.equals(noun1A[k])
                && relation.equals(relationA[k])
                && noun2.equals(noun2A[k]) )
    {
        return 1; // 1 means query matched database
    }
    else
    {
        return 0; // 0 means no match
    }
}
```

The choice of 1 to indicate a match and 0 to indicate no match is arbitrary. We could have chosen any set of values we wanted, as long as the two parts of the program agree on the system being used.

A new item here is the way we compare two strings. Unfortunately, we cannot simply use the == operator that we used in comparing int variables with int variables and double variables with double variables. Since strings are classes, we need to use a method of the String class. The String class has a method equals that does exactly what we want. So, to compare noun1 to the *k*th array element noun1A[k], we write noun1.equals(noun1A[k]). Note that we could also have written noun1A[k]. equals(noun1) because tests for equality are symmetrical. To combine the three tests to certify that all three are matching, we use the && operator, which stands for *and*. As stated before, we must make sure that noun1 = noun1A[k] *and* relation = relationA[k] *and* noun2 = noun2A[k].

This code functions as expected. If the user wishes to search for a given fact, that fact is typed as a query. If the fact is found, the system will print it. For example, after entering some facts and then asking if Mr. Mason is a chemist, we might see the display in figure 4.16.

We have developed the code to determine whether a given fact is in the database. If the fact is found, it is printed. If it is not found, the program will print nothing after the message THE RELATED FACTS. However, this is not a very exciting capability and certainly

Enter facts in the three fields below and press Enter button.

Mr. Mason	is	a chemist.

Enter	All	Enter query items in the three fields above and press Find button.

Find	THE RELATED FACTS Mr. Mason is a chemist.	∧ ∨

Figure 4.16

would not be very helpful to Inspector Brown. How is it possible to answer more interesting types of questions? Suppose it is known that someone visited today at 3:00 P.M., but it is not known who. That is, we query whether any fact appears of the form

(   ) (visited at) (3:00 P.M.)

and the answer will be found in the first of the three fields. Therefore, the way to find the answer is to search the database and print any fact that matches on the second and third fields. A good way to type this question to the machine is

(?) (visited at) (3:00 P.M.)

where the question mark means "the user does not know this information." Here is a modification to the QFCompare routine to handle this query:

```
int QFCompare(String noun1, String relation, String noun2, int k)
{
    if ( (noun1.equals(noun1A[k]) || noun1.equals("?"))
                    && relation.equals(relationA[k])
                    && noun2.equals(noun2A[k]) )
    {
        return 1; // 1 means query matched database
    }
    else
    {
        return 0; // 0 means no match
    }
}
```

If the first field noun1 of the question is not "?", then the code will function as before. If noun1 is "?", then the routine also will return 1 as long as we also have relation =

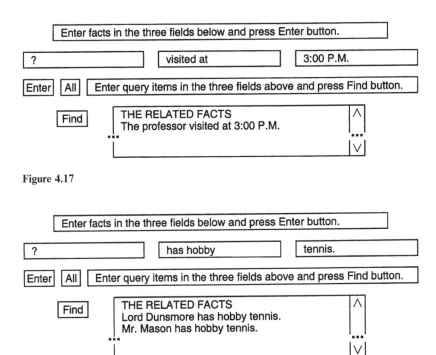

Figure 4.17

Figure 4.18

relationA[k] and noun2 = noun2A[k]. Thus, it will ignore the first field and print any fact that agrees on the second and third fields. We accomplish this by allowing either a match or a query "?" to result in a *true* result. We have introduced the logical operator for *or* to do this, namely ||. The vertical "or" bars give us powerful new flexibility. Figure 4.17 shows how the screen will look to the user. Success! This program is clearly going to be of use to Inspector Brown. Let's try another query (figure 4.18).

This greatly improved system was achieved by allowing a question mark in the first field of any query. The question mark means that the user does not know what belongs in that field and that the system should print all facts that match on the other two fields. The next obvious extension is to allow a question mark in any field. With this change, one may ask a huge variety of questions, as is shown by the following questions and corresponding query entries:

Mr. Mason visited at what time?
(Mr. Mason) (visited at) (?)

What was Mr. Mason doing at 3:00 P.M.?
(Mr. Mason) (?) (3:00 P.M.)

Give me every fact about Mr. Mason.
(Mr. Mason) (?) (?)
and
(?) (?) (Mr. Mason)

Who visited today and at what time?
(?) (visited at) (?)

What happened at 3:00 P.M.?
(?) (?) (3:00 P.M.)

Tell me everything you know.
(?) (?) (?)

This query system is now quite satisfactory for the inspector's use. He can easily ask any question required to find his prime suspect.

In summary, this chapter began with a seemingly large, complex task of writing a program that would make it possible to store information and to answer almost any question about that information. The solution was found by formulating the task to be one of simply storing and retrieving facts and by discovering a powerful method for doing the retrieval. The coding effort was cut down to manageable proportions through decomposition into subtasks, which were then implemented using subroutines.

Exercises

1. Show how to modify the QFCompare method to handle a question mark in every field.

2. Design a method called FindAll that receives one string from the user, such as "Mr. Mason" and then prints all facts that contain that string in any field. In this case, it would print facts such as

   Mr. Mason visited at 3:00 P.M.
   The Inspector is a customer of Mr. Mason.

Assembling the Database Program and Adding Comments

Most of the work of coding the database program was completed in the previous sections. But one more addition needs to be made to finish the program in a professional manner. It is the inclusion of enough comment statements to document the code properly for anyone who may later wish to read it or change it. A properly commented program includes sufficient information regarding its input-output characteristics and method of operation to enable a reader of the code to use it, understand its functioning, and modify it if necessary. The program comments should also identify the author and give other nominal information such as the date and application.

Most of the programs in this book do not have many comments because the surrounding text includes the necessary information and the comments might distract attention from the code. But in other situations programs must stand alone without such explanatory material, and the programmer should carefully add the needed information to preserve their usefulness. Most industrial organizations have standards for their programmers specifying how code should be written and documented.

A reasonable policy for code documentation includes four kinds of comments:

1. The program header. This appears at the beginning of the program and includes (a) the programmer's name and other nominal information, (b) the input-output specification for the program, and (c) a brief description of how the code works.
2. Code block headers. Well-written code is always organized into "blocks" of self-consistent code that do well-defined tasks such as reading, sorting, or calculating. Each block should begin with enough comments to identify its purpose and its essential operation. Blocks usually are 5 to 20 lines in length and in many cases are organized as subroutines. In some cases, the author of a block may not be the same as the main author, and proper credit should be included in the header.
3. Method preconditions and postconditions. The precondition is placed directly below the method header and tells what information is expected by the method and what constraints that information has to allow the method to work correctly. The postcondition states what we can expect of that method. It is like a "contract" that says, If the preconditions are met, the resulting data will meet the standards spelled out in the postconditions.
4. Line comments. You should write code that is so straightforward that its operation is obvious to any reader. But occasionally it is helpful to add a short comment just to the right of a line of code to clarify its meaning. Comments are especially helpful at array declarations or at assignment statements where key computations occur.

Adherence to these standards should result in a completed program that can be read, used, or modified by any competent programmer. Here is the database program fully commented:

```
//          Database Program
//          by Alan W. Biermann
//          January 1996
//          Modified by D. Ramm September 1999
//
//
```

```
//Inputs: In input mode, "facts" are read in three fields:
//noun phrase, relationship, noun phrase. For example, "John is a
//boy." is separated into three parts, "John," "is," and "a boy."
//These parts are entered into the program in three TextFields
//
//Input a fact. Enter three fields, the press "Enter" button
//[John     ] [is    ] [a boy. ]
//
//In query mode, queries are read in the same
//format as facts except that some fields may have a question
//mark instead of data.
//
//Outputs: In query mode, the program prints into a TextArea all facts
//that match the query on fields that do not have question marks.
//
//Method of operation: The facts are stored in three arrays
//called noun1A, relationA, and noun2A. The k-th fact has its first,
//second, and third fields in the k-th entries of, respectively,
//noun1A, relationA, and noun2A. The program answers a query by
//sequentially examining every stored fact and printing it if it
//matches the query on the fields that do not contain a question
//mark.

import java.awt.*;
import java.awt.event.*;

public class DataBase extends java.applet.Applet
                    implements ActionListener
{
    TextField gN1, gRel, gN2, mInstruct, mInstruct2;
    String noun1A[], relationA[], noun2A[]; // Facts stored in these
    TextArea mResults;
    Button bEnter, bAll, bFind;
    int last; // last tells how many facts are stored

    public void init()
    //postcondition: all class data members created, initialized, with
    //layout specified, listener activated for any buttons
    {
        last = -1;
        noun1A = new String[100];
```

```
        relationA = new String[100];
        noun2A = new String[100];
        mInstruct = new TextField(70);
        mInstruct.setText
        ("Enter facts in the three fields below and press Enter button.");
        mInstruct2 = new TextField(70);
        mInstruct2.setText
        ("Enter search in the three fields above and press Find button.");
        gN1 = new TextField(25);
        gRel = new TextField(25);
        gN2 = new TextField(25);
        mResults = new TextArea(10, 60);
        bEnter = new Button("Enter");
        bAll = new Button("All");
        bFind = new Button("Find");
        //register buttons to listeners
        bEnter.addActionListener(this);
        bAll.addActionListener(this);
        bFind.addActionListener(this);
        //specify layout
        add(mInstruct);
        add(gN1);
        add(gRel);
        add(gN2);
        add(bEnter);
        add(bAll);
        add(mInstruct2);
        add(bFind);
        add(mResults);
    }
public void actionPerformed(ActionEvent event)
//postcondition: Correct method is invoked to handle the
//processing corresponding to a particular button press
{
    Object cause = event.getSource();

    if (cause == bEnter)
    {
        InputFact();
    }
    if (cause == bAll) //mainly for debugging
```

```
        {
            DumpData();
        }
        if (cause == bFind)
        {
            Find();
        }
    }

void InputFact()
//precondition: Facts have been entered in the TextFields: first
//noun phrase in gN1, relation in gRel, and second noun phrase
//in gN2. "Enter" button has been pressed.
//postcondition: last has been incremented to point to next
//empty slots in arrays. The information extracted from gN1, gRel,
//and gN2 has been stored in noun1A[last], relationA[last], and
//noun2A[last]. TextFields have been cleared.
//known bugs: No explicit check is made to avoid exceeding array
//bounds.
    {
        last = last + 1;
        noun1A[last] = gN1.getText();
        gN1.setText(" ");
        relationA[last] = gRel.getText();
        gRel.setText(" ");
        noun2A[last] = gN2.getText();
        gN2.setText(" ");
    }
void DumpData()
//precondition: last facts have been stored in the String arrays
//noun1A, relationA, and noun2A. "All" has been pressed.
//postcondition: All information stored is displayed, in the same
//order as entered, in TextArea mResults.
    {
        int k;
        mResults.setText("Dump of data\n");
        k = 0;
        while (k <= last)
        {
            mResults.append(k + " " + noun1A[k] + " " + relationA[k] +
                    " " + noun2A[k] + "\n");
```

```
            k = k + 1;
        }
}
void Find()
//precondition: last facts have been stored in the String arrays
//noun1A, relationA, and noun2A.
//Query facts or a ? have been entered into each of TextFields
//gN1, gRel, and gN2. "Find" has been pressed.
//postcondition: All information stored was compared to the query
//facts read from TextFields. If QFCompare decides there is a
//match, the facts are displayed in the TextArea mResults
{
    String noun1, relation, noun2;
    int k;
    noun1 = gN1.getText();
    relation = gRel.getText();
    gN2.getText();
    mResults.setText("THE RELATED FACTS\n");
    k = 0;
    while (k <= last)
    {
        if (QFCompare(noun1, relation, noun2, k) == 1)
        // 1 means match
        {
            mResults.append(noun1A[k] + " " + relationA[k] + " " +
                noun2A[k] + "\n");
        }
        k = k + 1;
    }
}
int QFCompare(String noun1, String relation, String noun2, int k)
//precondition: parameters noun1, relation, and noun2 contain
//either a query fact or a "?". k is the index to properly
//stored facts in arrays noun1A, relationA, and noun2A
//postcondition: If for each of the three arrays, the k-th element
//matches the corresponding query fact or the query fact is
//a ?, QFCompare returns a 1 to indicate a match. Otherwise
//returns a 0.
{
    if( (noun1.equals(noun1A[k]) || noun1.equals("?"))
            && (relation.equals(relationA[k]) ||
```

```
                    relation.equals("?"))
                    && (noun2.equals(noun2A[k]) ||
                    noun2.equals("?")) )
        {
            return 1; // 1 means query matched database
        }
        else
        {
            return 0; // 0 means no match
        }
    }
}
```

This code can be shortened somewhat by following a rule allowed by Java. Whenever the form

```
{
    a single statement;
}
```

falls within an `if-else`, `if`, or `while` statement, it can be replaced by

```
a single statement;
```

Thus the braces are not needed if only one statement is being used. As an example, this rule can be applied to

```
if (cause == bEnter)
{
    InputFact();
}
```

to obtain this equivalent and shorter code:

```
if (cause == bEnter)
    InputFact();
```

This rule is not generally used in code presented in this book because it can cause confusion.

The time has finally come for us to discover the prime suspect for the murder mystery. Here is the database that the inspector used to draw his conclusion. Use the program to store the information and then type the necessary queries to find the prime suspect.

Lord Dunsmore is married to Lady Emily.
The gardener is married to the maid.
Poison can be gotten by a person for a blood relative.
Mr. Mason visited at 3:00 P.M.
A shared hobby causes friendship.
The gardener was recently dismissed by Lord Dunsmore.
Lord Dunsmore has hobby tennis.
The maid set tea on the table at 2:45 P.M.
Lord Secrest has hobby philosophy.
The gardener has hobby music.
Lord Dunsmore has rival Lord Secrest.
Mr. Mason is a chemist.
The Inspector is a customer of Mr. Mason.
Lord Secrest has daughter Miss Secrest.
The butler owes 10,000 pounds to Lord Dunsmore.
The butler helped serve lunch at 12:00.
The professor has hobby philosophy.
The professor visited at 3:00 P.M.
Lord Secrest is a customer of Mr. Mason.
The professor often brings gifts to Lady Emily.
Tea is always taken at 3:00 P.M.
Miss Secrest visited at 5:00 P.M.
Poison is sold by a chemist.
Lady Emily has hobby music.
Poison can be gotten by a person for a friend.
Mr. Mason has hobby tennis.
Poison takes one hour to take effect.
The professor was once a suitor of Lady Emily.

The set of three-field facts in this problem is known as a relation. This technical definition of *relation* should not be confused with more ordinary uses of the word that may appear elsewhere in this book. The database system is referred to as a relational database system. Many such systems are in use in commercial applications, though often they are much more complex. It is quite common to have dozens of relations and dozens of fields in each relation.

One shortcoming of the database system described here is that it includes no inference system. Suppose as an illustration that "Jill is a sister of Nancy" and "Nancy is a sister of Barbara" are facts in the database. If a query appears requesting the sisters of Jill, one would like to have both Nancy and Barbara listed. However, the database of this chapter will not discover that Jill is a sister of Barbara. An inference is required, of the form "If X is a sister of Y, and Y is a sister of Z, then X is a sister of Z." No such inferential capabilities were programmed. Commercial database systems usually do include such features, and another programming system with such abilities is described at the end of chapter 16.

Exercises

1. Complete the assembly of the database program, and try it on a simple problem.

2. Which character in the story is most likely to have had a motive, access to the poison, and an opportunity to lace the lord's food? Can you reconstruct the events that probably led to the crime?

3. A problem with the database program is that it provides no method for deleting facts. A simple way to delete a fact is to replace all its fields with an asterisk. Add a command to the system that requests the number of the fact to be deleted and then replaces its three fields with asterisks. Then change the print routine so that it skips over asterisks when they are encountered.

4. Write a delete program similar to the one described in exercise 3, but use a deletion procedure that is not so wasteful of space.

5. Prepare a database for the courses taught in a university department. The database should include such information as times the courses are taught, instructors' names, and the associated prerequisites. Then a user should be able to obtain answers to such questions as

   Which professors are teaching this semester?
   Who is teaching Psychology 11?
   What are the prerequisites for Psychology 207?
   Are there any courses being taught at 4 P.M.?

6. Some relations are called symmetrical because the order of the noun groups does not affect meaning. An example of such a relation is sisterhood. If one can say

   Julie is the sister of Ann.

   then one can also say

   Ann is the sister of Julie.

   The database program does not account for this possibility and will thus answer some questions incorrectly. If the single fact

   (Julie) (is the sister of) (Ann)

is stored, it will not correctly answer the question, Who is the sister of Julie?:

(?) (is the sister of) (Julie)

Design a feature for the database program that can ask which relations are symmetrical, and then use this information to process queries that refer to them.

7. Solve some retrieval problems with the database program. Discover some of its shortcomings, and write code to correct them.

---

*Recursion

A major strategy for solving a problem is to divide it into parts, solve the parts, and then combine the solutions of the parts to obtain a solution to the whole problem. As an example, suppose we wish to compute the factorial of 5. It is $5 * 4 * 3 * 2 * 1 = 120$. A way to do this calculation is to split it into the two parts—5 and $4 * 3 * 2 * 1$—and calculate each part separately: $5 = 5$ and $4 * 3 * 2 * 1 = 24$. Then we can recombine the parts to obtain the answer: $5 * 24 = 120$. This strategy can be represented with the following notation:

$$\text{factorial}(5) = 5 * \text{factorial}(4)$$

More generally, if n is greater than zero, one can write

$$\text{factorial}(n) = n * \text{factorial}(n - 1)$$

This is a very special calculation because it is circular in nature. The strategy for computing factorial(n) requires finding factorial($n - 1$) first. But how does one compute factorial($n - 1$)? The answer is that one must compute factorial($n - 2$), and so forth.

But the formula

$$\text{factorial}(n) = n * \text{factorial}(n - 1)$$

fails if $n = 0$. In the case $n = 0$, we write

$$\text{factorial}(n) = 1$$

This special situation corresponds to what is often called the *base case* or the *halting case*. In fact, the general definition of factorial is

$$\text{factorial}(n) = \begin{cases} 1 & \text{if } n = 0 \\ n * \text{factorial}(n - 1) & \text{otherwise} \end{cases}$$

This is called a *recursive* calculation because the function being defined is used in the definition. Here is a general algorithm for such calculations:

Method for Doing Computation C
on Data D to Obtain Result R
1. If the calculation is trivial, then do it and return result R.
2. Otherwise,
   a. Divide D into two parts D_1 and D_2.
   b. Do part of the calculation on D_1 to obtain R_1 (possibly using C).
   c. Do part of the calculation on D_2 to obtain R_2 (possibly using C).
   d. Combine R_1 and R_2 to calculate and return result R.

This can be illustrated by showing how it works on a factorial:

Method for Computing the Factorial of n
to Obtain Result f
1. If $(n = 0)$, $f = 1$. Return f.
2. Otherwise,
   a. Separate n into parts $D_1 = n$ and $D_2 = n - 1$.
   b. Do part of the calculation on D_1 to obtain $R_1 = D_1$.
   c. Compute the factorial of D_2 to obtain R_2.
   d. Combine R_1 and R_2 to obtain $f = R_1 * R_2$.
   e. Return f.

Here is the factorial method in computer code:

```
int factorial(int n)
{
    int D1, D2, R1, R2;

    if (n == 0)
    {
        R1 = 1;
        return R1;
    }
    else
    {
        D1 = n;
        D2 = n-1;
        R1 = D1;
        R2 = factorial(D2);
        return R1 * R2;
```

```
        }
}
```

This, of course, uses more data locations than necessary. The program can be shortened to this:

```
int factorial(int n)
{
    if (n == 0)
    {
        return 1;
    }
    else
    {
        return n * factorial(n - 1);
    }
}
```

(If this program is run, it will overflow the integer variables for values of *n* that are not small.) You can better understand this program for obtaining a factorial if you carry through a computation by hand. Here is a trace of its major actions when it computes the factorial value for 3. All computations from a single call are indented equally.

```
Call factorial(3)
    i = 2
    Call factorial(2)
        i = 1
        Call factorial(1)
            i = 0
            Call factorial(0)
                return 1
            return 1 * (value from previous call) = 1 * 1 = 1
        return 2 * (value from previous call) = 2 * 1 = 2
    return 3 * (value from previous call) = 3 * 2 = 6
```

Recursion Is Not as Strange as It Seems

At first you might think that this recursive approach is very strange and unnatural. But, in fact, packaged a bit differently, we use recursive approaches all the time.

Imagine that a visitor has come to the United States from another country and is learning English, so he makes heavy use of a dictionary. The dictionary provides an excellent analogy to a recursive method.

Our visitor needs to look up the meaning of *prime* as in a "prime number." The dictionary gives us (simplifying a bit) "Divisible by no number except itself or 1."

That seems straightforward to us, but our visitor doesn't know the meaning of the word *divisible*. Is he stuck now? No, he has the dictionary, and he uses it recursively to look up that word. He may have to consult it several times before he finally understands what *prime* means. However, it should be clear that, in general, the use of a dictionary is a recursive process.

The dictionary also illustrates a problem we may encounter with poorly formulated recursive algorithms. If our visitor's knowledge of English is extremely limited, he might find that a definition he has come to, after several steps, includes the word he was originally looking up. In other words, he has extracted a completely circular definition. Unfortunately, he is stuck now. A dictionary is inherently circular, defining English words in terms of English words. What is needed to make it work is a basic vocabulary that will allow us to halt after one or maybe a few references.

Recursive algorithms always require one or more base cases or halting cases for which recursion is not used. Otherwise, the algorithm would be completely circular and its implementation would lead to an infinite loop. For our factorial example, the base case is $n = 0$.

Recursion in Sorting

Recursion is a difficult concept to learn. But if you master it, you will discover that it makes many programs easy that otherwise might be very difficult to code correctly. Let's examine a method for sorting a list using recursion:

Method for Sorting a List L
1. If L has length 1 or less, do nothing (this is the base case).
2. Otherwise,
   a. Choose a member of L, which we call the pivot.
   b. Let D_1 be the members of L less than the pivot.
   c. Let D_2 be the members of L greater than or equal to the pivot (but D_2 does not contain the pivot).
   d. Rearrange L so that D_1 is to the left of the pivot and D_2 is to the right of the pivot.
   e. Sort D_1 to obtain R_1.
   f. Sort D_2 to obtain R_2.
   g. The final sorted list is R_1 followed by the pivot followed by R_2.

As an illustration, suppose the list 2, 5, 7, 6, 3, 1, 4 is to be sorted. The method of calculation chooses one member of the list—say, the last one, 4—and moves the numbers that are less than 4 to the left end of the array and the numbers that are greater than 4 to the right: 2, 3, 1, 4, 5, 7, 6 Here we have pivot = 4, D_1 = 2, 3, 1, and D_2 = 5, 7, 6. Next

D_1 is sorted to obtain 1, 2, 3, and D_2 is sorted to obtain 5, 6, 7. The final sorted list is D_1 followed by pivot followed by D_2: 1, 2, 3, 4, 5, 6, 7. Following is the subroutine for this sorting algorithm. It is a famous sorting method, known as `quicksort`. The routine `quicksort(ar, i, j)` sorts the portion of the integer array, ar, beginning at entry i and ending at entry j: (normally, we start the process by specifying the entire array. Thus, $i = 0$ and $j =$ the number of elements in the array minus 1.)

```java
void quicksort(int[] list, int first, int last)
{
    int pivot;

    if (first < last)
    {
        pivot = rearrange(list, first, last);
        quicksort(list, first, pivot - 1);
        quicksort(list, pivot + 1, last);
    }
}
```

There are many strategies for coding `rearrange` and its auxiliary routine `exchange`, and we will not discuss them here. The following is one Java version of these routines that you may wish to study:

```java
void exchange(int[] list, int x, int y)
{
    int temp;
    temp = list[x];
    list[x] = list[y];
    list[y] = temp;
}

int rearrange(int[] list, int first, int last)
{
    int pivot, pval, p, k;
    pivot = (first+last)/2; // Find middle
    exchange(list, first, pivot); // Move to front of sublist
    pval = list[first];
    p = first;
    k = first + 1;
    while (k <= last)
    {
```

```
        if (list[k] <= pval)
        {
            p = p + 1;
            exchange(list, p, k);
        }
        k = k + 1;
    }
    exchange(list, first, p);
    return p;
}
```

In conclusion, the strategy of dividing a problem into simpler parts and solving each one separately was explored earlier in this chapter. In this section, the approach for computing function C divides the data into parts, calculates partial results using C, and combines those results to obtain the final answer. The methodology is called *recursion*, and it is both subtle and powerful. Some writers also refer to the methodology of splitting the data into parts and solving the parts *the divide and conquer methodology*.

Recursion can often be used as an alternative to writing ordinary looping programs. For example, you can probably write a program to compute factorial easily without recursion. However, other problems are extremely difficult to write unless you use recursion. An example of such a problem is given in exercise 4: the computation of all the orderings of a set of symbols. Other examples of problems that need recursion for straightforward solution are tree-searching problems, as described in chapter 16 on artificial intelligence.

Exercises

1. Study the routine `rearrange` and explain how it works. Write a program that reads a series of integers and then uses the `quicksort` program to sort them.

2. The Nth Fibonacci number is computed by adding the $(N-1)$th and the $(N-2)$th Fibonacci numbers. The first two are 0 and 1. Thus, the Fibonacci numbers can be enumerated as 0, 1, 1, 2, 3, 5, 8, 13, 21, ... Write a recursive program that reads a number N and then prints the Nth Fibonacci number. (When this program is run, its execution time can be long if N is not small. Why is this? Program execution time is studied more in chapter 13.)

3. The sum of N numbers in an array can be computed as follows: Add the first $N-1$ numbers, and then add that sum to the last number. Use this method to design and program a recursive procedure for adding an array.

4. Write a program that receives an array of symbols and then prints every arrangement (permutation) of those symbols. For example, if the program receives the array a, b, c, it will print out

a, b, c
a, c, b
b, a, c
b, c, a
c, a, b
c, b, a

Use a recursive strategy to solve this problem.

Summary

The central problem of computer science is the discovery of methods for managing complexity. The two techniques that have historically been most effective involve finding the best representation for the problem and then systematically decomposing it into simpler parts. These strategies appear to be universally applicable to all problem-solving situations, and mastering them seems fundamental to all education.

This chapter has illustrated both strategies in a series of examples. The first was the database problem, where the original statement of the task seemed to involve programming far beyond the grasp of novice programmers. Yet with careful structuring of the solution, a way was found to achieve the target behaviors with a single loop program and relatively little additional complexity.

Java and most other programming languages provide syntactic support to the decomposition process through the subroutine feature. A subroutine or method is a module of programming that solves a part of the total problem. Whenever the solution to any task seems complex, we section off parts of it into subroutines that will be written later. Each part of the solution should be cut down to such a proportion that it seems straightforward and obviously correct.

The use of the subroutine feature requires care in designing communication between the subroutine and its calling program. This communication is carried out through the parameter list. When the higher-level program needs to have a job done on its data structures, it calls the subroutine to do it. The subroutine references only the needed structures in the calling program through the parameter list. If the subroutine needs additional memory locations to do its work, they should be declared internally.

The database program developed in this chapter introduces the concept of a database and shows how it organizes data. An excellent way to retrieve information from such a database is to search for data patterns where some but not all of the fields are specified.

One of the shortcomings of the program studied here is its inability to do inferences when the needed facts are not explicitly in the memory. Chapter 16 will reexamine this shortcoming and describe a method for overcoming it.

This chapter completes our study of the Java language. The features described in chapters 2–4 do not include the whole language, but they are sufficient to do essentially any program. A description of the syntax used in these chapters appears at the end of chapter 2. The full Java language includes a long list of other features, but they are primarily embellishments of the constructions covered here: additional looping, branching, and subroutine constructions and additional data structure types and declaration facilities. Also, Java has many graphics features; some are described in chapter 5.

In the early days of computing, an interesting competition arose related to the power of computer languages. One researcher would show that his or her language could be used to compute every function that some other language could compute. Then someone else would show that the second language could compute everything that the first one could. The implication was that neither language could compute anything more than the other; both were capable of computing the same class of functions. Such comparisons occurred many times with the same surprising result: any nontrivial computer language that one can invent is apparently capable of computing no more and no fewer functions than all the other nontrivial programming languages. This is known as the *Church-Markov-Turing Thesis*, and it applies to the part of Java described in this book. You have learned all the computational features needed to compute any function that can be programmed by any language yet invented. Additional features provide convenience but not increased computational capability.

The Church-Markov-Turing Thesis has even more profound implications. Consider the portion of the English language appropriate for discussing computation in very concrete terms. This widely used sublanguage includes such sentences as, "Find the largest number in this finite set that is prime" and "Sort the set of records on the fifth field." Let's call this portion of English C-English and think of it as just another programming language. As far as anyone can tell, the power of C-English is similar to any other programming language: it is capable of describing any calculation that any standard programming language can do, and no more. The Church-Markov-Turing Thesis in its extended form thus asserts that any algorithm that anyone can describe in concrete English (or any other natural language) can be translated to any modern programming language, including the Java presented in this book. This thesis is embraced by most computer scientists, and it implies a kind of completeness to modern programming languages. It says that if you can specify an algorithm concretely in English, you can program it. Modern computer languages are powerful enough; no new languages will enable us to compute more functions than are now possible unless some currently unimaginable new paradigm for computing is created.

You should now be able to solve many problems of moderate size using the Java language. However, this is only a brief introduction to programming, and substantial additional study is needed in order to become an accomplished programmer. If you wish to become an expert, learn the rest of the Java features, as well as one or two other languages. Then undertake an extensive study of data structures and the multitude of ways that can be used to represent data in computers.

Associated with this study, learn to analyze the execution times of programs so that you can create efficient as well as correct programs. Also, learn methodologies for proving the correctness of programs, so that they can be guaranteed to meet the specifications that are claimed for them. Finally, you should gain experience applying all these methodologies to the analysis and coding of a variety of problems.

5   Graphics, Classes, and Objects

Calling All Artists

This is your chance to show the creativity that you have been storing up for so long. If you wish to create beautiful graphics that can be displayed on your own terminal or any terminal connected to the Internet, read on. You can draw something like figure 5.1 or anything else you can imagine. Fortunately, we have now covered the basics of Java and will call on Java facilities using familiar constructions.

In this chapter, we study a set of graphics primitives that will enable us to create essentially any picture on a computer screen. The only major limitation will be the resolution of the hardware screen, which has a limited number of pixels per centimeter. We will be able to draw the graphics within the context of applets as described in earlier chapters, and we will be able to activate them in response to buttons in the usual way. In the process, we will gain additional experience with Java constructions, including the ability to define new classes and use them in a variety of ways.

Graphics Primitives

We begin by studying the `Graphics` class, which is similar to other classes we have studied. This class enables us to put two-dimensional images on the screen in the same way that the `TextField` class enables us to put strings of characters on the screen. Thus, if we have a `TextField` called Q, we can put the characters Yes on the screen with the statement `Q.setText("Yes")`. If we have a `Graphics` object called G and want to put a straight line on the screen, we type `G.drawLine(...)`.

In our examples, we will assume we are drawing on a `Canvas` (another class, discussed later) that measures 200 by 200 pixels. You can think of each pixel as a point source of light that can radiate any color you choose, and the `Graphics` code will have the job of

Figure 5.1

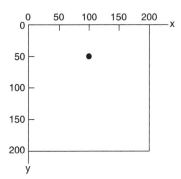

Figure 5.2

lighting up the ones we want. Each pixel has a set of coordinates that measure from the upper-left corner across and down. The across measurement is called the *x*-coordinate, and the down measurement is called the *y*-coordinate. Figure 5.2 shows a 200 by 200 grid with the point ($x = 100$, $y = 50$) plotted.

Our first new method for drawing will be `drawLine`, which takes four coordinates, the *x*, *y*-coordinates for the beginning and ending points of the line:

```
void drawLine(int x1, int y1, int x2, int y2)
```

This draws a line from point ($x1, y1$) to point ($x2, y2$). Notice that `drawLine` is a routine requiring four `int` declared arguments and does not return a result. Its only action is to place the line on the screen. On our sample `Canvas`, we have the `Graphics` object `G`; the execution of `G.drawLine(50, 50, 150, 100)` produces the graphic shown in figure 5.3.

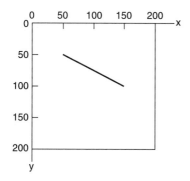

Figure 5.3

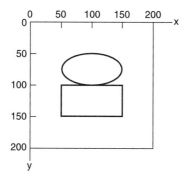

Figure 5.4

Similarly, we can draw a rectangle with the method `drawRect`:

```
void drawRect(int x, int y, int width, int height)
```

This draws a rectangle with upper-left corner at point (x, y). The width and height are given by the parameters `width` and `height`. We can draw an oval (an ellipse) with the method `drawOval`:

```
void drawOval(int x, int y, int width, int height)
```

It will be drawn inside an (unseen) rectangle with upper-left corner at point (x, y) and with the width and height given. If we execute `G.drawOval(50, 50, 100, 50)` and `G.drawRect(50, 100, 100, 50)`, we will obtain the graphic shown in figure 5.4.

Besides creating line drawings, rectangles, and ovals, we can also create solid objects with

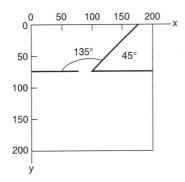

Figure 5.5

```
void fillRect(int x, int y, int width, int height)
```

and

```
void fillOval(int x, int y, int width, int height)
```

If we want to draw a curved line, we do it by using a part of a lined oval:

```
void drawArc(int x, int y, int width, int height, int startAngle,
int arcAngle)
```

This form is identical to `drawOval` except that only part of the oval is drawn starting at the angle `startAngle` and moving through the number of degrees shown. Figure 5.5 shows the result of `G.drawArc(50, 50, 100, 50, 45, 135)`. There is also a fill version of `drawArc`:

```
void fillArc(int x, int y, int width, int height, int startAngle, int
arcAngle)
```

You can present a series of characters to label your graphic by using the following, where s gives the `String` to be presented and x and y give the coordinates of the beginning of the `String`.

```
void drawString(String s, int x, int y)
```

There are a number of features that enable you to set the font and size of the string, but you must obtain these from a Java manual.

Note that everything we described must be done in a color. We designate the color with

```
void setColor(Color c)
```

where `Color c` can be a designated color such as `Color.red` or `Color.green` or a color defined by you specifying the amounts of red, green, and blue you want. You do this by defining a color with something like

```
Color c1;
```

and

```
c1 = new Color(200, 30, 40);
```

where the integers are `int` declared and between 0 and 255. The color `c1` will have red to degree 200, green to degree 30, and blue to degree 40. You should try this feature and find some shades that you like.

The `Graphics` class has many other features not discussed here. But the ones we have studied are enough to enable us to do a lot. You should consult standard manuals for the complete list of features.

Let's Draw Some Pictures

Let's create a demonstration applet for some of the preceding `Graphics` methods. This program uses a class called `Canvas`, which sets up a display area for our `Graphics` object. In fact, we get our `Graphics` object from the `Canvas` class with the `Canvas` method called `get.Graphics`.

```
import awb.*;
import java.awt.*;
import java.awt.event.*;

public class GDemo extends java.applet.Applet
                    implements ActionListener
// A demonstration program for the Graphics methods drawLine,
// drawOval, and drawRect.
{
    Graphics g;
    Canvas c;
    Button b1, b2, b3, b4;

    public void init()
    {
```

```
        c = new Canvas();
        c.setSize(200,200); // Set the size of the Canvas.
        add(c);
        g = c.getGraphics(); // Get the Graphics object from c.
        b1 = new Button("Start");
        b1.addActionListener(this);
        b2 = new Button("Line");
        b2.addActionListener(this);
        b3 = new Button("Oval");
        b3.addActionListener(this);
        b4 = new Button("Rectangle");
        b4.addActionListener(this);
        add(b1); add(b2); add(b3); add(b4);
    }

    public void actionPerformed(ActionEvent event)
    {
        Object cause = event.getSource();
        if (cause == b1)
        {
            g.setColor(Color.white);
            // Color the whole canvas white.
            g.fillRect(0, 0, 200, 200);
        }
        if (cause == b2)
        {
            g.setColor(Color.blue);
            g.drawLine(50, 50, 150, 100); // Demonstrate drawLine.
        }
        if (cause == b3)
        {
            g.setColor(Color.green);
            g.drawOval(50, 50, 100, 50); // Demonstrate drawOval.
        }
        if (cause == b4)
        {
            g.setColor(Color.red);
            g.drawRect(50, 100, 100, 50); // Demonstrate drawRect.
        }
    }
}
```

By running this applet and pushing the buttons, you can see some of the figures presented earlier in the chapter.

The next step is to draw a picture; the following applet draws a simple house:

```java
import awb.*;
import java.awt.*;
import java.awt.event.*;

public class DrawHouse extends java.applet.Applet
                    implements ActionListener
// A graphics demo applet that draws a simple house.
{
    Graphics g;
    Canvas c;
    Button b1, b2;
    int hx, hy; // The x and y coordinates of the upper left
               // corner of the house.
    int hwidth, hheight; // The house width and height.
    public void init()
    {
        c = new Canvas();
        c.setSize(200, 200);
        add(c);
        g = c.getGraphics();
        b1 = new Button("Start");
        b1.addActionListener(this);
        b2 = new Button("House");
        b2.addActionListener(this);
        add(b1); add(b2);
    }

    public void actionPerformed (ActionEvent event)
    {
        Object cause = event.getSource();
        if (cause == b1) // Set background.
        {
            g.setColor(Color.white);
            g.fillRect(0, 0, 200, 200);
        }
        if (cause == b2) // Draw the house.
        {
```

```
hx = 50; hy = 90; // x,y coordinates for upper
                  // left corner of the house.
hwidth = 100; hheight = 80; // House width and height.
g.setColor(Color.blue); // Color of front of house.
g.fillRect(hx, hy, hwidth, hheight);
// Draw front of house.
g.setColor(Color.black); // Color of roof.
g.fillRect(hx - (hwidth/20), hy,
        hwidth + (hwidth/10), hheight/3);
        // Roof with some overhang.
g.setColor.green); // Color for door and window.
g.fillRect(hx + (2 * hwidth/3), hy + hheight/2,
        hwidth/8, hheight/2); // Draw the door.
g.fillRect(hx + hwidth/4), hy + (hheight/2),
        hwidth/8, hheight/8); // Draw the window.
g.setColor(Color.red); // Color of chimney.
g.fillRect(hx + (3 * hwidth/4), hy - hheight/8,
        hwidth/.8, hheight/8); // Draw the chimney.
    }
  }
}
```

Figure 5.6 shows the graphic you get if you run the DrawHouse applet. Of course, your machine will show this in full color whereas we have only black and white here.

So you now have all the tools you need to create color images. Have fun!

Exercises

1. Here is the code to draw a simple cartoon face. Write the rest of the applet that will be needed to display this face.

Figure 5.6

```
facex = 60; facey = 50; facew = 80; faceh = 100;
g.drawOval(facex,facey,facew,faceh);
mouthx = facex + facew/4;
mouthy = facey + faceh * 9/16;
mouthw = facew/2;
mouthh = faceh/4;
g.drawArc(mouthx,mouthy,mouthw,mouthh,190,160);
g.drawLine(facex + facew/4,facey + faceh * 7/16,
                  facex + facew * 3/8,facey + faceh * 7/16);
g.drawLine(facex + facew * 5/8,facey + faceh * 7/16,
                  facex + facew * 3/4,facey + faceh * 7/16);
earx = facex - facew * 3/32;
eary = facey + faceh * 5/16;
earw = facew/8;
earh = faceh/4;
g.drawArc(earx,eary,earw,earh,50,240);
earx = facex + facew * 31/32;
g.drawArc(earx,eary,earw,earh,250,240);
g.setFont(new Font("TimesRoman", Font.BOLD,12));
g.drawString("Java Graphics!!!!", facex, facey + faceh * 5/4);
```

2. Draw a figure of your own design using Java.

Let's Create a Class Called House

We are now going to pretend that the house drawing we made in the previous section is really important. We are going to be drawing lots of houses, and maybe other programmers will be wanting to draw them as well. In fact, it will be so important that future Java users will learn about TextFields and Houses (which we have invented). Thus, we will create a class called House, and once we will have done it, people will be able to declare House objects in the same way as they declare TextFields:

```
TextField t1;
House h1;

t1 = new TextField(20);
h1 = new House(50, 90, 100, 80, g);

t1.setText("Great Ideas");
h1.draw();
```

We can do this easily by simply typing the correct Java syntax. We need to say we want to create a new class: public class House. And we should declare the key internal variables for this class as "protected." This means that our class can reference these data but no program outside the class can reference them. Thus the data are not "public." The reason we protect the data is to prevent a user of the class House from accidentally changing a variable within House when the intention was only to be carrying out an external computation. The only way a protected item can be changed is to have a method associated with House do that change. Here is the beginning of our new class definition:

```
public class House
{
    protected int hx, hy, hwidth, hheight;
    protected Graphics hg;
```

Next we need what is called a *constructor method*, which will be used to construct a new house. We want a programmer to be able to type

```
h1 = new House(50, 90, 100, 80, g);
```

and have a new house come into existence in the machine with all of its parameters, hx, hy, and so forth, set correctly. The house will not necessarily be displayed on the screen; it will only exist internally. The syntax for the constructor method is the following:

```
public House(int a, int b, int c, int d, Graphics h)
{
    hx = a;
    hy = b;
    width = c;
    height = d;
    hg = h;
}
```

This is a somewhat boring method because it seems to do nothing. But it does its job—to take value a and put it into hx, to take value b and put it into hy, and so forth.

As an example, suppose we have these internal protected variables:

```
hx =
hy =
hwidth =
hheight =
hg =
```

Suppose the user wants to create a house with

```
h1 = new House(50, 90, 100, 80, g);
```

This call has identified each input parameter with a value:

```
a = 50
b = 90
c = 100
d = 80
h = g
```

You can see this by looking at the definition of the constructor method House.

But what does the constructor method do? It loads a into hx, b into hy, and so forth. The result is that we now have our new constructed house, and its internal parameters are

```
hx = 50;
hy = 90;
hwidth = 100;
hheight = 80;
hg = g;
```

After you become accustomed to this, it will seem like much ado about nothing. But it can be confusing at first.

We are still not done. We must have a method to draw the house. So far it only exists as a set of parameters. We will call the method draw; here is the code:

```java
public void draw()
{
    hg.setColor(Color.blue); // Color of front of house.
    hg.fillRect(hx, hy, hwidth, hheight); // Draw front of house.
    hg.setColor(Color.black); // Color of roof.
    hg.fillRect(hx - (hwidth/20), hy, // Roof with some overhang.
                hwidth + (hwidth/10), hheight/3);
    hg.setColor.green); // Color for door and window.
    hg.fillRect(hx + (2 * hwidth/3), hy + hheight/2,
                hwidth/8, hheight/2); // Draw the door.
    hg.fillRect(hx + hwidth/4), hy + (hheight/2),
                hwidth/8, hheight/8); // Draw the window.
    hg.setColor(Color.red); // Color of chimney.
    hg.fillRect(hx + (3 * hwidth/4), hy - hheight/8,
                hwidth/.8, hheight/8); // Draw the chimney.
}
```

This is all that is necessary to define the new class House. Here is the whole applet with the definition of the House class and its proper use in the program. This applet is identical in function to the DrawHouse applet in the previous section except that it does the profoundly important thing of defining the class House and using it.

```java
import awb.*;
import java.awt.*;
import java.awt.event.*;

public class HouseClass extends java.applet.Applet
                    implements ActionListener
// A graphics demo applet that creates the House class and uses it.
{
    Graphics g;
    Canvas c;
    Button b1, b2;
    House h1;

    public void init()
    {
        c = new Canvas();
        c.setSize(200, 200);
        add(c);
        g = c.getGraphics();
        b1 = new Button("Start");
        b1.addActionListener(this);
        b2 = new Button("House");
        b2.addActionListener(this);
        h1 = new House(50, 90, 100, 80, g);
        add(b1); add(b2);
    }

    public void actionPerformed (ActionEvent event)
    {
        Object cause = event.getSource();

        if (cause == b1) // Set background.
        {
            g.setColor(Color.white);
            g.fillRect(0, 0, 200, 200);
        }
```

```
            if (cause == b2) // Draw the house.
            {
                h1.draw();
            }
        }

        public class House
        {
            protected int hx, hy, hwidth, hheight;
            protected Graphics hg;
            public House(int a, int b, int c, int d, Graphics h)
                (Code shown previously for the constructor method)

            public void draw()
                (Code shown previously for the draw method)

        }
    }
```

Here is one final note regarding terminology. When we define House, we are defining a *class*, as has been described in this and previous chapters. When we create h1, we are creating an *object*, which is an instantiation of the class House.

Exercise

1. Draw your own picture using Java graphics. Create a class that names your picture and that enables one to create it and draw it by using the class definitions.

Adding Features to the House Class

If Houses are going to be important, we may want to add some methods to the class to make it more useful. We might want to move the houses around on the screen, change their size or color, or modify their dimensions or design in various ways.

Here is a method which will simply move the house left or right:

```
public void moverl(int j)
{
    hx = hx + (j * (1 + hwidth/10));
}
```

If we set j to be 1, the routine will increase hx by about one-tenth of the width of the house. (If hwidth is very small, it will move the house right at least one pixel.) If we set $j = -1$, the routine will decrease hx by that amount.

This method would be even better if we had it erase the house in its current position and redraw it in the new position:

```
public void moverl(int j)
{
    erase();
    hx = hx + (j * (1 + hwidth/10));
    draw();
}
```

(How do you erase the house? One simple method is to create an erase routine that is exactly like the draw routine except that the drawing is done in Color.white, which is the background color. This is a naive method for erasing, but it is satisfactory for the present.) With this new method available, we can now move the house h1 to the right with the code h1.moverl(1) and to the left with the code h1.moverl(-1).

Similarly, we can create a method to move the house up or down (by making changes to hy). Or we can create a routine that will make the house larger or smaller by changing both the width and height parameters:

```
public void size(int j)
{
    erase();
    hwidth = hwidth + (j * (1 + hwidth/10));
    hheight = hheight + (j * (1 + hheight/10));
    draw();
}
```

Here is the applet with the House class improved:

```
import awb.*;
import java.awt.*;
import java.awt.event.*;

public class HouseClassE extends java.applet.Applet
                    implements ActionListener
// A graphics demo applet that creates the House class with
// move and size changing features and uses it.
{
```

```
Graphics g;
Canvas c;
Button b1, b2, bleft, bright, bup, bdown, bsmaller, blarger;
House h1;

public void init()
{
    c = new Canvas();
    c.setSize(200, 200);
    add(c);
    g = c.getGraphics();
    b1 = new Button("Start");
    b1.addActionListener(this);
    b2 = new Button("House");
    b2.addActionListener(this);
    bleft = new Button("Move left");
    bleft.addActionListener(this);
    bright = new Button("Move right");
    bright.addActionListener(this);
    bup = new Button("Move up");
    bup.addActionListener(this);
    bdown = new Button("Move down");
    bdown.addActionListener(this);
    bsmaller = new Button("Smaller");
    bsmaller.addActionListener(this);
    blarger = new Button("Larger");
    blarger.addActionListener(this);
    h1 = new House(50, 90, 100, 80, g);
    add(b1); add(b2); add(bleft); add(bright);
    add(bup); add(bdown); add(bsmaller); add(blarger);
}

public void actionPerformed (ActionEvent event)
{
    Object cause = event.getSource();

    if (cause == b1) // Set background.
    {
        g.setColor(Color.white);
        g.fillRect(0, 0, 200, 200);
    }
```

```
            if (cause == b2)  // Draw the house.
            {
                h1.draw();
            }
            if (cause == bleft)
            {
                h1.movelr(-1);
            }
            if (cause == bright)
            {
                h1.moverl(1);
            }

            and similarly for the other four buttons.
        }
        public class House
        {
            protected int hx, hy, hwidth, hheight;
            protected Graphics hg;

            public House(int a, int b, int c, int d, Graphics h)
                (Code shown previously for the constructor method)

            public void draw()
                (Code shown previously for the draw method)

            public void erase()
                (This is left as an exercise)

            public void moverl(int j)
                (Code shown previously)

            public void moveud(int j)
                (Code similar to mover)

            public void size(int j)
                (Code shown previously)


        }
    }
```

Exercise

1. Design some modifications to your class of the previous section and code them into your class definition.

Creating a Village

Once we have a new class, we can gain many benefits that Java offers. One illustration is the use of the array feature for the new class. We can create an array of ten houses with the same syntax as an array of ten integers:

```
House h1[];
```

```
h1 = new House[10];
```

We can create the first House h1[0] with h1[0] = new House(...) and the second with h1[1] = new House(...), and so forth. We can draw the first house with h1[0].draw(), the second house with h1[1].draw(), and so forth. Also you can use the other methods to modify these houses. Here is the code to enlarge house h1[4]: h1[4].size(1);.

The code for the applet that enables one to create ten houses is easy to write. The IntField which tells which house is to be created or modified by pushing a button.

```
import (as before)
```

```
public class Village extends java.applet.Applet
                    implements ActionListener
// A graphics demo applet that creates the House class and
// an array of ten houses.
{
    Graphics g;
    Canvas c;
    Button b1, b2, bleft, bright, bup, bdown, bsmaller, blarger;
    House h1[];
    IntField which;
    int i;

    public void init()
    {
        (Same as init in HouseClassE applet except for two statements)
```

```
        h1 = new House[10];
        add(which);
    }

    public void actionPerformed (ActionEvent event)
    {
        Object cause = event.getSource();

        if (cause == b1) // Set background.
        {
            g.setColor(Color.white);
            g.fillRect(0, 0, 200, 200);
        }

        if (cause == b2) // Draw the house.
        {
            i = which.getInt();
            h1[i] = new House(30 * i,100,20,15,g);
            h1[i].draw();
        }
        if (cause == bleft)
        {
            i = which.getInt();
            h1[i].movelr(-1);
        }

        And similarly for the other buttons.
    }

    public class House
    {
        (Same as previous definition of House)
    }
}
```

Exercise

1. Use the array feature to create a set of objects for some class you have defined.

Subclasses and the Java Class Hierarchy

One of the great powers of Java is that one can use code written by someone else easily. One can do this even if the other code is not exactly what you wanted. Suppose you have used the House class and found it nearly satisfactory, but you still want additional features. You may be able to extend the definition of House to give you the special things you want while still using the main features of House.

Let's assume the House class is usable except that we want to be able to stretch the house out very long or stretch it vertically to be tall. We can create a class StretchHouse that extends the definition of House in the direction that we want. Here is the code to do that. It needs little explanation.

```
public class StretchHouse extends House
{
    public StretchHouse(int a, int b, int c, int d, Graphics h)
    {
        super(a, b, c, d, h);
    }

    public void stretchw(int j)
    {
        erase();
        hwidth = hwidth + (j * (1 + hwidth/10));
        draw();
    }

    public void stretchh(int j)
    {
        erase();
        hheight = hheight + (j * (1 + hheight/10));
        draw();
    }
}
```

The constructor method simply takes its values and passes them on to the constructor method of the routine that is being extended. This is done with the call to super(a, b, c, d, h). The name "super" refers to the constructor of the class being extended. All the capabilities of the class House are maintained by StretchHouse. So if h1 is to be a StretchHouse object, then one can create h1 with the following code:

```
StretchHouse h1;
h1 = new StretchHouse(...);
```

One can draw h1 with

```
h1.draw();
```

One can move h1 right with

```
h1.movelr(1);
```

and up with

```
h1.moveud(-1);
```

and make h1 larger with

```
h1.size(1);
```

and so forth.

The power of the extend feature should therefore be clear. Notice that the user has created a new class with just the desired new features while enjoying the use of possibly vast amounts of code that were incorporated into the extended class House. Every time you create an applet, you are doing an extension of the java.applet.Applet class, which does vast amounts for you, including linking your code to an HTML page and displaying the things you want in the way you have requested in your applet.

Just to make the point again, let's assume someone is using your StretchHouse class and wants to add the feature that a house can be reversed (with the door on the left side and the window on the right). He or she can write an extension of your class:

```
public class ReverseHouse extends StretchHouse
{
    protected int rev;

    public ReverseHouse(int a, int b, int c, int d, Graphics h)
    {
        super(a, b, c, d, h);
        rev = 0;
    }

    public void reverse()
    {
```

```
                erase();
                if (rev == 0)
                    {rev = 1;}
                else
                    {rev = 0;}
                draw();
        }

        public void draw()
        {
            if (rev == 0)
            {
                (Code to draw house as usual)
            }
            else
            {
                (Code to draw the reverse of the usual house)
            }
        }
    etc.
}
```

Notice that with this extension, we want to use the code from the previous routines except that we do not want to use draw. We need a new draw that can do both normal and reversed houses. When Java runs objects of the ReverseHouse class, it will notice that draw is defined in ReverseHouse, and it will not use the inherited version of draw. But it will use the inherited versions of the rest of the code.

At this point, you become aware of the huge hierarchy of classes in Java. In fact, every class in Java has a parent or a superclass except the highest class of all, Object. The class hierarchy is a very large tree extending down from Object. A tiny fraction of that tree is shown in figure 5.7. Most classes are specified as extensions of other classes. If they are not specified, then they are extensions of Object. Figure 5.7 shows a few of the classes included in the awt package; some of them should look familiar. However, you should be aware that we touch on only a few of the many available options in this book. You also can see our locally defined classes from this chapter, House and its subclasses. Since House was not defined to have a superclass, its superclass is Object.

Exercises

1. Define a subclass of one of the classes you have defined in earlier sections. Code it in Java and demonstrate it.

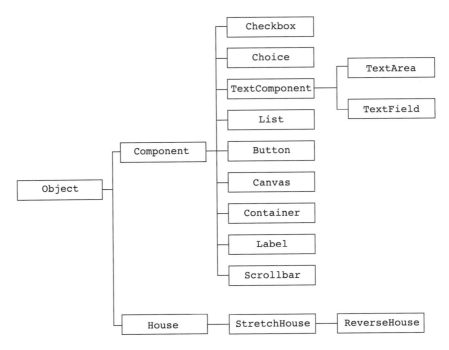

Figure 5.7

2. Define a subclass of ReverseHouse called ColorHouse, which enables you to specify the colors of the house. Code it in Java and show how all the capabilities of the superclasses of ColorHouse continue to function properly.

3. (a) Define a class called Book, which holds the title, author's name, ISBN number, and price of a book. Code it in Java and show its ability to hold the required information. Include methods to retrieve or modify any of the information fields.

   (b) Define an array that can hold 100 such books, and code a program in Java to store and retrieve the information on all those books.

   (c) Define a subclass of Book called BookHS, which holds the same information as Book except that it also has a field telling whether the book is hardcover or paperback.

   (d) Define a subclass of BookHS called BookInventory, which holds an additional field telling the number of copies a local bookstore has on hand. Include methods that enable the user to increment or decrement the inventory. Show how to create an array of 100 of these, and use all the capabilities of the superclasses as well as the BookInventory class.

Summary

This chapter introduced a set of `Graphics` methods and showed how to use them to construct simple graphics on the screen. The technique is to declare a `Canvas` and to craft your design on the screen using those `Graphics` methods. The approach follows the applet structure used throughout this book.

Once this technique is clear, you can move the graphics drawing code into the definition of a class. That is, you can define your own class for drawing scenes on the screen and then just call your `draw` method to create the image. The class definition can hold all the details. The advantages are that you can package some complex code in a bundle that can be used by yourself or others as needed. Another advantage arises when you want a series of objects of that class type. You can create an array of those objects.

Finally, the chapter shows how to create extensions of a defined class. If the class does not completely conform to the needs of the programmer, an extension can be created that will use the superclass but that can have its own definitions of methods to satisfy more specialized needs. The methods of the subclass can be methods that were not included in the superclass, or they can be rewritten versions of methods in the superclass.

A side effect of the study of extensions of classes is the observation that all Java classes are defined in one great tree with the `Object` class at the root. Thus, when we use Java, we are employing thousands of lines of code written by others, even though we may not be aware of it. A prime example of this is the `java.applet.Applet` code, which is the superclass of all the applets in this book. This code does the many tasks related to connecting our computation to the HTML call, allocating the areas on the screen, and executing the Java processor on a browser.

6 Simulation

Predicting the Future

The sun is a layered sphere of superheated materials: it has a dense core, where nuclear fusion produces energy resulting in astronomical temperatures—perhaps 15 million degrees Centigrade; a middle layer called the radiative zone, which transmits the energy outward—its temperature is possibly around 4 million degrees; and an outer layer, at perhaps 2 million degrees, which is made up of dense gases churning violently and bubbling the energy toward the surface. Scientists predict that the sun will continue to burn in roughly its current state for several billion more years, when it will begin to exhaust its resources. Then it will enter a "red giant" phase and expand its diameter from less than a million miles to possibly over 50 million miles. Instead of being a bright disk in our sky, it will *be* a large fraction of our sky. It will burn itself out in this phase and eventually collapse to a "white dwarf," which may be about the size of the earth.

This chapter introduces a powerful tool of science for studying complex systems like the sun and for understanding their mechanisms. Knowing the basic facts about the sun now, or any other system, we would like to make predictions about it. What will happen next? How long will each phase last, and what will its characteristics be? The answers to these and other questions can often be answered by *simulation*.

Our methodology will follow three steps:

1. We will devise a model that captures the essence of the system we wish to study. It usually consists of some equations or other relationships that indicate how the significant measures of the system relate to each other.
2. We will develop a next-step function. The input for this function will be a listing of the significant information about the system at a given time. The output will be the new state the model will change to after a given interval of time.
3. We will set the model in an initial state and apply the next-step function repeatedly to discover future states.

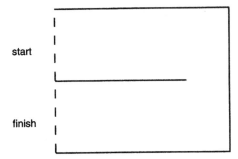

Figure 6.1

Simulation enables us to observe a system as it goes through a sequence of steps. A simulation can help scientists understand the system; it can help a designer of a system predict behavior so that it is possible to optimize design decisions; it can provide us with a subjective view of the proposed system so that we can enjoy, appreciate, and understand it even though it does not exist in reality.

How Do You Win an Auto Race? A Simulation

Suppose we wish to run a race over the track shown in figure 6.1. The auto starts anywhere along the start line as shown and drives in the direction toward the right, around the barrier in a right-hand turn, and back across the finish line. It should reach the finish line in the shortest amount of time. The auto is capable of accelerating and decelerating at 3 meters per second per second, and it has no maximum speed. The lateral acceleration on the curve may not exceed 9 meters per second per second without the auto's losing traction and sliding off the track. The main goal is to find the strategy that attains the fastest possible coverage of the track. The simulation will enable us to propose any strategy we wish and then find out how well it works. By trying several strategies, we should be able to converge on one that works really well.

In order to proceed with this study, it is necessary to go through the three steps listed previously. First, we need a model of the system we are studying. The model must represent the information about the system that interests us. In the current situation, the items of interest are the position of the car, its velocity, its direction, and its state (e.g., running normally, skidding, crashed into the wall). These will all be `double` numbers except for the state, which will be an integer.

State description   *x* coordinate
                     y coordinate

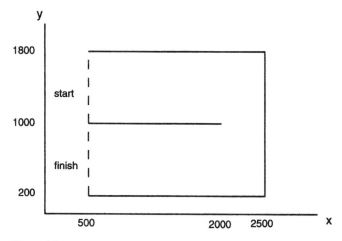

Figure 6.2

> *x* velocity
> *y* velocity
> running state (1 for under control;
>   0 for skidding; −1 for crashed; −2 for successful completion)
> *t* time in seconds since the beginning of the race

The model also must include a description of the race track indicating where the walls and finish lines are (figure 6.2). Let's decide that the start and finish lines are at $x = 500$. The top and bottom lines are at $y = 1800$ and 200, respectively. The far wall in the x direction is at $x = 2500$. The dividing line in the middle is at $y = 1000$, extending from $x = 500$ to $x = 2000$.

Second, we need a next-step function. We define an `Automobile` class and the next-state function as a method of that class. This method will receive as input a state description of the auto, and it will compute the next state after 1 second of driving. The name of this function is `drive`, and it has two arguments, as follows:

a   The acceleration, a `double` number, that we have decided to apply. It may not exceed 3 in a positive or negative direction. (A negative acceleration corresponds to applying the brake.)

turnr   The turn radius. For example, `turnr = 100` means turn right in an arc with a center that has a distance of 100 meters from the vehicle. A negative turn radius means the same thing except turn left. If `turnr = 0`, the auto will go on a straight course.

The `Automobile` class has been coded and is available on the Internet, as described in the introductory chapter, along with the main program and the other code needed for the simulation.

Summarizing, if we have `auto1`, which has been declared to be an instantiation of the `Automobile` class, we can invoke `auto1.drive(a,turnr)` to obtain a 1 second simulation of `auto1`. The method `auto1.drive` uses the values of the position, velocity, and so forth specifying the state of `auto1`. These values are internal to the `auto1` object. The method `auto1.drive` also receives as parameters the desired acceleration a and turn radius `turnr`. It then computes the new values of position, velocity, and so on, after 1 second of driving and enters them as the new state of `auto1`.

As an example, suppose `state` holds the position $x = 1000$, $y = 1400$ and velocity 30 meters per second in the x direction. Also, a $= 0$ and `turnr` $= 0$. Then `auto1.drive(a,turnr)` will compute a new state with position $x = 1030$, $y = 1400$ and velocity in the x direction of 30 meters per second.

Now, we can program the simulation to do any driving sequence we may wish to try. As a first test of the system, let's place the auto at the location $x = 500$, $y = 1400$ with velocity zero aimed in the x direction. (We place the car just at the start line at $x = 500$.) Then let us accelerate for 10 seconds at a rate of 3 meters per second per second in a straight line.

```
a = 3;
turnr = 0;
time = 1;
while ((time <= 10) && (not complete))
{
    auto1.drive(a,turnr);
    time = time + 1;
}
```

This should get the car moving at a rate of 30 meters per second in the x direction down the track. (If you accelerate at 3 meters per second per second for 10 seconds, you will be traveling at 30 meters per second.) In the location `not complete`, of the program, we place a test to check that the race has not ended with a success or a crash.

Next, we drive at a steady rate until we are even with the corner. (Here `corner` has the value 2000.)

```
a = 0;
turnr = 0;
while ((x < corner) && (not complete))
{
```

```
auto1.drive(a,turnr);
time = time + 1;
}
```

Next, we turn with a radius of 400 meters until we are going in the opposite direction. Since we are 400 meters from the end of the middle barrier, we will be rotating around that corner.

```
a = 0;
turnr = 400;
while (((y > middle) || (x > corner)) && (not complete))
{
    auto1.drive(a,turnr);
    time = time + 1;
}
```

(The symbols && and || stand for "and" and "or", respectively.) Finally, we accelerate maximally in a straight line until we cross the finish line.

```
a = 3;
turnr = 0;
while (not complete)
{
    auto1.drive(a,turnr);
    time = time + 1;
}
```

That is the program. We simply join the four pieces of code and insert them into the simulation program. Let's run the simulation and observe the path and the total time required to finish the course (figure 6.3). The total time was 121 seconds. (If you actually run this simulation, you will find the car stays on the curve around the track a bit too long and does not make a perfectly straight path toward the finish. The reason for this and the fix is left to you to figure out.)

Summarizing, we proposed a strategy for completing the auto race course and coded the simulation to check whether it would be successful. Then we ran the simulation and determined that the auto finished the course successfully in a time of 121 seconds. Presumably, if this course and automobile actually exist somewhere, someone could drive the sequence we have programmed and, on the condition that the model is accurate, observe the path shown and a completion time of 121 seconds.

Of course, we wanted to complete the race in the minimum amount of time, so we should try to find a strategy that will do better than our first attempt. Let's accelerate the car continuously from the start line to the curve. Then we will hold that speed around the curve before accelerating maximally again to the finish. The code in this case begins with

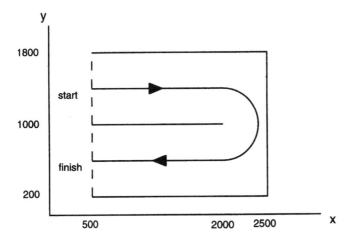

Figure 6.3

```
a = 3;
turnr = 0;
while ((x < corner) && (not complete))
{
    auto1.drive(a,turnr);
    time = time + 1;
}
```

and finishes with the last two segments in the previous strategy.

Unfortunately, when we run the new version, the auto goes into a skid at the turn and crashes into the far wall at $x = 2500$. It was traveling too fast at the curve to make the turn. This attempt was unsuccessful. (Aren't you glad you found this out by doing a simulation instead of driving a real auto?) There must be a better strategy, and we leave it as an exercise for you to find it.

Exercises

1. Write a program to simulate the following racing strategy. Begin at the same position as previously. Accelerate maximally in the x direction until reaching the point $x = 1000$. Then decelerate maximally to a velocity in the x direction of 30 meters per second. Then make the curve as before, but with a radius of 300 meters and accelerate maximally across the finish. What result does this strategy achieve?

2. Find the best strategy you can for completing the race course in minimum time.

*Avoiding the Plague: A Simulation

A problem of great interest to public health officials is the life cycle of a disease as it spreads through a population. When the disease is discovered, we would like to know how many people will be affected, how long the disease will be a problem, and how preventative and curative efforts may change the situation. A way to study these things is to develop a model of the disease characteristics and to run a simulation to try to predict its behaviors.

Step 1 in our development of the simulation is to devise a model of a set of individuals and the characteristics of the disease as it spreads through the population. We use an especially simple model because it is easy to program and still shows a variety of interesting behaviors. We will think of our population as a linear set of individuals and model it as a linear array. We place a 0 in each individual's entry if that person is well and a positive integer if the person becomes infected. The positive integer indicates the number of days since the individual was infected.

The model works as follows: All individuals start in the well condition with zeros in their associated locations. One individual in the population is infected by placing a 1 in that individual's location:

0000000000000000000000000000100000000000000000000000000000000

You can think of it as a row of houses with one containing a sick person. Or it could be a row of tomato plants.

Then a contagion rule models the process of infecting other individuals. It randomly selects individuals near the currently ill individual and places 1's in their locations. They become ill on the next day, and the individual that is already ill has its number of days incremented:

0000000000000000000100000000201000000000000000100000000000000

On the third day, the newly infected individuals infect additional individuals, and the number of ill individuals multiplies:

0000000000000001010020110000030201001001010100200000000000000

We then model the process of getting over the disease and having an immune period afterwards in which an individual cannot be reinfected. We have a parameter `infectious`, which gives the number of days that the illness will last, and a parameter `immune`, which tells the number of days past the first day of infection that an individual cannot be reinfected. Thus, if an individual is ill for 3 days after infection and remains immune to the disease until 7 days after the infection began, we set `infectious` = 3 and `immune` = 7.

Step 2 is to consider the next-step function. The core of this is the computation that finds which individuals are infected by an existing ill individual. This is done by a routine `infect`, which receives as input the number of the individual that is infecting and makes entries into the array showing which new individuals are becoming infected on the current day. Here is a first attempt at writing the `infect` routine. Variable k tells which individual is doing the infecting.

```
int [] infect(int [] B, int k, int rate)
{
    int i,j;
    i = 1;
    while (i <= rate)
    {
        // Select individual j to be infected and infect it.
        B[j] = 1;
        i = i + 1;
    }
    return B;
}
```

This routine infects several individuals, namely, the number given by `rate`. It infects individuals by placing 1's into their associated array entries.

We need to decide how to compute `j` each time a new individual is to be infected. We do this by calculating a *pseudo random number*, a number that is computed by a carefully designed function that delivers a variety of numbers if used repeatedly. The design of this computation is a complex matter that is not discussed here.

Here is the revised subroutine with the pseudo random number generator included. The `%` operator divides the left operand by the right operand and yields the remainder.

```
int [] infect(int [] B, int k, int iInc, int rate);
{
    int i,j;
    i = 1;
    while (i <= rate)
    {
        // Select individual j to be infected and infect it.
        iInc = ((iInc * 23) % 31);
        j = k + iInc - 13;
        if ((j > 0) && (j <= 60))
        {
            B[j] = 1;
```

```
        }
        i = i + 1;
    }
}
```

The task of step 2 is to begin with a matrix of individuals, some well, some ill, and some immune, and to call `infect` repeatedly so all the ill individuals infect new ones. In our current study, we choose the infection rate to be 3. The complete code for the simulation is given on the World Wide Web.

Let's execute the simulation and see what we can expect from a disease with the given characteristics: `infectious = 3`; `immune = 7`; `rate = 3`. The result shows each sick individual with an asterisk *, each immune individual with a 1, and all others with a 0:

```
day 1  000000000000000000000000000000*000000000000000000000000000000
day 2  000000000000000000000*00000000*0*0000000000000*0000000000000
day 3  000000000000000*0*00*0**00000*0*0*00*00*0*0*00*0000000000000
day 4  000*00*0000**00*0*******0***010***0****0*0*****00000*0**000
day 5  00**00****0***0*****1***0****1*1**************1***0*0*0***0
day 6  *0***0********01*1**1*11*****1*1*1**1**1*1**1*************
day 7  ***1*01****11**1*1111111*111*1*1111*1111*1*11111*****1*11***
day 8  **11**1111*111*111111111*11110111111111111111111*1*1*1111*
day 9  1*111*11111111*11111*1111111101*111111111111110111111111111
```

Here is a statistical summary of what happened over the nine days:

Day	Well	Ill	Immune
1	59	1	0
2	56	4	0
3	47	13	0
4	27	32	1
5	11	45	4
6	3	44	13
7	1	26	33
8	1	11	48
9	2	5	53

The simulation shows that all individuals eventually become infected by the disease. However, the immune period after the sickness enables essentially all individuals to become immune, and the disease appears to die out. (Actually, it might not die out. This is left as an exercise.)

In summary, we wanted to investigate the progress of a contagious disease as it makes it way through a population. We built a model for the population and a rule for the spread of the disease. Then we ran the simulation and saw what would happen and when. The exercises involve further investigations with this model.

Exercises

1. Does the disease that we modeled die out as expected? Investigate this and explain. Use the program given on the Internet.

2. What happens in the disease model if the immunity period is longer, say, 8 or 9 or 10 days after the first infection? What happens if the immunity period is shorter?

3. It is quite possible that the contagion rate selected is not correct in a given situation. If the disease is modeled by `infectious = 3` and `immune = 7`, show what happens if the infection rate changes.

4. Can you discover a systematic relation between any two of the variables, such as contagion rate and the probability that the disease will die out?

5. Suppose that a very infectious disease has arrived in town. It has the property that if a resident of a given house on a street becomes infected, both neighbors (one on each side) become infected on the next day. Write a new `infect` routine that has this property, and replace the existing one with it. Using the same disease model described in exercise 3 (`infectious = 3`, `immune = 7`) and the new infection routine, discover what the life cycle of the disease is.

6. A better simulation might result if the state were stored in a two-dimensional array measuring, perhaps, 20 by 20. Revise the simulaton program to handle this model. Use the graphics capabilities studied in chapter 5 to show the state of the population. Repeat a set of experiments of the kinds suggested in the previous exercises.

---

*Have You Ever Observed Evolution in Action? A Simulation

Let's create a model world and populate it with beings. Then let's watch the beings survive in the world and evolve to become a better species. We can make up any rules we want and watch the consequences of our decisions.

We create an 8 by 8 grid and propose that the beings can wander around the grid looking for food and, from time to time, mating. These beings are called neds, a name given to them by their creator, Joshua D. Carter. (This simulation was developed as a term project in a course at Duke University.) We propose that each ned must eat some food each day. The amount of food is an integer computed by $(age/20) + 1$, where *age* is an integer giving the number of days the ned has lived. Thus, a ned of age 25 days would eat 2 units of food per day.

There are three more rules related to food. First, each grid square starts with some food units and has more food units added to it each day. The amounts are controlled by a random number generator. Second, the ned can pick up as many as three units of food each day if these are available and put them in a bag. Thus the ned can store ahead a quantity of food and use it later as needed. However, its food requirements will not allow it to reach an age a lot older than 40 days. Finding the reason for this is left as an exercise. Third, the ned uses up two extra units of food if it mates.

The activities of a ned on a given day are first to eat the required amount and second to make a move given by one of the following activity codes:

00 Move forward one step (if a wall is hit, stand still).
01 Rotate right by one-eighth of a full turn.
10 Mate (if a member of the opposite sex is present in the same square).
11 Mate (if a member of the opposite sex is present in the same square).

How the ned gets these codes is the next question.

Each ned is created with a gene code, its DNA, so to speak. This is a 40-bit binary string of digits created as follows. When the mating of its parents, a male and a female, occurs, a random number i is selected between 1 and 40. Then the first i bits from one parent are combined with the bits starting from $i + 1$ on to the end for the other parent. This becomes the gene code for the new ned. As an example, suppose the parents have these gene codes

0000010000110000011110101111111111100111
1111111101110101010101010101010101010101

and the random number selected is 17. Then the new gene code would be

0000010000110000010101010101010101010101

Each ned's behavior is governed by its gene code. Specifically, it executes the first two bits in its code on one day using the given activity code, the next two bits on the next day, and so forth. Thus, the preceding child ned would follow these actions on its first few days:

day 1   00   move forward one step
day 2   00   move forward one step
day 3   01   rotate
day 4   00   move forward one step

: noop

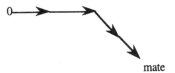

mate

Figure 6.4

day 5   00   move forward one step
day 6   11   mate

Figure 6.4 shows a diagram of its path.

Now let's run the simulation and see what kinds of neds evolve. We use a random number generator to create four neds, two males and two females, with random genetic codes. Then we place them in random cells on the grid and watch what happens in the first three days (figure 6.5). An asterisk means an attempted mate. A dollar sign means death from lack of food.

It turns out that these neds are not doing very well. There are not enough of them to find each other and mate. The simulation goes only a few steps (not shown to end) until the last lonely ned dies from lack of food.

Let's start again with 20 neds. This time the simulation lasts for about 100 days and then dies out. Apparently, this environment is difficult for the neds to survive in. We try several similar simulations and one goes for 491 days. This is unusual. Let's investigate the neds that were evolved in the last generation. They must have a fairly good genetic code to have survived such a long time. Here is the code for the last surviving ned.

100000101101110110100100100101101111010

You should, as an exercise, analyze this ned and describe why its genetic code and thus its evolved behavior enabled it to survive for a long time.

In summary, we wanted to observe evolution in action. We wanted to allow beings in a very severe environment to attempt to survive and to pass on to the next generation at least part of their characteristics. Those that survived well and that regenerated successfully passed on their genes to later generations. Those with poor genetic codes disappeared. The methodology was the same as for the previous examples. First a model was designed, then a next-step function was created that executed each ned's next move and updated the state description, and finally the system was set in an initial state and run. We started with random codes and allowed evolution to proceed. After a number of attempts, one population survived an unusually long time, and we had the opportunity to see what its code had become. We can now use this model to study evolution as an abstract phenomenon. We can vary the many parameters and mechanisms in the system and observe the results.

(a) Day 1

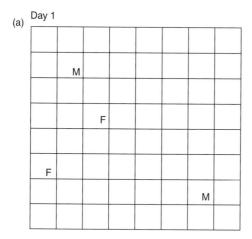

(b) Day 2

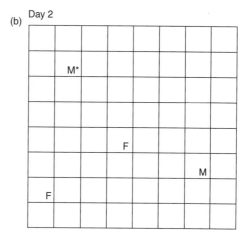

(c) Day 3

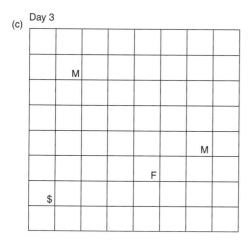

Figure 6.5

You can obtain a program in C written by Josh Carter to do this computation. Use the Internet as described in the introductory chapter.

Exercises

1. Analyze the code of the final ned evolved in the long simulation (491 days), and tell why its design enabled it to succeed so well.

2. Repeat the simulation with parameters that you set. Try to evolve a being whose genetic code is more successful than the one in exercise 1.

---

*What Will It Look Like? A Simulation

There are many scientific, engineering, and even recreational reasons to want to view something that does not, in reality, exist. With computers, we can create an object in *information space* and then use the graphical capabilites of the system to view that object. An example is the design of buildings where the architect can create the building graphically and allow people to put on head-mounted displays so that they can actually "walk through" a building before it is built. People can try out the design, critique its functionality and aesthetics, and make suggestions for improvement.

In this section, we create a program that allows us to enter a new world of both recreational and scientific interest. It is the world of fractals, and it is a study that could not progress practically until computer graphics came into existence.

We begin this study with the concept of a point transformation on the geometric plane. We represent such a transformation with the functional notation f. Suppose we have the point z_0 on the x, y plane; then $f(z_0)$ will find a new point on the plane. Our example for the moment will be as follows: if (x, y) gives the coordinates of a point on the plane, we define $f((x, y))$ to be (x_1, y_1), where

$$x_1 = x * x - y * y + c_1$$

$$y_1 = 2 * x * y + c_2$$

and c_1 and c_2 are constants. Thus, if we choose $c_1 = 0.36$ and $c_2 = 0.10$, then the point $(0, 0)$ is transformed into the point $(0.36, 0.10)$ by the function f. This is shown in figure 6.6 by drawing an arrow from $(0, 0)$ to $(0.36, 0.10)$. We can then apply the function f to the point $(0.36, 0.10)$ and obtain yet another point:

$$x_1 = (0.36)^2 - (0.10)^2 + 0.36 = 0.48$$

$$y_1 = 2 * (0.36) * (0.10) + 0.10 = 0.17$$

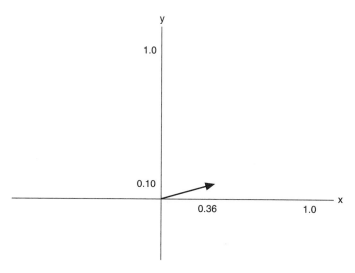

Figure 6.6

We can apply f again and again to the new points as they are generated and obtain a sequence:

$$f(0.36, 0.10) = (0.48, 0.17)$$

$$f(0.48, 0.17) = (0.56, 0.27)$$

$$f(0.56, 0.27) = (0.60, 0.40)$$

$$f(0.60, 0.40) = (0.57, 0.58)$$

$$f(0.57, 0.58) = (0.34, 0.76)$$

$$f(0.34, 0.76) = (-0.10, 0.62)$$

$$f(-0.10, 0.62) = (-0.01, -0.02)$$

$$f(-0.01, -0.02) = (0.36, 0.10)$$

$$f(0.36, 0.10) = (0.48, 0.17)$$

$$\vdots$$

Figure 6.7 shows a graph of this sequence of points. Notice that this sequence has the property that it bends back on itself. The last two points are, in fact, the same as the first two points (to the level of accuracy shown).

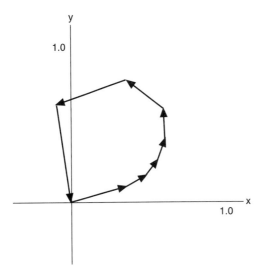

Figure 6.7

In the theory of fractals, we are interested in sequences of points like the one shown in figure 6.7. Specifically, we are interested in points that have converging sequences like $(0,0)$, where the resulting sequence of points stays close to the origin of the plane. We are also interested in diverging sequences, where the later-generated points go off into infinity. An example of one of these sequences, with beginning point $(0.70, 0.70)$, is the following:

$$f(0.70, 0.70) = (0.36, 1.08)$$

$$f(0.36, 1.08) = (-0.68, 0.88)$$

$$f(-0.68, 0.88) = (0.05, -1.09)$$

$$f(0.05, -1.09) = (-0.83, 0.00)$$

$$f(-0.83, 0.00) = (1.04, 0.10)$$

$$f(1.04, 0.10) = (1.43, 0.31)$$

$$f(1.43, 0.31) = (2.32, 1.00)$$

$$f(2.32, 1.00) = (4.75, 4.72)$$

$$f(4.75, 4.72) = (0.69, 44.97)$$

$$f(0.69, 44.97) = (-2021.58, 62.48)$$

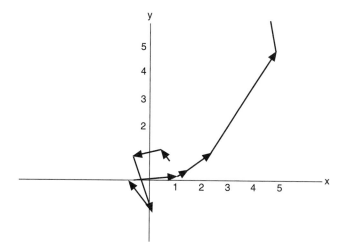

Figure 6.8

$$f(-2021.58, 62.48) = (4,082,867.15, -252,602.95)$$

$\vdots$

Figure 6.8 shows a graph of this sequence of points.

Now the time has come to pose a question. Let's color black all points that result in converging sequences using the tranformation f and color white all points that result in diverging sequences. We know that $(0,0)$ should then be colored black and $(0.70, 0.70)$ should be colored white. Figure 6.9 shows the beginning of the diagram. The question is, What figure will result if we apply this rule to the coloring of all the points on the plane? Maybe it will be a simple circle or something. Actually, what you get using $c_1 = 0.360284$ and $c_2 = 0.100376$, as recommended by Robert L. Devaney in his book *Chaos, Fractals, and Dynamics*, is shown in figure 6.10.

This figure is known as a *fractal*, and our experiment can form the beginning of an exploration of the world of fractals. By varying the constants c_1 and c_2, one can obtain an astounding variety of complex figures. The program is given on the Internet with the others so that you can try it out yourself. By varying the way the figures are drawn, one can get full color and an even wider variety. An interesting characteristic of fractals is that they have endlessly interesting detail if you magnify the individual parts. If a part of the figure were generated in magnified form, it would be as complex as the overall figure no matter how great the level of magnification.

Fractals have provided mathematicians in recent years with a delightful area for research. Fractals give us a bridge from the very simple, as exemplified by the preceding

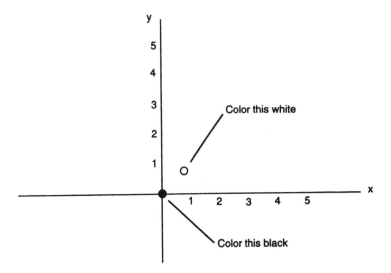

Figure 6.9

Figure 6.10

equations, to the very complex, as shown in figure 6.10. From an intellectual point of view, one might suspect that one must have extremely complex generators to produce complex phenomena. Fractals are an amazing example to the contrary.

A possible application for fractals is in coding theory. If one wishes to transmit information over a channel, how many bits need to be sent to convey a picture like figure 6.10? (A bit is defined as a single binary digit, 0 or 1.) The answer is that possibly millions of bits of information will be needed. But how much information is needed to transmit the equations for the generation of the figure? Possibly only a few hundred. Then the figure could be generated from the equations at the receiving end. So a coding strategy for transmitting pictures might begin with a picture, code it into fractal images in some way, transmit the equations of the fractals, and then reconstruct the picture at the other end using those equations. This could lead to dramatic reductions in the number of bits required to transmit pictures.

Exercises

1. Repeat the fractals experiment using the constants $c_1 = -1.0$ and $c_2 = 0$. Try $c_1 = 0.3$ and $c_2 = -0.4$. Try $c_1 = -0.1$ and $c_2 = 0.8$. These are all examples recommended by Devaney in his book.

2. Look for other examples of c_1 and c_2 values that produce extremely interesting figures.

Summary

In almost every discipline or endeavor, people find themselves wanting to try out ideas and discover how they will work out. It might be the building of a structure, the playing of a symphony, the creation of a new form of government, the exploding of the sun, or almost anything else. In many of these cases, trying out the idea in the real world would be very costly or impossible, but with computer simulation one can often, at not too high a cost, get a close enough approximation to the desired real object or event to find out what would happen.

The process of doing a simulation usually follows the three steps given and illustrated in this chapter. Specifically, one must build a mathematical model of the phenomenon to be simulated and a next-step function to apply to it. Then one can place the system in an initial state and apply the next-step function repeatedly to discover what events will occur over a period of time. The chapter presented examples of simulations of an auto race, a disease epidemic, and a species evolution. It also demonstrated simulation techniques in the creation of a complex graphical construction. (The Java programs for the auto race, disease epidemic, and fractal image were written by Ben Allen.)

2 MONTHS INTO 6 MONTH PROGRAMMING EFFORT

4 MONTHS INTO 6 MONTH PROGRAMMING EFFORT

6 MONTHS INTO THE PROGRAMMING EFFORT

7   Software Engineering

The Real World

A recent honors graduate in computer science from a prestigious university, whom we shall call Brian, accepted an industrial programming job. Brian, an able programmer, had worked in that capacity in university laboratories during his student days and had earned a string of A's in computer courses. He was accustomed to looking at a problem, sketching out a solution method, and accurately estimating both the size of the desired program and the amount of time needed to write and debug the code. For planning purposes, he was wise enough to multiply estimates by a factor of 2 to make sure he had "breathing room," and even then he sometimes found himself up late the night before the deadline getting things into perfect order. But he had a reputation for doing a good job, and he was usually on time.

After accepting his new position, Brian was given a specification for a program and asked to develop a plan for getting it done. He followed his usual procedures and then went to his boss with a set of algorithms for the various subroutines, data structure descriptions, and a time schedule. He said he could finish the job in three months and described at length how he would do it. His boss, whom he respected immensely, listened carefully to the plan and studied the problem himself. Then he made an announcement that astounded Brian: he assigned five programmers to the job and set the deadline a year hence.

Brian went home that night confused and amazed. How, he wondered, could a company afford to spend such tremendous resources on this program? He believed they should reassign four programmers and let him do the job.

But Brian's boss had had plenty of experience in the industrial world, and he knew the difference between personal computing and industrial computing. He knew about standards that had to be met, interfaces that had to be negotiated, documentation that had to be written, and perhaps revised specifications that might be introduced from time to time.

He had seen deadlines like Brian's set and then missed. He had seen the number of programmers on a project doubled and doubled again. He had seen a system running except for a few bugs, but when those bugs were fixed, the changes introduced new bugs in an unending chain. He knew that entering into an industrial-scale programming project is a fiscally dangerous undertaking and should be done with care.

Such is the case for large-scale programming projects. Experience gained with one or two people writing programs a few pages long does not extrapolate well into massive efforts. Extensive communication among programmers, requirements for documentation, the intrinsic complexities of large programs, and many other factors contribute to greatly reduced efficiency. Too many times large programming efforts have marched forward to produce a product that still has bugs, is many months late, and overruns the budget. Frederick Brooks in his book *The Mythical Man-Month* likens the world of industrial programming to the tar pits of old where "many great and powerful beasts have thrashed violently" only to become more and more entangled.

It is important to know that large-project programming is very different from personal programming. It is important to understand the characteristics of such projects, the problems that can occur, and the remedies that can be tried. The following sections describe lessons that have been learned from large-scale projects, improved technologies that lead to better team effectiveness, and the life cycle of an industrial program.

Lessons Learned from Large-Scale Programming Projects

The first lesson is that a *program* is much easier to produce than a *programming system*, which in turn is easier to produce than a *programming system product*. Brooks (in *The Mythical Man-Month*) has defined these three entities and estimated that each higher stage is at least three times more expensive to produce than the previous one. A *program* is the entity that students write in universities. Its specifications are given in a small document, and it computes the target behavior on a single machine and under the control of its author. A *programming system* involves a group of interacting components coordinated to do a central task. Each component must have carefully designed interfaces that match specifications with other components and may need to conform to other specifications. For example, components may have to meet restrictions related to size and speed. A *programming system product* must be documented thoroughly, usable in many environments, and robust in its operation. It must be sufficiently well described that its maintenance, revision, and operation can be carried on in the absence of the author.

The last class of entities is the most typical goal of an industrial project and, by Brooks's estimate, is at least nine times as costly to produce as a simple program. In fact, this factor alone is nearly sufficient to account for the heavy investments that Brian's boss was prepared to make.

The second lesson is that programming is not necessarily an easily divisible task. If one is not to wait several years for Brian to produce a programming system product, more programmers will be needed. But these additional people will be communicating with each other and perhaps even arguing about how the design should proceed. They will have to develop precise specifications of the interfaces between the various parts of the code and may have to do additional work to meet these demands. Testing and debugging of the interacting modules may be more complex than for the more unified architecture that one person would build. Thus the per-person productivity for a multiperson effort usually will be lower than it would be for one programmer working alone. Halving the time required to finish a project requires more than doubling the number of programmers.

The more that programmers must interact with each other in order to do a job, the lower will be their productivity in terms of amount of code written. Brooks presents the following rough guidelines (by Joel Aron) for programmer productivity in terms of number of instructions written per programmer-year for design and coding activities:

Number of interactions	Instructions per year
Very few	10,000
Some	5,000
Many	1,500

These figures roughly summarize the kinds of results that have been observed in various studies of programmer productivity. They can be off by a factor of 2 or more in some situations, but they give the order of magnitude for typical performance.

Programmers do not spend all their time planning and writing code, so these figures may be high as an overall performance measure. Brooks estimates that, in the course of a project, programmers spend roughly half their time in testing and debugging activities.

Therefore, the addition of programmers to speed up a project increases the complexity of the programming task and does not result in time improvements proportional to the number of added people. In fact, too many additional programmers can saturate the team and yield no improvement whatsoever. Most programming tasks require a certain minimum amount of time to reach maturity regardless of the number of programmers assigned.

Another effect observed in large projects is that large programs may be disproportionally more complex than smaller ones. That is, a larger program, say 500,000 lines of code, may require more than twice as much effort as a project half that length. This effect may occur regardless of the number of programmers.

The combination of all these effects sends average programmer productivity plummeting in a way that Brian could not be expected to appreciate. While he was able to write and debug comfortably 100 lines of code per day, the figures indicate, assuming 250 working days per year, that industrial programmers may code as few as 6 lines of code per day.

If Brian's original estimate had been used, he probably would have worked very hard for a month or two only to realize that he was not generating a product to meet the required standards. He would then have asked for additional programmers and a delayed deadline of perhaps two months. Next, he would have tried to convince the new people that he had much of the task completed and would have invested much effort in educating them to understand his theory of operation and his code. One way or another, they would finally have gotten into the swing of the project, but the second deadline would be hard upon them. They would then ask for another slippage of the deadline. They also might ask for more programmers, who would also have to be trained and integrated into the effort.

Exercises

1. Suppose you are a manager and need to have a simple stand-alone program coded that will be approximately 500 instructions in length. How many programmers would you assign to the job, and when, based on figures given in the text, could you expect to have the program completed?

2. Suppose you are a manager and wish to have a programming system product coded that will be approximately 40,000 instructions in length. This, for example, might be the size of a compiler for a programming language. Assuming the guidelines in the text are applicable to your situation, how many programmers would you need in order to complete the job in three years? How would you revise your estimate if the time allotted were only two years? If your boss demanded that the program be completed within three months, how would you respond?

3. Repeat exercise 2 for the case where the target program will be approximately 200,000 instructions. This might be the length of an operating system for a moderate-sized machine.

4. What can you say about the amount of programming effort required for a large program such as a modern telephone switching system, which could involve 10 million instructions? Assume the time allowed for coding is four years.

Software Engineering Methodologies

The tremendous cost of software has become a major concern to the computing industry. In the mid-1950s, software costs were less than 20 percent of total computing costs, but now they exceed 80 percent. This has led to a major emphasis on discovering ways to improve programming methodologies and to the birth of a new field, *software engineering*.

The goal has been to change programming from a hit-or-miss, one-person-at-a-time operation to a sophisticated art and science where groups of people cooperatively work together to produce, reliably and efficiently, a worthy product. Three areas of software engineering are discussed here: the development of strategies to improve the correctness of programs, the invention of new organizational schemes for programmers, and the creation of better programming tools.

Correctness

The specification of a system will often state the allowed error rates, and the product is required to stay within them. For example, the specification might require that the software system process inputs successfully at some high rate, say, 99.95 percent. Software engineers enter into a project with the sobering knowledge that the ultimate product will be rejected if it does not achieve such a high level of reliability.

Therefore, the required strategy is to adopt a philosophy that brings correctness to the forefront of every designer's and coder's mind from the early stages of design to the day of product delivery. The philosophy asserts that correctness cannot be added as an afterthought but must be meticulously designed at every stage. It disallows common attitudes that errors are natural and inevitable, and asserts that errors exist in programs because people put them there. It asserts that correctness is a consequence of responsible programming practice and that no alternative should be contemplated. The generation of correct programs is important because the ultimate product must be correct and the cost of removing errors from running code can be tremendous.

Correctness considerations begin with the design of the program specifications—a careful, detailed, and exact description of every aspect of the product behavior. These specifications are to prescribe every detail that the external world will see but carefully avoid implying how the program will actually work. It is the job of the implementers to produce code that performs precisely as guaranteed in the program specifications. At these early stages, correctness must be carefully attended to because errors here will radiate into the product in unpredictable ways. Barry Boehm has estimated, in *Software Engineering Economics* (1981), that specification errors repaired in the later stages of software development can cost as much as 100 times more to fix than if they had been caught at specification time.

Next, the system designers build a mental image of how the internals of the system will work and write specifications for the various modules proposed to do the job. Then smaller groups of programmers or individuals will be assigned these modules. Their task is to produce code with behaviors that are guaranteed to match the interface specifications. This means that programmers must have verification techniques for checking that the code advances through the proper steps and delivers precisely what is specified. These techniques usually involve studying each sequential statement, considering every possible situation that could arise, and showing that, in every case, the statement does the right thing. During the 1970s, methodologies evolved that enable a person to prove mathematically that a program achieves its specifications. However, such rigorous procedures are too expensive for most applications and are used only in rare situations where extreme measures are justified.

One of the most important innovations was the idea of top-down structured programming. It is an approach that encourages clear and systematic thinking about large programs and plays an essential role in the art of writing correct code. Before the days of structured programming, programming methodologies allowed the use of a "go to" statement that enabled the program control to jump from any point in a program to any other point. It was found that the use of such statements enabled programmers to write code that would make many jumps from place to place in the code, resulting in a program that could be a nightmare to understand and debug. The elimination of the "go to" statement forces the programmer to use constructs with a more straightforward flow of control. It can be read in a linear fashion from beginning to end.

Another technology aimed at the correctness issue concerns adequate test procedures for programs. Once a program has gone through the laborious design, coding, and verification procedures, it should be run on a carefully constructed set of inputs that will exercise every branch, activate every combination of submodules, and explore endpoints and extreme values. The hope is that every conceivable test will go smoothly, but where failures occur, the responsible individuals will be called upon to do the repair.

Organizational Schemes

The second area for improved programming methodology concerns the way the programmers are organized. Various innovations have evolved that encourage people to help each other and that attempt to utilize the special talents of each.

A way to encourage good group dynamics in a programming environment is to break up the sense of ownership that programmers have in the code they have written. Consider, as an example, the case of a lone student in a classroom situation who has spent countless hours conceiving of the design, writing the code, and adding some much-loved special features. If later this program is said to be of poor quality or is discovered to have errors, the person justifiably will feel threatened or uncomfortable. In the environment of a programming team, the person could become protective, secretive, and defensive about the code when the goals of the group require openness and cooperation. Another model encourages so-called egoless programming where the code is considered to be a product of the group activity and where criticism and improvements from any member are always welcome. It may be that person A wrote the first draft, person B rewrote the code and got it running, and person C found some errors and made improvements. All three individuals accept each other as both contributors and mistake makers, and the code is viewed as a separate entity that can be praised or criticized without threatening any individual. All team members want to get it right, and the best talents of each are aimed at the common goal. (Some software engineers object to the idea of egoless programming on the grounds that they want individuals to take responsibility for sections of code. They feel that if no single person is answerable for that code, its correctness and performance may not get proper attention.)

Often an organization has programmers who are star performers, and a special arrangement is appropriate to utilize their talents properly. Unlike most other human activities where excellence involves being perhaps 20 percent above the norm, in programming the highest achiever may be ten times more productive than lesser contributors. Good management requires that such able people be freed to practice their trade and that others should gather around and do everything possible to help. This gives rise to the *chief programmer team*, which centers all activities on a single person.

The common organization for such a team begins with the *chief programmer*, whose job is to conceive of the code, write it, debug it, and perhaps write the major documentation. The second most central individual is the *backup programmer*, who observes every action of the chief and knows the code and documentation. This person performs support activities such as verification of correctness, development of required subroutines, background research, and documentation. If the chief programmer becomes unavailable at any point, the backup must step in and keep things going forward without delays. A third major player is the *programming librarian*, who types, formats, stores, and retrieves code and documentation for the group. The team may also contain various other players who may be programming, testing, writing documentation, or doing other tasks. The chief programmer team idea has been used on many occasions, often breaking records for programmer productivity and for quality of the final product.

Programming Tools

The third field of software engineering discussed here is the area of software tools for productivity. The new image of a programmer is no longer that of a person with a pencil, paper, and a terminal nearby. Instead it involves a large-screen workstation capable of displaying windows into a variety of facilities—libraries of code, a language editor, a run-time monitor, a debugging package, programming manuals, a theorem prover for verification activities, graphics subsystems, communications facilities to other programmers, and much more. The programmer then assembles code with the assistance of this collection of support systems, bringing in aid as needed. Object-oriented programming, as described in this book, provides a major aid in code reuse because of its emphasis on libraries of code and the individual's ability to modify such code for his or her specific purposes.

In the ideal scenario with a modern environment, the programmer may write relatively little code. Instead, he or she will have an extensive knowledge of existing software and will attempt to find ways to assemble the target program from these pieces. A complete programming task might begin with the coder writing a top-level program to organize the computation. Then the person would peruse the code library for the correct classes to finish the programming job. In the future, it may be that the programmer will be able to check some menu items and have the routines automatically altered to fit the application.

With the code assembled, the programmer might have a way to generate test data automatically, and then immediately run the code on the examples. If an error is observed, the programmer would study the code in one window, the data structures in another, the computation history in another, and so forth, to try to determine the cause of failure. Later, with the code fixed and running, the person might send it via e-mail to another team member for verification, modification, or use. Later, he or she might receive the code back with comments and updates. Perhaps it would then be archived and indexed for later use.

Not all the facilities mentioned here are in routine use in all programming organizations. But many of them are in use in many organizations, and reality approaches the ideal situation a little more each year.

Exercises

1. Select a program from an earlier chapter or from your own experience, and carry out a detailed study of its correctness.
   a. Write exact specifications for the class of legal inputs to the program. State explicitly every characteristic a legal input must have, including the lengths of allowed input strings, the number of significant digits and sizes of allowable numbers, and so forth. Give examples of legal and illegal inputs.
   b. Write complete and exacting specifications for the outputs of the program. Tell clearly what is to result in every possible computation that could result from inputs as specified in part (a).
   c. Study every line of code and write down careful arguments to show that it will do the proper action assuming the input meets the specifications given. Show with your arguments that the collection of the statements, in fact, computes the outputs exactly as they have been given in part (b). Be sure to check behaviors at endpoints, where inputs may have length zero or otherwise stretch the performance of the program.

2. Study the topics covered in this section and suggest a field of software engineering that you believe should be studied but is not described here. What kinds of results do you think could be obtained if this field were undertaken?

The Program Life Cycle

Software engineering does not restrict its vision to the program synthesis task. Economic investments with regard to a program begin early and may continue for many years after the program is written. This is because a program may have a long life cycle that substantially engages the organization at every stage. Decision making should account for this larger picture and attempt to optimize benefits for the long term. A system architecture optimized at the design stage but not amenable to later upgrade or maintenance will not be successful. A set of terminal specifications written to make programming easy but without regard to later training and usage requirements can lead to catastrophe. Thus, the software engineer must keep the larger picture in mind at each stage to achieve a long-term success. We briefly examine the life cycle of a typical software product and some of the concerns that appear at each stage.

Defining the Product

The first question to ask is, What need is to be addressed? The answer may be in terms of new information the client needs to compile, labor-intensive jobs that need to be automated, or the improvement of some already automated function. Whatever the goal, extensive interviews with the client and possibly market surveys need to be carried out to determine the nature of the problem.

Then automated solutions to the problem can be proposed in rough terms and measured against the originally stated need. Rough estimates can be made as to the cost and effectiveness of the solution, and judgments can be offered concerning their relative desirability. Sometimes an inexpensive prototype for a proposed system can be assembled and tested in the user environment to provide data regarding a proposed system's value. If one of the alternatives appears to be desirable, it can be selected, and the organization can begin steps toward its implementation.

Selecting the Programming Team

Assuming that the decision is to code a programming product to solve the problem, the organizers can begin choosing the members of the programming groups, making estimates as to the kind and numbers of people needed. As system specification and architecture develop, better estimates will become possible and more team members can be chosen.

Developing the Program Specification

Here the rough estimates of the earlier stages are made precise. An exact specification of the system's external characteristics is written down in a possibly voluminous document. In some cases, certain features of the ultimate product have not been decided. When this occurs, the required "hooks" are defined where later features can be inserted.

Designing the System Structure

The form of the system organization needs to be designed and the major data structures must be specified. At first, the design will be sketched in rough form, but these ideas must then be solidified in another set of specifications. These working documents, which could be longer than the external specifications, will set forth the list of the subcomponents and their complete interface characteristics. Individual programming teams will be given these subcomponents as tasks and will have little guidance except what is stated in these documents.

Coding the System

Next, the staff will write the program. Typically the implementation effort results in the discovery of errors or poor decisions at earlier stages, which must be corrected. Thus, the original specifications and other working documents will be revised occasionally as the group changes its view of the whole project. If the original conception was good, changes will have only second-order effects, and the basic form of the architecture will remain.

Testing the Code

As individual parts of the system become operative, they can be tested to confirm that they meet the requirements given in the working documents. Many times special software is written to test system modules. Testing often results in revisions to the code, but truly professional programmers can usually achieve early, if not immediate, convergence on acceptable performance. As larger subsystems come into existence, parts that were finished and tested earlier can be integrated into the whole.

Revision

As members of the group tend to mature in their conceptualization of a system, continual improvements may be made in the system design. Even updates to the original system behavioral specifications will be made from time to time. This involves modifying documentation and rewriting parts of the code.

Documentation

All stages of the project require much documentation, especially when many programmers are involved. In addition to the documentation of code, user manuals must be created for training and explanation of the principles of operation, installation, and maintenance. These documents will accompany the product into the user environment.

Delivery and Training

The product needs to reach the user and come into useful operation. This may involve sending project participants to the user organization to help with installation, early operation, and training of users.

Maintenance and Upgrade

Once a product is in field operation, the organization can expect to receive notification of errors in its behavior and requests for additional features. It is quite common for the vendor to keep a group of programmers working on the project for many years after its original development carrying on these maintenance and upgrade activities. Users can be sold contracts for such services so that these efforts can be profitable ventures on their own.

Positioning for the Next Product

Success on one project engenders opportunities for others. A reputation gained by delivering one successful system can open the door to projects that complement the original one or lead to follow-on projects.

Summarizing, the life cycle of a programming project includes many stages that can span a period of years. In order for a system to be successful, decision making must account for the whole life cycle and the best long-term interests of the project.

Exercise

1. Draw a set of boxes on a page, each labeled with one of the headings in this section. Then show the time flow of the stages in a product life by drawing arrows from box to box. Notice that, in realistic situations, the flow may not be linear.

Summary

Software engineering is the collection of disciplines that enable a group of people to build and maintain computer software systems. These include mathematical subfields that deal with program correctness and performance, numerous technologies related to programming languages and systems, some economics, and the psychology and sociology of team efforts.

The industrial programming of a software product is a substantially more ambitious undertaking than the construction of individual programs of the type students or laboratory workers may do. While isolated programmers may be able to assemble hundreds of lines of code per day to satisfy their own needs, programmers in an industrial project may produce on average fewer than ten lines of code in a programming systems product per day.

Many technologies have developed to aid the task of industrial programmers, including strategies for designing correctness into programs, methods for organizing programming groups, object-oriented programming methodologies, and automated systems for assembling code.

THE INSTRUCTIONS COME IN FROM MEMORY OVER THERE. THEN THEY ARE DECODED DOWN THERE.

THE DECODING CIRCUITRY TELLS THE COMPUTATION REGISTER WHAT DATA TO USE AND WHICH OPERATION TO CARRY OUT.

INSTRUCTION REGISTER DEPT.

DECODING DEPT.

COMPUTATION DEPT.

• ADD
• SUB.
• MULT.
• DIV.
• COPY

8 Machine Architecture

When You Buy a Computer

When you buy a computer you get a box full of circuit boards, silicon chips, disk hardware, connectors, wires, and more. You wonder what it all amounts to, and you open the manual to see what you have. You will probably find a diagram that looks something like figure 8.1.

Actually, this architecture diagram is for an Intel class machine (with some details removed), but if you had bought a different brand, the diagram would be quite similar. There will be a *central processing unit (CPU)* with a series of registers for doing computations. The central processor might include special hardware for doing computations on *floating-point numbers*, which are known as `double` numbers in Java. There will be a *memory* for storing the programs and data as the machine does the calculations. There will be a *cache memory*, which exists between the main memory and the CPU; its purpose is to download items from the main memory that are needed by the CPU at a given moment and then to supply them at very high speed to the CPU when they are called for. There will be a *disk* for storing your programs and data when you are not using them. There will be accommodations for various *input-output devices* such as your keyboard, video display, network connections, and printer.

We wish to study this architecture but do not have time to examine all the details shown. We examine a portion of the total architecture to understand its basic mechanisms and leave it to the reader to obtain the full manual for the details of any particular machine that may be of interest. We lift from figure 8.1 just enough of the essential components of the machine to get a working model of a modern computer and study that. We lift a CPU with only four registers and twelve machine instructions; a modern Pentium has over a dozen registers and over 100 machine instructions. We leave out the floating-point processor, the memory cache, and any considerations related to long-term storage or input-output devices. Some of these devices are discussed in chapter 10. We call our model of the CPU a P88, which stands for "part of an Intel 8088." The instructions we

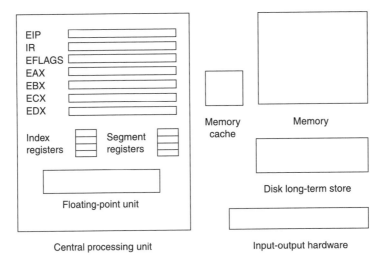

Figure 8.1

describe for the P88 are taken from the Intel manuals (sometimes with modifications for the purposes of this book), and they are realistic in the sense that they continue to work on current-day Pentiums.

A Sample Architecture: The P88 Machine

Our simplified machine is shown in figure 8.2. The CPU and its four registers are the major concern of this chapter. They are the place where the machine does its work. Their individual roles are as follows:

- Instruction pointer, IP. This register holds the address in memory of the instruction that will be executed next.
- Instruction register, IR. This register holds the instruction to be executed when it is brought in from memory.
- Condition flag, CF. This register tells what condition has just been observed. It is affected by only certain instructions.
- Computation register, AX. This is where a computation occurs, such as addition or multiplication of two data items.

The memory is the place where machine instructions and data are stored. Figure 8.2 shows in the memory five instructions (each bracketed by asterisks) and four data items

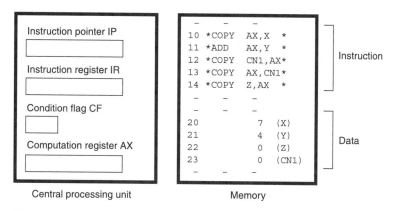

Figure 8.2

(7, 4, 0, 0). Both the CPU registers and the memory store sequences of 0's and 1's; that is, all information is represented in binary form. Typical sizes for registers or memory locations are 16, 32, or 64 *bits* (or binary digits).

A typical instruction for this machine is COPY AX,X, as is described later. This is called an *assembly language* instruction. When such an instruction is stored in the memory or in a register, it is usually coded as a binary number, such as 0010110101011011. This is called a *machine language* instruction. However, we do not use these binary codes in our discussion but write *COPY AX,X*, where the surrounding asterisks indicate that the instruction has been translated into binary code. That is, COPY AX,X is an instruction to the machine, and *COPY AX,X* represents its binary code.

The functioning of the computer proceeds by repeatedly executing the following two steps:

Repeat without end

1. Fetch—Find the instruction in memory at the address given by IP and put that instruction into IR. Increment IP to give the address of the next instruction.
2. Execute—Execute the instruction in IR.

These two steps constitute the *fetch-execute cycle*, and they can best be understood by going over an example. Suppose that the machine instruction codes

```
*COPY AX,X*
*ADD AX,Y*
*COPY CN1,AX*
*COPY AX,CN1*
*COPY Z,AX*
```

reside in memory at locations 10 through 14 and that the machine is about to execute these codes (figure 8.3a). Then the address, 10, of the first such code, *COPY AX,X*, will be in IP.

The first step of the cycle, fetch, involves loading IR from the location given by IP (see figure 8.3a). Then IP is incremented to give the address of the next instruction (figure 8.3b).

The second step of the cycle, execute, carries out the instruction in the instruction register, IR. In this case, *COPY AX,X* is decoded and executed (D&E) (figure 8.3c). As is explained next, the contents of memory location X will be copied into register AX.

The fetch-execute cycle continues without stopping. On the next cycle, the instruction is fetched from location 11 in memory. This is an add instruction, *ADD AX,Y*. It adds the contents of memory location Y to the contents of register AX and leaves the result in register AX (figure 8.4a).

Another pass through the fetch-execute cycle results in the third instruction's being executed. This instruction causes the contents of the AX register to be copied into the memory location CN1 (figure 8.4b).

Thus the machine sequentially loads the string of commands in memory and carries them out. Occasionally a "jump" instruction will load a new value into IP, which begins a new sequence of commands. For example, in this case, it is possible that some instruction would cause 10 to be loaded into IP again and result in another execution of the this sequence.

The fundamental operation of every digital computer is built around the fetch-execute cycle as described here. This is, in fact, the only thing that modern digital computers are designed to do—to fetch instructions and execute them. There is no need to be impressed with the intelligence of any modern computer, no matter how large, with its blinking lights, complex displays, and many workers huddled over their terminals. The giant machine is doing nothing more than fetching instructions and executing them. It never has in the past, cannot now, and never in the future will be able to do more or less than this. (Later chapters suggest other architectures, such as neural network computers, that do not use the fetch-execute approach to computing. But that is another story.)

Exercises

1. Trace the execution of the final two instructions in the text example—the instructions in memory locations 13 and 14. Show every detail of the fetch-execute cycle.

2. In the text example, the instruction pointer IP increases one on each cycle and will apparently soon reach 20. An error will occur if it does. Explain the nature of the error. What instruction must be included after location 14 but before location 20 to avoid this error?

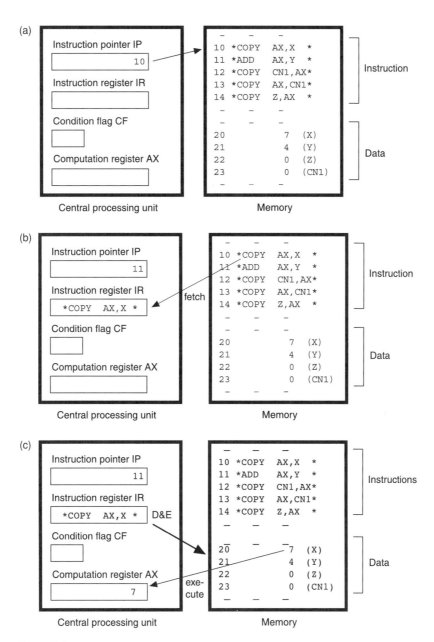

Figure 8.3

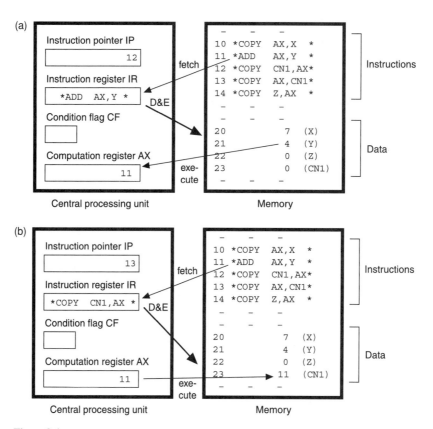

Figure 8.4

Programming the P88 Machine

The P88 has 12 instructions, as shown in table 8.1. Each individual instruction is simple in its operation, as described by the Action entry in the table. Thus, the first instruction is called a "copy" and is written COPY AX,mem, where mem refers to a location in memory. If this instruction is executed, the contents of memory at location mem is copied into register AX. Another copy instruction, COPY mem,AX, copies the contents of AX to memory location mem. As an illustration, one can use these two instructions to move data from memory location A to memory location B:

```
COPY AX,A
COPY B,AX
```

Table 8.1

Instruction	Format	Action
Copy from memory	`COPY AX,mem`	`AX = mem`
Copy to memory	`COPY mem,AX`	`mem = AX`
Add	`ADD AX,mem`	`AX = AX + mem`
Subtract	`SUB AX,mem`	`AX = AX - mem`
Multiply	`MUL AX,mem`	`AX = AX * mem`
Divide	`DIV AX,mem`	`AX = AX/mem`
Compare	`CMP AX,mem`	`if AX < mem then CF = B else CF = NB`
Jump	`JMP lab1`	Go to instruction with label `lab1`.
Jump if not below	`JNB lab1`	Go to instruction with label `lab1` if CF = NB, otherwise go to next instruction.
Jump if below	`JB lab1`	Go to instruction with label `lab1` if CF = B, otherwise go to next instruction.
Input	`IN AX`	Input an integer into register AX.
Output	`OUT AX`	Output an integer from register AX.

The P88 has four arithmetic instructions—ADD, SUB, MUL, and DIV—which perform their respective operations on AX and a memory location and leave the result in AX. Thus, ADD AX,B adds the contents of memory location B to AX and leaves the result in AX.

Notice that the following instruction is illegal: ADD mem,AX. The only instructions that allow a reference to memory to immediately follow the instruction name are COPY, JMP, JNB, and JB.

The P88 also has instructions for reading and printing integers, IN and OUT. These instructions can be used for writing some P88 programs. Here is a P88 program for reading an integer into register AX and then printing it:

```
IN AX
OUT AX
```

Or one could read an integer, square it, and print the result:

```
IN AX
COPY M1,AX
MUL AX,M1
OUT AX
```

As another example, one could read two numbers, divide the first by the second, and print the result:

```
IN AX
COPY A,AX
IN AX
COPY B,AX
COPY AX,A
DIV AX,B
OUT AX
```

Another type of instruction is the "jump," which loads a new address into IP and causes the machine to jump to an instruction that is not next in sequence. As an example, consider the following program, which adds the number in memory location A to AX repeatedly:

```
L1 ADD AX,A
   JMP L1
```

This program adds A to AX, and then the next instruction causes a jump to the instruction labeled L1. Here A is again added to AX. Then the jump instruction sends the machine back to L1 again, and so forth. This program loops forever, adding A to AX an unlimited number of times.

Of course, it is usually preferable to write a loop that will halt after an appropriate number of repetitions. This is done with the combination of the compare, CMP, and conditional jump instructions, JB and JNB. An example of this type of program is the following code, which prints the numbers from 1 to 10 before exiting. This program assumes the numbers 0, 1, and 10 appear in memory locations M0, M1, and M10.

```
   COPY AX,M0
L1 ADD AX,M1
   OUT AX
   CMP AX,M10
   JB L1
```

The compare instruction, CMP, loads B into register CF if AX is less than (below) M10. The "jump if below" instruction JB jumps to L1 if CF is B, that is, if AX is below M10. A paraphrase of this program shows its method of operation:

```
   Put 0 into AX.
L1 Add 1 to AX.
   Print the contents of AX.
   Check whether AX is less than 10.
   If it is, go to L1.
```

Another example of a program that uses the compare and jump commands is the following, which reads a number and changes its sign if it is negative. This program thus computes what is called the "absolute value":

```
     IN AX
     COPY M1,AX
     SUB AX,M1
     CMP AX,M1
     JB NEXT
     SUB AX,M1
     COPY M1,AX
NEXT COPY AX,M1
     OUT AX
```

The final example is a program to add a series of non-negative numbers. If a negative number is read at any time, the program prints the sum of all non-negative numbers read and exits:

```
     IN AX
     COPY M1,AX
     SUB AX,M1
     COPY ZERO,AX
     COPY SUM,AX
     COPY AX,M1
LOOP CMP AX,ZERO
     JB FIN
     ADD AX,SUM
     COPY SUM,AX
     IN AX
     JMP LOOP
FIN  COPY AX,SUM
     OUT AX
```

The language of machine instructions written in symbolic form as described here—COPY, ADD, CMP—is called assembly language. This type of language was heavily used during the 1940s and 1950s before higher-level programming languages like FORTRAN, PL/I, and Java were available. Each instruction in assembly language can be directly translated into a binary code, the machine language, denoted in this chapter by instructions surrounded by asterisks. The machine language instructions can be loaded into the IR register and executed as explained.

Exercises

1. Explain what function the following program computes:

```
        IN AX
        COPY M1,AX
        SUB AX,M1
        CMP AX,M1
        JB LAB1
        OUT AX
        JMP LAB2
LAB1 COPY AX,M1
        DIV AX,M1
        OUT AX
LAB2 END
```

2. Write an assembly language program that reads two integers and prints the larger one.

3. Write an assembly language program that reads two integers—a small integer followed by a larger one. Then it prints all the integers between but not including them.

4. A programmer noticed that a machine was running more slowly each day and wondered why. Furthermore, it acted erratically from time to time. She studied the code running in the machine, and after considerable effort, found the following code that she could identify as being of unknown origin:

```
V1      JMP   BEGIN
ZERO    0
ONE     1
TEN     10
FIFTY   50
LENGTH  33
COUNT   0
N1      0
BEGIN   COPY  AX,RANDOM
        COPY  N1,AX
        DIV   AX,TEN
        MUL   AX,TEN
        SUB   AX,N1
        CMP   AX,ZERO
        JB    EXIT
        COPY  AX,ZERO
        COPY  COUNT,AX
```

```
LOOP1   COPY   CX,RANDOM
        COPY   AX,COUNT
        CMP    AX,FIFTY
        JNB    EXIT
        COPY   BX,ZERO
LOOP2   CMP    BX,LENGTH
        JNB    NEXT
        COPY   AX,V1+c(BX)
        COPY   c(CX),AX
        ADD    BX,ONE
        ADD    CX,ONE
        JMP    LOOP2
NEXT    COPY   AX,COUNT
        ADD    AX,ONE
        COPY   COUNT,AX
        JMP    LOOP1
EXIT
```

In fact, the programmer had found a computer *virus*, and your job is to analyze it and discover how it works. This is a program that might be inserted into a computer system by an unfriendly person. It sits quietly in the middle of any program that it is inserted into until the right moment. Then it springs into action and duplicates itself many times around the machine memory.

Can you answer the following questions about the virus: How does it make the decision to go into action? How does it hide when it is not doing anything? What mechanism does it use to duplicate itself? How many times does it duplicate itself? Why does the virus cause the machine to seem to slow down? Why does it cause the system to act erratically sometimes? What should the programmer do to get rid of this virus? What problem does this virus have in carrying out its destructive job? How can it be changed so that it can more discreetly sneak around in the machine undetected?

The virus uses some features of the P88 machine not discussed before. It references a location called RANDOM, which contains a random number. Every time that location is referenced, it gives a different random number. Two additional registers are assumed: they are called BX and CX. The notation c(CX) refers to the memory location with the address equal to the number in CX. Thus, if register CX contains 100, then COPY c(CX),AX will put the contents of AX into location 100 in memory. The expression V1+c(BX) refers to the memory location found by starting at location V1 at the beginning of the program and counting BX locations beyond it.

This virus would not be dangerous in a typical modern computer because such machines usually have memory protection mechanisms that would quickly stop it. A successful virus that runs on contemporary machines will also need a scheme to trick the protection system, an issue not discussed here.

Summary

This chapter describes the classic architecture of the great majority of digital computers. They have a CPU that runs the fetch-execute cycle on sequences of instructions, and these instructions are stored in memory with the data of the computation. This is called the *von Neumann architecture*, and the only common deviations from it are the parallel machines described in chapter 14.

When we buy such a machine, we are told it runs at a certain speed, such as 800 megahertz. This speed refers to the number of clock cycles the internal electronics complete per second; in this case, it would be 800 million cycles per second. The execution of the machine instructions is synchronized by these clock cycles. For example, the machine may fetch an instruction on one cycle, decode it on the next, and carry out its computation on the third. Another machine might bring in several instructions simultaneously and execute them all in a single clock cycle. Some instructions on a given machine may require many clock cycles, whereas others may require one cycle or less. One can think of the specified speed as an approximation to the number of assembly language instructions executed per second; but this is clearly a very rough approximation.

If we own a machine of the kind described here, we can program on it in assembly language, but we cannot use a higher-level language such as C++ or Java. Chapter 9 examines the translation technology that enables us to automatically convert such higher-level languages into assembly language so that we will be able to program in C++ or Java on our machine.

9   Language Translation

Enabling the Computer to Understand Java

The primary vehicle for communication is language, and many languages have developed over the millennia. The advent of computers has brought many more. But most languages have no meaning to us unless we can translate them into familiar terms. So translation is a process of great importance to people and machines. We wish to understand and use many languages, and the process of translation can give us access to them.

Computer scientists have developed a powerful technology for language translation. This chapter introduces the methodology, a general technique applicable to many translation problems, and thus familiarizes you with another great idea of the field. The methodology has been quite successful for computer languages and can handle small subsets of natural languages, as described in chapter 16.

Our concern here is the translation of a higher-level programming language like Java into a lower-level language like assembly language or machine language. Machines do not understand higher-level languages, but they do understand machine language or, with the help of a very simple translator, assembly language. For example, we ask how the Java statement

```
Z = (X + Y)
```

is translated into the following assembly language code, which correctly expresses the desired meaning:

```
COPY AX,X
ADD AX,Y
COPY CN1,AX
COPY AX,CN1
COPY Z,AX
```

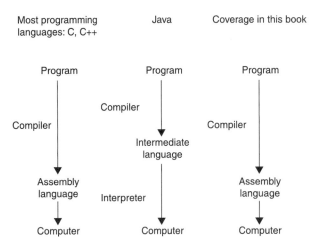

Figure 9.1

If we can understand the mechanisms that do this simple translation, we will understand fundamental processes of translation applicable in almost any domain. (The assembly language translation shown here is not of minimal length, and you can probably find a shorter program to do the same job. Automatic translators have the task of producing correct translations, but they do not always produce optimal ones, as is the case here.)

In fact, Java compilers do not translate Java into assembly language, as we do here. Most languages, such as C, C++, and others, historically have been translated directly into assembly language or machine language. However, Java compilers translate into an intermediate language that is interpreted by the Java processing system (figure 9.1). The main reason for this is to provide a software barrier between the computer and the Java program that prevents the Java program from threatening files and the normal operation of the machine. However, we ignore this extra level of processing in order to keep the complexity of our discussions under control.

This chapter introduces some fundamental ideas related to the theory of languages and translation. Then it shows how to assemble these ideas to build a translator for a small part of Java, and it gives many examples of translation.

Syntactic Production Rules

Language is embodied in sequences of symbols. In order to understand language, we must have a mathematics for sequences of symbols. This mathematics will show how to generate and analyze such sequences and will supply the necessary mechanisms for doing translation.

The first idea is that of the *production rule*. Such rules were introduced in chapter 2. They are discussed in more detail here and provide the basis for our translation mechanisms. Conceptually, a production rule changes a given object or set of objects into something else—a different object or set of objects. An example of a production rule from chapter 2 is

```
<name> ==> any string of alphanumeric symbols that begins with a
                          letter
```

which will be written in a modified form here as

R1. $<\text{i}>_j$ ==> *any string of alphanumeric symbols that begins with a letter*

This rule has been given the name R1, and it means "change $<\text{i}>_j$ into a sequence of letters and/or digits that begins with a letter." The term `<name>` has been modified to `<i>` (for *identifier*) and given a subscript j. Each time R1 is used, j will have a specific value, and a specific alphabetic string will be used on the right-hand side of the rule. An example *instantiation* of R1 is

```
<i>₇ ==> HEIGHT
```

which means "change $<\text{i}>_7$ into `HEIGHT`." We will study *syntactic production rules* like R1, which convert symbols like $<\text{i}>_7$ into strings of symbols like `HEIGHT`. All of these rules will be simplifications of the rules given previously for a much larger fraction of Java than is considered in this chapter.

Once we have a rule, we can then *apply* the rule to modify some string. For example, suppose we have the string $(<\text{i}>_7 + <\text{i}>_{19})$. Let's use this version of R1 to change this string:

```
(<i>₇ + <i>₁₉)
```

The rule $<\text{i}>_7$ ==> `HEIGHT` says that $<\text{i}>_7$ can be changed to `HEIGHT`, so the result will be

```
(HEIGHT + <i>₁₉)
```

Since the form $(<\text{i}>_7 + <\text{i}>_{19})$ has been changed to $(\text{HEIGHT} + <\text{i}>_{19})$, we can write

```
(<i>₇ + <i>₁₉) ==> (HEIGHT + <i>₁₉)
```

The $<\text{i}>_7$ in the first form has been replaced by `HEIGHT` in the second form. If we wish to apply R1 again, we could use the instantiation

```
<i>₁₉ ==> INC
```

to obtain

```
(HEIGHT + <i>₁₉) ==> (HEIGHT + INC)
```

In these rules, $<i>_j$ stands for "identifier name," and the string of symbols generated by $<i>_j$ is an identifier name.

It also may be desirable to apply rules to other things besides $<i>_j$. R2 is another useful rule; it enables us to convert $<e>_i$ into $<i>_j$:

R2. $<e>_i$ ==> $<i>_j$

For example, using the version $<e>_3$ ==> $<i>_7$ plus the R1 rule, we have

```
<e>₃ ==> <i>₇ ==> HEIGHT
```

The asterisk * is used to indicate that any number of rule applications has occurred. Thus, the preceding two-step derivation could be written

```
<e>₃ =*=> HEIGHT
```

In these rules, $<e>_i$ stands for "expression" or "arithmetic expression," as defined in previous chapters.

None of this looks like it has much to do with Java. But rule R3 introduces a familiar construction, the assignment statement:

R3. $<s>_k$ ==> $<i>_j$ = $<e>_i$

This rule says that $<s>_k$ can be replaced by $<i>_j$ = $<e>_i$. But the real meaning of the rule is that a legal statement $<s>_k$ in Java is the sequence of symbols $<i>_j$ = $<e>_i$, where $<i>_j$ is an identifier name and $<e>_i$ is an arithmetic expression. Using the combination of rules R1–R3, we can generate legal assignment statements. As an illustration, consider the generation of the Java statement

```
X = Y
```

Table A

Derivation	Rule
$<s>_1$	R3. $<s>_1$ ==> $<i>_2$ = $<e>_3$
$<i>_2$ = $<e>_3$	R1. $<i>_2$ ==> X
X = $<e>_3$	R2. $<e>_3$ ==> $<i>_4$
X = $<i>_4$	R1. $<i>_4$ ==> Y
X = Y	

In this derivation, we begin with $<s>_1$, which means we wish to generate a statement in Java. Then we use a case of rule R3 to convert $<s>_1$ to something else, namely, $<i>_2$ =

$<e>_3$. The conversion is done with the rule $<s>_1 ==> <i>_2 = <e>_3$. Next, we wish to change $<i>_2$ to X, and this is done with R1 of the form $<i>_2 ==> X$. The result of this change appears on the third line of the derivation: $X = <e>_3$. Finally, rule R2 is used to convert $<e>_3$ to $<i>_4$, and rule R1 is used to convert $<i>_4$ to Y.

Only two more rules are needed for our examples: R4 and R5, which make it possible to handle some complex arithmetic expressions:

R4. $<e>_i ==> (<e>_j + <e>_k)$
R5. $<e>_i ==> (<e>_j * <e>_k)$

This set of five rules makes up a *grammar* for some assignment statements in Java and is sufficient to provide many interesting examples for this chapter. The rules are simplifications of rules introduced in earlier chapters. A few sample derivations follow.

Table B

Derivation	Rule
$<s>_1$	R3. $<s>_1 ==> <i>_2 = <e>_3$
$<i>_2 = <e>_3$	R1. $<i>_2 ==> Y$
$Y = <e>_3$	R4. $<e>_3 ==> (<e>_4 + <e>_5)$
$Y = (<e>_4 + <e>_5)$	R2. $<e>_4 ==> <i>_6$
$Y = (<i>_6 + <e>_5)$	R1. $<i>_6 ==> XX$
$Y = (XX + <e>_5)$	R2. $<e>_5 ==> <i>_7$
$Y = (XX + <i>_7)$	R1. $<i>_7 ==> YY$
$Y = (XX + YY)$	

The following shows the generation of a more deeply nested arithmetic expression:

Table C

Derivation	Rule
$<s>_1$	R3. $<s>_1 ==> <i>_2 = <e>_3$
$<i>_2 = <e>_3$	R1. $<i>_2 ==> SUM$
$SUM = <e>_3$	R4. $<e>_3 ==> (<e>_4 + <e>_5)$
$SUM = (<e>_4 + <e>_5)$	R5. $<e>_4 ==> (<e>_7 * <e>_8)$
$SUM = ((<e>_7 * <e>_8) + <e>_5)$	R2. $<e>_7 ==> <i>_9$
$SUM = ((<i>_9 * <e>_8) + <e>_5)$	R1. $<i>_9 ==> X$
$SUM = ((X * <e>_8) + <e>_5)$	R2. $<e>_8 ==> <i>_{10}$
$SUM = ((X * <i>_{10}) + <e>_5)$	R1. $<i>_{10} ==> C$
$SUM = ((X * C) + <e>_5)$	R2. $<e>_5 ==> <i>_{11}$
$SUM = ((X * C) + <i>_{11})$	R1. $<i>_{11} ==> SUM$
$SUM = ((X * C) + SUM)$	

Of course, any nesting of multiplication and addition can be generated in the arithmetic expressions:

`<s>`$_1$ `=*=> Y = ((XX * YY) + (XY * (YX + XXX)))`

A question arises for all these derivations concerning how the indexes are determined. For example, if we have the string

`X = (Y + <e>`$_6$`)`

and wish to apply the rule `<e>`$_i$ `==> (<e>`$_j$ `+ <e>`$_k$`)`, what method should be used to determine i, j, and k? The answer is that the index on the left-hand side is determined by the symbol to be replaced. For example, the symbol `<e>`$_6$ is to be replaced in the statement, so the left side of the rule must be `<e>`$_6$: `<e>`$_6$ `==> (<e>`$_j$ `+ <e>`$_k$`)`. The indexes on the right-hand side can be anything as long as they are different from any indexes used previously in this derivation. Suppose that 8 and 9 have not been used. Then we can set $j = 8$ and $k = 9$ to obtain the form `<e>`$_6$ `==> (<e>`$_8$ `+ <e>`$_9$`)`. Applying this rule in the preceding statement results in

`X = (Y + (<e>`$_8$ `+ <e>`$_9$`))`

Summarizing the process for setting the indexes, we repeat the preceding example. We wish to modify this:

`X = (Y + <e>`$_6$`)`

And we wish to use this rule:

`<e>`$_i$ `==> (<e>`$_j$ `+ <e>`$_k$`)`

Then we set the index on the left-hand side of the rule to make it match the item to be replaced:

`<e>`$_6$ `==> (<e>`$_j$ `+ <e>`$_k$`)`

But the rule is not ready until all its indexes are set. Let's put any other numbers we want into the other slots, j and k, say, 8 and 9 (if 8 and 9 have not been previously used as indexes):

`<e>`$_6$ `==> (<e>`$_8$ `+ <e>`$_9$`)`

Now let's apply the rule to the original form, `X = (Y + <e>`$_6$`)`:

`X = (Y + (<e>`$_8$ `+ <e>`$_9$`))`

Once a grammar has been established for a language (or, as in our case, part of a language), the grammar can be used for either *generation* of the language or *analysis* (understanding) of it. The preceding examples illustrate generation; a person wanting to say something in Java begins with the decision to say a statement and then generates the thing to be said:

$$\text{<s>}_1 \implies \text{<i>}_2 = \text{<e>}_3 \implies X = \text{<e>}_3 \implies \cdot \ \cdot \ \cdot \implies X = (Y * X)$$

Each application of a rule further specifies what is to be said until the statement is completely defined. But the rules can also be applied in reverse to analyze or understand a statement. Thus, given

```
X = (Y * X)
```

we can use R1 to discover where the identifiers are:

$$\text{<i>}_1 = (\text{<i>}_2 * \text{<i>}_3)$$

Then rules R2 and R4 uncover the structure of the right-hand side:

$$\text{<i>}_1 = \text{<e>}_4$$

Finally, R3 tells us that a complete statement has been made:

$$\text{<s>}_0$$

So the same rules that were used in generation can be used in reverse to disassemble, analyze, and understand a Java statement.

Analogous processes probably account for human beings' processing of English. Presumably human beings have something like a grammar in their brains, and generation proceeds by applying the rules to create well-formed utterances. A person might decide to assert a declarative sentence

(declarative sentence)

and a grammar could indicate that such sentences have subjects and predicates:

(subject) (predicate)

Further rules could enable these symbols to be replaced by actual words:

The boy went to town.

Understanding would involve the reverse process: finding the parts of speech of the spoken words, finding how they assemble to become sentence constituents such as subjects and predicates, and finally, finding the structure of the complete sentence. This is discussed more in chapter 16.

This section has addressed the issue of the *syntax* of language. We have examined mechanisms for generating or analyzing the strings of symbols that make up language.

The next section is concerned with the *semantics* of language. There we study the concept of meaning and show how meaning is associated with the utterances of language, the syntactic strings of symbols.

Exercises

1. Apply the given rules to `<s>`₁ to generate strings of symbols.
   (a) Rules R3, R1, R2, R1
   (b) Rules R3, R1, R5, R2, R1, R2, R1
   (c) Rules R3, R1, R4, R2, R1, R5, R2, R1, R2, R1

2. Use rules R1–R5 to generate each of the following strings of symbols starting from `<i>`₁ or `<s>`₁:
   (a) `YXY`
   (b) `JACK`
   (c) `X = Y`
   (d) `X = (X * X)`
   (e) `YYY = (Y * (X + X))`
   (f) `XX = ((X + XX) * Y)`
   (g) `X = ((Y * Y) + (X * X))`

3. What new rules are needed to be able to generate the following statement?

   `SUM = FACT - X`

   Use your new rules to show the complete generation of this statement.

4. Build a grammar that can generate all of the following sentences.

   The boy knows the girl.
   This girl knows that boy.
   That boy knows this boy.
   Jack knows that boy.
   Jill knows Jack.
   Jack knows Jill.
   ⋮

Attaching Semantics to the Rules

The *meaning* of a language entity is a knowledge structure that the users of the language associate with that entity. An example language is English, and an example language entity is "John ran to the red house." Its meaning might be a picture that forms in your mind showing John running toward a house that is colored red. Another example of a language is the set of binary numbers, and an example member of the language is 101. We could decide that we will take the meaning of each binary number to be its decimal equivalent. Thus, the meaning of the string 101 would be 5. The *semantics* of a language refers to the mechanisms that attach meaning to the language entities.

The language being translated is called the *source language*, and this language is translated into the *object language*. The source language is presumably not usable by the recipient, but the object language is. We consider in this section the binary numbers as a source language, and we show how to translate them into decimal numbers, the object language.

We begin our study of language meaning by studying the semantics of binary numbers. First, let's create a set of rules for generating binary numbers:

P1. $\texttt{<s>}_i$ ==> $\texttt{<s>}_j 0$
P2. $\texttt{<s>}_i$ ==> $\texttt{<s>}_j 1$
P3. $\texttt{<s>}_i$ ==> 0
P4. $\texttt{<s>}_i$ ==> 1

We can use these rules to generate any binary number. Here is how we generate 101:

Table D

Derivation	Rule
$\texttt{<s>}_1$	P2. $\texttt{<s>}_1$ ==> $\texttt{<s>}_2 1$
$\texttt{<s>}_2 1$	P1. $\texttt{<s>}_2$ ==> $\texttt{<s>}_3 0$
$\texttt{<s>}_3 01$	P4. $\texttt{<s>}_3$ ==> 1
101	

Begin with $\texttt{<s>}_1$ and apply rule P2 to create a 1 on the right end of the string. Then rule P1 creates the 0, and P4 completes the derivation of 101. All this is just a review of the familiar rule mechanism, but it is being applied to generating binary numbers.

Here is the new idea. We now add a semantic part to each rule. The rules P1–P4 with semantics included look like this:

Table E

Rule Syntax	Rule Semantics
P1. $\texttt{<s>}_i$ ==> $\texttt{<s>}_j 0$	$M(\texttt{<s>}_i) = M(\texttt{<s>}_j) * 2$
P2. $\texttt{<s>}_i$ ==> $\texttt{<s>}_j 1$	$M(\texttt{<s>}_i) = M(\texttt{<s>}_j) * 2 + 1$
P3. $\texttt{<s>}_i$ ==> 0	$M(\texttt{<s>}_i) = 0$
P4. $\texttt{<s>}_i$ ==> 1	$M(\texttt{<s>}_i) = 1$

Therefore, each production rule now has two parts, the syntactic part and the semantic part. The notation M stands for "meaning," so the semantic part of rule P1 should be read as "the meaning of $\texttt{<s>}_i$ is equal to the meaning of $\texttt{<s>}_j$ times 2." The other semantic parts can be read the same way. The next concern is to find out how to use this semantic part.

The function of the semantics mechanism can be seen by examining the derivation of the string 101 and its meaning 5:

Table F

Derivation	Rule Syntax	Rule Semantics
$\texttt{<s>}_1$	P2. $\texttt{<s>}_1$ ==> $\texttt{<s>}_2 1$	$\texttt{M(<s>}_1) = \texttt{M(<s>}_2) * 2 + 1$
$\texttt{<s>}_2 1$	P1. $\texttt{<s>}_2$ ==> $\texttt{<s>}_3 0$	$\texttt{M(<s>}_2) = \texttt{M(<s>}_3) * 2$
$\texttt{<s>}_3 01$	P4. $\texttt{<s>}_3$ ==> 1	$\texttt{M(<s>}_3) = 1$
101		

This table is easy to understand because it is simply a copy of table D with the semantic parts of the rules added as specified by the definitions in table E. Next, we recopy table F, line by line and, after every line, write down the current version of the meaning, using all the semantic information up to that point:

$\texttt{<s>}_1$ P2. $\texttt{<s>}_1$ ==> $\texttt{<s>}_2 1$ $\texttt{M(<s>}_1) = \texttt{M(<s>}_2) * 2 + 1$

According to this entry, the first approximation to the meaning is $\texttt{M(<s>}_1) = \texttt{M(<s>}_2) * 2 + 1$.

MEANING FOUND: $\texttt{M(<s>}_1) = \texttt{M(<s>}_2) * 2 + 1$

But this expression for meaning has an unknown in it: the quantity $\texttt{M(<s>}_2)$. The next entry from table F will help:

$\texttt{<s>}_2 1$ P1. $\texttt{<s>}_2$ ==> $\texttt{<s>}_3 0$ $\texttt{M(<s>}_2) = \texttt{M(<s>}_3) * 2$

Specifically, we use the semantics from rule P1 to tell us the value of $\texttt{M(<s>}_2)$ and substitute that value into the "MEANING FOUND" expression:

MEANING FOUND: $\texttt{M(<s>}_1) = (\texttt{M(<s>}_3) * 2) * 2 + 1$

But this expression for meaning has the unknown $\texttt{M(<s>}_3)$ in it. The next entry from table F will help:

$\texttt{<s>}_3 01$ P4. $\texttt{<s>}_3$ ==> 1 $\texttt{M(<s>}_3) = 1$

Substitute the value of $\texttt{M(<s>}_3)$ into the "MEANING FOUND" expression:

MEANING FOUND: $\texttt{M(<s>}_1) = (1 * 2) * 2 + 1 = 5$

This completes the computation of the meaning of 101. The meaning is $M(\langle s \rangle_1) = 5$.

Table F, together with the "MEANING FOUND" expressions, shows every step of the computation needed to produce the meaning value. The steps are summarized in table G. You should study table G until you are sure you understand every step.

Table G

Derivation	Rule Syntax	Rule Semantics
$\langle s \rangle_1$	P2. $\langle s \rangle_1 \implies \langle s \rangle_2 1$	$M(\langle s \rangle_1) = M(\langle s \rangle_2) \ast 2 + 1$
MEANING FOUND: $M(\langle s \rangle_1) = M(\langle s \rangle_2) \ast 2 + 1$		
$\langle s \rangle_2 1$	P1. $\langle s \rangle_2 \implies \langle s \rangle_3 0$	$M(\langle s \rangle_2) = M(\langle s \rangle_3) \ast 2$
MEANING FOUND: $M(\langle s \rangle_1) = (M(\langle s \rangle_3) \ast 2) \ast 2 + 1$		
$\langle s \rangle_3 01$	P4. $\langle s \rangle_3 \implies 1$	$M(\langle s \rangle_3) = 1$
MEANING FOUND: $M(\langle s \rangle_1) = (1 \ast 2) \ast 2 + 1 = 5$		
101		

In conclusion, we have gone through all the details involved in finding the meaning for a language entity like 101. First, we found a sequence of syntactic rules that start with $\langle s \rangle_1$ and generate 101. Then we used the semantic parts of those rules to create the meaning $M(\langle s \rangle_1)$.

Exercises

1. Use the syntactic parts of rules P1–P4 to find a generation of the string 1011. Now add the semantic parts of the rules and use them to compute the meaning (the decimal equivalent) of the original string.

2. Repeat exercise 1 for the binary strings 10111 and 00111.

3. Explain the construction of the semantic parts of rules P1 and P2, and tell exactly why they compute the correct value for $M(\langle s \rangle_i)$.

The Semantics of Java

The previous section showed how to attach semantics to rules and how to use those semantic parts to compute a meaning for a language utterance. Now it is time to use these ideas on the problem of central importance here, the translation of Java into a language that the machine can understand—P88 assembly language or ultimately the binary-coded machine language.

The symbols $\langle i \rangle_j$, $\langle e \rangle_j$, and $\langle s \rangle_j$ on the left sides of the grammar rules R1–R5 are called *grammar variables*, and the grammar semantics assign meaning to them. We now add semantic parts to each of these rules in the same manner as in the previous section. The result will be a translator for the class of Java statements that they represent.

What should be the meaning associated with the simplest rule, R1?

R1. `<i>`$_j$ `==>` *any string of alphanumeric symbols that begins with a letter*

That is, if a variable is called X in the source language, what name should it have in the object language? Let's make things as easy as possible and let the variable have the same name in both languages:

R1. `<i>`$_j$ `==> w`   `M(<i>`$_j$`) = w`

where `w` is some identifier string. Thus, we might have the following instantiation of R1:

`<i>`$_9$ `==> HEIGHT`   `M(<i>`$_9$`) = HEIGHT`

Next, we consider the semantics associated with R2. The left-hand variable, `<e>`$_i$, has two parts to its meaning representation, `M(<e>`$_i$`)` and `code(<e>`$_i$`)`. Intuitively, the arithmetic expression `<e>`$_i$ will have a name, `M(<e>`$_i$`)`, and some lines of assembly language code, `code(<e>`$_i$`)`:

R2. `<e>`$_i$ `==> <i>`$_j$ `M(<e>`$_i$`) = M(<i>`$_j$`)`
                        `code (<e>`$_i$`) = nothing`

Thus, as an example, if `<e>`$_1$ `=*=> HEIGHT`, then `M(<e>`$_1$`) = HEIGHT`, and `code (<e>`$_1$`)` is a list of instructions (code) of length zero.

Rule R3 provides the first interesting semantics. If `<s>`$_k$ generates a Java statement, then `code(<s>`$_k$`)` will give its translation in terms of P88 assembly language.

R3. `<s>`$_k$ `==> <i>`$_j$ `= <e>`$_i$ `code (<s>`$_k$`) = code (<e>`$_i$`)`
                                    `COPY AX,M(<e>`$_i$`)`
                                    `COPY M(<i>`$_j$`),AX`

Thus, `code(<s>`$_k$`)` is the list of all instructions in `code(<e>`$_i$`)` followed by the two `COPY` instructions shown. This says that the code for `<s>`$_k$ should first compute the value of `<e>`$_i$, then copy the result of that calculation into `AX` and then into the location for `<i>`$_j$.

Notice that we follow a particular notational convention in this chapter. Fragments of code are typed as similarly indented sequential lines of programming. Such fragments should be regarded as units even though they are spread across several lines. In the previous definition, `code(<s>`$_k$`)` is defined as

`code (<s>`$_k$`) = code (<e>`$_i$`)`
            `COPY AX,M(<e>`$_i$`)`
            `COPY M(<i>`$_j$`),AX`

The convention requires that these three lines of code be considered a single unit. Thus, the definition states that $code(<s>_k)$ is equivalent to the three lines of code given, not just the single line $code(<e>_i)$.

To illustrate the use of the rules R1–R3 with their semantic components, let's do a complete translation of the statement

```
X = Y
```

into assembly language. From a previous section (table A), it is clear that the sequence of rules R3, R1, R2, R1 is sufficient to derive the source statement. So we write down the complete derivation that will determine the semantic rules required to find the translation. This derivation is identical to the one carried out in table A except that the semantic portion of each rule is set down next to the syntactic portion:

Table H

Derivation	Rule Syntax	Rule Semantics
$<s>_1$	R3. $<s>_1 ==> <i>_2 = <e>_3$	$code(<s>_1) = code(<e>_3)$ $\phantom{code(<s>_1) = }$ COPY AX,$M(<e>_3)$ $\phantom{code(<s>_1) = }$ COPY $M(<i>_2)$,AX
$<i>_2 = <e>_3$	R1. $<i>_2 ==> X$	$M(<i>_2) = X$
$X = <e>_3$	R2. $<e>_3 ==> <i>_4$	$M(<e>_3) = M(<i>_4)$ $code(<e>_3) = $ nothing
$X = <i>_4$	R1. $<i>_4 ==> Y$	$M(<i>_4) = Y$
$X = Y$		

In table H, the first two columns are taken from a previous section on syntax (table A). The third column is new; it gives the semantic portion of each of the rules used.

Now we want to use the third column in table H to compute some "MEANING FOUND" expressions. The beginning of discovering the meaning involves simply copying from table H the value for $code(<s>_1)$.

```
MEANING FOUND:  code(<s>₁) = code(<e>₃)
                           COPY AX,M(<e>₃)
                           COPY M(<i>₂),AX
```

This is a good start, but we wonder what the value of $M(<i>_2)$ will be. The answer is given by the second entry of table H, column 3: $M(<i>_2) = X$. So we can make that substitution into the preceding MEANING FOUND expression.

```
MEANING FOUND:  code(<s>₁) = code(<e>₃)
                           COPY AX,M(<e>₃)
                           COPY X,AX
```

The third entry in table H, column 3 enables us to fill in values for two more entities in the MEANING FOUND, $M(<e>_3) = M(<i>_4)$ and $code(<e>_3)$ = nothing. With those two substitutions, MEANING FOUND becomes:

```
MEANING FOUND:  code(<s>₁) = COPY AX,M(<i>₄)
                            COPY X,AX
```

There is still one more item to be completed. It is the evaluation of $M(<i>_4)$, which the fourth entry of table H makes possible: $M(<i>_4) = Y$.

```
MEANING FOUND:  code(<s>₁) = COPY AX,Y
                            COPY X,AX
```

The translation rules thus assert that the meaning of $X = Y$ in Java is

```
COPY AX,Y
COPY X,AX
```

in P88 assembly language. The Java statement says, "Find the value in Y and put it into X." The translation says the same thing in P88 assembly language: "Copy Y into AX and then copy AX into X." This example is worthy of careful study because it demonstrates all the essential mechanisms of the translator without undue complexity.

In summary, the *input* to the translation process was $X = Y$. Rules R1, R2, and R3 were applied, resulting in the semantic relations shown in the third column of table H, which are duplicated here:

Semantic Rules

```
code(<s>₁) = code(<e>₃)
            COPY AX,M(<e>₃)
            COPY M(<i>₂),AX
M(<i>₂) = X
M(<e>₃) = M(<i>₄)
code(<e>₃) = nothing
M(<i>₄) = Y
```

Finally, $code(<s>_1)$ was evaluated using these rules. The translation *output* was

```
COPY AX,Y
COPY X,AX
```

More interesting translations are possible only if semantics are available for our last two rules, R4 and R5:

```
R4. <e>_i ==> (<e>_j + <e>_k)    M(<e>_i) = createname
                                 code(<e>_i) = code (<e>_j)
                                              code (<e>_k)
                                              COPY AX,M(<e>_j)
                                              ADD AX,M(<e>_k)
                                              COPY M(<e>_i),AX
R5. <e>_i ==> (<e>_j * <e>_k)    M(<e>_i) = createname
                                 code(<e>_i) = code (<e>_j)
                                              code (<e>_k)
                                              COPY AX,M(<e>_j)
                                              MUL AX,M(<e>_k)
                                              COPY M(<e>_i),AX
```

These semantic rules use the function `createname`, which creates a name that has not been used elsewhere. Thus, if one encounters $M(<e>_7)$ = `createname`, the system might create the name `CN1` and assign it: $M(<e>_7)$ = `CN1`. If later one encounters, say, $M(<e>_9)$ = `createname`, the result might be $M(<e>_9)$ = `CN2`.

Examining the code semantics for the addition rule R4, you can see that the code segments for $<e>_j$ and $<e>_k$ are expanded to determine the value of these arithmetic expressions. Then the results are added into the register `AX` by two P88 instructions and finally stored away to be used by a later calculation. An analogous thing happens with the rule R5.

The use of these rules is demonstrated in the following two derivations. The first is the translation of `Z = (X + Y)`.

Table K

Derivation	Rule Syntax	Rule Semantics
$<s>_1$	R3 $<s>_1$ ==> $<i>_2$ = $<e>_3$	code $(<s>_1)$ = code($<e>_3$) COPY AX,M($<e>_3$) COPY M($<i>_2$),AX
MEANING FOUND:	code $(<s>_1)$ = code($<e>_3$) COPY AX,M($<e>_3$) COPY M($<i>_2$),AX	
$<i>_2$ = $<e>_3$	R1. $<i>_2$ ==> Z	M($<i>_2$) = Z
MEANING FOUND:	code $(<s>_1)$ = code($<e>_3$) COPY AX,M($<e>_3$) COPY Z,AX	
Z = $<e>_3$	R4. $<e>_3$ ==> $(<e>_4$ + $<e>_5)$	M($<e>_3$) = CN1 code($<e>_3$) = code $(<e>_4)$ code $(<e>_5)$ COPY AX,M($<e>_4$) ADD AX,M($<e>_5$) COPY M($<e>_3$),AX

Table K (continued)

Derivation	Rule Syntax	Rule Semantics
MEANING FOUND:	code ($<s>_1$) = code ($<e>_4$) code ($<e>_5$) COPY AX,M($<e>_4$) ADD AX,M($<e>_5$) COPY CN1,AX COPY AX,CN1 COPY Z,AX	
Z = ($<e>_4$ + $<e>_5$)	R2. $<e>_4$ ==> $<i>_6$	M($<e>_4$) = M($<i>_6$) code($<e>_4$) = nothing
MEANING FOUND:	code ($<s>_1$) = code ($<e>_5$) COPY AX,M($<i>_6$) ADD AX,M($<e>_5$) COPY CN1,AX COPY AX,CN1 COPY Z,AX	
Z = ($<i>_6$ + $<e>_5$) MEANING FOUND:	R1. $<i>_6$ ==> X code ($<s>_1$) = code ($<e>_5$) COPY AX,X ADD AX,M($<e>_5$) COPY CN1,AX COPY AX,CN1 COPY Z,AX	M($<i>_6$) = X
Z = (X + $<e>_5$)	R2. $<e>_5$ ==> $<i>_7$	M($<e>_5$) = M($<i>_7$) code($<e>_5$) = nothing
MEANING FOUND:	code ($<s>_1$) = COPY AX,X ADD AX,M($<i>_7$) COPY CN1,AX COPY AX,CN1 COPY Z,AX	
Z = (X + $<i>_7$) MEANING FOUND:	R1. $<i>_7$ ==> Y code ($<s>_1$) = COPY AX,X ADD AX,Y COPY CN1,AX COPY AX,CN1 COPY Z,AX	M($<i>_7$) = Y
Z = (X + Y)		

This completes the translation of the original statement, $z = (x + y)$. The *input* to the translation process was $z = (x + y)$. Rules R1, R2, R3, and R4 were applied. Their semantic relations are given in the third column of table K. The translation *output* was

```
COPY AX,X
ADD AX,Y
COPY CN1,AX
COPY AX,CN1
COPY Z,AX
```

Translators often produce nonminimal code, as has occurred in this example. Code segments of this kind can be optimized by many well-known techniques, but such studies are beyond the scope of this book.

The last example of this section demonstrates the translation of a more complicated arithmetic expression: $U1 = (x + (y * z))$.

Table L

Derivation	Rule Syntax	Rule Semantics
$<s>_1$	R3. $<s>_1 ==> <i>_2 = <e>_3$	code $(<s>_1)$ = code$(<e>_3)$ COPY AX,M$(<e>_3)$ COPY M$(<i>_2)$,AX
MEANING FOUND: code $(<s>_1)$ = code $(<e>_3)$ COPY AX,M$(<e>_3)$ COPY M$(<i>_2)$,AX		
	R1. $<i>_2 ==> U1$	M$(<i>_2)$ = U1
$<i>_2 = <e>_3$ MEANING FOUND: code $(<s>_1)$ = code $(<e>_3)$ COPY AX,M$(<e>_3)$ COPY U1,AX		
$U1 = <e>_3$	R4. $<e>_3 ==> (<e>_4 + <e>_5)$	M$(<e>_3)$ = CN1 code$(<e>_3)$ = code $(<e>_4)$ code $(<e>_5)$ COPY AX,M$(<e>_4)$ ADD AX,M$(<e>_5)$ COPY M$(<e>_3)$,AX
MEANING FOUND: code $(<s>_1)$ = code $(<e>_4)$ code $(<e>_5)$ COPY AX,M$(<e>_4)$ ADD AX,M$(<e>_5)$ COPY CN1,AX COPY AX,CN1 COPY U1,AX		

Table L (continued)

Derivation	Rule Syntax	Rule Semantics
U1 = (<e>$_4$ + <e>$_5$)	R2. <e>$_4$ ==> <i>$_6$	M(<e>$_4$) = M(<i>$_6$) code(<e>$_4$) = nothing

MEANING FOUND: code (<s>$_1$) = code (<e>$_5$)
           COPY AX,M(<i>$_6$)
           ADD AX,M(<e>$_5$)
           COPY CN1,AX
           COPY AX,CN1
           COPY U1,AX

Derivation	Rule Syntax	Rule Semantics
U1 = (<i>$_6$ + <e>$_5$)	R1. <i>$_6$ ==> X	M(<i>$_6$) = X

MEANING FOUND: code (<s>$_1$) = code (<e>$_5$)
           COPY AX,X
           ADD AX,M(<e>$_5$)
           COPY CN1,AX
           COPY AX,CN1
           COPY U1,AX

Derivation	Rule Syntax	Rule Semantics

U1 = (X + <e>$_5$)	R5. <e>$_5$ ==> (<e>$_7$ * <e>$_8$)	M(<e>$_5$) = CN2
		code(<e>$_5$) = code (<e>$_7$)
		        code (<e>$_8$)
		        COPY AX,M(<e>$_7$)
		        MUL AX,M(<e>$_8$)
		        COPY CN2,AX

MEANING FOUND: code (<s>$_1$) = code (<e>$_7$)
           code (<e>$_8$)
           COPY AX,M(<e>$_7$)
           MUL AX,M(<e>$_8$)
           COPY CN2,AX
           COPY AX,X
           ADD AX,CN2
           COPY CN1,AX
           COPY AX,CN1
           COPY U1,AX

Derivation	Rule Syntax	Rule Semantics
U1 = (X + (<e>$_7$ * <e>$_8$))	R2. <e>$_7$ ==> <i>$_9$	M(<e>$_7$) = M(<i>$_9$) code(<e>$_7$) = nothing

MEANING FOUND: code (<s>$_1$) = code (<e>$_8$)
           COPY AX,M(<i>$_9$)
           MUL AX,M(<e>$_8$)
           COPY CN2,AX
           COPY AX,X
           ADD AX,CN2

Table L (continued)

Derivation	Rule Syntax	Rule Semantics
	COPY CN1,AX	
	COPY AX,CN1	
	COPY U1,AX	
$U1 = (X + (<i>_9 * <e>_8))$ R1. $<i>_9 ==> Y$		$M(<i>_9) = Y$
MEANING FOUND: code $(<s>_1)$ = code $(<e>_8)$		
	COPY AX,Y	
	MUL AX,M$(<e>_8)$	
	COPY CN2,AX	
	COPY AX,X	
	ADD AX,CN2	
	COPY CN1,AX	
	COPY AX,CN1	
	COPY U1,AX	
	R2. $<e>_8 ==> <i>_{10}$	$M(<e>_8) = M(<i>_{10})$
$U1 = (X + (Y * <e>_8))$		code$(<e>_8)$ = nothing
MEANING FOUND: code $(<s>_1)$ = COPY AX,Y		
	MUL AX,M$(<i>_{10})$	
	COPY CN2,AX	
	COPY AX,X	
	ADD AX,CN2	
	COPY CN1,AX	
	COPY AX,CN1	
	COPY U1,AX	
$U1 = (X + (Y * <i>_{10}))$ R1. $<i>_{10} ==> Z$		$M(<i>_{10}) = Z$
MEANING FOUND: code $(<s>_1)$ = COPY AX,Y		
	MUL AX,Z	
	COPY CN2,AX	
	COPY AX,X	
	ADD AX,CN2	
	COPY CN1,AX	
	COPY AX,CN1	
	COPY U1,AX	

$U1 = (X + (Y * Z))$

This completes the description of the translator for a small class of Java assignment statements. The system uses the syntactic portions of the rules to find the structure of the unknown statement. The semantic portions of the rules are functions that compute portions of the meaning. The expansion of these functions and their combination provides the final translation. This general methodology is quite satisfactory for handling many translation problems and is the basis for many existing translators.

A program can be written to do all the translation steps for a complete programming language such as Java. Such a program is called a *compiler*. Many compilers have been written for the various programming languages. The following section gives several more translation rules for the compilation of simple looping programs. These rules show how the methodology of this chapter can be extended to handle larger programming constructions.

Exercises

1. Use rules R1 through R5 to translate the following statement into assembly language: `HEIGHT = (C * B)`.

2. Use rules R1–R5 to translate the following statement into assembly language: `I = (I + ONE)`.

3. Use rules R1–R5 to translate the following statement into assembly language: `X = ((T * U) * V)`.

4. Use rules R1–R5 to translate the following statement into assembly language: `TOTAL = ((C1 * MAX) + (C2 * MIN))`.

5. Examine very carefully the translations given in this section for the statements `Z = (X + Y)` and `U1 = (X + (Y * Z))`. Can you write assembly language code that will do the same task but with fewer instructions? Can you make a rough estimate of how much shorter minimal assembly language programs are on average than programs output by the translator? Can you guess how much faster optimal assembly language programs will be than computer-generated ones?

6. Study the construction of the syntactic and semantic parts of rule R5, and explain the function of every part of the rule.

*The Translation of Looping Programs

The previous sections gave a general approach to the design of translators. This section adds no new ideas to the theory but provides additional examples of rules and shows how larger code segments can be translated.

Two more rules are needed to enable translation of a sequence of statements rather than a single statement:

R6. $\langle q \rangle_i \implies \langle s \rangle_j;$ $code(\langle q \rangle_i) = code(\langle s \rangle_j)$
                    $\langle q \rangle_k$ $code(\langle q \rangle_k)$

R7. $\langle q \rangle_i \implies \langle s \rangle_j;$ $code(\langle q \rangle_i) = code(\langle s \rangle_j)$

Here $<q>_i$ stands for a "sequence of statements." To see how these rules work, apply R6 several times to $<q>_1$:

Table M

Derivation	Rule Syntax	Rule Semantics
$<q>_1$	R6. $<q>_1$ ==> $<s>_2$;	code($<q>_1$) = code($<s>_2$)
	$<q>_3$	code($<q>_3$)
$<s>_2$;	R6. $<q>_3$ ==> $<s>_4$;	code($<q>_3$) = code($<s>_4$)
$<q>_3$	$<q>_5$	code($<q>_5$)
$<s>_2$;	R6. $<q>_5$ ==> $<s>_6$;	code($<q>_5$) = code($<s>_6$)
$<s>_4$;	$<q>_7$	code($<q>_7$)
$<q>_5$		
$<s>_2$;		
$<s>_4$;		
$<s>_6$;		
$<q>_7$		

Three applications of R6 produce a sequence of three statements, $<s>_2$;, $<s>_4$;, and $<s>_6$;, each followed by a semicolon. Then we can apply R7 once to add a final statement to the sequence:

Table N

Derivation	Rule Syntax	Rule Semantics
$<s>_2$;	R7. $<q>_7$ ==> $<s>_8$	code($<q>_7$) = code($<s>_8$)
$<s>_4$;		
$<s>_6$;		
$<q>_7$		
$<s>_2$;		
$<s>_4$;		
$<s>_6$;		
$<s>_8$;		

Then the semantics rules can be applied to determine codes for the four statements $<s>_2$;, $<s>_4$;, $<s>_6$;, and $<s>_8$;. The following are the "MEANING FOUND" expressions for the creation of the final meaning of the set of four statements:

```
code (<q>₁) = code (<s>₂)     By first R6
              code (<q>₃)
code (<q>₁) = code (<s>₂)     By second R6
              code (<s>₄)
              code (<q>₅)
```

```
code (<q>₁) = code (<s>₂)        By third R6
                code (<s>₄)
                code (<s>₆)
                code (<q>₇)
code (<q>₁) = code (<s>₂)        By R7
                code (<s>₄)
                code (<s>₆)
                code (<s>₈)
```

The result is as expected. The translation of $<s>_2;$, $<s>_4;$, $<s>_6;$, and $<s>_8;$ is

```
code (<q>₁) = code (<s>₂)
                code (<s>₄)
                code (<s>₆)
                code (<s>₈)
```

But Java always embeds statement sequences between the braces { } to form a *compound statement*. A rule is needed for this:

```
R8. <c>ᵢ ==> {          code(<c>ᵢ) = code(<q>ⱼ)
                <q>ⱼ
              }
```

Using this rule with the others, we can then show that

```
<c>₀ =*=>
{
    <s>₂;
    <s>₄;
    <s>₆;
    <s>₈;
}
```

and the semantics rules are the same as in the previous example.

Summarizing, if a compound statement of n sequential statements is to be translated, rule R8 should be used once, followed by rule R6 $n - 1$ times and R7 once. This gives n statements whose translation will be n code segments. Illustrating this idea, suppose the following compound statement is to be compiled.

```
{
    X = Y;
    Z = (X + Y);
    U1 = (X + (Y * Z));
}
```

These individual statements were translated in the previous section, so those details can be omitted.

Table O

Derivation	Rule Syntax	Rule Semantics
$<c>_0$	R8. $<c>_0 \implies \{$ 　　$<q>1$ 　　$\}$	$\text{code}(<c>_0) = \text{code}(<q>_1)$
$\{$ $<q>_1$ $\}$	R6. $<q>_1 \implies <s>_2;$ 　　　$<q>_3$	$\text{code}(<q>_1) = \text{code}(<s>_2)$ 　　　　　　$\text{code}(<q>_3)$
$\{$ $<s>_2;$ $<q>_3$ $\}$	R6. $<q>_3 \implies <s>_4;$ 　　　$<q>_5$	$\text{code}(<q>_3) = \text{code}(<s>_4)$ 　　　　　　$\text{code}(<q>_5)$
$\{$ $<s>_2;$ $<s>_4;$ $<q>_5$ $\}$ $\{$ $<s>_2;$ $<s>_4;$ $<s>_6;$ $\}$	R7. $<q>_5 \implies <s>_6;$	$\text{code}(<q>_5) = \text{code}(<s>_6)$

We can show that

$$\text{code}(<c>_0) = \text{code}(<s>_2)$$
$$\text{code}(<s>_4)$$
$$\text{code}(<s>_6)$$

where

$$<s>_2 \overset{*}{\implies} X = Y$$
$$<s>_4 \overset{*}{\implies} Z = (X + Y)$$
$$<s>_6 \overset{*}{\implies} U1 = (X + (Y * Z))$$

and code($<s>_2$), code($<s>_4$), and code($<s>_6$) were computed in the previous section. Substituting the results of previous sections, we obtain

```
code (<c>₀) = COPY AX,Y
              COPY X,AX
              COPY AX,X
              ADD AX,Y
              COPY CN1,AX
              COPY AX,CN1
              COPY Z,AX
              COPY AX,Y
              MUL AX,Z
              COPY CN2,AX
              COPY AX,X
              ADD AX,CN2
              COPY CN1,AX
              COPY AX,CN1
              COPY U1,AX
```

This code is not precisely what is generated by the rules because we did not use new names CNi for each new assignment statement as it was generated. But this detail does not affect the computation, so it is not discussed here.

The final rule to be examined in this chapter will make it possible to do looping programs:

```
R9. <s>ᵢ ==> while (<i>ⱼ < <e>ₖ)   M(<s>ᵢ) = createname
                <c>ₕ             M'(<s>ᵢ) = createname
                                 code(<s>ᵢ) = M(<s>ᵢ)   code(<e>ₖ)
                                                        COPY AX,M(<i>ⱼ)
                                                        CMP AX,M(<e>ₖ)
                                                        JNB M'(<s>ᵢ)
                                                        code (<c>ₕ)
                                                        JMP M(<s>ᵢ)
                                        M'(<s>ᵢ) NO-OP
```

This rule translates loops that have a single test in them, $<i>_j < <e>_k$. One new assembly language instruction, NO-OP, appears in the code. It means "no operation" and is included only because a place is needed to put the label M'($<s>_i$).

Let's collect all the translation rules, with their syntax and semantics, in one place:

Table P

Rule Syntax	Rule Semantics
R1. $<i>_j$ ==> w	$M(<i>_j) = w$
where w = any string of alphanumeric symbols that begins with a letter	
R2. $<e>_i$ ==> $<i>$	$M(<e>_i) = M(<i>_j)$
	code $(<e>_i)$ = nothing
R3. $<s>_k$ ==> $<i>_j = <e>_i$	code $(<s>_k)$ = code $(<e>_i)$
	COPY AX,M$(<e>_i)$
	COPY M$(<i>_j)$,AX
R4. $<e>_i$ ==> $(<e>_j + <e>_k)$	$M(<e>_i)$ = createname
	code$(<e>_i)$ = code $(<e>_j)$
	code $(<e>_k)$
	COPY AX,M$(<e>_j)$
	ADD AX,M$(<e>_k)$
	COPY M$(<e>_i)$,AX
R5. $<e>_i$ ==> $(<e>_j * <e>_k)$	$M(<e>_i)$ = createname
	code$(<e>_i)$ = code $(<e>_j)$
	code $(<e>_k)$
	COPY AX,M$(<e>_j)$
	MUL AX,M$(<e>_k)$
	COPY M$(<e>_i)$,AX

R6. $<q>_i$ ==> $<s>_j$;
      $<q>_k$
	code$(<q>_i)$ = code$(<s>_j)$
	          code$(<q>_k)$

R7. $<q>_i$ ==> $<s>_j$;	code$(<q>_i)$ = code$(<s>_j)$

R8. $<c>_i$ ==> {
      $<q>_j$
      }
	code$(<c>_i)$ = code$(<q>_j)$

R9. $<s>_i$ ==> while $(<i>_j < <e>_k)$ $<c>_h$	$M(<s>_i)$ = createname
	$M'(<s>_i)$ = createname
	code$(<s>_i)$ = $M(<s>_i)$ code$(<e>_k)$
	COPYAX,M$(<i>_j)$
	CMP AX,M$(<e>_k)$
	JNB $M'(<s>_i)$
	code$(<c>_h)$
	JMP M$(<s>_i)$
	$M'(<s>_i)$ NO-OP

The use of these rules is illustrated in the translation of a program to compute a factorial. This program computes $1 * 2 * 3 * \cdots * N$ and leaves the result in FACT. Thus, if $N = 5$, it will compute FACT $= 1 * 2 * 3 * 4 * 5 = 120$. The process of translating variable declarations is not considered here, but it is assumed that I, FACT, N, and ONE have been declared as integers, that ONE contains 1, and that N contains the argument for the calculation:

```
{
    I = ONE;
    FACT = ONE;
    while (I < (N + ONE))
    {
        FACT = (FACT * I);
        I = (I + ONE);
    }
}
```

The compilation of this program using rules R1–R9 follows. Some steps are omitted.

Table Q

Derivation	Rule Syntax	Rule Semantics
$\langle c \rangle_0$	$\langle c \rangle_0 \implies \{$ $\quad \langle q \rangle_1$ $\}$	code($\langle c \rangle_0$) = code($\langle q \rangle_1$)
$\{$ $\langle q \rangle_1$ $\}$	$\langle q \rangle_1 =*\Rightarrow \langle s \rangle_2;$ $\quad \langle s \rangle_4;$ $\quad \langle s \rangle_6;$	code ($\langle q \rangle_1$) = code($\langle s \rangle_2$) code($\langle s \rangle_4$) code($\langle s \rangle_6$)
$\{$ $\langle s \rangle_2;$ $\langle s \rangle_4;$ $\langle s \rangle_6;$ $\}$	$\langle s \rangle_2 =*\Rightarrow$ I = ONE	code($\langle s \rangle_2$) = COPY AX,ONE COPY I,AX
$\{$ I = ONE; $\langle s \rangle_4;$ $\langle s \rangle_6;$ $\}$	$\langle s \rangle_4 =*\Rightarrow$ FACT = ONE	code($\langle s \rangle_4$) = COPY AX,ONE COPY FACT,AX

Table Q (continued)

Derivation	Rule Syntax	Rule Semantics

{
I = ONE;
FACT = ONE;
$<s>_6$;
}
	$<s>_6$ =*=> while ($<i>_7$ < $<e>_8$)
	$\qquad\qquad\qquad<c>_9$
		$M(s_6)$ = CN6
		$M'(s_6)$ = CN7
		$code(s_6)$ = CN6 code(e_8)
		$\qquad\qquad$ COPY AX,M($<i>_7$)
		$\qquad\qquad$ CMP AX,M($<e>_8$)
		$\qquad\qquad$ JNB CN7
		$\qquad\qquad$ code($<c>_9$)
		$\qquad\qquad$ JMP CN6
		$\qquad\qquad$ CN7 NO-OP

{
I = ONE;
FACT = ONE;
while ($<i>_7$ < $<e>_8$)
$\qquad<c>_9$;
}
	$<i>_7$ =*=> I	$M(<i>_7)$ = I
		$code(<i>_7)$ = nothing

	$<e>_8$ =*=> (N + ONE)	$M(<e>_8)$ = CN8 code ($<e>_8$) = COPY AX,N $\qquad\qquad$ ADD AX,ONE $\qquad\qquad$ COPY CN8,AX

{
I = ONE;
FACT = ONE;
while (I < (N + ONE))
$\qquad<c>_9$;
}
	$<c>_9$ =*=> {
	$\qquad<s>_{10}$;
	$\qquad<s>_{11}$;
	$\qquad$}
		$code(<c>_9)$ = code($<s>_{10}$)
		$\qquad\qquad$ code($<s>_{11}$)

{
I = ONE;
FACT = ONE;
while (I < (N + ONE))
$\qquad${
$\qquad<s>_{10}$;
$\qquad<s>_{11}$;
$\qquad$}
}
	$<s>_{10}$ =*=> FACT = (FACT * I)	code (s_{10}) = COPY AX,FACT
		$\qquad\qquad$ MUL AX,I
		$\qquad\qquad$ COPY CN9,AX
		$\qquad\qquad$ COPY AX,CN9
		$\qquad\qquad$ COPY FACT,AX

{ I = ONE;	$<s>_{11}$ =*=> I = (I + ONE)	

Table Q (continued)

Derivation	Rule Syntax	Rule Semantics

```
FACT = ONE;                                          code (<s>₁₁) = COPY AX,I
while (I < (N + ONE))                                             ADD AX,ONE
        {                                                        COPY CN10,AX
        FACT = (FACT * I);                                       COPY AX,CN10
        <s>₁₁;                                                   COPY I,AX
        }
}
{
I = ONE;
FACT = ONE;
while (I < (N + ONE))
        {
        FACT = (FACT * I);
        I = (I + ONE);
        }
}
```

Applying the semantics rules, we obtain the final translation:

```
code (<c>₀) =       COPY AX,ONE
                    COPY I,AX
                    COPY AX,ONE
                    COPY FACT,AX
                CN6 COPY AX,N
                    ADD AX,ONE
                    COPY CN8,AX
                    COPY AX,I
                    CMP AX,CN8
                    JNB CN7
                    COPY AX,FACT
                    MUL AX,I
                    COPY CN9,AX
                    COPY AX,CN9
                    COPY FACT,AX
                    COPY AX,I
                    ADD AX,ONE
                    COPY CN10,AX
                    COPY AX,CN10
                    COPY I,AX
                    JMP CN6
                CN7 N0-OP
```

Comparing the source language program with its translation, it is easy to see the tremendous gains in clarity and simplicity that come from using the higher-level language.

Exercises

1. Show how rules R1–R9 can be used to find the translation for the following program.

```
{
    INC = TW;
    J = (J + INC);
}
```

2. Fill in the details for the translation of the factorial program.

3. Show how rules R1–R9 can be used to compute the translation of the following program. Assume that ZERO and ONE are integers that are initialized at 0 and 1, respectively. Assume that N is a non-negative integer and x is an integer; both have been initialized as data items, perhaps from read statements.

```
{
    J = ZERO;
    POWER = ONE;
    while (J < N)
    {
        POWER = (POWER * X);
        J = (J + ONE);
    }
}
```

What does this program compute?

4. Write a Java program that is within the generative scope of rules R1–R9. Use the rules to find its translation.

5. Design an `if-then` construction and create a rule R10 to translate it. Write a program using your `if-then` construction, and show how it can be translated using rules R1–R9 with your new rule R10.

Programming Languages

Once compiler design came to be understood during the 1950s and 1960s, it was relatively easy to invent new higher-level languages and write compilers for them. In the years since, hundreds of computer languages have been developed.

A few well-known computer languages are mentioned briefly here to give a glimpse of the rest of the programming world. Most of the early programming languages were not object-oriented in the manner of Java. This means that they did not have classes or methods or inheritance of the kind we have studied here. Those languages each have looping and branching constructs, data types like integer, double, and String, and a subroutine feature. They did not ordinarily have much more than these basic features. Examples of such languages are FORTRAN, BASIC, PL-I, Algol, Cobol, Pascal, C, and many others. The object-oriented paradigm became popular in the 1980s, and C++ was the first widely used such language. Java is derived largely from C++. Java drops some of the features of C++ while adding the features of security and network compatibility (applets).

But there are also some important languages that differ dramatically in their form from Java and other popular languages. APL is one such language; it features a large number of single symbol operators that are designed to manipulate arrays. As an example, the program to add up the entries in array A and put the result into SUM is as follows:

```
SUM <- +/A
```

Larger programs can be created by assembling a sequence of operators. Here is a program to compute prime numbers:

```
PRIMES N (2=+/[1]0=(ₜN)o.|ₜN)/ₜN
```

The powerful operators of the language enable a programmer to obtain a lot of computation with just a few symbols. The programs, however, are typically somewhat difficult to read.

Another well-known language outside the Java family is LISP, a language designed for symbolic rather than numerical computation. Its constructs are designed to make it easy to build and manipulate complicated structures such as trees. It uses recursion heavily for control, as described at the end of chapter 4. It is sometimes useful for quickly assembling a prototype program in a situation where execution time may not be critical. The column sum program can be written in LISP as follows:

```
f(A) = (cond ((atom A) 0)
             (T (plus (car A) (f (cdr A))))))
```

Here is a paraphrase of this program, which adds up the list A:

$f(A) =$ on the condition that A has length 0, return 0, otherwise, add the first entry of A to
$\quad f(A$ with first entry removed) and return the answer.

Another important language is Prolog, which uses a declarative style rather than an imperative form for programs. Note that all the languages discussed in this book and almost all languages in regular use are imperative in nature. The programs are of the form

Do this.
Do that.
Do something else.
$\vdots$

Thus, the programmer uses the program to tell the machine what to do. Prolog programs are of the form

This is a fact.
That is a fact.
Something else is a fact.
$\vdots$

Here the programmer does not use the program to tell the machine how to do a calculation. The program merely states facts, and the machine automatically finds the facts needed to answer a question.

Here is an example of the use of Prolog. We state four facts regarding height relationships:

```
fact(jill, tallerthan, sally).
fact(sally, tallerthan, renee).
fact(renee, tallerthan, nancy).
fact(nancy, tallerthan, mary).
```

Then we ask questions such as, Who is taller than Mary? Here is how the question is asked:

```
fact(X, tallerthan, mary).
```

The system will respond with X = nancy. Or we could ask, Who is taller than who?

```
fact(X, tallerthan, Y).
```

The machine will respond:

```
X = jill, Y = sally
X = sally, Y = renee
X = renee, Y = nancy
X = nancy, Y = mary
```

Actually, this feature acts exactly like the database program of chapter 4. It even has the shortcoming that the database program had: it does not infer information that was not explicitly given in the facts.

But Prolog allows much more powerful assertions. We can also state generalized facts of the following type:

```
fact(X, tallerthan, Z) :- fact(X, tallerthan, Y), fact(Y, tallerthan,
Z).
```

This should be read as "X is taller than Z if X is taller than Y and Y is taller than Z." Using the previous four facts and this one, let's again ask the question, Who is taller than Mary?

```
fact(X, tallerthan, mary).
```

This time the system will use all the original information plus the generalized fact to infer new facts:

```
X = nancy
X = renee
X = sally
X = jill
```

Thus, the Prolog system uses the total of the facts given to assemble the answer even though the programmer has not explicitly indicated how to do the computation. It has done a kind of inference that our database program could not do, and this property makes it an extremely important kind of language.

A programming language of this type is quite different from Java and other languages in ordinary computations. Here is a Prolog program to add a list of numbers:

```
f(0,[ ]).
f(S,[X|Y]) :- f(Z,Y), S is X + Z.
```

The first fact says, "f associates 0 with the list with no entries." The second fact says, "f associates S with a list beginning with X and ending with a list Y of other entries if f associates Z with Y and S is $X + Z$." In other words, the sum S is found by adding up everything Y except the first entry X in the list $[X|Y]$ to obtain Z. Then X is added to Z to obtain the result S. This is another recursive program that can be understood only if recursion is understood. But we can demonstrate how to use it to add numbers. We type

```
f(X,[7,3,9,2]).
```

and the system will respond X = 21.

Many languages are available to computer scientists, and an experienced programmer must choose which to use in a given application. Some languages resemble Java in form but have special characteristics that may make them better or worse than Java in one situation or another. Some languages are very good for graphics, others may be very fast, others may be compatible with many different kinds of machines, others may be excellent for numerical computation, and so forth.

Exercises

1. Show how the LISP program for addition works. (`atom A`) is true if `A` is a list of length zero. The function (`car A`) returns the first entry of list `A`, and the function (`cdr A`) returns `A` with its first entry removed.

2. Analyze the Prolog program for addition. The notation `L = [X|Y]` means that `L` is a list of objects where `X` is the first entry on the list and `Y` is the list containing the rest of the entries of `L`.

Summary

This chapter has explained a methodology for translating one language to another. Translation rules are described that build a linkage between the two languages. Each rule has two parts—a syntactic part and a semantic part. The syntactic parts of the rules are used to discover the form of a sentence in the source language; one finds a way to generate the source language sentence from an initial symbol such as $<s>_1$, and the rules needed to do the generation identify the parts of the source statement. For example, the discovery that the multiplication rule R5 is needed at a particular point to generate a Java statement is an indication that a multiplication is to be done, and the rule discovers what is to be multiplied.

Once it is known which syntactic rules generate the source statement, the structure of that statement is known, and its translation can be determined. This is done by the semantic portions of the rules that were used in the syntactic analysis. Straightforward substitution and combination of these semantic definitions yields the result, the translation in the object language. All of these ideas were demonstrated in the first several sections by the rules R1–R5, which can be used to translate some Java assignment statements to assembly language. In a later section, rules R6–R9 were introduced, showing how to translate complete code segments, including some loops, into assembly language.

A translation program from a source language such as Java to a lower-level language such as P88 assembly language is called a *compiler*. The compiler is composed of all the translation rules, code to use the rules to do the syntactic and semantic analyses, and many other routines to optimize the code, send messages to the user, and so forth.

Another way to use a computer language on a computer besides compiling it is to use an *interpreter* for it. Interpreters are programs that execute a program without a translation into assembly language. From the user's point of view, they may seem to function in the same way as compilers, but their execution time will be slower. Many times interpreters are able to produce debugging information that will aid the programmer who is developing new code. Their principles of operation are beyond the scope of this book.

Java uses both a compiler to translate the source program to a lower-level language and an interpreter to execute that lower-level language.

   This chapter completes the two chapters of the book that trace the mechanisms of a computer hardware and software system necessary to run a program in a language like Java. The story goes from the program at the highest level to the architecture of the machine at the register level. A review of the chapters is worthwhile to understand the total view. We summarize by once again tracing all processing for a single Java statement:

```
Z = (X + Y)
```

Using the rules R1–R5 of this chapter, this statement is translated or compiled into a lower-level language. To simplify our coverage, we assume the Java is compiled into equivalent assembly language. (In truth, Java is compiled to an intermediate language that is executed on the host machine by an interpreter.)

```
COPY AX,X
ADD AX,Y
COPY CN1,AX
COPY AX,CN1
COPY Z,AX
```

These instructions are then translated in a process called *assembly* into a set of binary codes, which we have written as

```
*COPY AX,X*
*ADD AX,Y*
*COPY CN1,AX*
*COPY AX,CN1*
*COPY Z,AX*
```

but which really look something like this:

```
0010101010011001
0100000101101100
0010011101000111
0010111100110101
0010101000101001
```

These are loaded into the memory of the machine, and when they are used, the instruction pointer, IP, gives their location. Chapter 8 catalogs the events associated with their execution.

10   Virtual Environments for Computing

Use Your Imagination

This book has presented a variety of computing processes, including numerical computation, graphics generation, and data storage and retrieval. Now it is time to create an environment within which we can comfortably do those things. We can create almost any kind of environment that we can think of; almost anything that we can imagine, we can program.

Suppose, for example, that we think of computing as a hallway with a series of rooms that we might enter. Then we can have the computer draw on the screen a hallway and a series of labeled doors. Each door opens the way to a place where we might do a certain kind of computing. Thus, we might have a room for editing, a room for compiling programs, a room where mail is handled, and other rooms for other computing tasks. We will think of computing as just going down the hallway and entering the place where we can do the current job (figure 10.1).

After we enter the room we want, we find a series of images related to that job. Thus, if we go into the room for editing, we find objects and things to do related to editing, and we will use them for our job (figure 10.2). If we decided to compile a program, that room would have in it whatever objects we might need for compiling. What would you suggest for that room?

On the other hand, we could decide to think of computing in another way and build some other model. For example, we could think of the systems inside the machine as tools and of computing as the process of grabbing tools and applying them to the job. You use an editor to create a program. Then you grab a compiler to translate the program and an execution system to run the program. Maybe there is a debugging tool to help find the errors and a mail tool to send the final program to the course instructor.

As a third paradigm for computing, maybe we are uncomfortable with the machine, and we want it to be our friend. It could smile at us in a friendly way and greet us with a warm hello. We could smile back and respond with spoken requests.

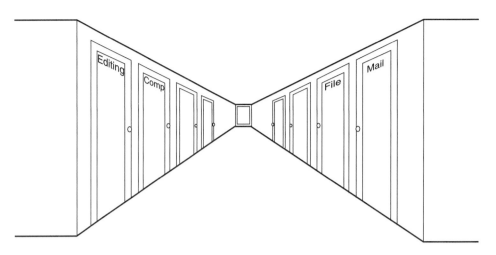

Figure 10.1

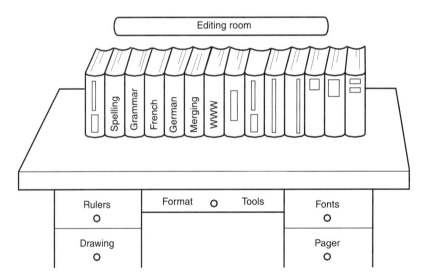

Figure 10.2

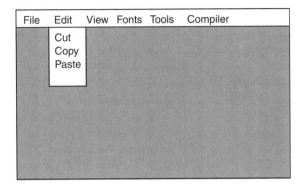

Figure 10.3

Or maybe we think of computing as a menu of choices and just want to have an easy way to select the right item from the menu (figure 10.3). This is a view of computing presented by many current-day computing systems.

Whatever the facade we want for our computing environment, we can program the machine to look that way. We learned in earlier chapters how to get the machine to draw a picture. We can use those methods to draw any picture on the screen and create our desired environment for computing. If the machine has audio capabilities, we can program it to provide us with an audio environment, and if it controls any other aspects of our surroundings, we can program it to enhance the environment with those. If we have a wearable three-dimensional head display, we can program that to make us feel like we are actually inside of some kind of world that has been coded into the computer.

When a computer is programmed using visual, audio, and possibly other media to create the impression of a specific environment, that environment is called a *virtual environment*. One of the great ideas of computer science is that we can use computers to create such environments. We may create a specific environment just to make ourselves more comfortable, to improve our efficiency, or to give ourselves the chance to experience something that we could not easily experience otherwise.

This chapter is a study of *operating systems*. They are the programs that deliver the virtual environments that we have been considering. If you have been writing the programs discussed in earlier chapters, you are already familiar with some operating system. It might be Windows, Macintosh, UNIX, or some other one. So you have done already many of the things we discuss in this chapter, such as create a program with an editor, compile it, run it, use mail, store files, and so forth.

The purpose of this chapter is to teach you that an operating system is just another program, and of course you already know a great deal about such programs. In fact, you know so much that you could write many of the parts of an operating system without much help. For example, you have written the `actionPerformed` command-control loops that receive commands from a user and execute them, and this is one of the main functions of an operating system. In the following sections, we examine how some of the standard tasks are done with a well-known operating system. We look at both the user's point of view and the mechanisms inside the system.

Exercise

1. Design an interface for computing that you would like to have for your own machine and that does not resemble interfaces that you have seen before.

Using an Operating System

We start where we were at the end of chapter 8, with a central processor, its registers (IP, IR, CF, AX), and the memory. We also assume there are additional hardware devices, such as a disk system for storing files, a keyboard and display, a printer, and so forth. Let's examine how to create and run a Java program and think about the facilities that are needed to make this possible.

First we want to gain access to the machine; we want to *log in*. We use the UNIX operating system for our examples. You should repeat these steps using the operating system of your choice. The first message we receive is

```
login:
```

and we have a registered identifier to tell who we are. For example, one author of this book would type awb.

```
login: awb
```

Then we see the request

```
password:
```

and can type in our personal secret password. (This should be a more or less random sequence of characters with a few odd choices such as #, }, or +. A good password might be t$}7wg2, which would be hard for another person or a password-breaking program to guess (see chapter 11 on security).

What kind of program is needed to carry out this interaction? It must have a database of users and their passwords. It must be able to display the two requests and check the database. This subprogram is part of the operating system, and it runs on the architecture we described previously.

The designers of UNIX decided the best facade to present to the user would be a simple prompt such as %, which can be answered by the user with very brief typed commands. This system was created in the early days of computing when the standard terminal was little more than a typewriter.

If we wish to create a Java program, we can invoke an editor with a short command. Let's use the famous editor created at MIT, called emacs. We follow this command with the name we will attach to our new Java program:

```
% emacs GDemo.java
```

The operating system will then activate the program we request, and emacs will show the blank page for editing. It is next our job to use emacs to create (or edit) our program:

```
import java.awt.*;
public class GDemo extends java.applet.Applet
.
.
.
```

After completing this edit, we can exit emacs and check to see whether the program file exists in our directory. So we type ls to list all the files in our current directory, including, we hope, the one we just created:

```
% ls
File1
File2
File3
GDemo.java
.
.
.
```

Aha! There it is. The edit was sucessfully stored. But will it compile correctly? Let's try by calling the Java compiler javac:

```
% javac GDemo.java
```

The compiler returns some error messages, so we return to the editor (% emacs GDemo. java) and revise our code. After a few tries we obtain a successful compilation and can see the compiled object (GDemo.class) code appear in the directory:

```
% ls
File1
File2
```

```
File3
GDemo.class
GDemo.java
  .
  .
  .
```

Now let's try the program out. We need an HTML page from which to call the program. Using the editor, we create that as well:

```
<HTML>
<HEAD>
<TITLE> Graphics Demonstration <\TITLE>
<\HEAD>
<BODY>
<P> This tests the program GDemo.java <\P>
<APPLET code = "GDemo.class"> <\APPLET>
<\BODY>
<\HTML>
```

Finally, we try our program out by calling a browser and linking to the new HTML file.

Now let's look at our computing system. We have the hardware described previously and the security software that enables us to log in. We also have a command interpreter that receives the commands `emacs`, `ls`, `javac`, and others, and calls in the requested software. The command interpreter must know where the called programs are and must activate them to get them to do the requested jobs. The operating system is the software that receives our commands and brings in the software to get our jobs done.

Exercise

1. Show how to do all of the preceding steps on the operating system of your choice.

Hardware Pragmatics

We wish to understand as well as possible the operating system that can deliver all the described behaviors and more to the user. The task of the operating system is to provide the bridge between the hardware and the higher-level behaviors we want. This section reviews basic hardware facts, some of which you may have gathered from earlier chapters or from other experiences. Later sections then describe the operating system itself.

The two main parts of the computer are the central processing unit (CPU) and the memory. The CPU has the job of executing instructions that do such things as bring in data from the memory, manipulate them, and store them back into the memory. There are usually a hundred or more instructions for a CPU, and they typically are designed to process a fixed amount of data in each operation. That is, there will be some number N, and each CPU instruction will copy or manipulate N bits of data. For many early microprocessors, N was 8 or 16, but more recently most have N of 32 or 64. Many large mainframe machines process 32 or 64 bits per operation, but a variety of other sizes have been built.

Memory is usually constructed with very large numbers of tiny electric circuits, each of which can hold a 0 or a 1. A single binary digit of information (a 0 or a 1) is called a *bit*, and the usual module of memory is the *byte*, which ordinarily contains eight bits. This is a convenient size because most coding schemes allocate one byte per character for text processing. Thus a one-million-byte memory can hold one million characters, a *megabyte* of characters. Typical machines have a few megabytes up to a few hundred megabytes. For example, a machine with 64 million bytes of memory is said to have 64 megabytes. Memory is often called *random access memory* (RAM).

Besides the main memory, machines often have a smaller auxiliary memory called a *cache*. The cache is designed to deliver information at extremely fast rates to the CPU so that it does not have to wait for the next data or instruction after a given one is executed. Thus, a computation might involve loading a lot of data into the main memory, which has a moderate access rate, and then moving small blocks of data into the cache for very fast access during the calculation. Typical sizes for cache memories are a fraction of a megabyte. In some machines, there can be several levels of cache, with the fastest access rates being closest to the CPU.

When a program or a set of data is not being used, it is typically stored on a *disk*. This is called *secondary storage*. These disks are coated with a ferrous material and hold information using magnetism, as does an ordinary tape recorder. A *disk drive* spins the disk and either reads information from or stores information on the disk surfaces. A *floppy disk* is a disk made of thin plastic material that can be carried around with its stored information and inserted into a machine's floppy disk drive if the information—programs or data—is needed. A variation on the magnetic disk is the *CD-ROM*, a compact disk read only memory, which can hold large amounts of data and is often used to hold large databases or programs. A *hard disk* is a high-precision disk permanently mounted in a closed case. A floppy disk can store possibly a few hundred thousand (a few hundred K) bytes up to many megabytes of data. Typical CD-ROM disks hold 660 megabytes. Hard disks can store from a few dozen megabytes to many thousands of megabytes. (One thousand megabytes is called a *gigabyte*.)

The information on a disk is organized into packages called *files*. A file contains a program, a set of data, or both and is moved around the computer as a unit in the same way that an envelope of pages might be handed around an office. A file can be stored on a disk, brought into computer memory, modified in a machine, stored back onto the disk, printed, or transmitted on a network. A file will always have a name so that it can be referred to in commands.

An *input-output device* is a special-purpose hardware system to deliver or receive information for the computer. An example of such a device is a printer, which will have machinery to manipulate paper and place figures or text on the pages. Most printers actually have their own imbedded computers: a memory to store the information that is to be printed and a central processor to control the printer functions—receive the characters and graphics from an external source, manipulate the hardware to print them out, and send messages to the external source giving the status of the job. Other examples of input-output devices are the keyboard and the video monitor. There are also scanners that lift information from a page and code it into electronic form for computer manipulation, sound input-output devices, robotic arms, and wearable head displays.

Exercise

1. Find the nominal hardware specifications for your machine. What is the number of bits processed by a machine instruction? How many machine instructions are there, and what is their speed? What is the size of the memory and disk system? Is there a cache memory on your machine? How many bytes fit on a floppy disk on your system?

The Operating System

The *operating system* is a computer program that provides a virtual environment and that executes the actions the user requests. On the one hand, it gives the user convenient visual and other media images with comfortable means for interaction. On the other, it carries out immensely complicated and detailed actions inside of the machine to accomplish requested tasks. This section describes many of the major functions of the operating system.

In order to appreciate the operating system, it is useful to consider what a computer would look like without it. You would have a memory with no entries in it, empty computer registers, empty disk files, a display with no information, and input-output devices that do not work. All these devices would be dead because they are all driven by programs. They only come to life when programs are there to direct them. Furthermore, you would have no way to enter your programs or any other programs because even the process of reading a program requires software, the input-output drivers that operate the input-output devices. Figure 10.4a gives a symbolic representation of the computer hardware in its naked and useless state.

The operating system is a large program with subroutines to operate and manage all the devices of the hardware system. Each device responds to an array of commands that control its operation and special formatting rules for transmitting information to and from its local memory. Thus, a printer might require a special activation code to prepare

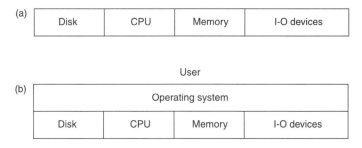

Figure 10.4

to print, and it might return a status code to indicate its readiness to proceed. It might receive a sequence of, say, 1,024 printable characters to begin its job and then send a message when it has printed them and is ready for more. The operating system enables the Java programmer or other user to print documents without knowing any of these details. It simply receives the request to print and then executes all the needed actions to complete the job. The other devices all have their own characteristics, which one can learn from their associated manuals, and they must be programmed individually to function properly.

Symbolically, we represent the operating system, which contains all these programs and a lot of other systems described later, as a layer of software that separates the user from the hardware (figure 10.4b). When we want to use any of these devices, we issue commands to the operating system, and it delivers the proper instruction sequences to the devices to get the job done.

The operating system is read into the computer main memory from the disk or another external source by a special hard-wired program in the machine called the *bootstrap* code. This is the first and essential operation needed to bring any computer to life—the loading of the operating system. (It is called *booting the system*.)

Once the operating system is loaded, it provides four major kinds of services to the user.

Providing Access to Computing Functions

The most important task of the operating system is to provide the user with access to computing functions. Some of the functions of the operating system can be better understood if you consider the example of an editor. To the user, it is simply an object on the screen to be selected and used. To the operating system, the editor is a piece of code that exists on a storage device with an address, a size, and possibly many special characteristics such as communications requirements with other programs or internal parameters to be set. When the user calls for the activation of the editor, the operating system must find that code and locate a place in the memory to put it. Then it must move that code into memory and set up communication between it and the user so that an edit can take place.

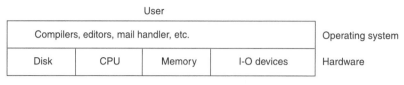

Figure 10.5

Figure 10.6

The operating system has access to many special programs like the editor to enable it to do its jobs. These may include compilers for various languages, editors, a mail system, and many other subsystems (figure 10.5).

Providing a File System

A second major function of the operating system is to provide a *file system* (figure 10.6). This is a program that organizes and manages files. When any program creates a file, it will be able to call on the file system to store it. If any program later needs that file, it will be able to request the file system to retrieve it. The file system can also be asked to move, rename, or delete files, or to provide a listing of them. An example file system is described in a later section.

Providing a Secure Computing Environment

A third major function of the operating system is to provide security of many kinds. Three primary kinds of security are important: (1) *Computing resources protection.* The system can store user identifiers and passwords and prevent unauthorized persons from obtaining any service from the machine. (2) *Internal file and function protection.* Once a user is on the machine, it can prohibit that person from accessing data that he or she is not allowed to see or from using unauthorized functions. The system must also prevent the user from either purposely or accidentally interfering with the other running programs. As an illustration, you would not want the display routines on your computer to stop functioning because you made an error in your Java code. The storage areas, where code and data exist that are not meant to be under user control, need to be protected. (3) *Protection from*

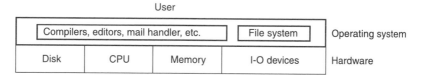

Figure 10.7

hardware failure. Another kind of security relates to the safety of your programs and data in case of a failure of the machine. Here it is necessary to store the contents of the files that are in the machine on a permanent medium such as a tape or floppy disk. Usually such backups are performed manually by the operators of the computer using file-handling facilities provided by the operating system. In figure 10.7, the thick lines dividing the major parts represent security. That is, no subsystem or person is allowed to damage any other entity in the process of the computation. All subparts should have secure boundaries.

Providing for Multiprogramming

The final major function of the operating system that is discussed here is the management of many tasks simultaneously. Users may not directly need or want all the computing capabilities that the machine's fetch-execute cycle can offer. While our program is not running, the machine will still be grabbing instructions from memory and executing them. Perhaps we should organize things so that another user can be running a program while we look at a printout or decide what to do next.

We will define a *process* to be our program or any program on the machine in some state of execution. Our process may be running and computing answers for us; it may have stopped to wait for us to type in the next item of data; or it may have been temporarily halted by the operating system while some other job is being done. Whatever its state, our program will have many needs, and the operating system has the job of providing them. First, our program will need a place to reside in memory, and the operating system will find such a place that is not currently being used. Next, if the program needs additional memory for execution, the operating system will find that. If the program needs to access files on the disk system, either for reading or writing, the operating system will make the access available. The program might also need to send items to the printer, receive data from some outside device, or otherwise use outside equipment. In all these cases, the program will transmit requests to the operating system, which will carry out the needed protocols to get the job done.

A process continues to execute until an *interrupt* occurs. An interrupt is a halting of the current computation to allow for other processing, and it can come from various sources. The operating system can initiate an interrupt to allow some other user to have some computation time. An external device, such as a printer, which has information-processing needs, can initiate an interrupt. For example, the printer may have completed output of the lines it was given and may be calling for the next segment of data. The computer hardware may also initiate an interrupt because an error condition such as a register overflow has occurred. A variety of interrupt types can occur in most machines, and an algorithm selects which ones to honor and in what priority.

When the system interrupts a process, it must store all information related to its state of computation so that the process can be continued later without error. It must store the state of the program data, a note of which program instruction is to be executed next, and the contents of certain machine registers. Later the system will be able to raise this process to high priority, restore register contents, and continue the computation at the correct next instruction.

The idea of multiprogramming is that the operating system has the ability to keep track of many processes simultaneously. Then it sequentially services each process, giving it some fetch-execute cycles and other support that it may need. If the machine is very fast, as most modern machines are, the operating system may be able to keep many processes running without the individual users ever realizing that they do not have complete control of the machine. In fact, the picture should be as follows: The machine may have many processes in some state of execution at one time. Each of these will have its own segment of memory and its own current status and needs. One process may be in midcalculation and waiting to get a chance to use some more cycles; another may have come to a stopping point until it gets its next data item from its user; another may have just sent a block of characters to the printer and will send more when the printer is ready; another may have finished its computation and will be removed from memory when the operating system gets back to it. In the meantime, the operating system has a priority schedule that tells it what to do. It will give one program a *time slice* of several milliseconds, then another, and another. At each point, it will check the status of that particular program and supply it with its momentary needs before going on to the next.

In summary, the operating system can be thought of as the keeper of the resources of the computing environment and the benevolent provider for the processes as they have needs. It tirelessly selects process after process and executes each one for a short time before moving on to the next. As it does its work, new processes come into existence and old ones occasionally disappear. But the operating system's only job is to keep grabbing processes and executing them. Figure 10.8 reminds us that the operating system can keep track of many users or processes simultaneously.

Exercises

1. Log in to the machine on which you have been doing your programming, and run through a typical programming session. Create a program, store it, compile and run it, print it out. But as you do all these things, write down every command you give to the operating system and describe with the command all the functions the operating system

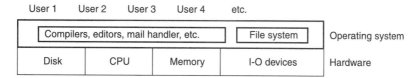

Figure 10.8

is delivering to you and all the devices it is using. Describe all the processes that are running besides the ones that you have coded with your own program.

2. List all the operating commands that you know and what their functions are.

3. Describe the file system on your computer. What are the commands that you need to store, print, delete, and otherwise access those files?

Files

Processes, have the task of manipulating information, and this information is usually organized as files. A file may be stored on the disk system, brought into memory, modified in a computation, sent abroad on a network, or read or printed by an input-output device. A file may contain data, a program, or both.

Files are usually accessed through a directory. In UNIX, one would enter the directory named `awb` from the directory above it with the change-directory command:

```
% cd awb
```

Then one would list the files in the directory with the command `ls` (figure 10.9):

```
% ls
javatest
letdr
.
.
.
```

File systems commonly allow for the creation of directories within directories. As figure 10.10 shows, the whole file system emanates from a single root directory. Each directory, represented as a boldface rectangle, lists a set of directories or files that can be found immediately below it in the hierarchy. The terminations of the descending branches come when files are reached. One common naming system simply traces the branches down the tree. Thus the full name of the sample Java program shown would be `/compsci/awb/`

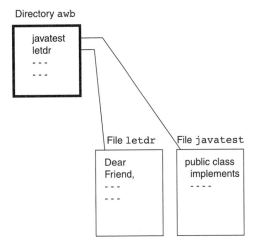

Directory awb

File `letdr` File `javatest`

Figure 10.9

`javatest`. This is known as the *path name*; you can find the path name of any file using the command `pwd`. If you want to explore such a tree, you can sequentially use the commands `cd` and `ls` to see what is there. Suppose you are in the root directory and type `ls`. You will obtain

```
% ls
compsci
english
   .
   .
   .
```

You can see *all* the lower directories by using a modification of `ls`:

```
% ls -R
compsci english ...
compsci:
awb dr ...

compsci/awb:
course11 ToJ javatest letdr

compsci/awb/course11:
schedule students syllabus ...
```

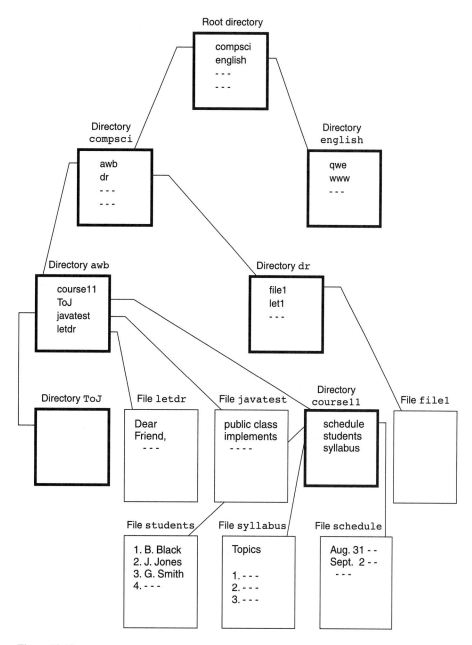

Figure 10.10

```
compsci/awb/ToJ:

compsci/dr:
file1 let1 ...

english:
qwe www ...
```

Or you can go to one of these subdirectories, one at a time, with the command `cd` and use `ls` to see its contents:

```
% cd compsci
% ls
awb
dr
.
.
.
```

The file system usually includes a security mechanism that allows or prohibits access to the various directories and files. For example, a directory and all its subdirectories and files might be closed to all users except the owner. Or certain directories and their associated files might be available to be read by anyone, but security locks could prevent their modification by anyone. Thus, an academic department might be glad to allow anyone to read the schedule of courses for the coming semester but would object to having people change that schedule. However, the computer administrative personnel usually have *superuser* status that enables them to access all files in the system to any extent that they wish. This is usually necessary in order for them to do maintenance and repair on the system.

Once the tree of directories and files has been created, it can be used in a variety of ways. For example, when a floppy disk is loaded into a drive, the system can grow a new subtree that holds the directories and files from the disk. All file manipulation operations can be the same whether or not the files exist on the floppy disk. As another example, sometimes input-output devices are made to look like files so that they can be accessed using the same system calls that are used for manipulating files. Thus, reading from an input device might be represented internally as if that device were simply a file to be read like any other file.

Exercises

1. Assuming the name of the Java program in file system shown in figure 10.10 is /compsci/awb/javatest, give the names of all of the other files in that tree.

2. Show how to create a duplicate of the directory-file tree shown in figure 10.10 on your own computer system using commands available on your operating system.

*Contention for Memory and Paging

The advent of multiprogramming puts new demands on the computer memory. If only a single program is to run on the machine and there is enough memory to run that program, historically we have felt certain that we could run that program on that machine. However, when there are many programs in contention to run on the machine, suddenly memory space seems scarce. We must look carefully at how we are using that space.

As an example, consider a program A which, for our purposes, will be divided into six parts, A1, A2, ..., A6. We call these six parts *pages*, and think about that program as it runs and its use of the memory. (These pages are convenient partitions for the purposes of machine internal functioning and do not correspond to the ordinary pages of computer printouts.) First, say, page A1 runs for a while, then page A2, and so forth. Possibly at some point, page A1 will run again or A2 will run again, and these repetitions could recur many times. The point is that when A1 is running, the memory that holds A2 and beyond is being wasted. It is holding unused and unneeded code. When another section is running, the memory holding A1 is being wasted. It is holding unused code.

A good solution to this problem is to create a partitioning scheme that separates every program into pages and that keeps only a few pages of each running program in memory at a time. The operating system then can run one program (process) for a short time, then another, then another, and so forth, giving each its appropriate time slice. The currently active pages of each program can all be resident in the memory simultaneously, and the inactive pages can be kept on the disk ready to be brought in as needed. In figure 10.11, three running programs, A, B, and C, are resident on the disk, and the active pages from each are loaded into memory. The operating system can run the active pages of the three programs, first one, then the other, and bring in new pages for each program as needed. The cache is also shown, to remind you that it is there. It is shown holding a part of C6, which is currently being executed.

The act of moving programs or pages in and out of memory is called *swapping*. Sometimes a machine gets caught in a very wasteful mode where it spends too much of its time swapping. This is called *thrashing*, and it occurs when the method for selecting which pages to bring into memory is always unlucky and the system at almost every step needs to bring in yet another page.

An important by-product of this paging and swapping scheme is that the individual programs no longer need to be small enough to fit into memory. You could have a 30-megabyte program that runs on a machine with a 10-megabyte memory. We say the machine has a large *virtual memory*; it appears to have a large memory even though its memory may actually be small.

Disk

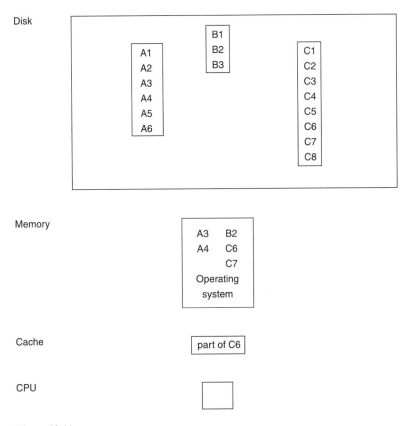

Memory

Cache

CPU

Figure 10.11

Exercises

1. Consider the following Java code. Suppose that it is to be divided into five roughly equal pages and that the computer memory is so small that only one page will fit at a time. Show how to divide it, and describe how much swapping will be done in the process of its execution. Assume that the routines sub1, sub2, and sub3 are defined elsewhere. Repeat the exercise, dividing the code into four roughly equal pages. Repeat again, dividing the code into three and two roughly equal pages.

```
{
    int i,N;
    N = 1000000;
    i = 0;
```

```
    while (i < N)
    {
        sub1;
        i = i + 1;
    }
    i = 0;
    while (i < N)
    {
        sub2;
        i = i + 1;
    }
    i = 0;
    while (i < N)
    {
        sub3;
        i = i + 1;
    }
}
```

2. In figure 10.11, assume that programs A, B, and C are to be run simultaneously. Assume that A is linear, executing A1 through A6 in a sequence and then halting; however, we do not know how long A will take. Assume that B executes similarly. Assume that C executes C1 through C3 once, then a loop consisting of C4 through C6 with one million repetitions, then the linear sequence C7 to C8 once. How should the pages be loaded into memory in order to minimize swapping, assuming that the memory will hold no more than six pages at one time.

Summary

The facade that the machine presents to the user is completely programmable. Therefore, the designer of a system can decide what image he wants the user to have when the system is used and write the code to make it happen. The designer thus creates a virtual environment for the user. The purposes of the virtual environment are to enable the user to function more efficiently and comfortably.

The operating system is the program that presents the user with the facade and that translates his or her commands into low-level instruction sequences that can be carried out by the hardware. The primary concepts related to operating systems are the idea of the process and the idea of the file system. Processes are the programs in active execution at any given time; the operating system's central loop simply keeps grabbing processes and executing them according to some priority schedule. The file system maintains the files stored on the machine and makes them available to the operating system for its many tasks.

The study of hardware and software involves an examination of a series of levels of abstraction. The place where the actual computations occur is in the electric circuits, where voltages and currents tell the story of what is happening. But when we discuss computation at the register level, we seldom mention the electricity; we usually talk about a representation of the register contents such as its binary form:

```
1100101001000011
```

At a higher level of abstraction, we might discuss a computation at the assembly language level, in which case the same register contents might appear as

```
ADD AX,X
```

The next level of abstraction is the level of a programming language, which is Java in this book. In Java, one might write

```
Z = (X + Y);
```

At the level of the operating system, the entities being manipulated are programs and files. Here one might type something like

```
emacs GDemo.java
```

In order to understand computer science, it is necessary to be able to deal with all these levels of abstraction.

Another view of the abstraction hierarchy is as a set of *virtual machines*. A virtual entity in computer science is an entity that seems to exist because of the view presented by the machine but that does not exist in reality. For example, when one programs in Java, the machine looks like a Java machine. It seems to understand Java statements and respond as if that were its native language. When one is using another language, say assembly language, Prolog, or C++, the machine appears to become, respectively, an assembly language, Prolog, or C++ machine. All these examples are cases of virtual machines created by the authors of the language-processing facilities for the convenience and efficiency of users.

11   Security, Privacy, and Wishful Thinking

What's Really Going on Here?

Suppose you are away from your room and you want to check your e-mail. You go to one of the machines that have been thoughtfully placed in public areas to allow you to do that. Everything looks normal. The computer asks you to identify yourself and then to enter your password. The layout of the instructions and everything about the process seem just as usual. Then the computer responds, "Password incorrect," as it usually does when you make an error in entering your password. So you type your password again, and everything seems okay. You read your e-mail, and your day is off to a good start.

Or, *is* everything okay? Let's look at the following scenario. The previous user of the machine you are using (let's call him Pat) ran a carefully crafted program that perfectly mimics the standard log-in process. When you thought you were logging in, you were actually dealing with Pat's program, and when you typed your password Pat's program read it and stored it in a file. Then his program printed a message, again imitating the official program, stating that your password was incorrect. Then his program exited, allowing the normal system log-in program to take over. The second time you tried it, you were dealing with the real system, and you successfully logged in and read your e-mail. Meanwhile, Pat has your password.

So, what just happened? Did you just mistype your password, or did Pat get your password? You may never know unless he uses it in an overt way. Short of having a video camera aimed at your hands, so you can replay your actions, it is very difficult to be sure that you, or even a sticky key, weren't responsible for the glitch. An experienced computer user who is paranoid about security would immediately change his or her password. And what about that security camera in the computer room? Was it aimed at your hands so someone could record and recover your password from your hand motions? Are we getting a little paranoid here?

Paranoia

We are long past the era of "Gentlemen don't read other people's mail." On the Internet or in any computer environment set up for communication, one must assume that there are risks to security and risks to confidentiality. We include under security challenges any malicious threats to proper and efficient operation. A breach of confidentiality means that someone else has been able to copy your data without your authorization. Often one is not aware of this breach.

Crimes of this type are far from new, but they are now much easier to perpetrate anonymously, leaving little or no evidence behind. This makes computer crimes especially difficult to detect or prosecute. Unfortunately, there are also many, often young, computer users who see perpetrating this kind of crime, and getting away with it, as a challenge to their skill and intelligence. They will climb to the peak "because it is there." Some of them will do no more than leave a "Kilroy was here" kind of message. Others will be more malicious and try in some way to damage your system. Of course, the classical motivation for crime, financial gain, is also a big factor.

Authentication

The process of having a computer program or system verify the identity of the person using the program is called *authentication*. You are probably already logging into one or more computer systems, and on these systems you are asked to supply a password. The system assumes that if you can supply the correct password, you must be the person authorized to use that computer account. This is the most common form of authentication and, as such, is in most cases the first line of defense against a computer account's being compromised. The stakes have gotten fairly high because even the most minimal computer user is these days using e-mail and the World Wide Web. Most people would prefer that others not be able to access their e-mail.

A password is just a word or string of characters that is ideally known only to the legitimate user of the account. It should not be easy for others to guess, and it should not be written down anywhere where it could get into the wrong hands. (A close analogy is the combination to a safe at home or in the office.) At first sight, that would seem to be reasonable and sufficient to ensure the account's safety. But in an even slightly hostile environment one needs to see if one is being watched when typing in the password (or opening the safe). Some people are pretty good at watching hand movements to see what is being typed. If a compromise is suspected, the password needs to be changed.

Good Passwords and Cracking

A Brief(case) Example

What prevents the person trying to get your password, called a cracker (probably from safe-cracking), from just trying all the possible passwords? This is called a brute force attack. For the simple kind of combination lock found on many briefcases, only three digits are needed, each in the range of 0–9. The cracker could simply try all possible combinations. In this case, the number of possibilities is the product of the possible number of entries for each digit, or $10 * 10 * 10$. That is, if the cracker tries all 1,000 possible numbers, he is guaranteed success. Since it is a matter of luck as well—he could succeed on the first try, or not until the last try—on average the cracker would succeed after 500 tries.

Since success is guaranteed, does that mean that a three-digit combination lock is worthless as far as security goes? Not necessarily. It takes time for each trial. If we assume we can try a new number every 2 seconds, then on average we will succeed after 1,000 seconds, or about 17 minutes. That may be long enough to deter most thieves (and there's an alternative: a sharp knife that cuts through the cover of the briefcase).

What have we learned from this briefcase example? Four major factors are involved in the security afforded by the lock:

1. The number of digits involved in the combination. With three digits, we multiplied together three numbers to get all the possible codes. A four-digit combination lock would be much safer because then there would be $10 * 10 * 10 * 10$, or 10,000, possibilities and it would take almost three hours to try all combinations.
2. The number of possibilities for each position. Using only digits 0–9, we have ten possibilities at each position. If we had a combination lock that used 26 letters at each position, then even a three-position system would allow $26 * 26 * 26 = 17,576$ possibilities. With the previous assumptions, a break-in would take an average of five hours instead of 17 minutes.
3. How long it takes for each trial. We assumed 2 seconds per new number try. If it took 20 seconds for each try, that would considerably change the picture. A system that would make us wait, say, one minute after three failed attempts in a row would also enhance the security of the system.
4. The fourth factor is less straightforward: that is, what are the alternatives? A briefcase could be broken or cut open. For some kinds of crime, that's what will probably happen. But for more subtle attacks, where the attacker does not want the victim to know that the information was compromised, that may not be an option.

Generally, the complexity of the security system must have a reasonable relation to the value of what is being protected and to the brute force alternatives. Even a high-security safe will "fail" if an attacker puts a gun to the victim's head and says, "Open it, or else!"

Password System for a Computer

If we translate our briefcase example to the computer, we find that our basic four points still hold but that we need to update the practical details.

One of the most important changes is that the time it might take the computer to try out each combination is considerably smaller. If we had a computer system that could try out a different combination every millionth of a second, then even a six-position system would be compromised in less than a second. However, if the system made us wait one minute after three incorrect attempts in a row, security would be considerably enhanced. Unfortunately, in many cases, the cracker can get a copy of whatever is needed to try the various combinations on her own system. She can then try combinations as fast as her computer resources will allow.

Obviously, on a computer system, we need to increase the number of positions in the password and the number of values each position can have. Most systems allow a password to contain not just numbers but also letters of the alphabet and punctuation marks. Most keyboards will support 96 different characters, including the space. To keep the arithmetic simple, we round that to 100. That means a six-position password will have $100 * 100 * 100 * 100 * 100 * 100$, or 10^{12}, possible combinations, and a computer-cracking program would have to try all of these. If it could try 1 million (10^6) combinations per second, it would still take 1 million seconds, or about 17,000 minutes, or about 275 hours, or a little more than 10 days. That's not the best security, but it is a deterrent. Note that by adding a seventh position to the password, we would get 1,000 days, or about 3 years; an eighth position would give us 300 years. Now that's security. However, a computer that is 100 times faster brings that back down to 3 years. Another approach is to use 100 different computers, each trying one 1 million combinations per second, also yielding 3 years. This is still a deterrent but not wonderful security.

Dictionary Attacks

The lesson from the previous analysis is that you might have pretty good security if you used an eight-position password and you allowed letters, digits, and punctuation marks in each position.

Unfortunately, there's another risk. Instead of using a brute force attack, trying all possible combinations, the cracker is likely to try something much more selective first. If the cracker is in possession of any personal data about you—telephone numbers, birth dates, names of family members—he will try those first. And he will try them backwards as well as forwards. Suddenly the multiyear cracking task is over in a millisecond.

If that doesn't work, or if the cracker doesn't know you or anything about you, he will try various dictionaries. Any English or foreign-language word makes the cracker's task easier. He will also have lists of names of people, places, companies, and organizations. Lists of almost anything will help the cracker do much better than a brute force attack. With a fast computer, a run through several dictionaries should take only a few minutes.

A Good Password

A good password is one that will survive the dictionary attack. In other words, it should not be a word or name in any language. Unless you are a language expert, you might find that a daunting task. However, if you include a sprinkling of punctuation marks in your password, you are probably on the right track. Just remember that any "system" you may come up with may also be known to the cracker.

Exercises

1. Using the simple briefcase combination lock as a model, calculate the number of combinations possible if the lock were reduced to two positions with ten numbers each. How many combinations are possible for a six-position lock of this type?

2. Explain why the following are not good choices for passwords:

   ```
   influenza     Versailles     Gesundheit     061282
   ```

Encryption

In addition to (or in place of) a good password protection system, there is another line of defense for preserving confidentiality. Even if it does nothing for security, encryption allows us to transform useful information into a form that an outsider would find incomprehensible. *Encryption* is the systematic transformation of a message (or any information) into a form that obscures its original meaning. Since this is key to many systems of providing computer security and privacy, we explore this topic in some detail. (Encryption can play a very important role in authentication and password protection.)

Cryptoquote™

Many daily newspapers carry a wise quotation or other message that has been encrypted. As a form of entertainment, the reader is expected to decipher (or decrypt) the message. What is employed here is a mono-alphabetic substitution cipher. Each letter of the alphabet has been replaced by another letter. For example, if we substituted *X* for *a*, *R* for *b*, *A* for *c*, *Y* for *d*, *F* for *e*, *I* for *f*, and so forth, for the whole alphabet, then the word *face* would appear encrypted as IXAF. This brief example suggests that we could obtain rather good privacy in this manner. There is no way, short of knowing the letter substitutions used, to guess that IXAF means *face*. On the other hand, the newspaper wouldn't be providing much entertainment if no one could solve these Cryptoquotes. Several things make most of them easy to break. For any but the shortest text, letter frequency gives away the solution. When dealing with English messages, whatever letter appears most frequently is likely to be the letter *e*; the next most frequent is often the letter *t* or *a*. In other words, the distinctive letter frequency usually yields valuable information. After fixing two or three letters, it is usually easy to guess additional letters, and very soon you've solved the cipher. (Additional clues are provided if the spacing and punctuation have been preserved in the encrypted version. Single-letter code must be either an *a* or an *i*. Single letters after an apostrophe are typically *s* or *t*.) For many centuries, this approach and its variations were the main means of preserving the privacy of diplomatic, military, and commercial messages that were deemed sensitive.

In summary, for lightweight encryption, we pick a substitution alphabet for the original message and make sure that all people who are allowed to read the message have a copy of the substitution alphabet. Often the substitution alphabet is summarized as a key word or phrase. For the preceding example, the substitution alphabet is

XRAYFILMSBCDEGHJKNOPQTUVWZ

and the key is

XRAYFILMS

This does result in *Z* representing *z*, but that does not hurt the encryption very much.

Here is another encrypted English message. See if you can solve it.

IFOJ LKFJN DCE LNPNC XNDJL DVF FOJ
IDMRNJL UJFOVRM IFJMR FC MRSL
KFCMSCNCM, D CNQ CDMSFC, KFCKNSPNE
SC BSUNJMX, DCE ENESKDMNE MF MRN
GJFGFLSMSFC MRDM DBB ANC DJN KJNDMNE
NHODB. —D BSCKFBC

The letter frequencies in the encrypted message are

A	1	H	1	O	4	V	2
B	6	I	3	P	2	W	0
C	16	J	11	Q	1	X	2
D	14	K	7	R	6	Y	0
E	7	L	6	S	10	Z	0
F	15	M	15	T	0		
G	2	N	18	U	2		

Polyalphabetic Substitution

Even efforts to obscure the letter frequency by substituting several different cipher letters for *e*, for example, were not sufficient to preserve privacy. Edgar Allan Poe challenged readers of a newspaper to send him encrypted messages of this type, and he deciphered every one he received.

The next level of security was provided by using more than one substitution alphabet. For this discussion, let's assume we have four different alphabets, A1, A2, A3, and A4. We encrypt the first letter of our message using A1, the second letter of our message using A2, the third letter of our message using A3, and the fourth letter of our message using A4. Since we have only four alphabets, we use A1 to encrypt the fifth letter of our message, A2 to encrypt the sixth letter, and so forth. In the end, letters 1, 5, 9, 13, 17, . . . are all encrypted using the first alphabet, A1. Letters 2, 6, 10, 14, 18, . . . are all encrypted using A2. We continue on in the same manner using A3 and A4. With four different substitution alphabets, the distinctive frequency for the letter *e* and other common letters will not be apparent. That is because *e* will have different translations depending on which of the four alphabets was used at each point.

This form of cipher was considered to be extremely secure until Charles Babbage, the designer of the Difference Engine and other mechanical computers, figured out that if you did the frequencies separately for each group of letters, for example, letters $1, 5, 9, 13, 17, 21, . . .$, you could use the old trick to determine which was an *e*, which a *t*, and so forth. (The official credit for this breakthrough goes to the Prussian Friedrich Kasiski, who discovered it independently and actually published his solution. Babbage never bothered to do that.) You just had to do the frequencies separately for each set of letters. For this example, you had to discover four different alphabets. For very short messages or systems using a very large number of different alphabets, poly-alphabetic encryption was still quite secure, but for long dispatches there were tricks that let you guess the number of different alphabets used. Once you knew that, you could break the problem down into the appropriate number of mono-alphabetic substitution problems.

It is very important to realize that reusing the same alphabets for multiple dispatches also makes it easier to break the ciphers. Short messages don't allow the statistical accuracy of figuring out which is an *e*, and so on. But collecting a number of messages that you know or suspect were encrypted using the same alphabets lets you accumulate the statistics. So, as a general rule, reusing passwords and alphabets makes it much easier to break them. On the other hand, if you want to use a new password for each message, then the recipient of your message must be sent a large batch of these. Transporting the codes and related materials between correspondents is a security problem in its own right.

One-Time Pads

An absolutely secure means of encryption is the one-time pad. Each page (or sheet) in such a pad consists of a list of random numbers. The sender and the receiver each have a copy of the pad, but presumably no one else does. A simple form of the one-time pad would have each of the random numbers be in the range 0–25. Each letter of the original message would be shifted in the alphabet by the number of places dictated by the random number. Figure 11.1a shows two sheets that could have come from a one-time pad:

Let's go through an example using the left-hand sheet. (A summary of what we are doing is shown in figure 11.b.) We want to encrypt the text "Listen, my children, and you shall hear of the . . ." from Longfellow's *Paul Revere's Ride*. The first letter of the message is an *l*, and the first random number in the left-hand sheet is a 3. So the *l* is shifted three places in the alphabet to become an *O*. (This is illustrated in figure 11.1b as follows: First, we write the letter *l*. Below it we show a 12 because *l* is the twelfth letter in the alphabet. Below that we show the 3 from the one-time pad. Below that we sum 12 and 3 to get 15. Below that we show the encrypted letter *O*, which is the fifteenth letter of the alphabet.) The second letter in the message is an *i*; the second random number on the pad is a 4. Then *i* shifts four places to become *M*. (In figure 11.1b, below *i* we see 9 because *i* is the ninth letter in the alphabet, then 4 for the shift, then $9 + 4 = 13$, then *M*, which is the thirteenth letter in the alphabet.) The third letter, *s*, is the nineteenth letter in the alphabet, and it is paired with the random number 19. Summing these, we get 38. Since the alphabet has only 26 letters, identifying the "thirty-eighth" letter involves "wrapping around" to the beginning of the alphabet again and finding the twelfth letter in this case. (In figure 11.1b, 12 is shown in the *s* column.) The twelfth letter of the alphabet is *L*, so the *s* that we are encrypting becomes an *L*.

Proceeding in this manner, we obtain the cipher

OMLQID VA ORJCZZDV CVZ
YQH MWABS TOQI GN OGR

Since each letter of the original message is paired with its own random number, the resulting encrypted text is absolutely secure and can only be deciphered by someone having an identical sheet of random numbers to help the recipient shift the encrypted letters back to the original letters.

A tool used in simple encryptions is a cipher disk. Figure 11.2 shows one set to encrypt (only) the first letter of the Longfellow message. The middle circle's *A* has been lined up with the 3, the first number on our one-time pad. We then see that the letter *L* in that circle is next to the *O* in the outer circle. So, when adding 3, *L* translate to *O*. To continue, we next set the *A* in the middle circle to the next number on the one-time pad: 4. Then we can read off the translation of the letter *I* to an *M*. Remember that the middle circle must be turned to align with the appropriate number from the one-time pad for each character in the message. (The cipher disk can aid decryption in a similar manner.) (A historical

(a)
```
  3   4  19  23   4  16   9   2  12  10          12   3  25  10  25  15  18  24  25  16
  1  17  22   8  25   8   2   8  21   0          10  23  24  11  10  19  14   8  13  24
  2  13   3  17   0  16   7  12  10  16          20  24   4  15  25  14  24   7  16   5
 17  18   8  21  25  13  14   0   6   5          23  24  21   5   4  22  23   5  15  20
  6   1   3  23   6   1  21  15   3  10           1   4  14   3   0  23  16   2   0   6
  1   2  13   7  23  13   7   3   8  13           2  19   5   8  19   7  12  15   7  21
 22  13  16  13  15   0  18  21  15  10           9  17   0  14  11   3  14   6  12  24
 21   2   7   6   7  15  19  13  19   1          13   1   4  20  22  19   2  21   5  24
  6   9   2  15  25  17  25  14  11   5           9  18   3  23  18   6   7   6   5   4
 23   6   9  15  24   0   0   7  20  13           6   2  24  19  18  22   8  18   8   2
```

(b)
```
  l   i   s   t   e   n       m   y       c   h   i   l   d   r   e   n       a   n   d
 12   9  19  20   5  14      13  25       3   8   9  12   4  18   5  14       1  14   4
  3   4  19  23   4  16       9   2      12  10   1  17  22   8  25   8       2   8  21
 15  13  12  17   9   4      22   1      15  18  10   3  26  26   4  22       3  22  25
  O   M   L   Q   I   D       V   A       O   R   J   C   Z   Z   D   V       C   V   Z

  y   o   u       s   h   a   l   l       h   e   a   r       o   f       t   h   e
 25  15  21      10   8   1  12  12       8   5   1  18      15   6      20   8   5
  0   2  13       3  17   0  16   7      12  10  16  17      18   8      21  25  13
 25  17   8      13  23   1   2  19      20  15  17   9       7  14      15   7  18
  Y   Q   H       M   W   A   B   S       T   O   Q   I       G   N       O   G   R
```

... midnight ride of Paul Revere,
On the eighteenth of April, in Seventy-Five:
Hardly a man is now alive
Who remembers that famous day and year.
...

H W Longfellow

Figure 11.1

note: the disk as shown in figure 11.2 is set up to show the Caesar cipher used by Julius Caesar. He just shifted all letters by three positions. You can ignore the numbers for this application. "*Veni, vidi, vici*" becomes "YHQL, YLGL, YLFL.")

As long as the numbers on one-time pads are truly random and the sheets are not reused, security is guaranteed. However as with codes and alphabets, physically getting the one-time pads to your correspondent (behind enemy lines) can be a problem. Note that we've left one clue that could compromise the system: spacing. If the message were known or guessed to be a copy of some published work, then matching known texts by word length and spacing might give it away. Serious encryption using one-time pads would first reduce the original message to five-letter groups regardless of original spacing and would drop any punctuation works.

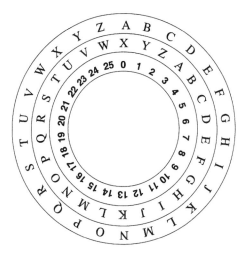

Figure 11.2

Computers and Cryptography

It should be clear that all the techniques discussed are labor-intensive and require careful transcription of message, alphabets, and code words. This is clearly an area where a computer would be very useful. Programs to generate character frequencies for messages are easy to write and can save hours of work.

Computers and Random Numbers

Computers can generate pseudo random numbers. We say *pseudo* because computers cannot in fact generate truly random numbers. Pseudo random number algorithms require a starting number or seed number. Using this seed, they will produce a repeatable pseudo random sequence. So if you use the same seed, you get the same sequence of numbers. It is tempting to imitate the methodology of the one-time pads. You would only need to be in possession of the starting seed for your random number generator and make sure your recipient has the same seed. In other words, you are using the seed number as your encryption and decryption key. However, since the number sequence is generated by an algorithm, there are probably techniques to break this kind of cipher. But if the techniques for such an attack are not in circulation, you may be able to achieve reasonably good privacy using this methodology.

Exercises

1. Solve the encrypted message shown in the Cryptoquote section.

2. What key word (or key phrase) was used to define the encryption alphabet in exercise 1?

3. Use the right-hand one-time sheet in figure 11.1a to encrypt a brief message. Ask a friend if he can decrypt it. Make sure to state that it is unbreakable—that should be a real incentive.

4. It has been suggested that when encountering a message encrypted with a one-time pad, we should just guess the values on the pad and when the resulting message makes sense, we've solved the encryption. Identify two major problems with that approach.

Modern Encryption

The material discussed in previous sections is intended to give you a historical background and give us a base to build on. The encryption techniques described next are fairly current and, when properly implemented, are virtually unbreakable. This is sometimes called strong encryption.

Those Darn Keys!

One thing that all the techniques described before have in common is the necessity for the sender and receiver to share certain information. In some cases it is a simple key word or phrase. In the case of one-time pads, a stock of these unique pads needs to be distributed to all possible recipients of encoded messages. Other forms of protected correspondence require the distribution of extensive code books. Even under ideal conditions, the key distribution problem is a nuisance. At worst, the distribution process may allow the keys to get into the wrong hands.

A tempting solution is to use your encryption system to distribute keys to be used in future sessions. This is, however, an invitation to disaster. If the attacker breaks the cipher just once—maybe not through a weakness in the system but by espionage or luck—then all future sessions are compromised because then the attacker is able to read the future keys.

Is it possible to distribute keys securely electronically without risk of interception? The answer is yes, but it is not a trivial task. A very nice analogy is getting a secure metal box with a padlock. You put your message or password into the box and lock it with the padlock to which only you have the key. You mail it to your correspondent and with your lock, no one can open the box and peek along the way. When she receives the box, she can't open it either, but she attaches a padlock to which only she has the key and onto the box as well. Now the box has two locks, and she mails it back to you. Again, it's safe, doubly locked, en route. When you receive the box, you remove your padlock with your key. You can't open it now, but you don't want to anyway. You now send the box back to your correspondent, and since it's locked with her padlock, it's still safe from tampering while it's on the way. Finally, when she receives the box the second time, your correspondent can unlock the box with her key and extract the message. So, with triple postage and rather long delays, keys and other information can be securely exchanged over a distance using nontrusted intermediaries such as the post office or a courier service.

This suggests that there might be an electronic equivalent to this kind of exchange. Unfortunately, simply using encryption in place of a padlock does not work for most encrypting techniques. Although you can remove your padlock while hers is still on the box, you cannot remove your encryption after she's applied her encryption on top of your encryption. Mathematically we would say the two encryption processes are not commutative.

However, Whitfield Diffie, Martin Hellman, and Ralph Merkle came up with a mathematical procedure that allowed the generation of a mutually known key over insecure channels. It did require going back and forth a bit and so required two-way interaction. It also was not suitable for sending a general message—it just generated a secret key (which could then be used for sending messages by more traditional means). This solution to the key distribution problem was a major breakthrough but is still not as convenient as what was to come next.

Public Key Encryption

Let's go back to the padlock analogy. Suppose I have hundreds of identical padlocks made, and only I have the key. Then I mail these padlocks, still open, to anybody who might conceivably want to send me a secure message. If I could afford it, I'd just send millions of these padlocks all over the world, so that anyone wanting to correspond with me would have access to one of my padlocks.

Anyone wanting to send me a message would get a secure box, insert the message, close the padlock attached to the box (this doesn't require a key), and then mail it to me. As long as I have the only key, distributing the padlocks doesn't compromise the security.

Of course, distributing locks like that, in most cases, is totally impractical and rather expensive. Most padlocks aren't that secure anyway, and if a key got out (someone surreptitiously copied mine, say) all the padlocks would instantly become worthless.

Is there a password that I can distribute that people can use to encrypt messages that only I can decrypt? What we are looking for is an asymmetric encryption system that uses one password to encrypt and another to decrypt. Previously discussed systems used the same password or key to both encrypt and decrypt. If we could separate these two parts, then we could make the encryption key public while keeping the decryption key private. Whereas distributing padlocks is expensive, distributing a public key, say, in the electronic equivalent of a phone book, has very little cost associated with it. This conceptual scheme was proposed by Diffie in 1975, but no one knew a mathematical algorithm to implement it.

Rivest, Shamir, and Adleman (RSA) Encryption

In 1977, at MIT's Laboratory for Computer Science, Ronald Rivest, Adi Shamir, and Leonard Adleman finally came up with a practical algorithm to implement the conceptual framework proposed by Diffie. Let's review what we need. We need a public key that anyone can use to encrypt a message he desires to send us. This public key should in no way compromise a private key, known only to us, that we can use to decrypt the message.

The RSA system depends on the difficulty of factoring very large integers into component prime factors. Remember that primes are positive integers that divide evenly only by 1 and themselves. Seven is a prime number; 28 is a product of the primes 7 and 2, where 2 is employed twice:

$$28 = 7 * 2 * 2$$

To factor a number such as 28, we try to divide it by successively larger primes and see if it divides evenly. Thus, we started by dividing by 2. That went evenly, yielding 14. Using 2 again, we get 7. The next prime, 3, doesn't go evenly into 7, nor does the next prime, 5. So 7 is a prime, and the factors of 28 are 2, 2, and 7. This seems easy enough, but it is a brute force technique. There are no major shortcuts to use as the number gets larger. You just have to patiently try primes until you succeed or decide that the number you are trying to factor is itself a prime.

Let's up the ante a bit and use somewhat larger numbers. The number 73 is a prime and the number 61 is a prime. If we multiply the two, we get 4,453. Now, we know that 4,453 is the product of 73 and 61. If we give it to someone who doesn't know that, he would have to try successive primes to find those factors. In fact he would try 2, 3, 5, 7, 11, 13, 17, 19, 23, 29, 31, 37, 53, and 59, all with no success. On the next try, using 61, he would find that the other factor is 73. So, as the numbers get larger, it takes more and more work to factor them into their constituent primes. If you use integers with about 200 digits, even a computer will have a hard time discovering the factors. Indeed, it is fairly easy to come up with numbers so large that all the expected computing power for the next century will not be able to find the factors. Of course, we need to employ a computer to generate and manipulate these huge numbers. This is not a job for the average calculator.

We have established that factorization of very large numbers is hard, and we know we can make it as hard as we like simply by increasing the length of the numbers. How can we use this to produce a public and a private key suitable for encryption? We illustrate the RSA algorithm using very small numbers. This will allow you to follow the logic of the algorithm without drowning in hundreds of digits.

*An RSA Example

If we want to understand this public key encryption scheme, we need to follow these steps to generate our public and private keys:

1. Pick two primes, naming them P and Q. For our example, we use $P = 23$, and $Q = 29$. We also pick another working number, naming it K, preferably also a prime. We use $K = 31$. Remember that except where noted, all numbers need to be kept secret.
2. Create $N = P * Q$. In our case, $23 * 29$, or 667. This is the "big" number that must be factored to crack the encryption. That is easy in this example but hard for really big numbers.
3. Distribute N and the working number K. Together they represent our public key, and anyone desiring to send us a secure message must use these two numbers.
4. Generate the so-called private key or decryption key that will be used to decrypt any message. Call it G.

One important arithmetic tool you need in order to follow is modular arithmetic. This just means that we define a largest number and if we reach this, we "wrap around" to zero and continue. Most car odometers work modulo 100,000. That is, if we exceed 100,000 miles, the odometer starts over again.

Notice that this is the same as the Java remainder operator %. Thus, a car's odometer gives us the mileage % 100,000, that is, it only gives us the remainder after dividing by 100,000. In review: 8 % 100 yields 8; 88 % 100 yields 88; 888 % 100 also yields 88 because if we divide 888 by 100, we get 8 *with remainder* 88. Another set of examples: 12 % 13 yields 12; but 100 % 13 yields 9 because $100/13 = 7$ with remainder 9.

To begin, we define a value $V = (P - 1) * (Q - 1)$. For our example, $V = 22 * 28 = 616$. We need to find a value for G such that the following equation is true using modulo V (or mod V) arithmetic:

$$K * G = 1$$

At first it would seem that this could only be true if K and G were both equal to 1. But, that is why we are using mod V arithmetic: What we are saying is that after dividing $K * G$ by V, the remainder must be 1, or

$$(K * G) \% V = 1$$

Using our example values,

$$(31 * G) \% 616 = 1$$

Finding G is a bit tricky, but using a computer program and just trying different values works for these small examples. The correct answer for G is 159. To confirm this, $31 * 159$ yields 4,929. If we divide 4,929 by 616, we get a quotient of 8 with remainder 1. Thus, $G = 159$ is our private decryption key.

The end result is that $N = 667$ and $K = 31$ make up our public key. $G = 159$ is our private key.

We are now ready to try encrypting a message. We want to encrypt a message, call it M, using the public key and then show that with the private key we can recover the original number. With our small example, we can only encrypt a fairly small chunk of data. We'll have our correspondent send us a small integer, say $M = 65$. If we just want to send numbers, that is fine.

In practice, we want to send text, but since the computer represents each letter in a message as number anyway, then showing we can deal with numbers ensures that we could also deal with letters. We now show how she would encrypt the secret message, the number 65, and how we would decrypt it.

1. The encrypted message, named C, is arrived at when our correspondent calculates

   $$C = M^K \% N = 65^{31} \% 667$$

   That is, all calculations are made mod N. Now it turns out that in calculating M to the Kth power, we get the correct answer even if at each step along the way we apply the mod N operation. This keeps our number from getting too large. (What we are using is the identity $(x \% y) * (x \% y) = (x * x) \% y$.)
2. The result is $C = 103$. This bears no resemblance to the original 65 and would seem to be a fairly secure way of keeping that value a secret.
3. At our end, we receive the message 103 and now need to apply our private key to see what she was trying to send us. We use the formula

   $$M = C^G \% N = 103^{159} \% 667 = 65$$

Again, all the calculations are done mod N, and this results in our seeing her original message, 65.

Breaking the Code

To break this code, the attacker needs to get the decryption key. The only way known to obtain this from the public key is to factor N. If N can be factored, then the attacker can generate the private key, G, just as we did. For our example, where N is 667, it does not take much to arrive at the factors 23 and 29. To make this system secure, we are counting on the fact that factoring a number N that has several hundreds of digits is beyond any current and expected computing capability.

Digital Signatures

Signatures are used to authenticate items that are signed by a person. It is assumed that the signature is so unique in the way it is written that no one else could produce a signature exactly like the legitimate signer. Other ways to check out a person and have him or her validate their identity is if they know something only the person in question could have known. In each case we try to find something that could only have come from that person. Digital signatures consist of a message that could only have come from the person claiming to have sent the digital signature. RSA encryption allows a user to produce just that kind of message.

In the normal use of RSA public key encryption, messages are encrypted with the public key and decrypted with the private key. One nice property of the RSA algorithm is that it also works in reverse—that is, you can encrypt a message with the private key and decrypt it with the public key. So, assume that Juliet wants to send a message to Romeo. She wants to send it encrypted, but additionally, wants to include a digital signature that proves that she sent it. One way to do this is to break the message into two parts, the main body and the signature. The main body might be "Dear Romeo,... love,... love,... love...." (We'll spare you the details.) The signature might be "Sealed with kisses this 23rd day of April, 1595, at 10:30 P.M., your loving Juliet." First Juliet uses her private key to encrypt the signature. Then she encrypts the whole message, the body of the message with the encrypted signature portion attached, using Romeo's public key. So, the signature portion of the message is doubly encrypted, first by Juliet's private key, then by Romeo's public key.

Romeo receives the message and decrypts the whole message with his private key. That makes the body of the message readable. The signature portion, however, is still encrypted by Juliet's private key. He uses Juliet's public key to decrypt that signature portion. Since only she could have encrypted the signature with her private key, the message must have originated with Juliet. Note that the signature included more than just the name Juliet. It included the time, date, and other things. This is to help thwart replay attacks (discussed later in this chapter).

PGP, Encryption for the Masses

By entering the URL http://web.mit.edu/network/pgp.html in your Web browser, you can go to an MIT Web site that will allow you to download without charge programs that let you communicate with others using the strong encryption afforded by the RSA algorithm. The fact that this is readily available to anyone at no cost for noncommercial use is due to the effort of Phil Zimmerman. The RSA algorithms were published in the 1970s, and software to employ them was written the world over. To efficiently do arithmetic with the huge numbers involved is a nontrivial programming task. Making this all practical for the nonprogrammer, nontechnologist represents a major effort in dealing with human-computer interface. Also, Zimmerman reduced the computer power needed to communicate by not using RSA encryption for the whole message. He used it only for key exchange and for authentication using the digital signature approach. The body of the message is encrypted by more traditional and less computer-intensive methods than RSA. The process that Zimmerman used is an extension of the Data Encryption Standard (DES), which can be quite secure once the key exchange problem is dealt with using RSA. (We do not discuss DES, and you may want to go to a reference to look it up. It involves manipulations at the bit level, not just at the character level.) Zimmerman labeled his encryption method Pretty Good Privacy, or PGP.

Zimmerman expected to give away his software as freeware, but since he feared that the U.S. government would make it illegal for ordinary citizens to have access to strong encryption, he allowed an associate to make it available on computer bulletin boards, USENET, and the Internet. The government moved to punish Zimmerman for "letting the cat out of the bag," so to speak. He appeared in front of a grand jury in California, but in the end was not prosecuted.

Exercise

1. In amateur radio, the sequence 88 means "love and kisses." Encrypt and decrypt this message using the keys generated for the RSA example in the text.

Attacks

In the previous sections, we focused on the important but perhaps narrow issues of passwords and encryption, which allow us to ensure the confidentiality of our data and to put some barriers in the way of general access to our computer systems. Next, we take a wider view and look at a range of ways that an attacker could attempt to make our lives miserable.

Computer Break-ins

The break-in is the computer system administrator's nightmare. The first step is that the attacker somehow gets into the system. He may have gotten the password for a computer account that has been inactive. He may have been able to bypass password security altogether because of some operating system weakness. Whatever the mechanism, there is now an attacker using the system, masquerading as someone legitimate.

On most computer systems, normal users have limited privileges and powers. They usually have complete control over their own files but usually quite limited access to system files and the files of other users. They usually have complete control over any programs they run, but none over programs run by others and by the operating system. For maintenance reasons and for dealing with emergencies and other problems, there is another user class reserved for the people maintaining the computer systems, the *system administrators* (or *network administrators*). Users with these powers are sometimes called *superusers* or persons having *root privileges.*

The next step for an attacker is to obtain these sweeping privileges for himself, or herself. Usually it is easier to crack that next level after first logging in as an ordinary user. Then the cracker can use the computer's own power to help break the passwords or other impediments to that higher level.

Once the attacker is running his programs with superuser privileges, there are few limitations to the damage that can be inflicted. The compromised computer is often used as a stepping stone to launch an attack on another computer accessible over the network.

Defenses

This kind of outside attacker needs to get into the computer somehow, and there are two possible routes for an attack. If there are dial-in modems, then that is one possible path. In many educational, commercial, and industrial settings, there is a direct Internet connection. A computer not accessible from the outside because it lacks modem and direct network connections is fairly safe from direct outside attack (but see the section on viruses).

Many system or network administrators acquire special software generically called a *firewall* to guard a system at its network connection and to keep a special watch on the modem connections. These systems programs work by restricting the kinds of network traffic coming into the computer. Invariably, they also restrict the kind of traffic going out because accessing the World Wide Web, for example, is an interactive or two-way process. Firewalls often put severe restrictions on what legitimate users can do from the outside. Someone attempting to work from home might be severely hampered by the system's firewall.

A firewall can also give the user a false sense of security. Firewalls may have weaknesses as well and may fail under some attacks. Therefore, even behind a firewall, sensitive data should be encrypted, authentication procedures should be secure, and backups should be carefully performed.

Network Security/Network Attacks

The thing that makes network-based attacks so difficult to deal with is that the attacker is so hard to trace. Just as a bank robber often uses a stolen car as a getaway vehicle, the network attacker often works through a chain of compromised machines. If you detect a break-in from the network and trace it back to the originating machine, you've generally found another victim, not the attacker.

A compromised network connection often leaves no clues indicating that anything is wrong. What is wrong is that someone is able to copy all data that is being transferred because she is listening to, or monitoring, the traffic. For the attacker, often the most important things to copy are any passwords that are being typed as the connection is being used. These can then be used to compromise additional machines and networks.

Listeners can work as simply as the *promiscuous listener* described in chapter 12 on communications. This usually implies an inside job because the listener has to share the physical network with the victim. There could be physical wire-tap kinds of connections involved, or an attack could involve a much more sophisticated technique where the attacker sends out communications packets that claim to be coming from a machine other than their true origin. By masquerading as a "trusted host," the attacker may receive all kinds of privileges from the machine being attacked and may receive vital data actually intended for another machine. One form of this type of attack has been called *IP spoofing* because one's Internet Packets pretend to "be" someone else's.

Man-in-the-Middle

The most sophisticated form of masquerading interposes the attacker between two machines that are communicating. If machine X is talking to machine Y, all traffic from X to Y actually goes to attacker A, who then forwards the traffic to Y. Similarly, traffic from Y to X also goes via A. As long as machine A accurately copies everything received to the other party, X and Y will have no clue that anything is wrong although the connection may seem slower than usual. What is lost in this case is confidentiality because A has a copy of all information transferred. However, A can receive one thing from X and send something altered or entirely different to Y. Traffic going in the other direction may be similarly edited. Now what X thinks Y is saying is not what Y had actually intended but rather what A wants X to hear. As you can see, that can have extremely serious consequences.

For example, let's assume Arthur has a connection to his bank, BigBucks Savings and Loan. He asks BigBucks to transfer funds from his business account to his personal account. When he types in the account number for his personal account, the attacker substitutes a different account number that the attacker set up just for this purpose. Meanwhile, Arthur gives all the appropriate passwords to authorize the transaction. He may not realize until much later, after the rogue account has been emptied, that something went awry. (An entertaining Internet thriller named *Interception*, written by Graham Watkins, illustrates man-in-the-middle attacks in great detail.)

Prevention

When moving critical data outside of the local network that you physically control, it is safest to assume that someone is listening. And what could be more critical than the password that you type in to access a remote site? All remote sessions need to be encrypted. Kerberos, developed at MIT, was one of the earliest systems to encrypt sessions with remote machines. Thus, a password used to access a remote machine was never sent to that machine in a readable form.

This does not mean that whenever you browse the Web, everything must be encrypted. Usually the fact that you are looking at some Web site is not a critical piece of information. On the other hand, if you are working for a company that plans corporate takeovers, and you are doing research using the Internet, then even a leak of your browser's access history—which sites you have visited—might be considered a serious compromise.

Physical Attacks

Physical attacks mostly require that attackers have physical access to machines. Good physical security takes care of most of these problems. The most common problem is leaving machines unattended in a public or shared environment. You leave your machines to get a drink of water. You'll be back in a few minutes, so you stay logged in. While you're gone, someone sits down at your machine, types a few things, acts somewhat confused, and leaves. Maybe an accomplice has talked to you and asked a few questions—anything to delay you a few extra minutes.

When you come back to your machine, everything looks okay. There may be no clue that things have been tampered with. Yet maybe a Trojan Horse program has now been installed in your directory. Maybe copies of some of your e-mail or other files have been mailed out. Maybe the access permissions on some of your files have been altered. If you've left your machine unattended, you just don't know.

Our introductory section in this chapter raised the possibility of other physical attacks. A person sitting next to you may have been able to reconstruct your password from just watching your fingers as you typed it in. Video taping or watching from afar with binoculars might also assist in this process.

Another physical attack is the traditional wire-tap. Just as your phone line is vulnerable to a physical attack, so are communications cables anywhere along the way. And, insofar as microwave and satellite links are employed, even an appropriately tuned radio may be all it takes to record data.

The Replay Attack

In a replay attack, the attacker has somehow recorded a sequence of characters that represent a password or encryption key with the hope of using it again. With passwords, the attacker will usually succeed in subsequent attempts to use them until the password is changed. Some computer-based, security systems such as Kerberos thwart the replay attack by incorporating the current time and date in any keys and passwords. Thus, the keys change almost continuously and a stale key will not work. This does require, however, that all computers agree on what time it is. Network protocols include operations to keep the computers' clocks synchronized.

Denial of Service

A simple and not too subtle attack on your system is called the *denial-of-service* attack. Long before computers were ubiqitous, criminals would create diversions for the police or fire department so that they would have a better chance of performing their criminal acts undetected.

For example, if someone sends you thousands of e-mail messages, your e-mail file is effectively out of commission. Yet having a program mail you thousands of messages takes little computer skill. In open, semipublic systems, such as those often found at universities, running many jobs at the same time, using up all the temporary disk space, printing a 1,000-page job, and so on, are sometimes done even by accident, but if they are done intentionally, all are examples of denial-of-service attacks.

On the Internet, it is possible to overload facilities. Again, if done maliciously, this is a denial-of-service attack. As in our noncomputer examples, denial-of-service attacks are sometimes used to mask or divert attention from other kinds of attacks and in some cases to effectively disable software defense mechanisms.

Political/Social Issues

Some of the successes in encryption have raised social issues that have yet to be resolved. In the past, when law enforcement officials could show that there was likely criminal activity, they could go to a judge and obtain a warrant allowing wire-taps. With strong encryption, that option is disappearing. Encryption techniques can be used to scramble voice as well as data because any audio can be converted to data and then back.

Law enforcement officials have supported legislation to make strong encryption less strong or to require a system where law enforcement officials can obtain access to the keys with a court order. This would involve procedures similar to receiving authorization for a wire-tap and would make guaranteed privacy illegal. Yet it would give law enforcement a reasonable chance at tracking illegal activity.

The other side of the argument is that we have a right to privacy. To paraphrase a slogan used by the National Rifle Association, "If strong encryption were illegal, then only criminals would have strong encryption." Another argument is that since some criminals wear gloves to avoid leaving fingerprints, it should follow that gloves should be made illegal.

Interestingly, the business community, which often takes the more conservative positions, tends to be on the side of civil libertarians on this issue. Financial institutions, for example, are quite happy to know that their data are absolutely secure. To a large degree, it boils down to whether you trust your government or not.

Encryption as a Weapon

The government has also been worried that strong encryption might give foreign governments a means of communication that the National Security Agency has little chance of monitoring. Since there are laws that make it illegal to export munitions without a license, strong encryption software has long been labeled a munition, thus limiting its export. Operating systems and other systems have had to be formulated in special lower-security versions to allow their export.

With the international connections over the Internet, it is naive to assume that strong encryption software has not gotten out. It is also impossible to control the mailing out or carrying out of the country every floppy disk, tape, or CD-ROM.

Whom Can You Trust?

The more you think about security issues, the more you see that these are very difficult problems. If you obtain a software-based security package, be it an encryption system or a firewall, how do you know that the software is "clean"? How do you know that it does not have "back doors" or other surprises that allow access to someone else? Short of having access to the programs and carefully reading and understanding all the code, there is no way to be sure. It is important to deal with vendors whom you trust. Any software of questionable origin should be avoided. Free software and other bargains may be legitimate or may just lead to another Trojan Horse.

Viruses

A much publicized problem is that of computer viruses. A *computer virus* is an uninvited program that is loaded into your system without your intention or knowledge. Most viruses are hostile in that they subvert security, confidentiality, or both. A few are benign—someone showing off—and do nothing other than leaving a "gotcha!" message. A totally isolated computer is immune to viruses. However, direct Internet connections or modem connections provide a path for the entry of viruses. Often e-mail is used. If the recipient of strange e-mail does not try to execute it as a program, most attacks can be thwarted. Note that executing it includes the processing of some attachments by some mail reader programs. Of course, a computer break-in over the network can also introduce viruses, but usually the damage is much more direct.

Even a computer that is physically isolated is vulnerable when a user brings in outside software on floppy disks or CD-ROMs. Again, software of unknown provenance is a serious risk.

There are commercial programs available to help fight virus attacks. Just like influenza (flu) vaccines, they need to be constantly updated because new viruses are always evolving (with the help of malicious programmers). Again, these are no safer than the source of the programs. A pirated copy of anti-virus software or any software that seems too good to be true may in fact be a vehicle for introducing and spreading viruses.

Losing your Password or Encryption Key

Good security and privacy have their own risks. If you forget the password to your computer system, you usually have to go to your system administrator to retrieve it. If you can retrieve it, then it means that there is a copy of all passwords somewhere. This is in itself a potential problem. (How much is your system administrator being paid, and how much would these passwords be worth to someone else?) In many cases, the password is not retrievable and all that can be done is to have a new one issued. For most computer access issues, loss of a password is little more than a possibly embarrassing nuisance.

If you have encrypted files with a good system and lose the key, the consequences can be very serious. If it is a good encryption system, then it may be impossible to recover the data. If the system is not so secure, you may be able to get help in breaking into it. But this means that it can also be broken into without your knowledge. So, it is a two-edged sword. Sometimes encryption keys do need to be written down or otherwise backed up. This copy of the key will in one sense weaken the system but may represent a necessary compromise to avoid losing data entirely.

Exercise

1. Using the Web, search for and read news articles on the last three major viruses that have plagued computer users in the past year or two.

Summary

We saw that providing security and confidentiality requires a large array of tools, procedures, and even a suspicious state of mind. Seemingly innocent glitches in everyday computing may be a signal or clue that something undesirable has happened. If there are valuable data on your computer, you must assume that they are at risk unless you are extremely careful.

Authentication is an important part of providing protection. We explained passwords and the security they provide if we select them carefully, and how easy it is to crack poorly selected passwords using brute force and dictionary attacks.

We also explored encryption techniques from the simplest systems to more complex public key encryption systems such as RSA. We showed that the classical systems suffered from key exchange problems, whereas with public key encryption, using readily available packages such as PGP, the encryption key is made public.

We also looked at physical and network-related attacks such as denial-of-service attacks, common virus attacks, and the insidious man-in-the-middle attack. It is good to keep everything in perspective, however. If your security is so good that losing a password means that your data are gone forever, it may be too good (or too bad) for the kind of application you have.

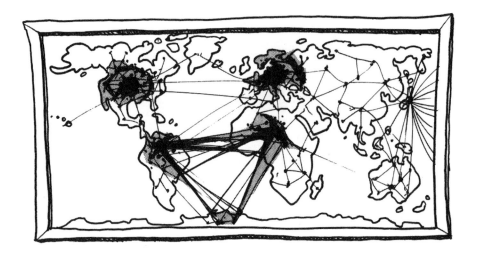

HOW MANY
COMPUTERS ARE
BEING SHOWN
HERE?

ACTUALLY,
ONLY ONE.

12   Computer Communications

Exploration

On the way back from a concert by your favorite rock group, you are almost cut off by an 18-wheeler with a huge trailer. You fume for a while, planning all kinds of revenge. You regret that you always seem to be fresh out of photon torpedoes just when that kind of thing happens. But there is another way. Why not send a note to the President noting your dislike of any laws allowing vehicles bigger than yours on the nation's highways. It is no longer necessary to get out paper, envelope, and stamps to do this. All you need to do is log into your networked computer and send electronic mail (*e-mail*) with your thoughts on this matter. You may not get a handwritten personal reply, but at least your opinion is likely to be heard. (Many of the examples in this chapter assume a UNIX (or LINUX) system. In most cases, you can obtain equivalent functionality on a Windows or Macintosh system by clicking on an appropriate icon.)

```
mail president@whitehouse.gov
Subject: Big, bad trucks
Dear Mr. President,
I'm afraid of the big bad trucks. Please help!
Sincerely,
Red
.
```

You are in luck, and the President would like to discuss your concerns with you in person. He replies that because of an upcoming governors' conference in Seattle, his meeting with you will have to take place there. The note asks you to suggest a nice place to lunch in Seattle. Before making a reservation, you want to find out what the weather will be like. It would be nice to meet in one of those outdoor establishments near the Space Needle.

SEATTLE METROPOLITAN AREA–TACOMA AREA–EVERETT AND VICINITY–
HOOD CANAL/KITSAP PENINSULA–
BREMERTON–SHELTON–BELLEVUE–EDMONDS–ISSAQUAH–PUYALLUP

NATIONAL WEATHER SERVICE SEATTLE WA
415 AM PST THU JAN 6 2000. . .NEXT FORECAST 330 PM PST THURSDAY. . .

(TEMPERATURES AND CHANCE OF MEASURABLE PRECIPITATION VALUES ARE FOR
TODAY. . .TONIGHT AND FRIDAY) WAZOO6–007–008–010–062330– SEATTLE METROPOLITAN
AREA–TACOMA AREA–EVERETT AND VICINITY–HOOD CANAL/KITSAP PENINSULA–
BREMERTON–SHELTON–BELLEVUE–EDMONDS–ISSAQUAH–PUYALLUP
TODAY. . .CLOUDY WITH RAIN DEVELOPING BY MIDDAY. . .PATCHY MORNING FOG HIGHS
IN THE LOWER 40S. SOUTHEAST WIND 5 TO 10 MPH.
TONIGHT. . .CLOUDY. . .RAIN DURING THE EVENING THEN DIMINISHING. . .LOWS IN
THE UPPER 30S.
SOUTH WIND 5 TO 15 MPH.FRIDAY. . .CLOUDY WITH RAIN AT TIMES. . .BREEZY. . .HIGHS NEAR 45

Location	Forecast	Temperature		Probability of Precipitation		
	Today	Tonight	Fri	Today	Tonight	Fri
SEATTLE	44	38	46	80%	80%	70%
EVERETT	44	37	46	80%	80%	70%
SHELTON	43	36	45	80%	80%	60%

SATURDAY AND SUNDAY. . .PERIODS OF RAIN. . .BREZZY. . .LOWS 35 TO 40. . .HIGHS
SATURDAY NEAR 45 AND SUNDAY NEAR 40.
MONDAY. . .RAIN. . .HEAVY AT TIMES. . .WINDY. . .LOWS NEAR 35. . .HIGHS NEAR 40 =

Figure 12.1

You fire up your Web browser and go immediately to your favorite search engine, which usually gets you just what you need. You search using the key words "Seattle weather". The search engine reports about half a million hits, but the first one seems just right: National Weather Service—Seattle, Washington. You click on that and then on the icon promising the local forecast. Figure 12.1 shows the response, direct from the National Weather Service. It looks like you might want to plan something inside after all. You could look at one of the many alternative sources of weather information on the Web that provide radar and satellite images, but rain is rain.

These are just two examples of the opportunities afforded by the Internet. Our goal in this chapter is to get a better understanding of how this marvelous network operates and how we might make the best use of it.

Layers and Local Area Networks (LANs)

One recurring theme in computing is that of layers. We looked at issues raised by two layers of programming when we studied Java and assembly language programming, and

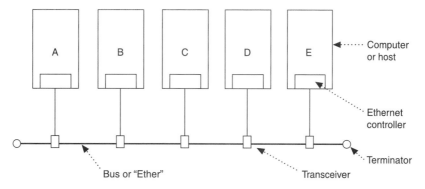

Figure 12.2

now we deal with issues raised by layers in communications software. The bottom layer is the actual hardware used for communications. The systems at this low level are often described as *local area networks*, or LANs. Two common low-level methods used for computer communications are call *Ethernet* and *Token Ring*. Token Ring is discussed briefly later. First we concentrate on Ethernet. Ethernet was developed by the Xerox Corporation and has now become a standard. It is called a *bus* architecture because many computers can share the same bus, as shown in figure 12.2. Generally, a bus is an electrical wire or cable that allows sharing via multiple attachment points. In the figure, the letters A through E designate computers (also called *hosts*). Each computer contains an Ethernet controller with a connection to the bus. The attachment point to the bus includes a *transceiver*, which provides the proper electronic interface to transmit and receive electrical signals to and from the bus.

The network works like many people trying to communicate in a large room. Helga might wait until the room is quiet and then say, "Alphonse, how did you like the book?" Everyone can hear the question, although it is intended for Alphonse, and in polite company only Alphonse will listen. Then he might wait for a quiet moment and reply, "Helga, the book was great!" As long as everyone is polite and orderly, any two people in the room can communicate, although no more than two can communicate at any one time. Even though everyone can hear all messages, all listeners are expected to ignore messages not intended for them.

Ethernet works like this except that the signals on the bus are electrical and the bus takes the form of a length of coaxial cable. (You may have seen coaxial cable as used in your cable TV hookup or in the connection between your VCR and TV.) The message length is limited in order to keep any two computers from monopolizing the bus. Each Ethernet controller has an address that is guaranteed to be unique (manufacturers coordinate through a central clearinghouse). This address is like a serial number and is a 12-digit hexadecimal (base 16) number written in the following form:

dest addr	source addr	message	check info

Figure 12.3

dest addr	source addr	Four score and	check info

dest addr	source addr	seven years ago,	check info

dest addr	source addr	our forefathers	check info

dest addr	source addr	brought forth	check info

. . .

Figure 12.4

5A 34 B2 31 90 1C

With a unique address, messages can always have an unambiguous destination. It would not be like the earlier example, where Alphonse would have problems if there were more than one Helga in the room.

Another problem dealt with at this low level is *collisions*. Even in polite company, two people may start talking at exactly the same time. For Ethernet this is called a collision. Ethernet controllers can detect a collision and know that this means the data is likely to be garbled. In this case, each controller wishing to use the bus waits for an approximately random amount of time before attempting to communicate again. This backoff procedure makes it unlikely that one collision is immediately followed by another.

A concept that is widely used in computer communications, including Ethernet, is that of packaging a message in chunks called *packets*. These packets are short enough to meet the Ethernet's size limitations. Each packet contains important control information (figure 12.3), including the destination address (where it is going) and the source address (where it came from).

The Format of an Ethernet Packet

Think of sending packets as mailing the parts of a manuscript on a series of standard postcards. Each postcard has independent address information on the front. At the destination, the postcards can be ordered and the manuscript reassembled in correct form. To aid in this, each packet includes sequencing information (figure 12.4).

Note that there is a potential security problem in the Ethernet communications method, since every controller on the bus can see every message regardless of it's destination. Standard software causes the controllers to ignore all messages not intended for that computer, but users may be able to obtain rogue software that does not follow that convention. Although this is in effect wiretapping and is illegal, such software is not too hard to obtain because it does have legitimate troubleshooting applications. Therefore, unless you are sure of the other machines and users on your local Ethernet, keep in mind that what you are typing may be monitored for undesirable purposes. Of course, you should keep this in perspective. Your phone may be tapped with a court order or illegally; police may intercept your mail if they have a warrant; and of course a thief can easily take something out of your mailbox (or trash).

10 Base T Ethernet and Beyond

You may be thinking, "What is this coaxial cable stuff? I make my connection to the Ethernet with a little plastic modular connector that looks like a telephone plug but is somewhat larger." What you are using is a very popular form of Ethernet called *10 base T*. It was designed to be able to operate on existing twisted-pair telephone wiring and to use compatible interconnection methodology.

One way to look at 10 base T is to shrink the Ethernet cable with its transceivers into a single box, called a *hub*, and then lengthen the connection between your Ethernet controller and the transceiver to whatever length is needed to go from the hub to your computer. It is important to realize that, logically, this is still a shared bus system.

In institutional settings the hub is usually placed in a communications closet and the connections are provided via wall jacks that look very much like telephone jacks. With 10 base T, the distance between the hub and your computer is typically limited to 300 feet. In contrast, some forms of coaxial-based Ethernet can extend almost a mile. The data capacity, as with the more traditional Ethernet, is 10 million bits per second. However, since this is shared among all users of the bus, the effective individual throughput may be considerably less.

More expensive switched hubs are also available. They get away from the bus approach and are somewhat more like a telephone switch in that they allow many simultaneous connections to take place at the same time. This means that some of the bus-related security problems disappear and that the average data capacity is much greater. One hundred million bit per second versions, called 100 base T, are also available.

Other Interesting LAN Technologies

Token Ring is somewhat like a bus whose ends are joined together to form a circle. Information travels in only one direction, say, clockwise. This means that to get to the nearest computer immediately counterclockwise from you, your message must go all the way around clockwise. You do receive confirmation that a message has gotten through: either the original message or an acknowledgment from the recipient of your message completes the circuit back to you. When the system is idle, a packet, called the token, is passed around the ring from machine to machine. To send a message on the ring, you must wait until the token reaches you, or you must just have received a message. When you receive a token, you replace it with your message. This token based procedure ensures that there are no collisions because you never transmit unless it is your turn.

Wireless LANs have also become available for certain niche applications. The protocols are similar to those used on a bus, but no physical connections are required. This can be very nice for a classroom or laboratory situation. The fact that all information is transmitted over the air means that anyone can receive the traffic. Encryption is advisable for sensitive applications.

Exercises

1. Suppose there are four people on an Ethernet. Each has a message to send to each other person, and each message requires 1 second to send. If they all send their messages as fast as possible, how long will it take to get them all transferred over the network?

2. Suppose we have the situation of exercise 1, but your Ethernet is implemented on a switched hub. This means that any two people can communicate with each other regardless of what the others are doing (it is possible to have several conversations going on simultaneously). How long would it take under these circumstances?

3. Give one obvious advantage that Token Ring has over Ethernet.

Wide Area Networks

Once we have mastered the idea of a network, we can consider the possibility of connecting several networks together. As an example, we can connect two Ethernet-based networks—network 1 with hosts A, B, C, and D, and network 2 with hosts W, X, Y, and Z (figure 12.5). They are connected using network 3. (Network 3 could have many more connections, but we consider only the two shown.) To accomplish this, we have set up machine A with two Ethernet controllers, connected to networks 1 and 3. Machine W also has two controllers, one for network 2 and one for network 3.

A machine that is connected to more than one network is sometimes called a *gateway*. (We can also buy a special-purpose piece of hardware called *router* to accomplish this.) These gateway machines can be used to enable universal communication. In figure 12.5, for example, machine C can now communicate with machine X by using gateways A and W. A message from C intended for X would first go from C to A using network 1. Then A would forward it, using network 3, to W. W would then forward the message, via network

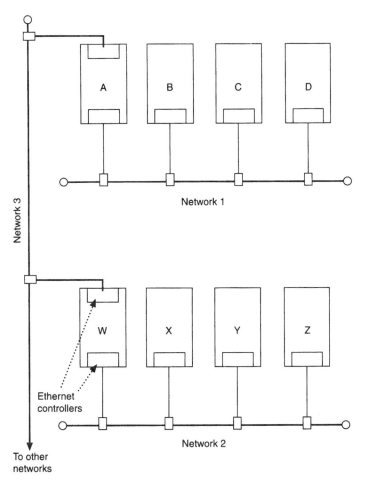

Ethernet controllers

To other networks

Figure 12.5

2, to X. If the message is long enough, it would be composed of a number of packets, each taking the same route.

A collection of networks connected together is called an *internet*. The large worldwide network that most computer users have access to is called the *Internet*.

Ethernets are designed to be fairly fast, but they have certain size restrictions placed on them. Under ideal conditions, an Ethernet bus can be almost a mile long. Other hardware and software constraints often reduce that to several hundred feet. With too many hosts on the same Ethernet bus, one would also have higher likelihood of congestion and collisions. This would mean that an internet consisting of only Ethernet-based networks would have to be fairly small physically, or it would take a very large number of "hops" from gateway to gateway to cover very large distances.

However, it is possible to replace the Ethernet in network 3 with other communications systems based on entirely different hardware. Such communications systems, often leased from a common carrier, can provide connections over very large distances. The physical basis for these systems can be the traditional means of forwarding telephone traffic, such as copper wire, and microwave links, both terrestrial and satellite-based. Most likely, the longer links will be implemented using optical fibers. The principles are similar to those used on Ethernet. Information is sent in the form of one or more packets, and each packet includes appropriate addressing and other control information.

Exercises

1. Suppose you are dealing with Ethernets that can each handle only four computers. Tell how many such nets you would need to connect 100 such machines, and tell how you would connect them. Assume that one machine can connect to no more than two networks simultaneously.

2. Define *network transfer* to be the passage of a message from one network to another through a gateway machine. Suppose that you wish to connect 100 machines with the networks of exercise 1 such that the number of network transfers required to get a message from any one machine to any other machine is as small as possible. More specifically, find k such that no two machines are more than k transfers apart and such that no smaller value for k would have this property. How would you do it?

The Internet Protocol (IP) Layer and Above

We have discussed one physical communications medium, Ethernet, in some detail. We have mentioned Token Ring (essentially a competing product) as another possibility, and there are others. In order to insulate the users of computer communications and the writers of communications software systems from having to become experts on many different kinds of communications hardware, a layer of software has been written, called the Internet Protocol, or IP. This layer provides a standard way of handling packets of information regardless of whether the underlying transport mechanism is Ethernet, Token Ring, or some other system. As long as someone writes the IP software for a particular new methodology, then any software using IP will be able to make use of it with minimum effort.

Each computer (or host) is given an IP address regardless of how it is connected. IP packets look a lot like Ethernet packets, with a source and destination address. If you know the IP address of the host you want to contact, the software will do the rest. It will automatically choose the appropriate networks (be they Token Ring, Ethernet, or another). The IP layer makes all networks seem the same.

If an IP packet is sent over an Ethernet, the complete IP packet is treated as data by the Ethernet packet. In other words, we have a packet within a packet. A (somewhat stretched) analogy is that if we sent our manuscript on postcards to a person in France, but that person was on a business trip in Belgium, the person's secretary might put the postcards into envelopes with French stamps and forward them to Belgium.

Error Handling and TCP

The IP layer does not fully deal with errors that might occur. Things can and do go awry. Random errors, essentially noise on the transmission medium, can alter or destroy information in a packet. Packets may be lost altogether because of overloading the end recipient of the packets or because of *network congestion*. There is also the possibility of duplicated packets—the message or parts of it may arrive more than once.

Errors are detected in two major ways. One is that each packet includes a kind of *checksum*. An example of a checksum would be if we were reading a series of numbers to a person on the other end of a telephone connection. After reading the list, we would report the sum of the numbers read as well. The recipient of our phone message, after having copied down all the numbers, would then add them up. The resulting sum should match the checksum that we gave. If these do not match, an error must be assumed. The checksums used in packets are somewhat more complicated and are designed to catch a variety of errors. The second way of detecting errors is with acknowledgments and a timer. Each packet is acknowledged (also with a packet) by the receiving host. If the sender does not get an acknowledgment within a certain amount of time, she must assume that the packet was lost.

The detection and handling of errors are mostly done in a higher-level software layer, called the *Transmission Control Protocol*, or TCP layer. The response to a damaged packet is to fail to send an acknowledgment. This in effect requests the sending computer to re-send the packet when the timer on waiting for an acknowledgment expires. (The reason for duplicate packets is that the actual packet may have been okay, but the acknowledgment may have been lost.) TCP ensures that the resulting, delivered message is error-free. It reassembles packets in the proper order, drops duplicates, and handles a variety of other tasks, including establishing a connection between two parties communicating.

The communications protocols used over the Internet are called TCP/IP for reasons that should be clear by now.

Exercises

1. Find a networked computer that is on an Ethernet with network access to the Internet. Determine its Ethernet address and its IP address. (This information is often displayed

when a machine is rebooted, but do not reboot the machine unless local policy allows users to do that.)

2. Draw a rough sketch of the format of an Ethernet packet forwarding an IP packet as data. Identify the major fields in a way consistent with the drawings used in this text.

*More on Addressing

Addresses are important in everyday life, and there are often alternative ways to address the same location. For example, "The White House" and "1600 Pennsylvania Avenue" would both work for the U.S. Postal Service in Washington, D.C. Terms like "Presidential residence" would probably also work. If you were already nearby and giving directions, you could use "third house on the right," "house on the corner," or "the white house with the columns." If you were a courier delivering something, an address would eventually translate to walking a certain number of steps, turning right or left, taking more steps, and so forth. Thus, we deal with any number of addressing schemes, and in the end we have to translate these into action.

When dealing with computer networks, we also need to be aware that there are several different ways of addressing. When Ethernet is involved, all addressing must be translated to the 12-digit hexadecimal number unique to the Ethernet controller you are trying to reach. Fortunately, we don't have to memorize such addresses because there are other addressing methods better suited to human use, and with the help of computer software we can use higher-level, more descriptive addresses.

Let's use a high-level address and follow the process that gets us to the right place. Assume we are sending a message to Tom at the University of California at Berkeley. If his log-in ID on his computer is

```
TOM
```

and the machine he is using is named

```
SIGMA
```

then we might type

```
mail tom@sigma.berkeley.edu
```

This uses a high-level addressing scheme called a *domain address*. The domain address is a hierarchical addressing scheme going (left to right) from local to general, just like a typical mailing address. For the United States, the last portion is one of the following:

com (commercial)
net (network)
edu (educational institution)
org (organization)
mil (military)
gov (government)

or a state code followed by `.us`. International extensions to this scheme end in a country code. Other levels are appropriately descriptive; their number depends on the size and complexity of the organization. The leftmost entry of the domain address is often the name of the host machine, `sigma` in the example, on which the user reads his e-mail.

This example domain address will cause a query to be sent to the machine `sigma` at Berkeley. There it will probably encounter a piece of software called the *name server*, which will produce a lower-level address called the IP address. This IP address is a number of the form 128.123.34.56 (four decimal numbers, each ranging from 0 through 255 and separated by periods). For all practical purposes, throughout the Internet, this IP address uniquely identifies the computer and the network. (Actually, more accurately, it identifies a connection point of a computer to a network. A gateway machine has more than one IP address. Most computers have only one connection point, thus only one IP address.)

Again, the beauty of the IP address is that it is independent of the kind of hardware it is used for. The actual lower-level hardware may be Ethernet or Token Ring or some other communications method. Since everything has an IP address, once we have the address we can start sending packets to our destination using the actual physical medium. In the case of Ethernet, an IP packet is carried as data in an Ethernet packet, which uses the 12 hexadecimal digits for addressing. Because this translation to the other addresses is done automatically, we normally don't have to worry about it. For our message to Berkeley, the software will figure out the addresses of the various Ethernet controllers that may be involved. If other types of communications hardware are being used, then the addressing specific to that method will automatically be utilized.

Exercises

1. Determine the e-mail addresses of several friends in your town and in distant towns. Send them messages.

2. Find both the IP address and the domain address for the computer you use most often.

Networked Servers

An extremely successful idea in computer networking is that of a *server*. A server is a program running on a networked machine that can provide certain services to other machines on the network. (If the server machine is also a general-purpose machine with users, it may also provide these services to local users.) Using a server is a common way of sharing scarce resources on a network or of using economy of scale to provide a service from a machine that is optimized to provide that service. Sometimes special *client* software is needed to utilize a server. Usually this is conveniently built into any application you are using.

One of the first ways that many computer users encounter servers is at home or in a small business where they have two or more computers networked together. Then they wonder, Wouldn't it be nice to share a printer between computers? Moving the printer from machine to machine by unplugging and plugging in printer cables would do the job but would be too cumbersome. The solution is to connect your printer to one machine and make the machine a *print server*. Then all computers on that network would have access to that printer. Appropriate server software queues up requests when more than one user attempts to print at the same time.

File Servers

Many computers users have used *file servers* without even knowing it. If you use a large general-purpose networked system like those often found at schools, it is common for all a user's personal files to be stored on one or more large file servers. This allows the user to log in to any machine on the network. The user's files appear to be local to that machine while actually being provided over the network by the file server. Two network file systems that are in common use are the Network File System (NFS) and the Andrew File System (AFS).

File servers are also used to organize and share software. There is usually no need to store a copy of every piece of software on every machine's local disk. Servers also afford some central control, as is required for certain licensed software where the fee paid restricts the access to a limited number of simultaneous users. A server can keep track of who has "checked out" the software and yet potentially allow access to that software to any user.

Servers Everywhere

The server approach is so powerful that many parts of modern computer systems use servers. We previously mentioned name servers. They help in resolving network addressing questions. Several of the applications that we discuss are typically implemented with servers. One of the most common servers in use today is the *Web server*. It serves the clients you have become familiar with: the Netscape or Microsoft browsers.

More Network-Based Applications

Our main illustration of Internet applications so far have been e-mail and the World Wide Web. This section considers some additional applications.

News

The interchange of general-interest information by computer started in 1979, when two graduate students at Duke University and a graduate student from the University of North Carolina at Chapel Hill started posting general information for others to read. The connections between the computers were made via modems over dial-up phone lines. (Only a small number of institutions had high-speed connections over the ARPA Net, an ancestor of the Internet.) Thus, they developed the software for posting and sending news (rather than e-mail, which was already in common use then). Soon several Duke University computers were involved, and the system went national when AT&T Bell Labs in New Jersey became the first non–North Carolina site to participate (and pay the long-distance charges). This system, dubbed *USENET*, grew rapidly, with participants all over the world. Most news is now forwarded over the Internet, and only a few sites depend on dial-up modem links.

Many news clients access the news server. Most Web browsers have news-reading capabilities built in. Others work in conjunction with some of the better mail readers and editors.

Using Remote Computers

If you have an account on any remote computer that is on the Internet, you can log in to it using the `ssh` command. For example, you could type

```
ssh truth.duke.edu
```

and provide your user ID and password to log in to the machine named `truth`. ssh is a secure version of the older telnet program, which performs the same services. ssh encrypts the session and makes sure that the password you send to the remote site to log in is not in readable form. (If the remote site does not yet support ssh, and you don't care if your password gets out, you may have to use telnet.)

If you just want to download files from such a computer, you can use the *file transfer protocol*, or ftp, by typing

```
ftp truth.duke.edu
```

and providing your ID and password and then using the appropriate download commands (e.g., `get filename`). Many Internet sites provide public information by allowing people to log in using the ID `anonymous` and using their own e-mail addresses as passwords. This is called *anonymous ftp*. Usually the same sites that provide anonymous ftp service also provide the same information through a Web site, and this is certainly more convenient. But not all sites are that accommodating.

Messaging Programs

There are a number of programs available that allow two people to communicate with each other in real time using their keyboards. Often the screen is split, and one field shows what you are typing and the other shows what your correspondent is typing. Some of these are descendents of the UNIX `talk` program, which first supported real-time messaging in this form. Currently popular versions include ICQ and AOL's (America On Line's) Instant Messaging.

Internet Relay Chat

Another popular Internet application that predates the Web is the *Internet Relay Chat*, more commonly referred to as IRC, which was developed in 1988 by the Finnish programmer Jarkko Oikarinen. With an IRC client, you can join one of hundreds of chat groups, called "channels," that are organized around every conceivable topic. The interface allows you to see what everyone is typing, much like the messaging systems just mentioned. However, there may be a large number of people on the channel, so it can get very busy and sometimes confusing. While many consider IRC use a fascinating (and to some, addictive) waste of time, this is an interesting way to meet strangers on-line. Since there are many foreign-language channels, it's also a good way to practice whatever language you are studying. At any given time, day or night, many thousands of users are logged on to an IRC client (see http://www.irchelp.org for more information).

Lynx

Another Web browser worth mentioning is *lynx*. This browser shows only text and bypasses all images on the Web. This is useful when your computer does not support graphics—you may be using a characters-only terminal. It is also useful when, for some reason, you have only a very-low-speed connection. Images require the transmission of large amounts of data.

Exercises

1. Read news on your local machine.

2. Try out the *lynx* Web browser.

3. Try out anonymous ftp to access some publicly accessible government documents. Most government Web sites give the addresses needed to get the files using ftp.

4. Find a friend who has installed an IRC client on his or her machine, and see if IRC might be of interest to you. If it looks like fun (and you have hours to burn) download your own client.

The Changing Internet

Over the years, many programmers used basic tools like telnet and ftp to gather information from other computers. Many computer sites keep special archives of programs and other information available for downloading. Some of the archives are sponsored by computer clubs or by the government. Institutions and individuals make general information available to people in this manner. Scientists keep copies of their latest publications on the computer so that other scientists can get copies of them. Historically, only people who were familiar with these basic tools had use of the Internet.

The World Wide Web has changed that. The nonprogrammer can be just as much at home on the Web as the computer professional. Many additional information services are now available because of this increased audience.

Another facet of the Internet that has changed is the support by advertisers. The earliest versions of the Internet banned commercial use altogether. Then personal flea-market-type newsgroups became popular. Now, much of what one finds on the Web has some kind of commercial basis or is supported by advertising. In many ways the Web now mimics commercial television. It's all free, but it has to be paid for somehow, and that often means a commercial sponsor with ads.

Problems in Paradise

The time has come to discuss a more sober side of communications. Ease in communications brings with it the increased chance that security or confidentiality may be compromised. Of course, if a computer is not connected to the outside world in any way, then many security problems are of no concern.

Some of the more obvious problems with bus-based Ethernet are taking care of themselves as users upgrade to more sophisticated switched hubs. Many of the other security issues were discussed in chapter 11. One main theme is worth repeating: *The only practical way to ensure privacy is through encryption.*

Kerberos

A widely used network-specific solution to the password security problem is named Kerberos (after the mythical three-headed dog guarding the entrance to Hades). By having a physically secure arbiter of passwords (the Kerberos server), you can have your computer send essentially encrypted versions of your password to a remote machine. (More accurately, the Kerberos server sends a "shared secret" encrypted by your password to the machine you are attempting to log in on. If the password you type in can decrypt this "shared secret," your password is assumed to be correct. Your password is thus never sent across the network while you are logging in.)

To defeat a replay attack, this encryption involves the time of day, so that just replaying a previously encrypted message recorded from eavesdropping will not work because the correct encrypted message changes with time. It does require that all the computers in the network be synchronized and agree on the time of day (within certain tolerances).

Summary

Computer communications are at the heart of the latest technology revolution: the World Wide Web. We took a look at the various layers used to provide connectivity. We started at the lowest level, using Ethernet as an example and noting the packet approach that permeates computer communications. We then moved to the higher layers, including the ubiquitous IP layer and the error-free services of the TCP layer.

We discussed the addressing schemes used at the various levels: Ethernet or machine addresses, IP addresses, and domain addresses. Then we looked at a sampling of applications, including ssh, telnet, ftp, news, and IRC.

The extremely important network-based server approach was discussed and related to Web servers and browsers, print servers, and file servers. Finally, some of the security questions first raised in chapter 11 were brought up again, because it is computer communications that makes us so vulnerable to anonymous remote attacks.

OUR UNITED NATIONS DELEGATION IS TO VISIT THE 300 LARGEST CITIES OF AFRICA OVER A 3-YEAR PERIOD.

WE NEED TO KNOW THE SHORTEST PATH THAT BEGINS IN CAIRO, GOES TO ALL THE CITIES, AND RETURNS TO CAIRO IN THE END.

WELL... IF YOU WANT THE VERY SHORTEST PATH, YOU'LL NEED TO TRANSPORT ME TO ANOTHER SOLAR SYSTEM.

WHY?!

BECAUSE THE SUN HERE WILL BURN OUT BEFORE I CAN FINISH!

13 Program Execution Time

On the Limitations of Computer Science

If one is a fairly experienced programmer, it is quite common to feel confident in one's ability to program almost anything. Programmers will often say, "If you tell me what you want done, I can code it for you." At the end of chapter 4, we discussed the Church-Markov-Turing Thesis, which hypothesizes that any procedure that can be precisely explained can be coded in any standard programming language.

It therefore may be surprising to learn that there are many useful calculations that we cannot do. This chapter and the ones that follow examine a number of problems whose solutions would be extremely useful but that computer scientists have not been able to solve. We examine the current limitations of the field, the topic areas for much modern-day research.

There are three major reasons that many useful calculations cannot be done:

1. The execution time of the program may be too long. Instead of simply yielding an answer after a few seconds or minutes, the program may require a year or even a century to find the answer. This may happen even though the fastest, most modern computer is used.
2. The problem may be what computer scientists call *noncomputable*. There are problems that no computer program can solve using current technologies or any technologies that can be foreseen. Many of these are of great practical interest and seem to form an impenetrable blockage to certain kinds of progress.
3. We may not know how to write the program to solve the problem. There are many problems that could conceivably be solved with present-day machines and languages, but methods are not known for solving them. Many of these are subproblems in the field of artificial intelligence—questions related to how to make machines "understand" language, visual data, and other concepts, and how to make machines learn.

These three topics related to the limitations of computer science are the concern of this and later chapters. In this chapter, we study the execution time of programs. In chapter 14, we examine parallel machine architectures that make it possible to speed up some computations. Chapter 15 presents the fundamental facts related to noncomputability and gives examples of important problems that are unsolvable by any known method. Chapter 16 gives an overview of the field of artificial intelligence, a study of problems that may be solvable but in many cases are beyond our present abilities to solve.

Program Execution Time

Ideally, a computation happens quickly. We would like to type the input to the machine, wait for no more than a few seconds, and then see the answer displayed. Most of the example programs examined in this book run satisfactorily, and in a learning environment it is not obvious that the execution time of programs can be a problem. But in industry, government, and research laboratories, program execution time is a matter of great concern. The quantity of data that needs to be processed can become astronomical, and even the fastest machines can require hours, days, or even years to complete certain tasks.

It is no longer enough to simply write a program and run it until the job is done. It becomes important to understand timing considerations for programs and to be able to predict how much time specific calculations will require before they are attempted. Before a U.S. government service attempts to sort the Social Security numbers of taxpayers, it is important to know how many hours, months, or years of computer time may be needed to do the job. Before a power company attempts to compute the most efficient routing of power lines around a region, it is advisable to estimate how many hours, months, or years of machine time will be expended. The cost of the calculation may be so high as to be prohibitive, forcing managers to look for alternative ways to manage their data and make their decisions.

This chapter examines the execution times of some programs and estimates how long they would require to handle some rather large blocks of data. The concept of a *tractable computation* is introduced; this is a calculation that can usually be completed on even large blocks of data within a reasonable time period. Then some *intractable calculations* are introduced that can require astounding amounts of computation for almost any problem beyond the most trivial examples. The conclusion of our study will be that computations divide themselves roughly into two classes: those that can be done with reasonable expenditures of time, and those that cannot be realistically completed except for rather small examples. Since problems in both classes are quite common in practical situations, these limitations are of substantial importance.

```
Name                    Height        Weight

0  John Jones         0  67         0  120
1  Sue Black          1  67         1  131
2  Bill Smith         2  73         2  166
3  Frank Doe          3  68         3  140
4  Jean White         4  67         4  131
5  Nancy Blike        5  71         5  162
```

Figure 13.1

Tractable Computations

For the moment, a tractable computation should be understood intuitively to be a calculation that can be done within a reasonable period of time even if large amounts of data are to be processed. A more precise definition of this term is given later in this section.

We begin by examining a particular computation, the task of collecting the names of all people with a specified height and weight. We assume three arrays are given, name, height, and weight, which hold in positions *i* the names, heights, and weights of several people (figure 13.1).

In the figure, John Jones has a height of 67 inches and a weight of 120 pounds, and the other five people have the associated heights and weights as shown. The program will store these arrays and then receive from the user two pieces of information, a target height and a target weight. The program will then display the names of all people who have this target height and weight.

A sample execution of the program would use the following algorithm:

Algorithm
Read in all entries in the arrays.

Prompt user to enter target height into IntField labeled Target height and store the integer.

Prompt user to enter target weight into IntField labeled Target weight and store the integer.

Compare user input to data in arrays. List all names of people who have the specified height and weight.

If a target height 67 and a target weight 131 are entered, the program will display the names of people who meet these targets:

Sue Black
Jean White

Let's examine a program to do this task:

```
import awb.*;
import java.awt.*;
import java.awt.event.*;

public class PersonSearch extends java.applet.Applet
                implements ActionListener
{
    String [] name;
    int [] height, weight;
    int i, n, targetheight, targetweight;
    IntField Theight, Tweight;
    TextArea FoundNames;
    Button b;

    public void init()
    {
        name = new String[100];
        height = new int[100];
        weight = new int[100];
        Theight = new IntField(15);
        Theight.setLabel("Target height");
        Tweight = new IntField(15);
        Tweight.setLabel("Target weight");
        FoundNames = new TextArea(10,60);
        b = new Button("Search");
        b.addActionListener(this);
        // Code to fill arrays with name, height, weight data
        // n contains the number of names in data
        add(FoundNames);
        add(Theight);
        add(Tweight);
        add(b);
    }
```

```
public void actionPerformed(ActionEvent event)
{
    Object cause = event.getSource();

    if (cause == b)
    {
        targetheight = Theight.getInt();
        targetweight = Tweight.getInt();
        FoundNames.setText("The names found:\n");
        i = 0;
        while (i < n)
        {
            if ((height[i] == targetheight)
            && (weight[i] == targetweight))
            {FoundNames.append(name[i] + "\n");}
            i = i + 1;
        }
    }
}
```

As you can see, this program is capable of holding the information for up to 100 people. Throughout this chapter, the symbol *n* will be used to measure the size of the task being undertaken. In this example, *n* represents the number of people whose records must be examined. For this example, *n* is 6, and for the given program *n* may not exceed 100 unless the type declarations are changed.

The loop in the program examines sequentially `weight[0]` and `height[0]`, then `weight[1]` and `height[1]`, and so forth, printing the associated name whenever the examined values both equal the target values.

The execution time for the program has two parts, the part required to fill the arrays and type in the target values, and the part required to perform the looping computation. We will consider only the second part; it is that part of the execution where the search through the data takes place. Thus, we are measuring the time required to examine the records of *n* people to find all cases that meet the two requirements. We are measuring the amount of time elapsed between the time the button is pushed and the time the last array data are examined.

A version of this program was entered into a computer and measurements were made of its search times. We assumed that the number of people might equal the number of students in a small university, up to 10,000 people. The results showed that this is a very inexpensive calculation even for this large number of people:

No. of People n	Execution Time (sec.) t
2,500	1.275
5,000	2.550
7,500	3.825
10,000	5.100

Ten thousand people can be checked in about 5 seconds on this particular machine.

These values can be graphed, showing that they form a straight line (figure 13.2), and algebraic methods can be used to find an equation for the line. In this case, execution time in seconds, t, and number of people, n, enter into an equation as follows:

$$t = 5.1 * 10^{-4} * n$$

The reader should check to see that if values of n from the table are entered into this equation, then the associated times t are correctly computed. Checking the second entry in the table, $n = 5000$, we get

$$t = 5.1 * 10^{-4} * 5000 = 2.55$$

It is often difficult to find formulas to compute execution times as was done here. But if they can be found, they are very useful. For example, one might ask how long it would

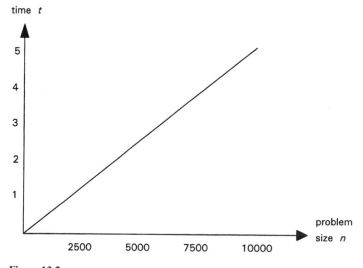

Figure 13.2

	A
1	47
2	12
3	46
4	10
5	41
6	33
7	44
8	86

(a)

	A
1	10
2	12
3	33
4	41
5	44
6	46
7	47
8	86

(b)

Figure 13.3

take to run this program on the total population of a large country. Assume $n = 300$ million; the execution time can be computed to be 153,000 seconds, or 42.5 hours. This program can search the whole population of that country in just a couple of days. This is a good example of an easily tractable computation. (In this example, we ignore the problem of how to fit the records of so many people into a single computer database. We only address the issue of execution time, the most severe constraint in most situations.)

Let's examine another computation, the process of sorting numbers into ascending order. That is, suppose an array A has values as shown in figure 13.3a. How long would it take a computer to put these numbers in order, as shown in figure 13.3b? This computation can be done by an algorithm called quicksort, and its running time was tested in the same way we tested the running time of the search program. Again, with a population of the size of a small university, this program was run for values of n up to 10,000:

No. of People n	**Execution Time (sec.)** t
2,500	59.261
5,000	129.021
7,500	202.745
10,000	279.042

Assuming that sorting names is roughly as time-consuming as sorting numbers, one could use this type of program to alphabetize the names of students at a small university of size 10,000. The required time would be slightly over 4 minutes. This is another example of a tractable computation.

These values also can be graphed, although the result is not quite a straight line (figure 13.4). However, one can still use algebraic techniques (not discussed in this book) to obtain an approximate formula for execution time, in seconds:

$$t = 2.1 * 10^{-3} * n * \log_2 n$$

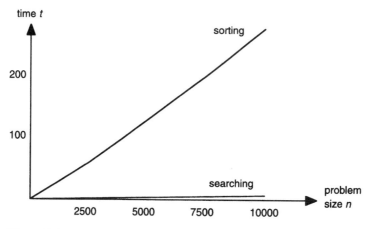

Figure 13.4

The function $\log_2 n$ commonly occurs in algebra and computer science. Some of its values are given here:

n	$\log_2 n$
1	0
2	1
4	2
8	3
16	4
32	5
2,500	11.2877
5,000	12.2877
7,500	12.8727
10,000	13.2877

One can check that the formula agrees with the values in the table. Thus, for $n = 5000$,

$$t = 2.1 * 10^{-3} * 5000 * 12.2877 = 129.021$$

The figure shows the run times for both sorting and searching. Sorting is clearly far more expensive than searching, but it is still classified as tractable.

Again, it is possible to calculate the cost of running this program on a huge population. Using the fact that if $n = 300$ million, then $\log_2 n = 28.1604$, the formula gives the sorting time as 205.34 days. This is a long time, but remember that the size of the job is huge. If a government service wants to do this calculation, it will presumably use large computers rather than our desktop model, and such machines might run a hundred or more times faster than our formula result would suggest. So the time required could probably be reduced to a couple of days or so. Thus, we conclude that sorting is another example of a tractable computation.

We are now able to give a more precise definition of tractability; this is the definition used by most computer scientists: A computation will be called tractable if its timing formula is a polynomial on n (and possibly $\log_2 n$). Such polynomials are sums of terms of the form $a * n^b$ or $a * n^b * (\log_2 n)^c$, where a, b, and c are fixed numbers. For example, the following formulas all give timings for tractable computations:

$$t = 3 * n^2$$

$$t = 4 * n^3 + 16 * n^2 + 7 * n + 8$$

$$t = 4 * n^2 * \log_2 n + 3 * n$$

$$t = 17 * (\log_2 n)^2 + n$$

The reader should check that the execution times for the preceding search and sort programs do have the required form and thus qualify officially as tractable computations.

In contrast to tractable computations, there are intractable ones, where the timing formula includes an n in the exponent. As an example, $t = 6^n$ is a formula that does not conform to the tractability definition. In this case, t increases in a profoundly different manner than in tractable situations, and at a much faster rate as n is increased. The next section gives an example of an intractable computation.

Exercises

1. Embed the following loop code in a program and run it for various values of n. Graph its execution time versus n. The formula for execution time should have this form, where C and D are numbers that you must determine: $t = C + Dn$.

```
i = 0;
while (i < n)
{
    i = i + 1;
}
```

What values do the constants C and D have for this program on your computer? How long would it take your program to count to 300 million?

2. Repeat exercise 1 for the following program. The execution time equation should have this form: $t = C + Dn^2$.

```
j = 0;
while (j < n)
{
    k = 0;
    while (k < n)
    {
        k := k + 1;
    }
    j = j + 1;
}
```

3. The program of exercise 2 was constructed by nesting a loop inside another loop. Revise to have three nested loops instead of two, and find a formula for its execution time.

4. The program to find all individuals of given height and weight will run faster if the data in the arrays are organized in a special way. Can you find that special way and show how to revise the program to run faster? Can you find a formula for its execution time and estimate the time required to process all the people in the United States?

Intractable Computations

A computation is called intractable if its execution time increases with increasing n faster than any polynomial of the form described for tractable computations in the previous section. An example of an intractable computation is the generation of all orderings of a set of n objects. (These orderings are called *permutations*.) As an illustration, suppose we have the three letters A, B, and C, and we wish to find all their orderings. The first ordering is just A, B, C. Another one is A, C, B. Here is a list of all the orderings of these three letters. There are of six of them.

A, B, C
A, C, B
B, A, C
B, C, A
C, A, B
C, B, A

A program is given in the exercise at the end of this section that will compute these orderings or permutations. Following the method of the previous section, we run the program for several values of *n* and find a function that will estimate the run time. (Actually, the code shown will need some modifications related to the size of the set being reordered. We do not describe those changes here.) We run the program with the usual values and record the observed timings:

No. of Objects	Execution Time (sec.)
n	*t*
2,500	?
5,000	?
7,500	?
10,000	?

Strangely, the measurement is not successful, and the program apparently runs forever when started on these values. What is wrong? Perhaps the program will not work if *n* is large.

In fact, there is a solution, and the program will solve it even for large *n*, but the execution time is large. Let's run the program on some small values of *n* and see how fast the run time grows:

No. of Objects	Execution Time (sec.)
n	*t*
1	<1
2	<1
3	<1
4	<1
5	<1
6	3.19
7	22.57
8	183.00
9	1,672.20

If we add these data to a graph like figure 13.4, it is clear that a new phenomenon is occurring (figure 13.5). The time to complete the task at $n = 9$ is greater than it was for sorting at $n = 10000$, and it is climbing on a line (labeled "permutations") that is nearly straight up.

We can find a formula to estimate the timing in seconds for this program:

$$t = 4.6 * 10^{-3} * n!$$

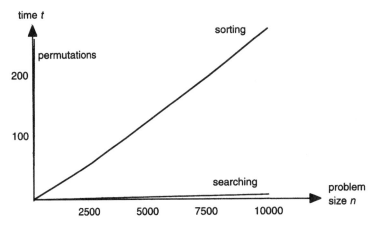

Figure 13.5

This comes from the fact that the number of orderings of n objects is $n!$ (which is spoken as n factorial). Thus, in the case of the three characters A, B, and C, the number of orderings is $3! = 1 * 2 * 3 = 6$, as was stated. One can use Sterling's formula to get a more easily understood version of the time estimate:

$$t = 4.6 * 10^{-3} * (2\pi n)^{1/2}(n/e)^n$$

where π and e can be approximated by 3.14159 and 2.71828, respectively. Then we can evaluate t for increasing values of n and see what computer scientists mean when they call something intractable.

n	t (approximate)
10	4.64 hours
11	2.13 days
12	25.50 days
13	331.53 days
14	12.71 years
15	191 years
16	3,052 years
17	51,882 years
18	933,883 years
19	17,743,767 years
20	354,875,356 years
21	7,452,382,483 years
22	163,952,414,630 years

The time required to process 14 objects is several years; 15 objects, a couple of centuries; and 18 objects, a period longer than all of recorded history. Physicists say that the sun will burn out in a few billion years, so the machine would not be able to process 22 objects unless it were moved to a different solar system. The history of the universe since the Big Bang, as theorized by cosmologists, is a mere 15 billion or so years, not enough time to have processed 22 objects.

Thus, in contrast with the examples of the previous section, where the calculations were completed for n of 10,000 or even 300 million, in the current example n may not exceed even two dozen. There is no comparison between the run times of tractable problems and intractable problems, such as the computation just discussed.

One might propose that future technology will be able to circumvent the problem of intractability. Large numbers of faster machines all working together may someday make it possible to handle even the problem discussed here for large n. Unfortunately, there is little hope that technology will help much for such problems. Suppose a rather substantial improvement in machines enabled them to run 1,000 times faster, and that a way were found to break the problem into small parts so that 1,000 such machines could all work in parallel on the solution. Even with this 1-million-fold increase in effort, it would be possible to solve problems with only half a dozen more objects than is currently possible in a given amount of time. The system could still do just a couple of dozen objects.

Finally, a question arises concerning the importance of this result. How many managers of contemporary industry really want to compute all the orderings of a set of objects? As we explain in the following section, this computation is at the heart of some very important kinds of problems and its efficient solution is very valuable. Furthermore, there are many computations that are very different in kind from this one but that have similar execution times. So a study of these problems presents a set of issues that are common over a large class of computations.

Exercise

1. Type the following subroutine and test it on your machine. A legal input is a string of characters without separators, and this is placed in the second parameter location, `original`. The first parameter should be a string of length zero. For example, if you want the subroutine to do the orderings of the characters A, B, and C, just load x with the null string "" and y with "ABC" and execute `permutation(x,y)`. Be sure to define a `TextArea` called `Found` in the environment of the subroutine and initialize `TextArea` with `Found.setText("The permutations:");`. Run the program on some short strings of lengths 2 to 6, and draw a graph of execution time versus n for your machine. Can you find a formula for its execution time? (This code utilizes recursion, so its operation is not necessarily easy to understand. But you can do this experiment without understanding it in detail.)

```
// A subroutine to list all of the orderings (permutations)
// of a set of characters.
//
// Input: A string of characters placed in the second parameter.
// The first parameter should be initialized as the null
//                  string "".
//
// Output: A set of strings giving every possible reordering
// of the characters in the original string. These are listed
// in the TextArea Found. For example, if the input is ABC, then
// the output will be ABC, ACB, BAC, BCA, CAB, CBA.
//
// Method of operation: The program maintains two strings, original
// and target. Original begins by holding the original string, and
// as the target string is constructed, characters are moved from
// original to target. The program makes every possible choice for
// what character should be in the first position, then every
// possible choice from the characters left for the second
// position, and so on.

void permutation(String target, String original)
{
    int i;
    String target1, original1;
    if (original.length() == 0)
    {
        Found.append(target + "\n");
    }
    else
    {
        i = 0;
        while (i < original.length())
        {
            target1 = target + original.substring(i,i+1);
            original1 = original.substring(0,i)
                    + original.substring(i+1,original.length());
            permutation(target1,original1);
            i = i + 1;
        }
    }
}
```

Some Practical Problems with Very Expensive Solutions

We examine three problems in this section that appear to be very expensive to solve computationally, as is finding all the orderings of n objects. The problems address the issues of finding minimum-cost paths on a flat plane, the most efficient coverage of an area with odd-shaped parts, and the discovery of the minimum number of colors for doing a certain kind of graph coloring.

Finding the Minimum-Cost Path

Suppose a traveling salesperson wishes to visit a series of cities, beginning at his or her home city, driving to visit each of the other cities exactly once, and then returning home. Suppose further that there are six cities, A–F (figure 13.6). The question is, Which route should he or she follow in order to achieve the shortest possible trip?

An example route might start at city A and then proceed sequentially to cities B, C, D, E, F, and back to A. The distance traveled (in miles) is easy to compute:

A to B   42
B to C   20
C to D   29
D to E   49
E to F   11
F to A   46

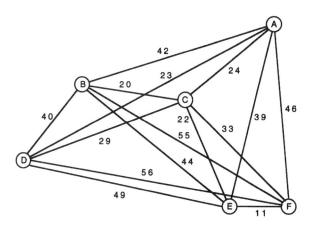

Figure 13.6

which comes to a total of 197 miles. But is this the shortest possible distance? Perhaps some other route would be better. The goal is to find it.

One way to find the shortest route is to find all routes, compute their lengths, and then select the best one. Here are a few of the routes that might be tried and their respective lengths.

Route	Length (miles)
AECDBFA	231
ACBDEFA	190
ABFEDCA	210
AEFDCBA	197
AFDECBA	235

The minimum one found here has a length of 190 miles, and there may be even shorter paths.

This calculation has a strange resemblance to the one we were doing in the last section. We start at a city, then we try an ordering of the cities that are left, then we return to the home city. So we must do a calculation for every possible ordering of the cities that are not the home city. There are $n - 1$ of them, so there must be $(n - 1)!$ such paths. Actually, if we count going around a loop in one direction the same as going around it in the other direction, we should divide by 2. So the number of paths is

$$s = (n - 1)!/2 = ((n - 1) * (n - 2) * \cdots * 1)/2$$

For $n = 6$ cities, one must check

$$s = (5 * 4 * 3 * 2 * 1)/2 = 60$$

different paths to solve the problem.

Clearly, this calculation for n cities is extremely expensive if no better solution method is found. This is called the *Traveling Salesperson Problem*, and it has been studied by many scholars over the past three decades. Some substantially better algorithms have been discovered, but even the best yield only intractable calculations. The details of such methodologies are beyond the scope of this book. However, if we were to write a program to implement any such procedure, the time chart would look very similar to the one for computing all the orderings of n objects, described in the previous section. Some problems have been solved for cases where n is a few hundred cities or more, but the amount of computer time can be large. Problems where n ranges in the thousands are completely out of the question unless they are special cases of some kind.

The Traveling Salesperson Problem is of great importance for two reasons:

1. Many practical problems involve finding such shortest-path solutions, for instance, setting up a truck route or an electric power distribution system.

2. The Traveling Salesperson Problem has been shown to be a member of a class called the *NP-complete* problems. The NP-complete problems are an important class in that they include many problems of practical importance. It has been shown that if a polynomial time algorithm can be found for solving any member of the class, then any other problem in the NP-complete class will also be solvable in polynomial time. Thus, if someone were able to find a way to solve the Traveling Salesperson Problem in tractable time, all the other problems in the class would become tractable also.

It is widely conjectured that no algorithm could exist that could solve the Traveling Salesperson Problem in tractable (or polynomial) time. Scientists have tried for many years either to prove that it cannot be solved in tractable (polynomial) time or to find a tractable (polynomial) algorithm to solve it. So far they have been unable to achieve either result, and this stands as one of the great unsolved problems in the field. In computer science jargon, Does P equal NP? That is, Does the class of problems solvable in polynomial time equal the class of problems in NP such as the Traveling Salesperson Problem?

Finding the Best Coverage of an Area

Suppose we have the following positive integers: 3, 21, 25, 31, 45, 57, 77, 87. We wish to find a subset of these integers that comes as close as possible to adding up to 110 but that does not exceed 110. For example, we could try the subset {3, 31, 57}. This adds up to 91. Let's try another one, {45, 57}; it adds up to 102. What about {25, 87}? It adds up to 112, but this exceeds the allowed maximum of 110. Let's be systematic and write down a lot of the possibilities:

Subset	Sum
{3, 31, 57}	91
{45, 57}	102
{25, 87}	112
{31, 77}	108
{3, 21, 25, 31}	80
{21, 87}	108

⋮

The best solution we have been able to find is a sum of 108, and we found two ways to get it. You should try to do some other sums to see if you can do better.

This problem is an example of the *Subset Sum Problem*, which is a special case of the much-studied *Knapsack Problem*. It is important for many reasons. First, it is a solution to the following practical question: Assume the set of integers represent the lengths of some boards that you need to build a certain structure. You have purchased a board that

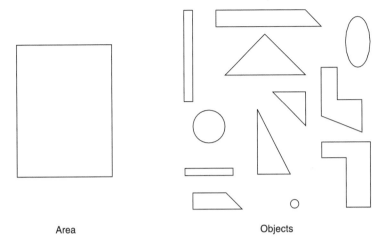

Area   Objects

Figure 13.7

is 110 units long, and you wish to cut some boards for your structure with as little waste as possible. Which set of boards should you choose so that as little will be left of the 110 unit board as possible?

A second reason the Subset Sum Problem is important is that a two-dimensional version of it is also quite common. If you have a set of odd shaped objects (figure 13.7), which ones should you choose and how should you arrange them in order to maximally cover a given rectangular area? Figure 13.8 gives a solution to that problem, and you can see that it is very difficult to find. Since the linear board problem is a special case of this two-dimensional problem, the latter must be at least as expensive to solve.

It turns out that the Subset Sum Problem is in the NP-complete class and thus has all the properties of those problems. We should not be too surprised at this because we have been solving it by looking at all subsets of n objects and there are 2^n of them. Thus, it is not known whether there is a tractable solution for it; it is generally believed that there is not. We can expect to find only very expensive (intractable) solutions to it. Consequently, we can expect to find only very expensive (intractable) solutions to the two-dimensional shape problem. So many parlor game puzzles that we are given to test our intelligence are problems whose only known solutions are very expensive.

Finding the Best Coloring of a Graph

Consider figure 13.9 and the task of assigning a color to each of the circular nodes. The *Graph Coloring Problem* is to find the coloring of all the nodes such that no two connected nodes have the same color and such that the minimum number of colors has been used.

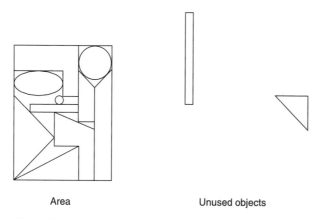

Area   Unused objects

Figure 13.8

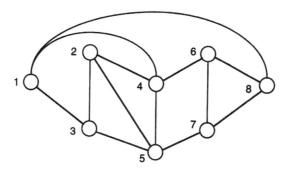

Figure 13.9

To find a solution, the first idea is to simply use a different color on every node. Call the colors C1, C2, C3, ..., C8. Then we could color the first node with color C1, the second node with C2, and so forth for the rest of the nodes. We can write this down as follows:

1. C1, 2. C2, 3. C3, 4. C4, 5. C5, 6. C6, 7. C7, 8. C8

This is a coloring such that no two connected nodes have the same color. But it uses too many colors.

Let's try a different coloring with fewer colors. Perhaps we should color node 8 the same as node 1:

1. C1, 2. C2, 3. C3, 4. C4, 5. C5, 6. C6, 7. C7, 8. C1

This has fewer colors but it is not acceptable because nodes 1 and 8 are connected.

Let's try another coloring with node 7 colored the same as node 1:

1. C1, 2. C2, 3. C3, 4. C4, 5. C5, 6. C6, 7. C1, 8. C8

This uses only seven colors and it is otherwise acceptable. Next, we should try to reduce it again. Can we get it down to six colors? What is the minimum number of colors?

The Graph Coloring Problem is another example of an NP-complete problem. Again, we can expect any algorithm to solve it to be intractable unless some new and unexpected discovery is made.

Exercises

1. Can you find a better solution to the six-city Traveling Salesperson Problem than the one given in the text?

2. If you wish to solve the Traveling Salesperson Problem for ten cities, how many different orderings of the cities do you have to examine in order to get the best one? How many do you have to examine in the case of 20 cities?

3. Can you find a better solution to the example Sum Subset Problem than the one given in the text that finds a subset adding to 108?

4. Find the solution to the Sum Subset Problem for the following set of integers: 11, 23, 34, 57, 90, 110, 331, 366, 423, 462, 622, 801, 1,277. The target number is 1,435, and your job is to find the subset with the largest sum that is not greater than 1,435. How many subsets exist for this set of $n = 13$ integers? Do you need to examine them all?

5. Find the optimum solution to the Graph Coloring Problem shown in the text.

6. Suppose the graph for the Traveling Salesperson Problem is examined as a Graph Coloring Problem. What is the minimum number of colors needed to color it?

7. Give an example of a practical problem that is equivalent to solving the Graph Coloring Problem.

Diagnosing Tractable and Intractable Problems

Let's look again at the tractable and intractable problems given in the previous section and try to determine some common features of each. Perhaps there are some rules that will help diagnose new problems that we encounter as either tractable or intractable. We speak here only in an intuitive way and try to catch the flavor of the two kinds of problems. We do not give iron-clad rules for making decisions but rather give reasonable guidelines that usually work.

The tractable problems can often be characterized as those in which the data items are processed one at a time and in which, once a data item is handled, it is not looked at again. As an example, in a sorting problem one might find the smallest number in the array and put it into the first location. It need not be examined again. Then one finds the second smallest item and puts it into the second location. It need not be referenced again. And so forth. Many tractable computations have this flavor.

Another feature of tractable problems is that one often knows of examples that have been solved for large n. Is it possible to schedule 10,000 students for their classes while meeting certain acceptability criteria? Yes, we know of many times when this has been done. So it appears to be tractable.

The NP-complete problems often have the characteristic that one cannot process a given item and be done with it easily. For example, in the Traveling Salesperson Problem, one might decide to start at city A and then go to D. Then you might go to C and then on to E. No matter what decisions you make, you can never be sure that the first decision to go from A to D was correct. You might have to go back and try to start by going from A to C first. Later you might decide to try going from A to E first, or something else.

The same thing happens with the Subset Sum Problem. If one decides that 25 is not going to be used in the current guess of the solution, one can never set it aside permanently. Later one might decide to use it.

NP-complete problems often have a kind of "keep on trying" flavor about them. Examine again all the NP-complete problems we considered. In each case, we examined all the data as a unit and tested them for acceptability. Then we examined some other way of doing the whole problem and tested it. In each case, there were many ways to try to find a solution, and this resulted in the large computation times.

These NP-complete problems are all intractable using known algorithms, and we can expect them to stay that way unless some amazing discovery is made. So the characteristics we have been observing for NP-completeness are effectively the signs of intractability.

You should study these examples and other examples, and try to develop an intuition for what constitutes tractability and intractability. For most common situations, you should be able to guess correctly. But in some cases, it takes a Ph.D. degree and years of experience to discover the answer.

Exercise

1. In each case, study the problem given and then use the guidelines given in the text to classify it as well as you can as either tractable or intractable.
   (a) The tenth from largest integer in a set of n integers is to be found. (Assume that n is greater than 10.)
   (b) A set of n positive integers is to be divided into two parts, and the sum of the integers in one part is to equal the sum of the integers in the other.

(c) A set Q of n positive integers is to be examined to determine whether any subset of Q adds up to equal one of the other integers in Q.

(d) A set of n integers is to be examined to determine whether any two of them are the same.

(e) A set of n integers is to be added up, where n is greater than 1 billion.

(f) A set of n rectangles of various sizes are to be assembled to cover, without overlap, a large given rectangle.

(g) An ordinary jigsaw puzzle with n pieces is to be assembled.

(h) A minimum-length path is to be found through a set of cities that touches every city exactly once. There is no home city nor any need to complete the loop.

*Approximate Solutions to Intractable Problems

We decided that the Traveling Salesperson Problem is very expensive to solve if the number of cities is greater than a few dozen. However, there are many salespeople who do seem to solve this problem on a regular basis. How can this be? The answer is that we require the path to be the smallest possible path, and the realistic salesperson does not worry about finding the best path. Any solution will do that is not too wasteful, and people just make a good guess.

We can do the same thing with computers. In this section, we do not require the best solution as long as some reasonable solution is found. As an illustration, let's return to the Traveling Salesperson Problem and try again. One could propose that the following algorithm will obtain a good enough path through the cities:

1. Select the home city.
2. From the current city, choose the shortest path leading out to a city that has not yet been visited. Follow that path to the next city. If there are still unvisited cities, repeat step 2.
3. Connect the final city back to the home city.

Following this algorithm, we might start at city A and note that the nearest unvisited city is D. From D, the nearest unvisited city is C; from C the nearest unvisited city is B, and so forth. This calculation is very fast, and it may lead to an acceptable solution. Many other fast algorithms have been developed, and they are often better than the one we propose here.

Here is a way to get an approximation to the Subset Sum Problem. Write down all subsets of size 3 or less. Add to each as many remaining items in the list as is possible (using any selection process) without exceeding the given limit. Choose the one with the largest sum. It has been shown that if this procedure is followed, the resulting sum will be at least three-quarters of the size of the optimum answer.

Exercises

1. Returning to the six-city Traveling Salesperson Problem, find the length of the path discovered by the approximation algorithm of this section when you start at home city A. How does it compare with the best other solution that you have been able to find?

2. Repeat exercise 1 except start at home city B.

3. Here is another Traveling Salesperson Problem. The cities are A, B, C, and D, and the distances are 1 between A and B, 2 between A and C, 10,000 between A and D, 1 between B and C, 2 between B and D, and 1 between C and D. Starting at city A, use the approximation algorithm to solve this problem. Can you make any general statements about this approximation after doing this problem?

4. Repeat the example Subset Sum Problem in the section Finding the Best Coverage of an Area using the approximation algorithm given in this section.

5. Repeat the example Subset Sum Problem given in exercise 4 of the section before last. Use the approximation algorithm.

6. Find an approximation algorithm for the Graph Coloring Problem.

Summary

This chapter began by noting that there are three reasons why it may not be possible to do a desired calculation. The first, studied here, is that the amount of machine time required to do the calculation may be unrealistically large. Later chapters examine the other reasons.

In fact, the study of execution times leads to the concept of tractable and intractable computations. The former can be done in a reasonable time in most cases, even if large amounts of data are to be processed. The latter usually require astronomically huge execution times if problems of nontrivial size are attempted. Both kinds of calculations are important in practice.

We studied the idea of NP-complete problems, which are intractable by all known algorithms. The question of whether there will ever be tractable means for calculating them is still unanswered. Most observers guess that they are intrinsically intractable.

But even if it turns out that the NP-complete problems can be solved in tractable time, there are other problems that are provably intractable, for instance, computing all the permutations of n objects. Since there are $n!$ such permutations, this will always be an intractable computation.

Some seemingly intractable computations are amenable to approximate solutions that can be computed in an acceptable length of time and that are accurate enough for many purposes. Many of these problems and their approximate solutions are the object of recent research in computer science.

An interesting survey of work on the Traveling Salesperson Problem appears in Miller and Pekny (1991). This article describes a number of approximation methods that have achieved solutions to n city problems with n in the range of thousands or hundreds of thousands. It describes in detail an algorithm that finds exact solutions for some special-case problems of similar sizes.

It is possible that a calculation could not be done because some other resource besides time is not sufficiently available. One can imagine that there may be calculations that require astronomical amounts of memory, for example, and that they could not be completed because of memory limitations. In practice, this is an uncommon situation and is not discussed further in this book.

14   Parallel Computation

Using Many Processors Together

A major point of chapter 13 was that execution time can be a problem. An excessively long computation can cause inconvenience and missed deadlines. Even more seriously, the computation may become useless if it is not completed on time. This is the case, for example, in computing the trajectory for a space vehicle course correction or in calculating inventory requirements for the next day's assembly operations. If the figures are not computed on schedule, the usefulness of the calculation is lost.

Computations must be completed on time, but it is not necessarily easy to build faster machines. A minimum amount of circuitry is needed to do a calculation, and the electricity can travel through the wires no faster than the speed of light. We can make the calculation go faster by shrinking the circuit to smaller and smaller dimensions, but this is a process that cannot go on forever.

The other way to speed up a calculation is to divide it into parts and let several processors work on it together. This is known as *parallel computation*, and it is the concern of this chapter. In fact, we study computers that are especially designed to do such computation. They have many processors, possibly of the kind described in chapter 8, each doing its own part. They communicate as needed for the purposes of the task and in most cases complete their work many times faster than a single-processor machine.

The next section describes a parallel machine and shows how it can be used to solve two problems from chapter 13: the retrieval of the names of individuals with specified height and weight, and the Traveling Salesperson Problem. Later sections describe a sorting method for parallel machines, problems that arise when the parallelism is of limited degree, communication schemes for parallel machines, and a new type of parallel computer, the connectionist machine.

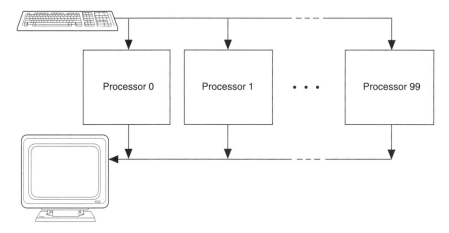

Figure 14.1

Parallel Computation

Parallel computation requires a parallel computer, and the first model to be studied here is composed of 100 machines placed in row (figure 14.1). These machines are nearly identical to the processor studied in all previous chapters. They all process a version of Java that has been slightly modified to account for the parallelism. All read from a single input source and simultaneously write to a very fast output device. They are numbered from 0 to 99.

Let's first program this parallel machine to solve the problem of finding the names of all individuals with a given height and weight. We begin by assuming the number of individuals n is 100 or fewer, so that one processor can be allocated to each. We later address the more general problem when n may be large.

Here is the program to do the computation. A copy of this code is loaded into every one of the 100 processors. Each processor has its own copy of *targetheight* and *targetweight*, and each processor holds the height, weight, and name of a particular person.

```
public class ParallelPersonSearch;

{
    double targetweight, targetheight, weight, height;
    String name;

    public void init()
    {
```

```
      // Put code here to enter data into weight, height, and name
      // for a single individual
      processor 0 output.setText("Give the target height.");
      targetheight = all input.getDouble();
      processor 0 output.setText("Give the target weight.");
      targetweight = all input.getDouble();
      if ((targetheight == height) && (targetweight == weight))
         {this processor output.setText(name);}
   }
}
```

The references to input and output are prefixed to indicate which of the 100 processors do the operation.

The functioning of the 100 processors as they do this computation is clear. First, each processor loads the weight, height, and name of one individual in a sequence of operations that does not interest us here. If there are fewer than 100 individuals, some of the processors will receive null values for height, weight, and name. Then processor 0 prints the message, "Give the target height." Next, all processors receive a value from the input, the target height. Then processor 0 prints, "Give the target weight," and all processors receive a second value, the target weight. Finally, each processor compares the target values with the values it stores for one person; if they match, it outputs that person's name. The output device prints all the names received from all the processors.

The input and output statements have prefix operators that designate which processors will do the action. If this code is running, for example, on processor 13, and that processor encounters `processor 0 output.setText`, it should ignore the statement and go on. If it encounters `all input.getDouble` or `this processor output.setText`, it should do the operation.

The timing of this parallel computation is dramatically faster than in the sequential case of chapter 13. Instead of finding the individuals in time

$$t_{\text{sequential}} = 5.1 * 10^{-4} * n$$

as before, the computation runs as fast as if there were only one individual in the database:

$$t_{\text{parallel}} = 5.1 * 10^{-4} * 1$$

The dramatic speedup that we were looking for has been obtained (figure 14.2). Of course, it is important to remember that these results pertain to a computation where there is a separate processor for each individual. The more general case when there may not be enough processors for all individuals is examined later.

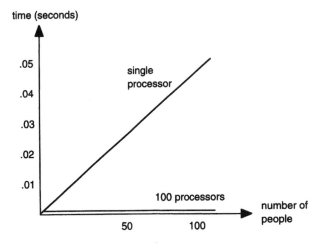

Figure 14.2

The Traveling Salesperson Problem provides an interesting second illustration of parallel computation. The methodology is to have each processor compute a different ordering for the cities and the length of the associated path. Then the different paths computed by all the processors are compared, and the best one is reported.

We do not examine the details of this program here but use the fact that the execution time for calculating one path can be estimated at about

$$t_{\text{parallel}} = 5 * 10^{-3} * n$$

which is substantially faster than the sequential version. If we have enough processors so that every possible path is computed on one of them, t_{parallel} gives a rough estimate of the total time required for a parallel machine to solve this problem. We assume that a reasonable time estimate for computing the exact solution to the Traveling Salesperson Problem on a single-processor machine is just to use the formula for computing permutations:

$$t_{\text{sequential}} = 4.6 * 10^{-3} * n!$$

Again, the power of parallel computing is dramatic, as is shown in figure 14.3 for values of $n = 1, 2, \ldots, 6$.

We are tempted to check how long the calculation would be for 22 cities using parallel computation if we had enough processors. In chapter 13, we discovered that the sequential machine would not finish the calculation before the sun burns out. Here, we find

$$t_{\text{parallel}} = 5 * 10^{-3} * 22 = 0.11 \text{ second}$$

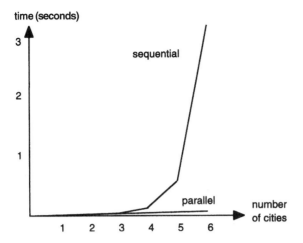

Figure 14.3

Hurrah! The infamous Traveling Salesperson Problem has been crushed by a parallel machine. But wait. The parallel machine will need $(n-1)!/2$ processors, one for each step in the solution. This can be computed at around 10^{19} processors. Thus, if we laid our machine out across the face of the earth, including the oceans, we would have to squeeze at least two dozen processors into every square inch to build a large enough machine.

Here is the program that computes the length of one path of the Traveling Salesperson Problem. After the program computes its sum, it passes that result to another set of processors, a comparator, which compares that result to the results from many other processors and chooses the best. The program assumes that the number of the current processor is in a location called `procnum`, and it employs a subroutine `findperm` that uses the processor number to decide which permutation it is to explore. Thus, every processor will explore a different permutation. The program stores the distances from city to city in an array called `distance`.

```
public class TSP;
{
    int [] permarray;
    double [] [] distance;
    int n, i, homecity, currentcity;
    double sum;
    public void init()
    {
        // Input n and array of all n cities and their
        // distances. Initialize arrays, etc.
```

```
permarray = findperm (procnum);
sum = 0;
i = 0;
homecity = permarray[0];
currentcity = homecity;
while (i < n - 1)
{
    sum = sum + distance[currentcity][permarray[i + 1]];
    currentcity = permarray[i + 1];
    i = i + 1;
}
sum = sum + distance[currentcity][homecity];

// Send sum to a comparator processor that
// works with other processors to decide
// the minimum sum and its associated
// permutation.
    }
}
```

This section has shown how two computations from chapter 13 can be spread out across a parallel architecture to obtain dramatic improvements in execution time. All these observations, of course, assume that *n* is small and that the number of processors is unlimited. The next sections show that not all computations are as easy to speed up as these two examples and they examine execution times when *n* is large in comparison to the number of processors.

Exercises

1. Show how to program the parallel machine to find which two people in a room have the same birthday if there are two such people. Assume that there are no more than 100 people in all.

2. Show how to program the parallel machine to compute all the prime numbers between 1 and 100.

3. Show how to program the parallel machine to do the database program of chapter 4.

4. Show how the parallel program for the Traveling Salesperson Problem solves the problem in the case of four cities. How many processors are needed? What is the task of each processor?

5. Describe how to program the parallel machine to finish the Traveling Salesperson Problem after the sums of all the paths are computed by the many processors. Code must be written to examine all these sums and find the smallest one.

Communicating Processes

The problems of the previous section were special in that they could be divided across a set of processors in a simple way. Next, we study a more difficult problem, the sorting of integers when they are distributed across our 100-processor machine. In this case, we need communication between the processes and the ability to pass the integers up and down the line.

Let's assume there are n integers located in processors 0 through $n - 1$, where n is 100 or less. Each processor has a location num, which contains one of the numbers in the list. It also contains n, an index i, and its own processor number (figure 14.4). The sorting algorithm requires that each processor except the first examine the number in the processor to its left. If the other number is larger than its own, it exchanges them. This operation is repeated with n repetitions, at which time the numbers should become sorted with the lowest in processor 0 and the largest in processor $n - 1$. Here is the program:

```
public class ParallelSort;
{
    int i, num, n, procnum;
```

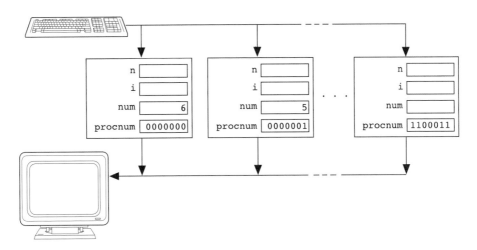

Figure 14.4

```
public void init()
{
    // Put code here to read num and n.
    if ((procnum > 0) && (procnum <= n - 1))
    {
        i = 1;
        while (i <= n)
        {
            if (num(left neighbor) > num(this processor))
            {exchange num(left neighbor) and num(this processor);}
            i = i + 1;
        }
    }
}
}
```

Let's examine this program in action. Suppose $n = 3$, and the first three processors contain 6, 5, and 4:

num	6	5	4
procnum	00	01	10

Program `ParallelSort` runs simultaneously on these three processors. On the first, it does nothing because procnum $= 00$. The second and third processors each see that their left neighbors have larger numbers, and they exchange their own numbers with those of their left neighbors. Thus, processor 01 will put 5 into processor 00 and 6 into itself. Processor 10 will put 4 into processor 01 and 5 into itself. Error! Processor 01 has just had both a 6 and a 4 loaded into its num location. Also both processors 00 and 10 have 5's. Something is wrong here. We thought we were going to end up with the numbers sorted like this:

num	4	5	6
procnum	00	01	10

Instead, we ended up with this:

num	5	?	5
procnum	00	01	10

Apparently the computations of one processor confuse those of its neighbor. Each processor looks at its own number and its left neighbor's and decides whether to do an exchange. But by the time it chooses to do the exchange, its own number and its neighbor's may both have changed. It cannot check any value and be sure it will stay that way because other processes may change it. This seemingly straightforward program is fraught with problems.

The solution is to have a set of flags called *semaphores* that guard locations from being changed by any but a selected single processor. That processor will maintain control over the specified locations until its job is done, and then it will change the flags to indicate that it has released the associated locations to other processors. This system of guards can become complicated, but it will restore sanity to the parallel computation.

Let's put a `flag` with each `num` location; `flag` is a location containing a value of 0 or 1. Then we will follow the rule that a processor is able to access and change its own `num` only if its `flag` is 1. If its `flag` is 0, it will not be allowed to affect its own `num` because that location is controlled by its neighbor to the right. Of course, a processor will never be able to exchange its `num` value with its left neighbor's unless it controls both. Its `flag` must be 1, and its left neighbor's `flag` must be 0. We indicate in the following table the conditions under which processor i can do an exchange. We say its activity is "on" if these conditions are met; otherwise, its activity is "waiting" or "off" if it is processor 0:

num		
flag	0	1
procnum	$i - 1$	i
activity	*waiting*	*on*

After a process completes a cycle, it should change its own `flag` and its left neighbor's to release them to other processes. There are two exceptions to this rule, however: `flag` of processor 0 should always be 0 because that processor never needs to do exchanges with its left neighbor, and `flag` of the last processor that holds data should always be 1 because the processor has no right neighbor to take control.

We can examine this strategy by repeating the preceding sort. We initialize the first `flag` at 0, the last `flag` at 1, all `flags` of other even-numbered processors at 0, causing them to wait, and all `flags` of other odd-numbered processors at 1, turning them on:

num	6	5	4
flag	0	1	1
procnum	00	01	10
activity	*off*	*on*	*waiting*

Remember that a processor never comes on unless its own `flag` is 1 and its left neighbor's is 0. Thus, only one of the three processors has the `flag` configuration to go on; it is processor 01, and it sees that its left neighbor has `num` larger than its own `num` and exchanges them. Also, it changes its own `flag`. (It would change the `flag` of its left neighbor too, if that processor were not the leftmost one.)

num	5	6	4
flag	0	0	1
procnum	00	01	10
activity	*off*	*waiting*	*on*

This puts processor 01 in the "waiting" state but releases processor 10 to compare its num with its left neighbor's. Processor 10 then finds the left neighbor's value larger and executes an exchange. Finally, it would change its own flag and its left neighbor's flag, but because it is the rightmost processor, it changes its neighbor's flag only:

num	5	4	6
flag	0	1	1
procnum	00	01	10
activity	*off*	*on*	*waiting*

Now processor 01 is "on" again, and it can do another compare, an exchange, and a flag change. This completes the sort:

num	4	5	6
flag	0	0	1
procnum	00	01	10
activity	*off*	*waiting*	*on*

Once this flagging strategy is designed, one can revise the parallel sorting program to work properly:

```
public class ParallelSortWithFlags;
{
    int i, num, n, flag, procnum;
    public void init()
    {
        // Put code here to read num and n.
        // We assume procnum holds the processor number.
        if (procnum is even)
            {flag = 0;}
        else
            {flag = 1;}
        if (procnum == n - 1)
            {flag = 1;}
        if ((procnum > 0) && (procnum <= n - 1))
        {
            i = 1;
            while (i <= n)
```

```
        {
            wait until ((flag(this processor) == 1) &&
                         (flag(left neighbor) == 0));
            if (num(left neighbor) > num(this processor))
            {exchange num(left neighbor) and num(this processor);}
            if (procnum > 1)
            {change flag in processor on left;}
            if (procnum < n - 1)
            {change flag in this processor;}
            i = i + 1;
        }
    }
  }
}
```

A common phenomenon in parallel computation occurs when one processor is waiting for another to complete its job while simultaneously the other processor is waiting for the first to complete its job. Each processor waits and waits, and neither ever takes another step. This is called *deadlock*, and it is a major concern for designers of parallel computations. In our sorting program, a processor waits until its flag and its left neighbor's flag have the correct configuration before it does anything. You should study the algorithm and determine whether it is ever possible for the sorting algorithm to reach a deadlock.

Finally, we examine the execution time of this algorithm. The program executes its loop n times, so the timing formula has the form

$$t_{\text{parallel}} = C * n$$

where C is some constant value. We noted in chapter 13 that it is possible to sort numbers in time

$$t_{\text{sequential}} = C' * n * \log_2 n$$

where C' is a constant. Since $\log_2 n$ is not a very large number, we see that t_{parallel} is not a lot faster than $t_{\text{sequential}}$. If we are using n processors, we would like to see a speedup by a factor of n. It is like hiring 100 people to help pick apples in your orchard and finding that they only get the job done seven times faster than one person could have done it. Thus, this sorting algorithm is somewhat of a disappointment, and we have not achieved the quality of success that we observed in the previous section. There are better parallel sorting methods available that obtain greater speedups, but they are more complex than the one shown here and are beyond the scope of this book.

In this section, we have found that not all computations are as easily divided for parallel execution as those initially presented. Whenever the programming involves interprocessor communication, the code can become very complex. Furthermore, the improvements in execution time may not be as large as one would hope.

Exercises

1. Suppose that the numbers $7, 2, 9, 6, 4, 1, 5, 4$ are spread out across processors 000 to 111 in a parallel machine and that they are to be sorted. Show how the program `ParallelSortWithFlags` would complete this sort. Show all the processors with their values for `num`, `flag`, and `procnum` at the moment when the computation is initialized. Then show them again after each significant step.

2. Suppose a programmer codes the preceding sorting program but makes one error: the flags are all initialized at zero. How will the program function in this situation? What new concept introduced in this section would apply here?

3. A sequence of n characters, where n is 100 or less, is spread across a parallel machine, with one character in each processor. Show how to program the processors so that a user can type in a short string of characters and find all the places where it appears in the original character sequence. The machine is to type out the numbers of the processors that hold the initial characters of the discovered substrings.

   As an example, suppose the initial string is "abcbc" and it is stored as follows:

   ```
   character      a    b    c    b    c
   procnum       000  001  010  011  100
   ```

   Then if the user types `"bc"`, the system will find two occurrences of this substring and print the locations of their initial characters: 001, 011.

Parallel Computation on a Saturated Machine

The previous studies have assumed that n is small enough to allow the computation to be divided among the available processors in a convenient manner. For the data retrieval problem, it was assumed that there would be a processor for every individual, and for the Traveling Salesperson Problem, it was assumed that there would be a processor for every ordering of the cities. In these cases, we say the computation does not *saturate* the machine because there are enough processors to divide the problem optimally.

Realistically, however, we must expect that n may be large, that we will not have as many processors as could be used effectively, and that it will be necessary to revise the organization of the code. This is the case when the processors are saturated, and there are two major results: the programming becomes more complicated, and some of the improvement in execution time is lost. This section investigates both of these effects.

Returning to the retrieval problem, let's assume that there may be thousands of individuals whose records are spread across the 100 processors. Then we should put 1 percent of the total population on each of the processors. Each processor will search its own 1 percent of the whole, and the result of the 100 separate computations will be a search of the complete population.

Here is the revised program prepared to handle a large number of individuals on each processor:

```
public class SaturatedParallelPersonSearch;
{
    double targetweight, targetheight, weight[], height[];
    String name [];
    int m, i;

    public void init()
    {
        // Put code here to find the number m of
        // individuals to be stored in this processor
        // and then read the data for those individuals.
        processor 0 output.setText("Give the target height.");
        targetheight = all input.getDouble();
        processor 0 output.setText("Give the target weight.");
        targetweight = all input.getDouble();
        i = 1;
        while (i <= m)
        {
            if ((targetheight == height[i]) && (targetweight ==
                                        weight[i]))
                {this processor output.setText(name[i]);}
            i = i + 1;
        }
    }
}
```

The execution time for this program can be discovered by carefully considering a series of cases. Suppose there are 100 individuals or fewer. This is the case considered earlier, and the execution time is the same as handling one individual on a sequential machine:

$$t_{1-100} = 5.1 * 10^{-4} * 1$$

If there are between 101 and 200 individuals, they can be distributed among the processors with two on some and one on the others. The execution time is the same as the sequential machine with two individuals:

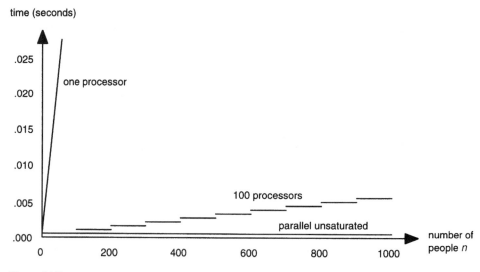

Figure 14.5

$$t_{101-200} = 5.1 * 10^{-4} * 2$$

The trend is now clear:

$$t_{201-300} = 5.1 * 10^{-4} * 3$$

and so on.

The result gives us a lesson about computing on a saturated machine. The incredible speedup that was apparent when there were enough processors is gone. But the parallel computation is still much faster than a sequential computation. At best, a machine with 100 processors will be 100 times faster than one with a single processor (figure 14.5).

A similar situation occurs with the Traveling Salesperson Problem. If $n!$ is larger than 100, we can no longer afford the luxury of putting one ordering of the cities on each processor. Instead, each processor must compute 1 percent of all the orderings, and this could be a large number. The execution time graph rises slowly if $n!$ is 100 or less but rises exponentially for larger n, as occurs in the sequential case. It is at best 100 times faster than a single processor. Unfortunately, this is not sufficient improvement to convert an intractable computation into a tractable one.

The sorting algorithm can also be programmed for large lists but with additional complexities. Furthermore, the timing advantage, which was difficult to achieve in the unsaturated case, cannot be maintained.

In summary, parallel computations offer the possibility of huge speedups in computation time, especially for problems that partition easily into many parts and where high degrees of parallelism are available. However, the introduction of parallelism often results in great increases in program complexity and for many problems does not yield dramatic speed increases.

Exercises

1. Build a chart summarizing the results of this chapter so far. It should have two columns—one for tractable and one for intractable computations. It should have two rows—one for computations on unsaturated machines and one for computations on saturated machines. In each cell, describe the degree of speedup that parallel computation can achieve.

2. Carefully analyze the speedup that can be achieved for the Traveling Salesperson Problem on the 100-processor machine in the case where n is greater than 6. Draw a graph of execution time versus n, and compare it with the cases of unsaturated parallel execution and sequential (one processor) execution.

Variations on Architecture

A variety of different interconnection schemes are possible for parallel machines. It is *not* true that all are organized in straight lines, as is the case for the model of the previous sections. The processors can be organized in a ring, a grid, a hypercube, a completely connected set, or any of a multitude of other ways (figure 14.6). The simpler schemes like the ring and the grid are easier to build. The more complicated ones offer greater potential performance.

One simple measure of performance is the number of transfers required for information to reach the most distant points in a network. For example, with 16 processors in a ring connection, the most widely separated nodes are on the opposite sides of the ring. The transfer of information from one to the other requires eight movements along communication lines. In general, a ring of n processors will require $n/2$ transfers to move information between the most distant processors. The following table gives the distance between the farthest processors for the four configurations shown in figure 14.6:

Configuration	Number of Processors		
	16	10,000	n
Ring	8	5,000	$n/2$
Grid	6	198	$2n^{(1/2)} - 2$
Hypercube	4	14	$\log_2 n$
Complete connection	1	1	1

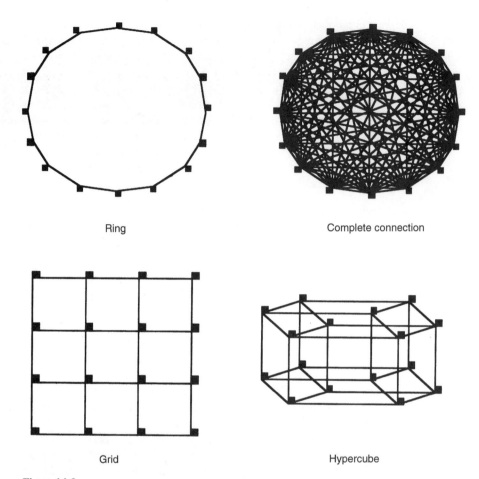

Ring

Complete connection

Grid

Hypercube

Figure 14.6

The parallel machine described in the previous sections is known as a *Multiple-Instruction Multiple-Data* (MIMD) machine. This means that each processor has its own program to manipulate its own data. Thus, each processor can have a completely different piece of code, giving total flexibility to the programmer in the organization of the calculation. Another common design is the *Single-Instruction Multiple-Data* (SIMD) machine, where one program controls all processors in the array. That single program broadcasts its commands to the complete network, and they all march in lockstep. This architecture is common in designs where there may be many processors, tens of thousands of them, and there is little possibility of generating individualized code for each one.

This brings up another issue in parallel architectures, the degree of *granularity* in the parallelism. A machine may have *coarse* granularity, with large processors at each node and relatively little communication, as in our model. Here there will be few processors, say a few hundred, and each will have full instruction sets and large memory—100,000 bytes or more. Or the granularity may be *fine*, with as many as hundreds of thousands of tiny processors with very tight communication between them. The next section gives an example of a parallel computer with very fine granularity.

Exercises

1. Suppose a three-dimensional cubical grid is proposed as a machine architecture.

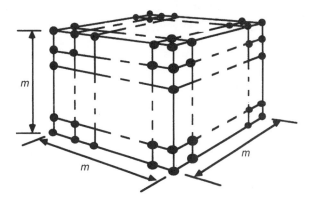

Thus, a cube might have m nodes along any edge and m^3 nodes in all. Fill in the table given in the text for the distance between the farthest nodes for this configuration.

2. Could you run the three problems discussed in this chapter on SIMD machines? Discuss each one, and show how it would succeed or fail.

3. Propose a parallel architecture not described in this chapter, and investigate its properties.

---

*Connectionist Architectures

There has been much excitement in recent years over a new kind of computer, the *connectionist* machine. Such machines lie at the extreme end of the spectrum in parallel computation with possibly millions of tiny nodes each capable of only very primitive

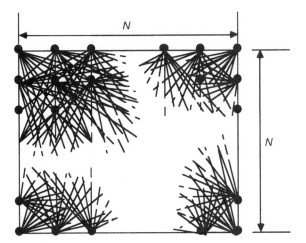

Figure 14.7

calculation. The connection schemes are massive, with large arrays of nodes communicating with each other and with other arrays of nodes. This kind of architecture is inspired by studies of the physiology of the human brain, and some researchers believe connectionist machines carry out computations in a similar way. We study one simple design for a connectionist machine here, and refer you to a fast-growing literature for additional readings.

Our connectionist architecture is typical of many of those currently under investigation: it is organized as an N by N square grid of nodes, where N may be in the hundreds (figure 14.7). Each node receives an input from every other of the N^2 nodes. Thus, the network is completely connected. Complete connectivity is not needed for many algorithms, but it is an excellent model for some interesting examples.

Each node receives either a 1 or -1 from every other node. It multiplies each of its inputs (1 or -1) by a real value called a weight and then adds up all the results. Finally, the node outputs 1 if this sum is greater than some constant c and -1 otherwise. The node then sends its output (1 or -1) to all the other nodes. All the nodes simultaneously carry out this computation to recompute their own outputs and broadcast them to their neighbors. If the nodes could all talk as they compute, there would be a tremendous din from their simultaneous chattering.

As an illustration of a single-node computation, consider the four-node grid shown in figure 14.8 and the calculation of the output of its upper left node. In this figure, the output of each node is shown on the node. All communication links are omitted except those needed for this example.

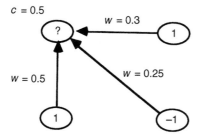

Figure 14.8

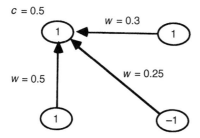

Figure 14.9

The upper left node receives the three inputs, multiplies them by appropriate weights w, and adds them:

$$0.3 * (1) + 0.25(-1) + 0.5(1)$$

The sum is 0.55. Since this is larger than $c = 0.5$ for this node, it will output a 1 (figure 14.9). After the upper left output becomes a 1, it is transmitted as input to all the other nodes, and they can compute their new outputs.

Consider a larger version of this machine, a 3 by 3 system. Suppose the upper left node is connected as shown in figure 14.10. The following array presents the information related to the node:

$$
\begin{array}{rrr}
 & -0.05 & \\
0 & -0.1 & -0.1 \\
0.1 & -0.1 & -0.1 \\
0.1 & 0.1 & 0.1
\end{array}
$$

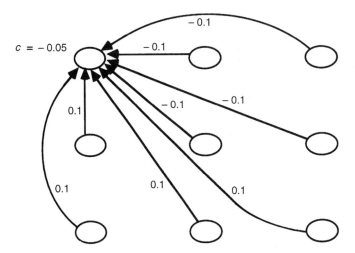

Figure 14.10

This array shows the values of all the arcs from other nodes back to the upper left node. It contains a zero in the upper left corner because the node has no transition to itself. The number above the array represents the constant c.

Remember that there are nine nodes, each with transitions coming into it. Thus, the whole connectionist machine can be represented by nine such arrays (figure 14.11). This specifies all the weights and constants for the machine. If you wish to know the weight from node i, j to node k, l, go to the k, l array and select the i, j entry in it.

Once the machine is specified, it is possible to compute with it. Let's set the outputs of all the nodes (figure 14.12a) and see what happens. All the nodes receive inputs from all the other nodes, and they compute new outputs. Examining the upper left corner, the next output can be computed by adding the weights times the inputs on all lines:

$$(-0.1)(-1) + (-0.1)(-1) + (0.1)(1) + (-0.1)(-1)$$

$$+ (-0.1)(-1) + (0.1)(1) + (0.1)(1) + (0.1)(1) = 0.8$$

Since 0.8 is larger than -0.05, this node will have a new value of 1 (figure 14.12b).

We can compute new values for the other entries also, but in this case, all remain unchanged. Thus, they all have reached stable values. If we consider the original configuration to be the input

$$-1 \quad -1 \quad -1$$

$$1 \quad -1 \quad -1$$

$$1 \quad 1 \quad 1$$

−0.05			0.05			0.05		
0	−0.1	−0.1	−0.1	0	0.1	−0.1	0.1	0
0.1	−0.1	−0.1	−0.1	0.1	0.1	−0.1	0.1	0.1
0.1	0.1	0.1	−0.1	−0.1	−0.1	−0.1	−0.1	−0.1

−0.05			0.05			0.05		
0.1	−0.1	−0.1	−0.1	0.1	0.1	−0.1	0.1	0.1
0	−0.1	−0.1	−0.1	0	0.1	−0.1	0.1	0
0.1	0.1	0.1	−0.1	−0.1	−0.1	−0.1	−0.1	−0.1

−0.05			−0.05			−0.05		
0.1	−0.1	−0.1	0.1	−0.1	−0.1	0.1	−0.1	−0.1
0.1	−0.1	−0.1	0.1	−0.1	−0.1	0.1	−0.1	−0.1
0	0.1	0.1	0.1	0	0.1	0.1	0.1	0

Figure 14.11

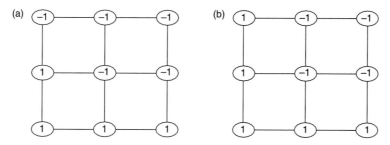

Figure 14.12

then this final stable configuration is the output:

1   −1   −1

1   −1   −1

1   1   1

Let's think of these nodes as neurons on a visual plane and assume 1 represents black and −1 represents white. Then an input of

has yielded an output of

This will be written as

Now we can experiment with this machine by repeatedly setting the inputs to be some image that interests us and then allowing all the nodes to recompute their values repeatedly until a stable configuration is found (figure 14.13a). It appears that every pattern that vaguely resembles an L shape will yield an L shape. Also, many patterns that contain mere fragments of the L pattern (figure 14.13b) also yield the L shape. But some configurations lead to something else (figure 14.14). The L shape is much preferred, and all configurations that look vaguely like an L result in an L's being formed. In fact, this machine is a recognizer of the L shape, and it attempts to make an L out of anything it encounters.

Summarizing, we began with a nine-node connectionist computer with its weights specified in a set of arrays. We examined its input-output characteristics and determined that there is one particular output configuration that is strongly preferred. Whenever any fragmentary information appears that may be suggestive of that pattern, the machine will generate that pattern as its output. This output may require many iterations of the basic node computation, but the final stable configuration will be that pattern.

This characteristic of bringing forth a total image after having observed only fragmentary evidence is believed by many to be a key aspect of intelligent behavior. Such a system is said to have *associative memory,* and this is clearly a characteristic of human minds. Suppose, as an example, that the stored image is a very complex structure containing information about a particular person. The structure would contain the person's name, an image of his or her face, and remembrances of his or her behaviors. Then if a fragment of that structure appears, say the name, part of the image, or some reminder of the behavior, the rest of the structure comes to mind: the name reminds one of the face, some behavior reminds one of the name, and so forth. The interesting thing about the connectionist

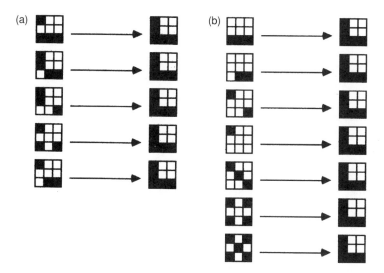

Figure 14.13

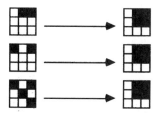

Figure 14.14

studies is that the model was derived as an analogue to the brain, and these behaviors seem to be reminiscent of brainlike activities.

Another interesting fact is the way the information about the L is spread across the machine. No particular weight or node is critical to the recognition, and in fact the weights can be varied somewhat randomly without greatly affecting behavior. If there are a few small changes, the pattern recognition will degrade relatively little. If large changes are made, more loss of function will occur but it still may not disable the basic behavior. This property of such machines seems again to resemble biological systems and is a desirable characteristic of intelligent machines.

As you study the particular weights given you can discern the L shape coded among them. However, the weights can be revised so that this machine is capable of recognizing many patterns, not only an L. When this occurs, the weights begin to look like random numbers, yet the L pattern and the other recognizable patterns will still be coded into them.

The final point about the connectionist approach that makes it attractive is that the computer need not be programmed to recognize patterns. It can be trained to do so. This is the subject of the next section.

Exercises

1. Suppose a 3 by 3 image with all four corners black and all other squares white is presented to the connectionist machine of this section. Calculate the new values of all node outputs to determine the output image.

2. Change some of the weights in the 3 by 3 connectionist machine and determine whether its ability to recognize an L has degraded.

*Learning the Connectionist Weights

Suppose that the 3 by 3 connectionist machine is to recognize some pattern, say L, but that the appropriate values for the weights are not known. Then we can assume that all the weights are zero and try to find a strategy to compute them. The usual method is to consider each weight individually and to try varying it slightly. If the system performs better when the weight is slightly larger or smaller, that change is made.

To see how this is done, return to the example of the upper left node, but this time assume all weights are zero (figure 14.15). The goal of our procedure is to find values for

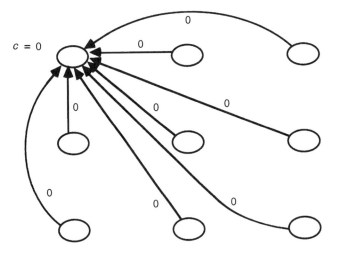

Figure 14.15

the weights so that they prefer to output the L shape. More specifically, the target pattern has this form

1   −1   −1

1   −1   −1

1   1   1

and it is necessary to find values for the weights that tend to compute a 1 in the upper left corner when given the other values. Assume the first weight to be examined is the one leading from the middle node in the top row to its left neighbor. We will increase it by 0.1 and then decrease it by 0.1, each time checking whether the change of weight helps or hinders the desired result (that the output in the upper left corner is a 1). Summing the eight values from the other nodes, we obtain the following results.

If the weight is 0.1, then

$$(0.1)(-1) + (0)(-1) + (0)(1) + (0)(-1) + (0)(-1) + (0)(1) + (0)(1) + (0)(1) = -0.1$$

Since −0.1 is less than $c = 0$, the output is computed to be −1. This is not the desired output for the upper left corner.

If the weight is −0.1, then

$$(-0.1)(-1) + (0)(-1) + (0)(1) + (0)(-1) + (0)(-1) + (0)(1) + (0)(1) + 0(1) = 0.1$$

Since 0.1 is greater than $c = 0$, the output is computed to be 1, which is the desired result. Of the two values tried, only the second was successful, so it is selected (figure 14.16).

Reexamining this computation, you can see that $w = -0.1$ will be preferred over $w = 0.1$ because the goal is to maximize the summation. Since the weight w is being multiplied by the pattern value at that cell, −1, $w = -0.1$ will do the job better than $w = 0.1$ because −0.1 results in a positive contribution to the sum. This generalizes as follows. When computing weights on arcs leading to a cell with a 1, all weights coming from cells with a 1 should be incremented, and all weights coming from cells with a −1 should be decremented.

A similar rule can be derived when the arcs lead to a cell with a value of −1. In this case, all weights coming from cells with a −1 should be incremented, and all weights coming from cells with a 1 should be decremented.

Let's see how these rules apply for finding a few more weights. Consider the weight on the arc from the upper right node. Its pattern value is −1, so its weight should be decremented. Its new value will be −0.1. Consider the weight on the arc from the node just below the upper left corner. This node has pattern value 1, so its arc weight should be incremented. Its new value will be 0.1 (figure 14.17).

This procedure was carried out for the rest of the weights, and a similar one was used to compute the constants c where variations of +0.05 and −0.05 were used. The result is the

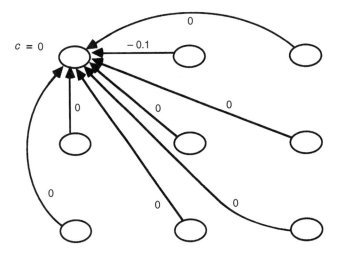

Figure 14.16

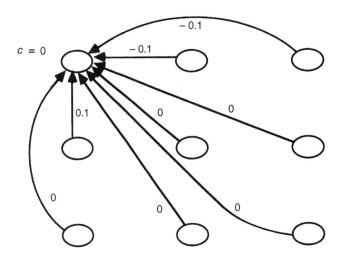

Figure 14.17

set of weights and constants shown in the previous section for the L recognizer. Other more complicated and less intuitive methods are used in computing these weights in some connectionist systems. The method given here is easier to understand and gives satisfactory results for the purposes of our study. Typically, in realistic situations where many patterns are to be recognized, this weight computation must be repeated many times before satisfactory values are found. The weights and constants will slowly migrate to acceptable values as the computation is repeated again and again. This process of slowly evolving a satisfactory set of weights and constants is called *learning*. (Other types of learning are examined in chapter 16.)

Presenting the connectionist machine with many different patterns to learn is called *training* the machine. Now that our machine has "learned" the L pattern, let's train it on a T. If we begin with the values of the weights and constants as shown for the L pattern and modify them again in the same way using the T pattern,

$$
\begin{array}{ccc}
1 & 1 & 1 \\
-1 & 1 & -1 \\
-1 & 1 & -1
\end{array}
$$

then a new set is derived (figure 14.18). Presumably after training on both an L and a T, these values code both images. A series of test inputs and their outputs is shown in figure 14.19. We see that the machine recognizes as an L any image with even the vaguest resemblance to an L. It does the same for a T. Only one of the test inputs yields a non-L, non-T response.

You might examine the weights and constants and wonder where the L and the T are stored. The answer is that they are stored everywhere in the sense that each weight contributes in a small way to all decisions. From another point of view, they are stored nowhere specifically because small perturbations on individual weights will have little effect on total performance.

The examples here are extremely simple and serve only to demonstrate principles. A more realistically sized machine could have a grid with tens of thousands of nodes as well as auxiliary arrays with more tens of thousands to do background computation. Training could involve thousands of examples, and the learning process could involve thousands of iterations to get the weights to converge to yield acceptable behaviors.

Larger systems are often studied in terms of *energy*. Given a set of weights and constants, a cell in the pattern is said to have energy

$E = c - s$ if the cell contains a 1

$E = -(c - s)$ if it contains a -1

$c = -0.1$

0	0	0
0	0	-0.2
0	0.2	0

$c = 0$

0	0	0.2
-0.2	0.2	0
-0.2	0	-0.2

$c = 0$

0	0.2	0
-0.2	0.2	0
-0.2	0	-0.2

$c = 0$

0	-0.2	-0.2
0	0.2	0
0.2	0	0.2

$c = 0$

0	0.2	0.2
-0.2	0	0
-0.2	0	-0.2

$c = 0.1$

-0.2	0	0
0	0	0
0	-0.2	0

$c = 0$

0	-0.2	-0.2
0.2	-0.2	0
0	0	0.2

$c = -0.1$

0.2	0	0
0	0	-0.2
0	0	0

$c = 0$

0	-0.2	-0.2
0.2	-0.2	0
0.2	0	0

Figure 14.18

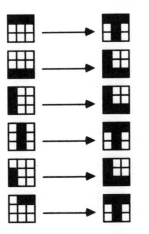
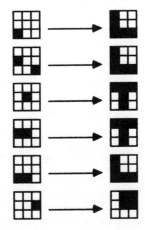

Figure 14.19

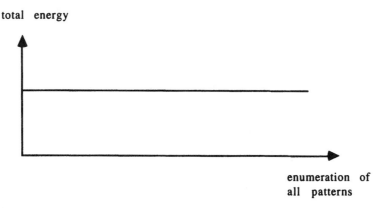

Figure 14.20

Here we define s to be the sum of inputs to the cell and c to be the threshold constant. For example the first cell in the section on connectionist architectures would have energy $E = 0.5 - 0.55 = -0.05$. If cells can have energies, then a pattern can have energy also; it is the sum of the energies of all the cells.

The concept of energy is quite useful for understanding large systems. Suppose a system has not been trained and all weights and constants are at initial values. Then all patterns will have the same energy (figure 14.20). But the effect of training is to lower the energy for training patterns and for patterns similar to them. Thus, if the system is trained on two patterns and their variations, there will be two regions of lowered energy (figure 14.21).

Once training is complete, one can present a fragment of an image to the system as input. This pattern will appear somewhere on the energy curve (figure 14.22). Then we can study the connectionist machine computation algorithm of the previous section to determine what it will do. Careful examination reveals that it tends to change cell outputs in the direction of reducing total pattern energy. Thus, in this example, the system will find its output by changing the values of individual cells in the direction of the nearby energy valley. In this case, it would converge on and output the image and name of Jill.

We can return to the previous example of the L–T recognizer and do a similar energy analysis. The L and T will appear in energy valleys, and when the system is started with an input, it will compute continuously until the pattern is reached in the nearest valley. A fragment of an L will migrate on the energy curve downward toward the bottom of the L valley. A fragment of a T will migrate toward the bottom of the T valley. Other fragments will migrate in unpredictable directions.

Connectionist systems are also capable of generalizing from examples. Such a system might be presented with images of many people and form a general image of people. They all tend to have a mouth, two eyes, a nose, and so forth. Then, being presented with a partial image, the system might conclude that it is a person and be able to fill in all the

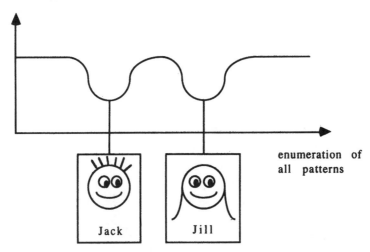

Figure 14.21

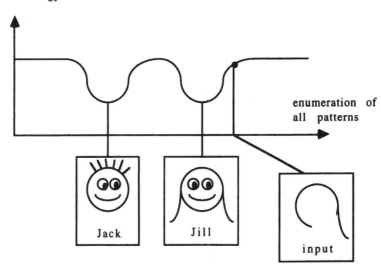

Figure 14.22

normal details for people. But it would not necessarily know which person to select. For a discussion of this and other connectionist phenomena, you should read the specialized literature.

Exercises

1. Use the set of weights and constants derived from the training set of L and T to determine the output if the input pattern is black in the upper left cell and white otherwise.

2. Vary the weights and constants and repeat the computation of exercise 1. How big must the changes be to cause the system to make a different decision?

3. Compute the total energy of the input pattern in exercise 1. Compute the energy of the output pattern in exercise 1. Notice that the second value should be less than the first.

4. Compute the total energy for patterns identical to and varying from the basic L pattern using the weights and constants computed for the L and T training set. Draw a graph showing total energy for patterns of varying nearness to the basic L shape.

5. Study the values of the constants c for the L recognizer and for the L–T recognizer. Can you discover the algorithm used to learn these values?

6. Train the 3 by 3 connectionist system on two patterns of your choosing and then test their performance.

7. The connectionist computation presented here tends to seek a minimum energy. However, we do not give a proof that this behavior will always occur. J. Hopfield (1982) has shown that machine processing is guaranteed to seek minimum total energy if it is built such that the weight from node i, j to node k, l always equals the weight back from node k, l to i, j. Revise the algorithms presented here to adhere to this restriction.

Summary

Parallel computation appears to be the only way to increase machine speed once limits of technology have been reached for traditional machines. Some problems divide rather naturally into parts that can be spread across a parallel architecture, and dramatic speedup is often possible, especially if the number of processors is large compared to the size of the problem. But other problems may be hard to speed up under any conditions. With a limited degree N of parallelism, as occurs on realistic machines, the speedup can be no greater than a factor of N, and this is often hard to achieve.

Parallel architectures can vary on many dimensions, including the degree and format of connectivity, the organization of the processors, and the granularity of the parallelism.

A recent trend in computing has been the development of connectionist machines whose architecture has been inspired by studies of the human brain. Large numbers of extremely simple computing devices are assembled in highly interconnected arrays. These machines are trained through the presentation of sample data, and their prominent characteristics include the abilities to do associative retrieval, to complete fragmentary information, and to maintain robust behavior despite perturbations of their mechanisms. The success of these studies shows the importance of research in brain biology for computer science.

15   Noncomputability

Speed Is Not Enough

From earlier chapters we know that some important calculations may not be possible because their execution times may be too long. This may lead to the wish for faster and faster machines and for new discoveries that will result in ever greater improvements in performance. Perhaps someday a computer will be built that will do as much work in 1 second as the combined effort of all the world's current machines could do in a billion years. But our studies in this chapter show that such impressive performance would not be enough to solve many of our problems. There exists a class of problems called *noncomputable*, and they have been shown to be unsolvable by any computer within the current paradigm of modern computing. This mystical and elusive class of problems will be the concern of this chapter.

In the next section, we study an argument that shows that there are functions that cannot be computed by any Java (or any other known language) program. This proof is simple and convincing. It solidifies the main idea of this chapter, but it has one shortcoming: it does not show us an example of a noncomputable function. The following sections give a series of ideas that lead to further understanding of the concept of noncomputability and then present specific examples of noncomputable problems. The final section gives a proof that one of the examples is, in fact, noncomputable.

On the Existence of Noncomputable Functions

We will call a function *computable* if a Java program exists that can compute it. In this chapter, we consider primarily functions that input a positive integer and return a positive integer. Four examples of computable functions, f_1, f_2, f_3, and f_4, are shown in table 15.1. The first function doubles its input and can be computed by this Java subroutine:

Table 15.1

f_1		f_2		f_3		f_4	
Input	Output	Input	Output	Input	Output	Input	Output
1	2	1	7	1	6	1	100
2	4	2	8	2	6	2	100
3	6	3	9	3	6	3	100
4	8	4	10	4	6	4	4
5	10	5	11	5	6	5	5
6	12	6	12	6	6	6	6

```
int q1(int x)
{
    return 2 * x;
}
```

The second function adds 6 to its input:

```
int q2(int x)
{
    return 6 + x;
}
```

Similarly, the third and fourth functions are easy to program:

```
int q3(int x)
{
    return 6;
}

int q4(int x)
    {
        if (x < 4)
            {return 100;}
        else
            {return x;}
    }
```

Our interest in this chapter is the computational capabilities of Java programs (and other languages). But we will usually talk about Java subroutines instead of programs simply to maintain simplicity in the examples. The main difference between programs and subroutines is that programs receive and deliver information through typed input and

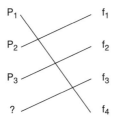

Figure 15.1

screen interactions whereas subroutines input via a parameter list and output via a return statement. Since the latter is much simpler to show in the examples of this section, we use subroutines as our examples in most cases. However, all the conclusions reached regarding subroutines carry over to programs because the only significant difference for our purposes is the input-output mechanism.

Sometimes functions are defined to be computable if they can be programmed in some language other than Java, but since any general-purpose programming language can be translated into any other, the definitions are equivalent. The class of computable functions includes all the functions studied thus far in this book and almost every function encountered in high school or early college mathematics.

A noncomputable function is any function that cannot be computed by any Java program. Initially you might think that there is no such thing—that every function can be computed. The fact that there exist noncomputable functions is a profound and fascinating discovery.

The argument that noncomputable functions exist is straightforward in concept. It states that there are many more functions than there are programs, so it is not possible to have a program for every function. There must be functions that do not have any corresponding programs, and they are the noncomputable functions.

This argument is easy to understand if we propose for the moment the rather extreme assumption that there exist in the world only three programs—P_1, P_2, and P_3—and the four functions listed previously. We may not know which program computes which function, but it is clear that no matter how the programs are paired with the functions, there will always be at least one function left unmatched. These leftover functions are the noncomputable ones because they have no associated programs. For example, if P_1 computes f_4, P_2 computes f_1, and P_3 computes f_2, then f_3 would be a noncomputable function (figure 15.1).

However, in practice there are more than three Java programs. There are infinitely many of them, so our argument needs to be improved. We use only Java subroutines in our arguments here, but the arguments hold for complete programs as well. Let's begin by listing all the subroutines that input an integer and return an integer. The first in the list will be a shortest such subroutine. Following the conventions of this book, the shortest possible subroutine that inputs an integer and returns an integer is as follows. It has a name of length 1, a variable name of length 1, and only one statement:

```
int p(int x)
{
    return x;
}
```

There are other programs that are equally as short as measured by the number of characters:

```
int p(int x)
{
    return 1;
}

int p(int x)
{
    return 2;
}

    .
    .
    .

int p(int x)
{
    return 9;
}
```

This is all the programs of this length (except for the renaming of identifiers), but if an additional character is allowed, more programs can be listed:

```
int p(int x)
{
    return 10;
}
    .
    .
    .
```

We can sequentially list every subroutine of one size, then every one of the next size, then the next, and so forth in an endless chain of subroutines. Every Java subroutine that

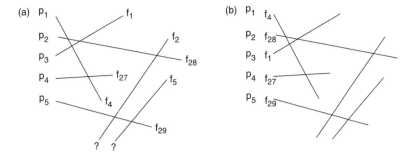

Figure 15.2

inputs an integer and returns an integer will appear somewhere in the list, although some of them may be long and appear very far from the beginning. However, we can in principle create such a long list and thus prove that this set of subroutines is a countable set, as defined in chapter 3. These subroutines can be placed in a row.

Let's place these subroutines in a row and draw a link from each to the function it computes (figure 15.2a). Suppose every function is computable and thus has a link to some subroutine. Then we could move the functions along their links and put the functions in a row also (figure 15.2b). However, we learned in chapter 3 that it is not possible to put all the functions in a row. The set of all functions is not countable. So it must be that we failed to link every function with a subroutine and that some functions do not have subroutines. Functions must exist that are not computable.

Summarizing, not all functions can be computed because there are not enough subroutines to cover them all. Some functions do not have associated subroutines that can compute them.

But what is an example of a function that cannot be computed? The next sections provide background and some very important examples of such functions.

Exercises

1. Consider the set of functions that receive a 10-digit binary number as input and compute a single binary output. Are these functions all computable, as defined in this chapter? Give a careful and complete justification for your answer.

2. Consider the set of functions that receive a positive integer and output a binary integer —a 0 or a 1. Are these functions all computable? Give a careful and complete justification for your answer.

Figure 15.3

Programs That Read Programs

The goal is to find some computations that cannot be done by any Java program. It would be interesting to specify a calculation that inputs integers but is noncomputable. While it is possible to do this, the most easily understood examples of noncomputability involve programs that read other programs and output something. These kinds of examples also illustrate some of the most commonly encountered forms of noncomputability. Thus, in this section, we study programs that input other programs (figure 15.3).

For the purposes of this section, assume that the programs input by other programs are simply sequences of statements separated by spaces all typed on a single line. Thus the program called *A* that is usually typed as

```
int A(int x)
{
    return 2 * x;
}
```

will be written on a single line as

```
int A(int x){return 2 * x;}
```

If we type this one-line subroutine into our usual compiler, it will compile and execute normally. We also assume that these subroutines do not call other subroutines when they do their computations.

Let's write a subroutine that can input subroutines like *A* and do something with them. We call the subroutine *B* and specify that *B* will input a subroutine and tell us whether the subroutine it has read has an "if" in it. Thus, if *B* were to read *A*, it would type "Has no 'if'." However, if *B* read one of the decision tree programs of chapter 2, it would print "Has an 'if' in it." (We assume all programs can be typed on a single line. If we attempted to account for multiple-line programs, the programs that read programs would be unnecessarily complex, a distraction worth avoiding.) Here is *B*:

```
String B(String p)
{
    if (p.indexOf("if") >= 0)
```

```
        {return "Has an 'if' in it.";}
    else
        {return "Has no 'if'.";}
}
```

The function of the `indexOf` method is to find where in `p` the characters `if` occur. If those characters are found, the method returns an integer indicating where they were found. If they are not found, `indexOf` returns −1.

Since the concept of a subroutine inputting other subroutines is strange, it may be helpful to type *B* into a machine and become comfortable using it. For example, try running *B* with *A* as input. Try running B with other subroutines as input. What happens if *B* is run on *B*?

We will examine other subroutines that input subroutines, but first it is important to introduce the idea of *the halting problem*. Some programs have the peculiar behavior that they run forever; they never halt. *C* is a subroutine with this characteristic:

```
int C(int x)
{
    while (x == x)
        {x = x;}
    return x;
}
```

This code will continue looping as long as *x* equals itself. But *x* always equals itself, so this program never halts regardless of what input is read.

Some subroutines may halt in some cases and fail to halt in others. The following code, *D*, will halt and return the input if it is less than or equal to 10. Otherwise, it will never halt:

```
int D(int x)
{
    while (x > 10)
        {x = x;}
    return x;
}
```

Most programs studied in this book halt on all inputs. Failure to halt is usually considered an undesirable property. The halting problem for computer programs thus addresses the question of whether those programs halt either on specific inputs or on all inputs.

We might like to write a subroutine that inputs other subroutines and checks whether they halt. Let us call the subroutine *E* and design it to determine, if possible, whether a

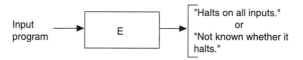

Input program → E → "Halts on all inputs." or "Not known whether it halts."

Figure 15.4

subroutine will halt on all inputs. If E reads a subroutine and finds that it will halt on every input, E will return the message "Halts on all inputs." Otherwise E will return "Not known whether it halts." (figure 15.4).

How can we write the subroutine E? This could be a complicated undertaking and only a simple version is attempted here. We could note, as a start, that if a subroutine has no `while` loops (and by assumption no internal subroutine calls), then it can be composed only of assignment statements, `if` statements, and the `return` statement. But such a subroutine would surely always halt because each such statement always executes and passes control to the next statement. The program end will be reached directly. The only way that nonhalting behavior can occur is if a loop captures control and never terminates, as occurs in C. A simple strategy for writing E is to have it check whether `while` appears anywhere in the input program. If E finds there is no `while` statement in its input program, it can be sure that program will halt on all inputs. If E does find `while` statements, it will not be able to guarantee any halting property. Thus, E can be written as follows:

```
String E(String p)
{
    if (p.indexOf("while") >= 0)
        {return "Not known whether it halts.";}
    else
        {return "Halts on all inputs.";}
}
```

Again, E is best understood if it is typed into a machine. It can then be run on various input programs such as A through E of this section and, in each case, will return the appropriate answer.

Unfortunately, E is more simplistic than we might desire. It does not give us any useful information beyond whether the string "while" appears in a given program, and we would actually like a definitive answer for any program. Does it halt on every input or does it not? We wish to create a new subroutine F and require that it be able to input any subroutine and halt after a finite time with the correct answer: either the given input subroutine halts on all inputs or it does not (figure 15.5). The next section describes the construction of F.

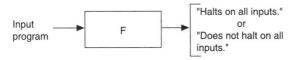

Figure 15.5

Exercises

1. Write a subroutine that reads another subroutine and tells whether the subroutine is known never to print anything. If your program cannot determine for sure whether the input program prints anything, it should give a message stating this.

2. Write a subroutine that reads another subroutine and gives its length. You will want to use the `String`-defined method called `length`, which returns the length of a given string as an integer.

3. Write a subroutine that reads a subroutine and then determines whether every variable declared actually appears in the main part of the program. If a variable is found that never appears after the declaration, your subroutine should return its name.

Solving the Halting Problem

The next task is to see how to write subroutine *F*. *F* will have lines of code that can check any input subroutine for its halting characteristics. *F* will check many features related to halting behavior, and if it finds a proof that the given subroutine will or will not always halt, it will print the appropriate message and stop.

The organization of *F* is as shown; a series of cases is examined. First, some lines of code check to see whether the current case is applicable. When a case is found that applies to the input subroutine, indicating its halting or nonhalting behavior, the appropriate message is returned, and all later cases are skipped:

```
String F(String p)
{
    String case1holds, case2holds, ... ;

    case 1 code
    if (case1holds.equals("true"))
        {return result of case 1;}
```

```
        case 2 code
    if (case2holds.equals("true"))
        {return result of case 2;}


        .
        .
        .


        case n code
    if (casenholds.equals("true"))
        {return result of case n;}
}
```

Thus, *F* can be completed as soon as all the cases are known. We now consider them in sequence.

Case 1

The easiest first phenomenon to cover is that addressed by *E*, the case where "while" does not appear anywhere in the input program. Here we know the message to be printed is "Halts on all inputs." so the case 1 portion of the *F* program is as follows:

```
if (p.indexOf("while") >= 0)
{
    case1holds = "true";
}
if (case1holds.equals("true"))
    {return "Halts on all inputs.";}
```

Case 2

A second phenomenon occurs in any program with a `while` loop that has `true` as a test. If the loop is ever entered, it will run forever, and this is a situation where *F* should print "Does not halt on all inputs." Subroutine *G* provides an example of this case:

```
String G(String x)
{
    while (true)
        {x = x;}
    return x;
}
```

The case 2 portion of F should be

```
Code that checks for a while loop that is entered and has true as a
                                test
if (case2holds.equals("true"))
    {return "Does not halt on all inputs.";}
```

Case 3

A slightly more complicated case is that represented by C, where a test is made in the loop but the test always produces a true result. If the loop is entered, the repetitions will not terminate. This is another situation in which F can return a "no halt" message. The case 3 portion of F can be written as follows:

```
Code that checks for a while loop that has a test that is clearly
                            always true
if (case3holds.equals("true"))
    {return "Does not halt on all inputs.";}
```

Case 4

D provides an example of another interesting class of programs. This is similar to case 3 except that it may not be clear whether the loop exit test will pass on the first encounter. In the case of D, the exit will occur if the input is not greater than 10. In other examples, more complicated situations may occur, and it is necessary to check whether any input could exist such that the loop exit will fail. Here is an example of a wide variety of constructions that might appear:

```
int H(int x)
{
    int y;
    if (x == 1772)
        {y = 1;}
    else
        {y = 0;}
    while (y == 1)
        {x = 1;}
    return x;
}
```

Handling all such examples is a complex undertaking that is not considered at length here.

Case 5

Another increment in complexity occurs if the loop test includes more than one variable. Here is a program that halts on all inputs, but it is not so easy to discover this:

```
int I(int x)
{
    int y;
    y = 2 * x;
    while (y > x)
    {
        x = x + 2;
        y = y + 1;
    }
    return x;
}
```

This is more complex than case 4 and is not considered further here.

Other cases need to be considered where three or more variables appear in the test or where very complex tests occur, as in this case:

```
while (((X * Z + 3) > Z - (Y/(Z1 * Z2 + 4)))
                && (X * (YY/Z1) < YY + Z1 + Z2))
```

Loops may also be nested to two or three or more levels, and there may also be deeply convoluted amalgamations of multiple `if` and `while` constructions. There may also be `while` loops with complicated indexing rules that could be mixed arbitrarily numbers of times with all earlier constructions.

So the job of writing a program F that will determine whether other programs halt is very difficult. Perhaps it could be a person's lifework. In fact, mathematicians have shown that no matter how many cases are considered and regardless of how completely each case is handled, the job will never be done. There will always be more cases, and there will always be more code to write on the given cases. *No finite program can be written that will check other programs and halt in a finite time giving a solution to the halting problem.* Thus, the goal of finding a noncomputable problem has been achieved. No program can exist that meets the specifications of F; this is proved later in this chapter.

In summary, we say that the halting problem is not computable. This does not mean that one cannot discover the halting characteristic of a particular program. We have determined the halting behavior for many programs in this chapter and others. What it does mean is that there is no single finite program F that will answer the halting question for all programs.

As an illustration, if *F* could exist, what would it do if it were given the following subroutine *J*?

```
int J(int x)
{
    int y;
    y = x;
    while (y > 1)
    {
        if (((y/2) * 2) == y)
            {y = y/2;}
        else
            {y = y * 3 + 1;}
    }
    return y;
}
```

(A special feature of this code is test `((y/2) * 2) == y`. This test will be true if *y* is even and false otherwise. So the program halves *y* whenever it is even and multiplies it by 3 and then adds 1 when it is odd.) If this subroutine inputs 17, it will compute these values for *y*: 52, 26, 13, 40, 20, 10, 5, 16, 8, 4, 2, 1. Then it will halt. We can give it thousands of other positive integers and probably discover it halts on them also. But will *J* halt on every positive integer? It is not likely that anyone knows, and there is no sure way to find out.

It is possible that someone will discover a way to solve the halting problem for *J*. As with some other programs discussed here, some solution may exist somewhere. Then we will not have to look far to find another program whose halting problem is not understood. There is no single program (or method) for solving all halting problems.

Exercises

1. Find a class of subroutines, not mentioned in the text, that halt on all inputs. Show how you have solved the halting problem for this class.

2. Find a class of subroutines, not mentioned in the text, each of which fails to halt on some input. Show how you can be sure that it will fail to halt on some input.

3. Run subroutine *J* on a number of inputs and observe its behavior. Do you believe that it halts on all positive inputs? How can we solve the halting problem for program *J*?

4. Find a program whose halting behavior is extremely difficult to determine.

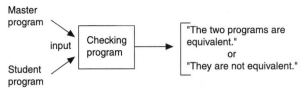

Figure 15.6

Examples of Noncomputable Problems

Suppose the instructor of a computer programming course wishes to have his or her students' programs checked automatically. A reasonable strategy would be for the instructor to write a master program that solves the assigned problem and then to check whether each student's submission is equivalent to the master. In order for two programs to be equivalent, they must print the same result for every input. The checking program would read the two problem solutions: the instructor's master and the student's submission. Then it would print the appropriate answer, either "The two programs are equivalent." or "They are not equivalent." (figure 15.6).

The analysis of this problem proceeds very much as with the halting problem in the previous section. It is often possible to determine that two programs are equivalent, as with

```
int A1(int X)
{
    return 2 * x;
}
```

and

```
int A2(int X)
{
    return x + x;
}
```

So, in some cases, equivalence can be discovered. It is also quite common to be able to show that two programs are not equivalent, as with program $A1$ and the following program:

```
int AA(int X)
{
```

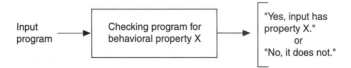

Figure 15.7

```
    return 3 * x;
}
```

However, there are many cases in which the discovery of equivalence is an exceedingly subtle, if not impossible, matter. Consider two programs, *J* from the previous section and *K*, and the difficulty in determining their equivalence assuming that the only inputs are positive integers:

```
int K(int x)
{
    return 1;
}
```

The first program, *J*, may halt on all inputs and return 1. It seems to do this, but we have no way of being sure that it always does. If it does, it is equivalent to *K*; otherwise it is not.

If we attempt to write a checking program as described here, we run into a series of cases resembling those encountered in the previous section, and we will not be able to complete the task. The *equivalence problem* is another example of a noncomputable calculation.

There are very large numbers of problems related to programs that are noncomputable, as are the halting problem and the equivalence problem. Suppose you want a program to check whether programs print something on every possible input. For some programs this is easy; but if *J* were redesigned to print its output, it would be very difficult. This is a noncomputable problem. Suppose you want a program to determine whether a specific line of code is always executed in other programs for all possible inputs. This is also a noncomputable problem. For example, does *J* execute the instruction `return y` for every (positive integer) input? Suppose you want a program to determine whether other programs double their input. This again is noncomputable.

In fact, almost every problem related to the behavior of programs is noncomputable in the sense described here. Almost every question related to halting, equivalence, printing, correctness, or any other behavioral property is unanswerable for the class of all programs. Anyone who proposes to write a program to check for property X in the behavior of all other programs is probably attempting the impossible (figure 15.7).

Are there any questions about programs that are computable? Yes, we can write programs to check almost any syntactic feature of programs. We can write programs that will measure the length of programs, the number of statements, the number of character A's, the number of arithmetic expressions, and many other things. We can write a program that will read a sequence of characters and tell whether it is a Java program or not. (The Java compiler does this.) We can write a program that will compute almost any property of the sequence of characters that make up the program. But we usually cannot write a program that will discover any general property of the program's execution when it is functioning as a program.

Exercises

1. We categorize functions in three different ways: noncomputable, computable-tractable, and computable-intractable. Study each proposed computation that follows and classify it, as well as you can, in one of the three ways:

   (a) A program is to be written that reads a list of n numbers and finds whether any one of those numbers is the sum of any two or more of the others.

   (b) A program is to be written that reads a program of length n. It then tells the number of characters that will be printed if that other program is run on the input of 17.

   (c) A program is to be written that reads a program of length n. If the program that was read computes a tractable computation, it prints "tractable." Otherwise, it prints "intractable."

   (d) A program is to be written that reads n numbers and prints the largest one.

   (e) A program is to be written that reads a program of length n and translates it into machine language.

   (f) A program is to be written that reads a Java program of length n. If there is a way to rearrange the characters of this program so that they become a legal P88 assembly language program, the program prints "yes." Otherwise, it prints "no."

   (g) A program is to be written that reads a program of length n and tells how many legal Java statements are in the program that was read.

2. The Church-Markov-Turing Thesis (chapter 4) states that any computation that we can describe can be computed. In this chapter, we have described some computations that we claim cannot be computed. Contradiction! What is the problem here?

---

*Proving Noncomputability

The previous sections have argued that writing programs to solve the halting problem and others would be very hard, in fact, impossible. However, no proof of this impossibility has yet been given. This section presents a classical proof that the halting problem is not computable. The other examples from the last section can be derived from this basic result.

The method of proof will be by contradiction. We assume that the halting problem is solvable and that a program has been found that solves it. We then study the ramifications of this assumption and come across ridiculous conclusions. We decide that since the assumption that a program exists to solve the halting problem leads to something obviously false, it must be that such a program does not exist.

The proof begins with the assumption that we have a Java subroutine called `halt` that inputs two things—a program `p` and its input `x`. We assume that `halt` will run for only a finite amount of time and then will return its answer. Either it will return "Halts." indicating that program `p` halts on input `x`, or it will return "Does not halt." indicating that `p` will run forever if given input `x`.

```
String halt(String p, String x)
{
    Body of the halt routine
    if (...)
        {return "Halts.";}
    else
        {return "Does not halt.";}
}
```

(This program is more specific than *F*, discussed earlier, in that it inputs both a program and that program's input. This program returns "Halts." if `p` halts on input `x`, whereas *F* reads only `p` and prints "Halts on all inputs." if `p` halts on all inputs. The subroutine `halt` checks only one input for program `p`, whereas *F* checks all inputs.) We do not know the details of the subroutine `halt`. We assume that someone has filled them in and wonder what the consequences are of having this program.

Next, we write two subroutines to help with this proof. One is called `selfhalt`, and the other is `contrary`. The former inputs a program `p` and then calls the subroutine `halt` to find whether `p` halts with itself as an argument:

```
String selfhalt(String p)
{
    String answer;
    answer = halt (p, p);
    if (answer.equals("Halts."))
        {return("Halts on self.");}
    else
        {return("Does not halt on self.");}
}
```

The second program, `contrary`, is designed to justify its name. It reads a program `p` and runs `selfhalt` to determine whether `p` halts on itself. If `p` does halt on itself, then `contrary` will never halt. If `p` does not halt on itself, then `contrary` will halt immediately:

```
String contrary(String p)
{
    String answer;
    answer = selfhalt(p);
    if (answer.equals("Halts on self."))
    {
        while (true)
            {answer = "x";}
    }
    return "Halt.";
}
```

This is all extremely simple. (It is very strange but simple!) But a real collision with reality occurs when `contrary` is allowed to run with itself as input. Let's analyze very carefully what happens.

Assume that `p` is the subroutine `contrary`, and that this routine `contrary` is executed with input `p`. Thus, we are running `contrary` on itself. The first statement of `contrary` is answer = selfhalt(p). Consider two cases:

1. Suppose `selfhalt` stops and returns the result "Halts on self." Then the second statement of `contrary` will check this and go into an infinite loop. That is, if it is found using `selfhalt` that `contrary` halts on itself, then `contrary` will run forever on itself. The infinite loop `while (true) {answer = "x";}` ensures this. This is a contradiction. The routine `contrary` cannot both halt on itself and not halt on itself.
2. Suppose `selfhalt` stops and returns the result "Does not halt on self." Then the second statement of `contrary` will be a test that fails, and `contrary` will halt immediately. Thus, we conclude that if `contrary` does not halt on itself (as determined by routine `selfhalt`), then it will halt on itself. Again, an equally ridiculous conclusion has been found.

This concludes the proof by contradiction. First, it was assumed that the program `halt` could exist as defined. Then the subroutine `contrary` was defined (with its subroutine `selfhalt`, which depends on `halt`). Then it was shown that if `contrary` halts on itself, then it does not halt on itself, and if it does not halt on itself, then it halts on itself. Something is wrong with this argument. But every step is extremely simple and logically sound. The only step lacking justification is the assumption that `halt` can exist. We conclude that it cannot exist.

Therefore, we have proved the noncomputability of the `halt` function. This proof may seem like so much mathematical magic because it is so involuted in its structure. It is, however, the classical proof of the mathematical literature translated into the notation and vocabulary of this book.

Once it is clear that `halt` cannot exist, we can prove many other noncomputability results. As an illustration, consider the program *F*, discussed earlier. This program, if it could exist, would read a program and tell whether it halts on all inputs. Knowing that `halt` cannot exist, how can we show that *F* also cannot exist?

We can do this proof by contradiction: If *F* did exist, then we could build `halt`, and this result has been shown to be impossible. Assume the program whose halting problem is to be solved has this form:

```
String p(String z)
{
    Java code that uses variable z
}
```

Then `halt` can be constructed as follows:

```
String halt(String p, String x)
{
    String answer;
    Code that removes variable z from the argument of p and replaces
                it with a new variable that appears nowhere in
                subroutine p. Call the new variable newz.
    Code that inserts a new statement at the beginning of p: z =
                (contents of x)
    answer = F(p);
    if (answer.equals("Halts on all inputs."))
        {return "Halts.";}
    else
        {return "Does not halt.";}
}
```

Here is how `halt` works. Assume it is called with argument p containing the preceding subroutine p and with x containing the input for p. First `halt` modifies p so that it has this form:

```
String p(String newz)
{
    Java code that uses variable z
}
```

Notice that this new version of p acts the same regardless of what its argument is. Variable newz is never used in the code. Also, this version has a bug in it because z, which previously received its input from the argument, now has no value. The next piece of code in halt fixes this error; it puts a statement into p that properly loads z. Now p has this form:

```
String p(String newz)
{
    z = The contents of x is placed here.
    Java code that uses variable z
}
```

The new subroutine p has the properties that it functions the same regardless of its input newz because newz is never used, and it does exactly what the old p would have done using the input in x. Thus, if the old p would have halted on x, the new p will halt on all inputs. If the old p would have run forever on x, the new p will run forever on all inputs.

Next halt calls F running on this modified program. According to the specifications of F, it will stop after a finite time and return the result "Halts on all inputs." if the revised p will halt on all inputs and "Does not halt." otherwise. But if the revised p halts on all inputs, the original p would halt on x, so halt should return "Halts." If the revised p fails to halt on all inputs, the original p would not halt on x, so halt should return "Does not halt." Summarizing, we have seen that if F could exist, then halt could be constructed, and this is impossible. This concludes the proof that the problem that F is specified to solve is noncomputable.

Exercises

1. Do a hand simulation of program contrary when it is run with program B as an input. Repeat with program E as an input.

2. Use the methodology of the section to prove that the following problem is noncomputable: A program is to be written that reads a program, and after a finite time the output is to tell whether the input program will ever print anything.

Summary

We began this chapter by asserting that there are numerical functions that cannot be computed by any Java program. Then we gave a proof of this assertion. The proof showed that there are noncomputable functions, but it failed to provide even one example. We could study some numerical examples, but they are both difficult to explain and less important practically.

Our study thus moved to a new domain—programs that read programs. Here it was found that if any proposed program is to read another program and determine almost any property of its execution behaviors, there is a good chance that noncomputability will be encountered; the proposed program will not be constructable using Java (or any other language that has been invented or proposed). Thus, programs cannot be written to solve the halting, equivalence, printing, correctness, or almost any other behavioral property of programs. This is an extremely important result for computer scientists because one of their main jobs is to write programs that manipulate other programs. Many of the tasks they may set for themselves are not within the realm of possibility.

But it should be noted that problems related to the syntax of programs very often are computable, and examples appear throughout this book. Thus, one can write programs that look for character sequences in other programs or that measure their syntactic properties. Also programs can read other programs and translate them into some other language, as shown in chapter 9.

This chapter and chapter 13 have shown two types of computations that cannot be done using current or proposed technologies. Chapter 16 studies another class of very difficult problems.

16   Artificial Intelligence

The Dream

The final frontier to be examined here concerns our limitations as programmers. At the beginning of a new century, it is reasonable to ask how large, how complex, how broad in capabilities, and ultimately how intelligent our programs will become. Considering any program created earlier in this book, we wonder how many improvements could be made to strengthen its capabilities and increase its usefulness. Could the program be improved to handle a larger class of problems? Could it be revised to make inferences beyond its current capabilities? Could it be designed to create alternative plans and to evaluate them and select the best one? Could the program recognize its own shortcomings and modify itself to give better performance?

As an illustration, consider the database program that was used to help the inspector solve a mystery. We have already noticed its lack of ability to infer new facts from the given information. A method for addressing this problem was suggested near the end of chapter 9. But how extensive could this inference mechanism actually be? For example, the system could be given the fact that every person must be somewhere at every instant of time, and then it could attempt to infer the whereabouts of every individual at critical times. It could formulate a plan for solving the crime by seeking a proof for each individual's story in relation to the key events. The program no longer would be a passive provider of information but an active developer of theories. Perhaps the program could handle a variety of English syntax instead of simply noun-verb-noun formats. We might, in addition, design mechanisms to remember successful strategies and then use them to improve the system's subsequent performance. Finally, we would want the system to be general enough in its design to manage various information-processing problems, not simply household facts.

Such is the dream of *artificial intelligence*: that machines may be programmed to become more and more powerful in the solution of problems until their abilities equal or exceed those of human beings. The artificial intelligence researcher looks on the human mind as an example of a very powerful computer, and his or her goal is to write programs so that electronic machines can achieve the abilities of these existing biological machines. Attempts have been made to develop systems that converse in natural language, solve puzzles, play games, understand visual images, walk on legs and manipulate the environment with hands, compose music, create new mathematics, and do long lists of other tasks. If the human mind-computer can do those computations, the argument is, electronic computers should be able to do them also.

Computers already can do some things much better than human beings. Certainly they can add numbers faster, millions of them per second, and they can remember facts better, billions of them without making even one error. So the question is not whether computers or human beings have better information-processing abilities but rather which problems are better handled by machines and which by human beings.

The difference between human and machine capabilities seems to depend on the intrinsic complexity of the task. If the complexity is low enough so that efficient programs can be written to do the work, machines will do a superior job. But if the complexity is too great, either the programs are too slow or the code is so complicated that no one knows how to write it.

Putting things into perspective, one can draw a rough graph showing task complexity on the horizontal axis and estimating human and computer capabilities on the vertical axis (figure 16.1). Machines clearly dominate in all situations where moderate-sized programs can be devised that run at acceptable speeds. No sensible person is proposing that standard industrial information processing such as computer language translation or payroll computation would be better done by human beings. However, machines are clearly inferior for tasks listed on the right half of the graph, such as in natural language translation, concept formation, and any kind of scientific theory formation.

Human performance, in contrast, is much more evenly balanced across the spectrum of possible activities. Human beings are moderately competent at simple tasks, such as adding numbers, at all the intermediate levels of complexity, and even at concept formation and the most profound of tasks.

This graph, of course, cannot be taken too seriously because none of the dimensions or terms is well defined. But it does organize our perspective in preparation for a study of artificial intelligence. The usual definition of intelligence roughly refers to the horizontal axis, where higher degrees of intelligence correspond to points farther to the right. When human beings and machines are being discussed, the definition of "intelligent behavior" typically begins somewhere around the crossover point for the machine and human performance curves. The goal for artificial intelligence researchers is to raise the level of the machine curve as much as possible, especially in the regions on the right.

As researchers attack profoundly more difficult problems, it is appropriate to have corresponding new intellectual paradigms. This chapter introduces the most important ones

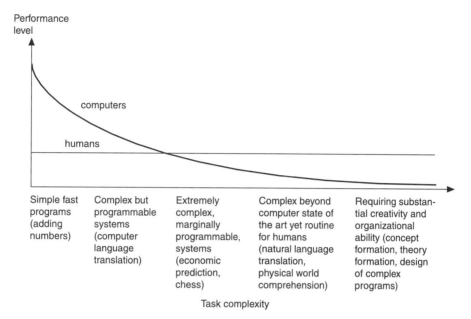

Performance level

computers

humans

| Simple fast programs (adding numbers) | Complex but programmable systems (computer language translation) | Extremely complex, marginally programmable, systems (economic prediction, chess) | Complex beyond computer state of the art yet routine for humans (natural language translation, physical world comprehension) | Requiring substantial creativity and organizational ability (concept formation, theory formation, design of complex programs) |

Task complexity

Figure 16.1

—the concepts of *knowledge* and *reasoning* as they relate to intelligent behavior. Instead of dealing with data such as numbers or strings, as in the previous chapters, we discuss larger structures of information, knowledge structures. Of course, these larger structures are composed of the same primitives as before—numbers and strings—but they will be thought of and manipulated as a whole rather than as one memory unit at a time. Instead of dealing with simple computations as before, such as addition or copy operations, we discuss steps in the reasoning process that may each involve many such individual operations. For example, a typical reasoning operation is to infer a new fact. The combination of our abilities to think at the knowledge level and to conceive of computations at the reasoning level enables us to approach more difficult problems. These provide the starting point for a study of artificial intelligence.

The following sections discuss the concepts of knowledge and reasoning at length. The first sequence of topics examines knowledge as a concept, its representation, the meaning of the word *understand*, the uses of knowledge, and methods for learning knowledge. Then reasoning methodologies and heuristic search are discussed, with applications to game playing and expert system design. Finally, the summary sections discuss the state of the art in artificial intelligence.

Representing Knowledge

The knowledge of an object or event is the set of facts and relationships pertaining to it. For example, one may have knowledge of a particular chair—its position, its material, its color, its size and shape, its owner, its cost, its age, its history, its current use, and many more facts. A particular data item is part of the knowledge of the chair if there are processing tasks related to the chair that reference that item. Thus, one might want to use the chair, move it, describe it, copy it, change it, or many other operations, and the data items related to the chair that are required to do these things compose the knowledge about the chair.

If the computer is to do these and other operations with regard to an object, it must have the required knowledge. The knowledge should be organized in such a way that the machine can use it efficiently to do its job. There are many ways of storing knowledge, and the method in this chapter uses *semantic networks*.

A semantic network is a set of labeled nodes with labeled arcs connecting them. The nodes can be used to represent objects, names, properties, and other entities, and the arcs can show the relationships between these entities. Figure 16.2 shows a semantic network that partly describes a chair that has been given the formal label *a1*.

This network describes an object called *a1* as represented by the node at the middle left of the figure. Following the arrow down, we see that the name of this object is "chair."

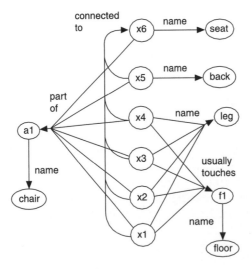

Figure 16.2

There are six other objects in the figure, labeled *x1, x2, . . . , x6*, and they all have pointers aimed at *a1*, which are labeled "part of." Thus, they are part of the object labeled *a1*. We can tell what these six objects are by their names. Some are legs, one is a back, and one is a seat. Finally, we can see the relationships of these objects to each other and to other objects. Some are connected, and a leg "usually touches" the floor.

This figure thus gives us a way to represent a more complex type of object than a number or a string. It enables us to manipulate inside a computer the kinds of objects that we would expect an intelligent agent to manage.

But how can we store this network in the machine? A method for doing it is to notice that every arc can be specified by listing its initial node, its arc label, and its final node:

```
x1    part of    a1
x2    part of    a1
.
.
.

a1    name    chair
.
.
.
```

This listing contains all the information in the network and is suitable for storage in the machine. In fact, we are experts at handling facts in three-part form because we studied this format extensively in chapter 4. For the remainder of this chapter, we continue to draw networks like the preceding one, assuming that you can fill in implementation details if needed by referring to chapter 4.

Knowledge can be represented in the machine with other methods than semantic networks. For example, one common technique is to write down a set of logical statements containing the significant relationships. Another is to specify the objects and relationships with an ordinary programming language such as Java, LISP, or Prolog. A third way is to store information in actual pictorial images in the machine. For this chapter, however, the only representation scheme will be semantic networks. They are easy to visualize and use in the tasks that we study here.

The next several sections discuss the concept of knowledge understanding, a method for learning new knowledge, structures for large knowledge modules, and an example of the usefulness of knowledge in natural language understanding.

Exercises

1. Remove one of the arcs between two nodes on the chair network. Describe the object that it represents after the change.

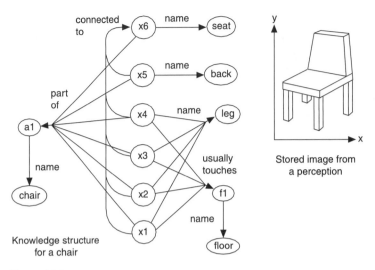

Figure 16.3

2. Draw a semantic network to represent a typical house. It should include each wall, the roof, each window, the doors, a chimney, and so forth. The network should show connectivity, support relationships, and some functional knowledge, such as where to enter.

Understanding

Suppose that the knowledge structure of the chair is stored in the machine (or perhaps the human mind). Suppose also that an image has been perceived from the outside world and is stored in a nearby memory region (figure 16.3). We would like to be able to use the knowledge to make sense of the image. If the knowledge can be linked in a satisfactory way to the lines and regions in the image, the system would be able to relate the knowledge to the image. In fact, it would be able to identify the object, to name its parts, to explain connectedness relationships of the parts to each other, and to give the uses of this object. It could find all other details that may be stored in its knowledge base (e.g., owner, cost, materials, history). If these linkages can be made, we say that the system *understands* this image with respect to this knowledge. Understanding will involve finding a linkage between these two structures.

Let's follow the process of searching for an understanding of the image with respect to this knowledge. Where, for example, is the seat of the chair? We link the node $x6$ asso-

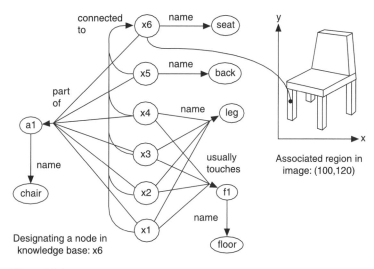

Figure 16.4

ciated with the name "seat" with a randomly selected region in the image (figure 16.4). Assume the selected region is specified by the coordinates of its central point $(x, y) = (100, 120)$. Then we store this linkage in a table:

Nodes in Knowledge Base	Associated Region in Image
x6	$(100, 120)$

Examining the knowledge structure, we see that five objects are connected to *x6*, "seat". In order to confirm the linkage that has been made, we scan the periphery of the selected region in the image to find those five objects. Unfortunately, a search of the surrounding area yields only one obviously connected part. Perhaps the linkage is incorrect.

Let's break the linkage and try connecting it to other regions. Other attempts may lead to the same result, but eventually the linkage in figure 16.5 will be tried and confirmed: the selected region has five objects connected to it.

Again, understanding requires continuous confirmation of as many associated relationships as possible. Perhaps the region designated $(100, 120)$ can be associated with some other node. Since it touches the floor, we propose that it is *x3*. The knowledge base asserts that *x3* is connected to *x6*. Can this be confirmed in the image? Yes. All linkages thus far appear to be consistent with expectations given by the knowledge base. Carrying this process on, three more objects can be identified as legs, and one can be identified as the back. In fact, a satisfactory linkage has been found between the nodes of the knowl-

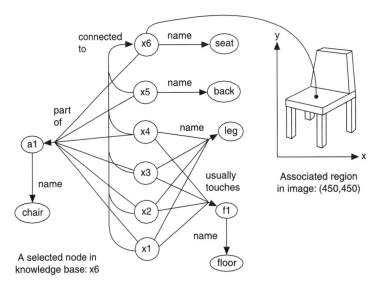

Figure 16.5

edge structure and the regions of the image. The predicted relationships given in the semantic network are confirmed, and the system can assume that the knowledge structure has been correctly related to the image (figure 16.6).

When the system has correctly made these linkages, we say that it *understands* the image. All of its knowledge related to the chair can be used. The system can now find the name of the object of which the identified regions are parts. It follows the "part of" links to *a1* and traces the name link to "chair." The system can now output, "This is a chair." Furthermore, it can follow the name links for all the parts and name them. Then it can follow the use link, if it exists, to discover the function of this object. It can follow ownership, cost, history, location, and other links, if present, to obtain as much additional information about the chair as its knowledge base may hold.

In summary, the understanding of a perception with respect to a body of knowledge involves finding a set of self-consistent links between the parts of the knowledge structure and the parts of the perceived data. After such a linkage is made, the intelligent being can follow arcs in its knowledge base to obtain innumerable useful facts, the name of the perceived object, the names of its many parts, their relationships to each other, the uses of the object, and all other information available in its knowledge base.

Of course, a being seeking understanding may incorrectly set up linkages with a knowledge structure. Then misunderstanding will occur, and incorrect inferences may be made. For example, for the wood block shown in figure 16.7, it may incorrectly conclude that an oaken object has been discovered that will be useful for sitting.

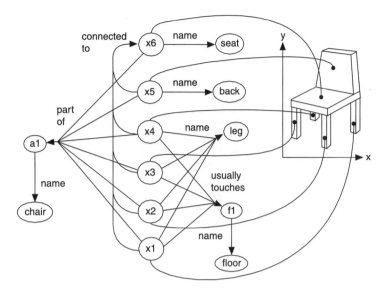

Figure 16.6

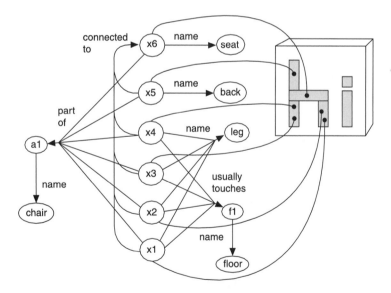

Figure 16.7

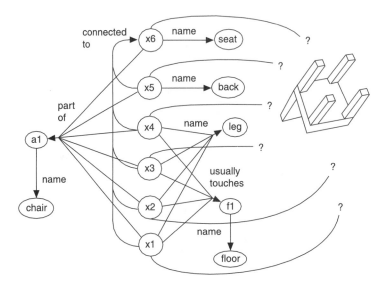

Figure 16.8

A being may also fail to understand a perception although its knowledge is adequate. The discovery of the proper linkages may involve a calculation outside its repertoire (figure 16.8). Here, parts that were supposed to touch the floor do not; parts that should not touch the floor do touch it. Either a teacher or additional computational exploration will be necessary to achieve understanding.

As a philosophical issue, some people have argued about whether computers can truly understand anything. If the preceding definition of understanding is accepted, then we must certainly agree that computers can understand many things. First, one should ask whether there are domains where significant knowledge can be stored, and second, we should verify that machines are capable of properly relating machine perceptions with such knowledge. On the first issue, it is clear that a computer can store all the relevant information on large sets of objects and their interrelations. These can include people in organizations, objects in an environment, objects or structures in a mathematical system or in a game, the data structures for computer programs, and an endless list of other examples. On the second issue, we assume the computer's "perceptions" are the sequences of inputs from keyboards, mouse clicks, or other input devices. Most certainly computers have been programmed to relate properly the input sequences to the internal structure. The image-understanding mechanisms just described provide an example.

As another example of computer understanding, consider the task accomplished by a processor for a computer language such as Java. The processor sets up linkages between the language constructs and the string of symbols that constitute the program. On the knowledge side, the machine has representations for such entities as keywords, identifiers,

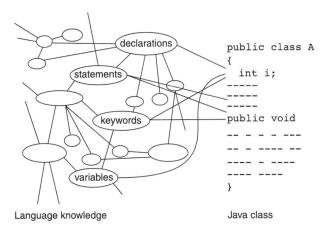

Figure 16.9

expressions, statements, registers, machine language, and much more. On the perception side, the system receives a string of characters that needs to be understood. The process of understanding involves finding expected objects and relationships in the perceived string as predicted by the knowledge of the language in the processor. This linking of internal structures to the string represents a rather complete understanding of that string as a program (figure 16.9).

While the processor will completely understand the input string as a program, it may not understand additional meanings the user has intended. Thus, there may be variables, such as X, that have particular meanings to the user, such as dollars earned. These cannot be known to the processor. However, if the machine had this additional knowledge, it could conceivably understand these facts as well.

At this point, we might begin to believe that machines can understand absolutely everything. After all, is it not reasonable to assume that all knowledge is representable in some kind of computer language? And is it not also reasonable to assume that if there is a linkage possible between that knowledge and perceptions, a computer could eventually find it? The discovery of the linkage might require much time, but the computer should be able to find it.

Careful reflection will lead us to another conclusion. There are kinds of knowledge that probably can never be satisfactorily represented in machines. The most important example is the knowledge of our own humanity—the knowledge that comes from being born human, growing up, and surviving in the world. We all have had parents, friends, and loved ones, and we have shared experiences with them over the years. We have struggled hard, suffered anguish, cared for people and for our values, celebrated successes, and wept over our failures. All these experiences build cumulatively in our psychobiological selves into an immense complex of memories and feelings. These experiences are unique to each of us but also shared to a great extent among us. This vast array of emotions and remembrances has been earned by each of us in a multitude of events that cannot be repeated. These are the kinds of knowledge that cannot be satisfactorily stored in a machine.

When a fellow human being says, "My baby just spoke her first word," or "My cousin died yesterday," we, as human beings, can link these observances into our human memories and understand them. We have plenty of representations for the emotions and ramifications of the statements, and our understanding involves our linking to them.

We could attempt to build a simulation of human experience and emotion into a machine and claim that it also understands these uniquely human utterances. We could have nodes for pain, hope, fear, love, and stored remembrances of associated events. All of these could be connected in complex ways, and the system might seem to understand and to respond, "Wonderful!" or "I am sorry" at the appropriate times. But the simulation will probably lack authenticity, and at best it will never be more than a simulation. It is not likely that human beings will ever agree that machines can understand the human experience.

In summary, this section gives a definition for the concept of understanding and indicates that machines are capable of this behavior in many domains. However, it argues that machines will probably never be able to understand some things, such as human emotion, in any satisfactory way.

Exercises

1. Draw a picture of a typical house and its associated semantic net. Explain the process a machine would go through in using the network to "understand" the image of the house.

2. Suppose the chair network were used to try to understand your house image of exercise 1. What processing would take place, and what mechanism would prevent the machine from recognizing your house as a chair?

3. Suppose a computer program is designed to receive digitized versions of paintings by the masters. Then it is supposed to "understand" these paintings and comment on them. What will the machine possibly be able to do and what will it probably fail to do?

4. A computer program has been designed to write music. Comment on the nature of music as a human endeavor and the role that music written by machines may play.

5. Discuss the replaceability of human beings by machines. Does the use of automated bank tellers foreshadow a day when most interactions between businesses and the public will be done by machine? Could teachers, counselors, or judges be replaced by

machines? What are the situations when a machine is preferred and when a human being is preferred?

Learning

Once the fundamental issues of knowledge are understood, the next problem is to discover how to build adequate stores of knowledge for the many purposes of intelligence. One way to build a knowledge base in a machine is to prepare it in an appropriate form and enter it directly as data. Another way is to have the system *learn* the knowledge; that is, it uses its own mechanisms to acquire and properly format its knowledge. This latter method is highly desirable if it can be achieved because the task of assembling knowledge is difficult.

We study two kinds of learning in this chapter: *rote learning* and *concept learning*. Rote learning refers to the most primitive kind of knowledge acquisition; information from the outside world is coded into internal formats and stored in a relatively raw form. The amount of memory space used is roughly proportional to the amount of information acquired. Concept learning is a much more profound type of knowledge acquisition because it attempts to build a small construction to represent a large amount of data. It attempts to find a summary that properly describes a multiplicity of data items. A learned concept may use relatively little memory in comparison to the amount of data it represents.

Chapter 14 examined connectionist networks that theoretically can achieve both kinds of learning. However, we use more conventional models of computing in this chapter because they are better understood and better developed for the purposes of the current study. This section begins with an examination of rote learning and then shows improvements in a basic mechanism that will lead to concept learning.

Suppose a being which is presented with the image in figure 16.10. The being has no concept "chair," has never seen a chair, and has never encountered the term *chair*. We

Figure 16.10

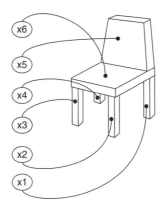

Initial understanding of the image

Figure 16.11

must assume, however, that the being can distinguish some primitive elements in the scene. Let's say it distinguishes a group of oaken boards but does not recognize the configuration to be anything special. Then its internal representation would indicate little more than the existence of the recognized objects (figure 16.11).

Next we assume that someone says, "This is a chair." This utterance asks the being to comprehend the image as something more than a pile of wood. It is a very special assembly of wood that has enough importance to have been given a name. The being thus notes more carefully the exact nature of the set of objects, assigns them a representation as a group, and attaches the name "chair" (figure 16.12). For further comprehension, we assume the teacher also names the components of the chair and demonstrates its use for sitting. Then the system would increase its knowledge structure to account for these additional data (figure 16.13).

Thereafter, the being should be able to see this object and recognize it as a chair. This is an example of what we call rote learning. A single data item has been observed, and a memory representation has been created for it. The system could similarly be given other objects to learn and name, such as a table, a lamp, a stool, a puppy dog, and so forth. Each new object has its own configuration and its own memorized structure. If a thousand such objects were so learned, a thousand such representations would be created.

Next if the system were given the three-legged image in figure 16.14 and asked to identify it, it would fail because there is no way to build a correspondence between the image and any existing internal representation. It does not match the description of a table, a lamp, a puppy dog, or any other object in memory. It is not a chair because a chair must have six major components, and this has only five. The system could not understand this image with respect to its current knowledge base.

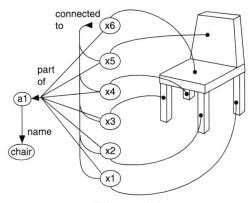

"This is a chair."

Figure 16.12

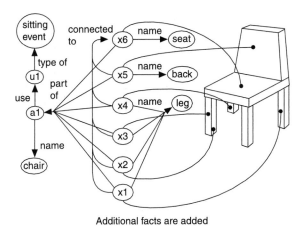

Additional facts are added

Figure 16.13

Figure 16.14

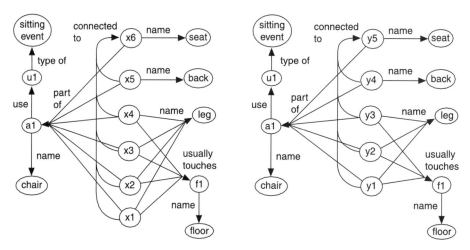

Two representations of "chair"

Figure 16.15

Let's indicate to the system that this new image is also a chair. We similarly name its parts and demonstrate it as a useful auxiliary for sitting. The system now has two representations of "chair" (figure 16.15). At this point, the system has two choices: it could continue its rote memory strategy for learning and store both of these representations, or it could attempt to combine them and perhaps generalize to some extent. Let's pursue the second strategy and note that these two drawings are identical except for the number of legs. So they can be merged if the difference between the numbers of legs can be accounted for (figure 16.16). The new representation asserts that something is a chair if it has a seat, a back, is useful for sitting, and has any number of legs.

A merger of this kind is called *concept formation*, and it has a number of advantages. First, it saves memory space because it enables the system to store information for

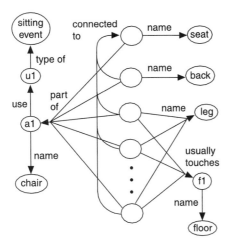

Merging the two "chair" representations

Figure 16.16

more than one data item. In fact, an unlimited number of data items can have a single representation, as is the case with the human concept of chair. Second, the merged representation allows the learner to deal with new situations that have never before been encountered. Thus, the system can recognize objects as chairs with perhaps one leg or no legs or a thousand legs if they meet the other prerequisites that chairs must have. The general concept has much greater usefulness than individual rote memory instances.

Concept formation of this type also has some dangers. It may be that an attribute may be observed to appear in a few examples and falsely generalized to be expected of all examples. For example, a being might observe that the winners of several U.S. presidential elections were taller than their major adversaries. On this basis, the system might conclude that the tallest candidate will always win, a typical but not necessarily reliable observation.

This section has described the acquisition of knowledge through rote memory and concept formation processes that enable a system to generalize from instances. The result of a lot of learning can be some large knowledge structures, as described in the next section.

Exercise

1. Draw semantic networks for two kinds of vehicles, say, a car and a truck. Show how to merge the two networks to obtain a more general description of a vehicle.

Frames

If one carries out extensive learning, rather large knowledge structures will evolve. These structures are called *frames*, and they are hypothesized to be of central importance in intelligent thought. They necessarily will be complicated and will include a variety of notations, indicating, for example, which relationships are obligatory, which are typical, which are possible although unusual, and which strange collections of relationships may occur. In realistic situations, frames may be built up over the years through a process of hundreds or thousands of concept learning mergers. These mergers result in huge numbers of auxiliary and extraneous connections that may include variations on the original template as well as seemingly unlimited numbers of related facts—history, associations, uses, special relationships, and long lists of other facts.

As an illustration, consider how much most people can say about their own knowledge of chairs. They can talk in considerable detail about a variety of chairs they have seen. They can probably give endless descriptions of chairs that are in their home, chairs they remember from schools or museums or theaters, chairs that were comfortable or not, chairs in stories, chairs that were broken, and other chairs. They can probably tell innumerable stories about chairs in their lives, chairs in literature or movies, and chairs in history. They probably can describe in detail the construction of chairs, their materials, their finishes, where they are built and sold, how much they cost, and much more.

Therefore, a semantic network that represents something close to a human being's knowledge of the concept "chair" will be a very large structure. It will include tens of thousands of nodes and arcs. Whenever the being needs information related to chairs, this frame will be called upon for understanding and for guiding correct action.

Researchers hypothesize that intelligent beings must have hundreds or even thousands of such modules and that thinking involves sequentially activating them as they are needed. This leads to the view of the intelligent being as a kind of frame-shuffling machine. Perceptions from the world impinge on numerous frames, and a few of those frames become successful in understanding those perceptions. Those activated frames prompt the being to appropriate action, and simultaneously additional changes may be observed. This leads to new perceptions, possible confirmation of current frame activity, and conceivably the activation of additional frames. The being is seen as perpetually grabbing frames that enable understanding, responding as dictated by those frames, receiving new perceptions, activating additional frames as needed, responding further, and so forth.

Consider the actions of a person walking down a hall. The theory might account for the sequence of actions as follows: A walking frame is activated to coordinate the eyes and muscular activities to achieve the walking behavior. A hall frame enables understanding of the visual images. Suppose the person turns into an office. The turning and visual door frames are activated to enable this movement. Suppose another person is encountered. Then a frame for that person is activated along with the frame for friendly conversation.

"Hi, how are you?..." The weather is mentioned, and the weather frame is activated. The appropriate words can now be understood: *rain, snow, cold, slippery*, and others. A newspaper is noticed on a nearby desk with the headline "Commission Appointed to Study Deficit." The politics and deficit frames come into action to permit relevant conversation: presidential proclamations, the appearance of positive actions, the requirements for large annual interest payments. The friendly conversation frame interrupts to indicate that the interaction should end. The person leaves the office, moving through the door frame and returning again to the walking and hall frames.

The frames system is called a *memory-rich* theory because it emphasizes the importance of memory and access to complex structures. It proposes that human beings depend primarily on remembrance in perceiving the world and in responding. It places less faith in inference or reasoning mechanisms as bases for typical behaviors. It asserts that the actions and thoughts of the person walking down the hall, meeting another person, conversing, and leaving are primarily governed by fast, efficient memory access methods. The claim is that the person did not calculate much to get the legs to move, to understand the visual images, or to converse.

One of the main arguments for memory-rich theories is that the elements of the human mind are too slow to do a large amount of sequential computation. The neurons of the brain respond in a time on the order of milliseconds, and the actions of a human being are too fast to allow for much more than memory access. For example, a tennis player observing a ball at a distance of 30 feet approaching at 30 miles per hour will have a fraction of a second to respond. This means that the player's mind has, at best, time for a few hundred sequential neural cycles. Yet the amount of computation for appropriate response includes the need to perceive the ball, calculate its trajectory, and properly activate a myriad of muscular responses throughout the body. It would seem that this is too much computation to complete in so few cycles even with tremendous parallelism. The memory-rich theory proposes that the player amalgamates the experiences of thousands of incoming balls perceived and properly answered into a massive frame for hitting balls. When the next tennis ball approaches, this huge structure comes into action to monitor the perceptions, to predict the trajectory, and to drive the body to hit the ball back. The player depends heavily on remembrance rather than on calculation to return the ball properly.

This section and previous sections have concentrated on concepts in knowledge representation and learning. The next sections show applications of some of these ideas to the problems of processing natural language, general problem solving, and game playing.

Exercises

1. Specify as well as you can remember all the details of the outside of some particular building. Then go and observe the building and check the accuracy of your memory. How many of the details did you correctly remember? How many details were supplied

by your general frames for all buildings? Did you "remember" some details that were not actually there but were filled in by your general frame for buildings?

2. Explain the meaning of the sentence "Make a wish." Then describe in some detail a frame for the events of a typical American birthday party. Suppose events have occurred that bring to the speaker's and hearer's mind the birthday party frame, and then the sentence "Make a wish" is uttered. What new meaning does this sentence have in the context of the party frame? What knowledge will the hearer associate with this sentence that could not have been possible without the party frame? Who spoke the sentence? Who was it directed to? Why was it spoken? What other events are associated with this action? What other sentences might be uttered in this environment, and how would the frame aid in their understanding? Is it possible to understand these sentences without the associated frame?

An Application: Natural Language Processing

In order to show an application of the preceding ideas, we examine methods for processing English-language sentences in the presence of a knowledge base. We suppose that the machine is in a place called *room1* and that it has a full representation of the objects in the room as well as other objects in its world. Our examples continue to be built around the chair example, and we list three chairs explicitly in the knowledge base (figure 16.17).

We assume the only active frame contains the set of objects in *room1*, but we list one object outside the frame to remind ourselves that there are other objects. A node is included, called *set*, which stands for the set of all chairs. Objects *a1*, *a2*, and *a3* are members of that set.

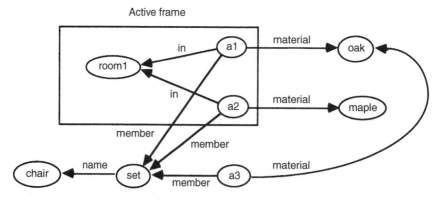

Figure 16.17

Rule syntax	Rule semantics
S => NP VP	M(S) = glue(M(NP),M(VP))
NP => PROPN	M(NP) = M(PROPN)
VP => V NP	M(VP) = glue(M(V),M(NP))
NP => ART NP1	M(NP) = M(NP1)
NP1 => ADJ NP1	M(NP1) = glue(M(ADJ),M(NP1))
NP1 => N	M(NP1) = M(N)

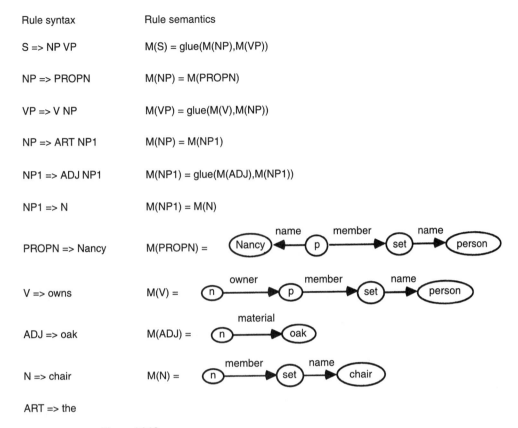

PROPN => Nancy   M(PROPN) =

V => owns   M(V) =

ADJ => oak   M(ADJ) =

N => chair   M(N) =

ART => the

Figure 16.18

We study methods for handling three kinds of sentences: (1) declarative sentences, (2) questions, and (3) imperative sentences. The function of a declarative sentence is to transmit information to the hearer, in this example, the machine. The declarative sentence enables the machine to add new nodes and transitions to its knowledge base. The purpose of the question is to solicit information from the knowledge base. The question specifies what information is to be retrieved, and the machine's task is to find it and generate a proper answer. An imperative sentence causes the machine to find the objects in the knowledge base that are referenced in the sentence and then to carry out the specified actions on those objects. This may also involve making some associated changes in the knowledge.

Considering declarative sentences first, assume someone speaks the utterance, "Nancy owns the oak chair," in the context of our knowledge base. Figure 16.18 gives a small

Generation	Rule syntax	Rule semantics
S	S => NP VP	M(S) = glue(M(NP),M(VP))
NP VP	NP => PROPN	M(NP) = M(PROPN)
PROPN VP	VP => V NP	M(VP) = glue(M(V),M(NP))
PROPN V NP	NP => ART NP1	M(NP) = M(NP1)
PROPN V ART NP1	NP1 => ADJ NP1	M(NP1) = glue(M(ADJ),M(NP1))
PROPN V ART ADJ NP1	NP1 => N	M(NP1) = M(N)
PROPN V ART ADJ N	PROPN => Nancy	M(PROPN) =
Nancy V ART ADJ N	V => owns	M(V) =
Nancy owns ART ADJ N	ART => the	
Nancy owns the ADJ N	ADJ => oak	M(ADJ) =
Nancy owns the oak N	N => chair	M(N) =
Nancy owns the oak chair		

Figure 16.19

grammar in the rules style of chapter 9 that is capable of generating this sentence. The `glue` function in the semantics rules is used to join separate graphs together.

The declarative sentence is processed as follows:

Declarative Sentence Processor
1. The grammar rules with their semantic components are used to create a semantic network representing the sentence meaning. This network is called $M(S)$, where S stands for the sentence.
2. The active frame for the sentence processing is selected. This is called the *focus*. It specifies the portion of the knowledge base that will be used in the processing.
3. A match is found between objects specified in $M(S)$ and objects in the knowledge base.
4. Additional nodes and linkages specified by the sentence are added to the knowledge base.

In our example, the sentence "Nancy owns the oak chair" results in the addition of several nodes and linkages to the knowledge base. These specify that a person named Nancy is associated with chair *a1* by the "owns" relationship. We now examine these steps in detail.

Consider step 1 first. Beginning with S, a generation of the target sentence must be found. Associated with each rule application is its semantic function (figure 16.19), which is used in creating the meaning representation $M(S)$. Following the methodology of chapter 9, the semantic portions of the rules in figure 16.19 can be applied (figure 16.20). $M(S)$ is a graph that represents the meaning of the original sentence. It states, with nodes and arcs, that Nancy is an entity p that is a member of a set of entities each with the name "person"; that is, Nancy is a person. Furthermore, this person is the owner of object n, which is a member of the set of chairs and is made of oak.

Step 2 of the processing procedure selects the active frame in the knowledge base, the set of objects in *room1*. Then step 3 attempts to match parts of the $M(S)$ graph with parts of the active portion of the knowledge base (figure 16.21). This match seems to imply that n in the sentence meaning corresponds to *a1* in the knowledge base. Notice that n does not match *a2* because the associated material is wrong. It does not match *a3* because *a3* is not in the active frame.

Once the correspondence has been found between some nodes in $M(S)$ and nodes in the knowledge base, the new information in $M(S)$ can be accounted for. Step 4 does this by gluing the nodes in $M(S)$ that are not found in the knowledge base to the appropriate nodes in the knowledge base (figure 16.22).

Summarizing, the knowledge base at the beginning of this section listed three chairs: *a1*, *a2*, and *a3*. In the context of *room1*, the sentence "Nancy owns the oak chair" was spoken. The meaning graph $M(S)$ was generated and matched against the active knowledge base nodes, those in *room1*. It was determined that *a1* is the object referenced by the noun phrase "the oak chair"; but the portion of $M(S)$ corresponding to "Nancy owns" was not found in the knowledge base, so it was added. The result of processing the sentence "Nancy owns the oak chair" is the addition of the nodes indicating that Nancy owns *a1*.

In a modern natural language processing system, a large variety of additional mechanisms are included that are not discussed here. Such systems must handle, for example, relative clauses, pronouns, ellipses, complex syntactic constructions, and a long list of other language behaviors. Furthermore, many contemporary systems use representations other than semantic nets. Thus, while the flavor of the kinds of processing needed to handle natural language utterances is conveyed by the description given here, the details of systems actually being built are often quite different.

Relatively few additions to these mechanisms are needed to enable the system to handle questions. First, we need more rules to handle question syntax (figure 16.23). Then an algorithm for question processing is needed:

Question Processor
1. Find the meaning graph $M(Q)$ for the question.
2. Select the active frame in the knowledge base, the focus.
3. Find a match between parts of $M(Q)$ and the active portion of the knowledge base.
4. The question mark in $M(Q)$ should match some node in the knowledge base. The system should return as an answer the contents of that matching node.

M(S) = glue(M(NP),M(VP))

    = glue(M(PROPN),M(VP))

    = glue(M(PROPN),glue(M(V),M(NP)))

    = glue(M(PROPN),glue(M(V),M(NP1)))

    = glue(M(PROPN),glue(M(V),glue(M(ADJ),M(NP1))))

    = glue(M(PROPN),glue(M(V),glue(M(ADJ),M(N))))

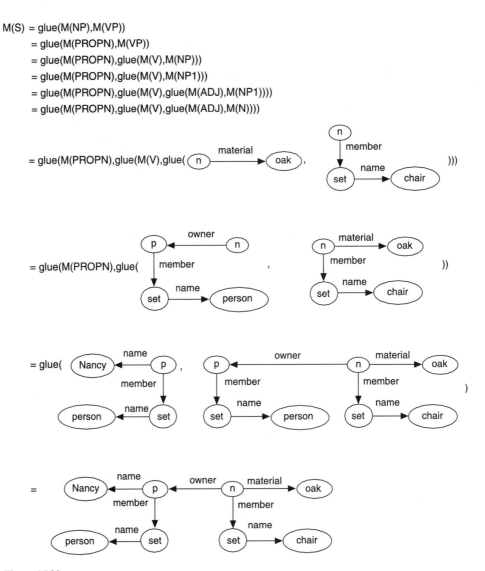

Figure 16.20

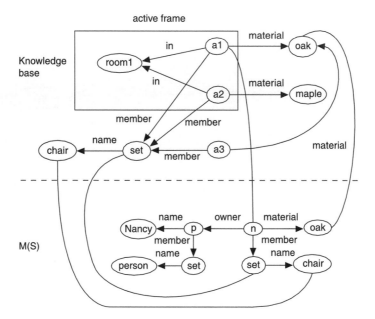

Figure 16.21

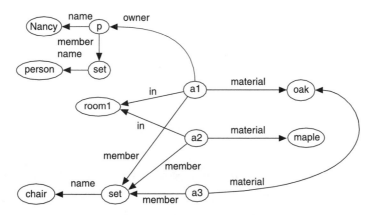

Figure 16.22

Rule syntax   Rule semantics

Q => WH VP   M(Q) = glue(M(WH),M(VP))

WH => who   M(WH) =

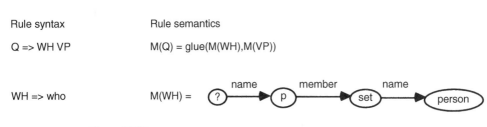

Figure 16.23

Rule syntax   Rule semantics

I => IMPV NP   M(I) = glue(M(IMPV),M(NP))

IMPV => pick up   M(IMPV) =

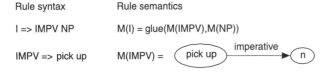

Figure 16.24

Using these added rules and the question-handling strategy, you should be able to carry out the processing of "Who owns the oak chair?" You should use the database that exists after the assertion "Nancy owns the oak chair." Most of the steps are similar to those for the previous example. But in the final step, the node with "?" will match the node with "Nancy," indicating that the answer to the question is "Nancy." This processing has some resemblances to the methodology of the database retrieval system in chapter 4.

Finally, we can examine a methodology for processing imperative sentences. Here the system is being asked to find certain objects in the active frame and do something to them. Some additional rules and an imperative sentence handler are needed (figure 16.24):

Imperative Sentence Processor
1. Find *M(I)*.
2. Select the active frame.
3. Match *M(I)* to the active frame.
4. Apply the action indicated by the imperative verb to the object referenced in the sentence.

You should be able to complete the details for an example sentence. Suppose the machine is a robot capable of navigating in the room and picking up objects. Then the command "Pick up the oak chair" will reference *a1*, and proper processing will cause the machine to "pick up *a1*."

This completes our discussion of mechanisms for processing natural language input to a computer. Many other topics in natural language processing must be omitted for lack of space. We have not, for example, considered the problem of how the system might generate natural language instead of recognizing it. We might like to have the system be able to respond to "Tell me everything you know about the oak chair." The system would then find the object *al* and create sentences from its associated arcs: "This chair is in *room1*. It is owned by Nancy...." We also have not examined mechanisms for handling indirect requests. Thus if a person is carrying *al* out of the room, the sentence "Nancy owns the oak chair" may not mean that the hearer should store this ownership fact in memory. It may really mean, "Put that chair back! It belongs to Nancy."

Exercises

1. Carry out the details for the processing of "Who owns the oak chair?"

2. Carry out the details for the processing of "Pick up the oak chair."

3. Design grammar rules to enable the processing of the following sentences:

   Nancy owns what?
   What is in this room?
   Don owns the maple chair.
   The oak chair is brown.

4. How would you build a mechanism to respond to the request "Tell me about the oak chair"?

Reasoning

Reasoning is the process of finding or building a linkage from one entity in memory to another. There must be an initial entity, a target entity, and a way of choosing paths from the initial entity toward the target. For example, if the system holds facts about family relationships, it might wish to determine the relationships between one member and a second. If it follows a parent link, a sibling link, and a child link, then it will *reason* that the second individual is a cousin of the first.

Rather than discovering existing links, reasoning often involves constructing links from the initial entity to the goal. If the being observes the state of the world, it may select some new goal state that it wishes to achieve and then reason a strategy for achieving it. Here it tries to discover a sequence of actions for going from the initial state to the goal. This sequence of actions is the desired linkage between the entities.

An illustration of this more complex type of reasoning comes from the monkey and bananas problem. Suppose the following are in a room: a monkey, a chair, and some

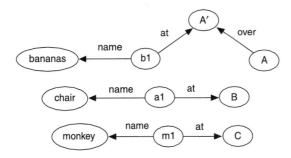

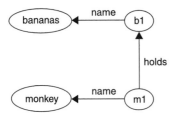

Figure 16.25

Figure 16.26

bananas hanging from the ceiling. If the goal is for the monkey to get the bananas, it is necessary to find a sequence of actions that begins at the current state and reaches the goal state. In terms of semantic nets, the initial state is represented as shown in figure 16.25.

Here A, B, and C represent positions on the floor below the bananas, the chair, and the monkey, respectively. A' represents a position well above A, which is reachable only by standing on the chair. The goal is represented by the subnet shown in figure 16.26. It is desired to achieve a state such that the monkey can hold the bananas (and presumably eat them).

The path from one state to another is a sequence of state-changing operations that converts the initial state to the target state. Five operations are available for this problem (table 16.1). The first operation, *go X*, takes the monkey from its current position to position X. We consider only three possible values for X: A, B, and C. But this operation cannot be applied if the monkey is already at X or if it is standing on the chair (at some Y'). As an illustration, suppose the monkey is at C and proposes to apply operation *go X* to go to A or B. Then we can construct the resulting states achieved in each case (figure 16.27).

The monkey and bananas problem thus requires that one find the correct sequence of actions from the initial state to any state having the condition that monkey holds bananas

Table 16.1

Operation	Meaning	Preconditions
go X	monkey goes to X	monkey is not at any Y' (not standing on chair), and monkey is not at X
push X	monkey pushes chair to X	monkey and chair are at Y, and Y is not equal to X
climbup	monkey climbs from current position X to X'	monkey and chair are at same location X
grasp	monkey grasps bananas	monkey and bananas are at X'
climbdown	monkey climbs from current position X' to X	monkey is at X'

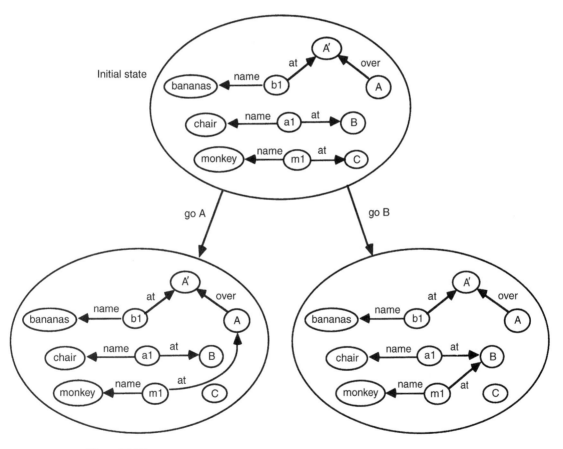

Figure 16.27

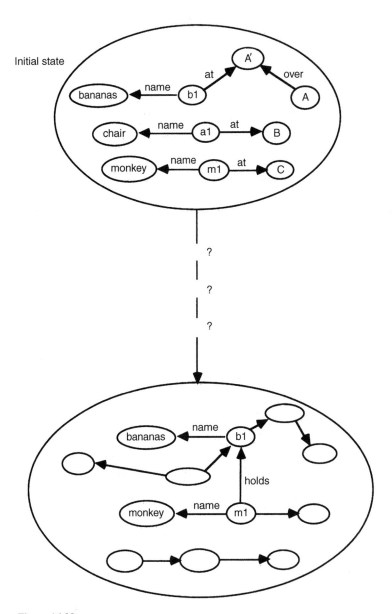

Figure 16.28

(figure 16.28). This is not necessarily an easy problem. If you consider the set of all possible action sequences, there are many things the monkey could do, and only a few of the possible sequences lead to success (figure 16.29). (The semantic net notation is abbreviated in the figure: M: and C: indicate the positions of monkey and chair, respectively.) If the monkey visualizes every possible sequence of actions, it will think for a long time before it finds a successful sequence.

Fortunately, human beings have a broad repertoire of remembered tool-using frames, so there is no need to do much reasoning in this problem. If the target is not instantly reachable, the human being has remembrances of successful quests on previous occasions. He or she will immediately search for tools to help achieve the goal. Is there a rock or a stick nearby? Or he or she might remember receiving help from a comrade if there is one available. In the current case, the chair is the only hope for help. Perhaps it could be thrown at the bananas or used as a stick. But if the human being had no experience using tools and had never before seen one used, he or she would probably have considerable difficulty reasoning a solution from first principles.

There are many methods for reasoning. You can start at the top of the tree of all possible actions and search down the branches for a goal. You can also attempt to reason backwards from the goal toward the initial state. You thus might argue that the goal cannot be achieved until a certain subgoal is reached, but that subgoal requires some previous achievement, and so forth. Or you might use a kind of distance measure as a guide toward the target: "If I can reach state S, I know I will be closer to success. I will do that first and then see what I should do next to reduce further the distance to the goal."

We examine a search algorithm that tries to find a path by searching downwards from an initial node toward the goal. It works by examining nodes farther and farther down the tree until the goal is found. Nodes that are about to be examined are called *active* nodes; those that have been examined and found not to be goals are called *closed* nodes.

Suppose the tree in figure 16.30a is about to be searched. The procedure begins by marking the top node active (figure 16.30b). Then this node (A) is examined to see if it is a goal. If it is, the search halts. Otherwise, its two successors are marked active, and it is marked closed (figure 16.30c). Then one of the active nodes is examined; assume the leftmost one is chosen in this case. If it is not a goal, its successors are marked active, and it is marked closed (figure 16.30d). This process continues either until a goal is found or until all the nodes of the tree have been examined.

Here is an algorithm for doing this search task. It searches a tree of possible actions until a goal is found. It uses a list, called *ACTIVE*, that stores the set of nodes that need to be examined next. It has a second list, called *CLOSED*, that stores the set of all nodes that have been examined:

(a)   Put initial node on *ACTIVE* list;
       The *CLOSED* list begins empty;
       While there are nodes on *ACTIVE* do

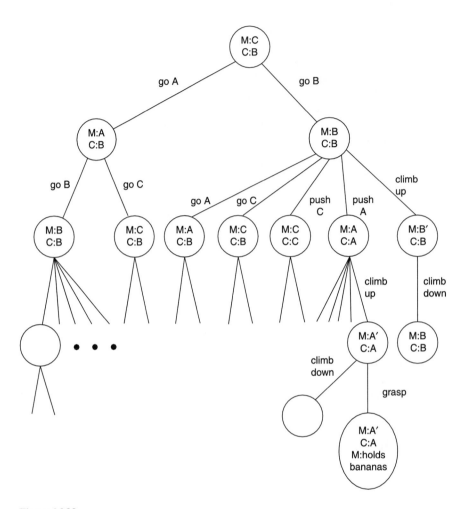

Figure 16.29

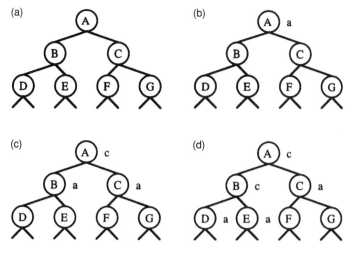

Figure 16.30

(b)   Remove a node from *ACTIVE* using criterion *C* and call it *N*;
(c)   If *N* is a goal, then
            Print "success";
            Print the list of actions on arcs from initial node to *N*;
            Halt;
(d)   Find all children nodes of *N* that are not on *ACTIVE* or *CLOSED* and add
                them to *ACTIVE*;
(e)   Add *N* to *CLOSED*;
        Print "failure";

Criterion *C* is the strategy for guiding the search. If no helpful strategy is available, *C* may choose the next node from *ACTIVE* randomly. But if there is a way to gauge the direction that the choice should take, *C* is the mechanism or subroutine that makes the decision.

The monkey and bananas problem can be solved with this search algorithm. We do not discuss here how *C* makes selections except to assume that it usually makes good decisions. Here is an outline of the computation:

(a) *ACTIVE* = {(M:C, C:B)}, *CLOSED* = { }.
(b) Criterion *C* selects *N* = (M:C, C:B). *ACTIVE* becomes empty.
(c) *N* is not a goal.
(d) Children of *N* are added to *ACTIVE*. *ACTIVE* = {(M:A, C:B), (M:B, C:B)}.
(e) *CLOSED* = {(M:C, C:B)}.

(b)   Criterion C selects $N = $ (M:A, C:B). *ACTIVE* is reduced to {(M:B, C:B)}.

(c) N is not a goal.

(d)   Children of $N = $ (M:A, C:B) are (M:B, C:B) and (M:C, C:B). But one is on *ACTIVE* and the other is on *CLOSED*.

(e)   *CLOSED* = {(M:C, C:B), (M:A, C:B)}.

(b)   Criterion C selects $N = $ (M:B, C:B). *ACTIVE* is reduced to { }.

(c) N is not a goal.

(d)   Children of N are added to *ACTIVE* (except for those already on *CLOSED*). *ACTIVE* = {(M:A, C:A), (M:C, C:C), (M:B', C:B)}.

(e)   *CLOSED* = {(M:C, C:B), (M:A, C:B), (M:B, C:B)}.

(b)   Criterion C selects $N = $ (M:A, C:A) from *ACTIVE*. *ACTIVE* = {(M:C, C:C), (M:B', C:B)}.

(c) N is not a goal.

(d)   Children of N not already on *ACTIVE* or *CLOSED* are (M:B, C:A), (M:C, C:A), (M:A', C:A). These are added to *ACTIVE*. *ACTIVE* = {(M:C, C:C), (M:B', C:B), (M:B, C:A), (M:C, C:A), (M:A', C:A)}.

(e)   *CLOSED* = {(M:C, C:B), (M:A, C:B), (M:B, C:B), (M:A, C:A)}.

(b)   Criterion C selects $N = $ (M:A', C:A). *ACTIVE* = {(M:C, C:C), (M:B', C:B), (M:B, C:A), (M:C, C:A)}.

(c) N is not a goal.

(d)   Only one child of N is not already on *ACTIVE* or *CLOSED*: (M:A', C:A, M holds bananas). *ACTIVE* = {(M:C, C:C), (M:B', C:B), (M:B, C:A), (M:C, C:A), (M:A', C:A, M holds bananas)}.

(e)   *CLOSED* = {(M:C, C:B), (M:A, C:B), (M:B, C:B), (M:A, C:A), (M:A', C:A)}.

(b)   Criterion C selects $N = $ (M:A', C:A, M holds bananas).

(c) N is a goal. Print "success". Print "go B, push A, climbup, grasp". Halt.

The selection criterion C greatly affects the operation of this algorithm. You can observe its effects by searching the same tree with different C (figure 16.31). Suppose C

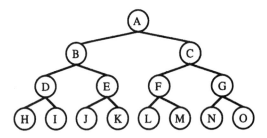

Figure 16.31

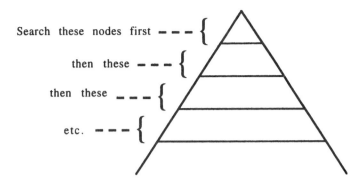

Search these nodes first ───{

then these ───{

then these ───{

etc. ───{

Figure 16.32

always chooses the node on *ACTIVE* that is shallowest (nearest *A*) and on the left when there are ties. Then the nodes will be selected in the order *A, B, C, D, E, F, G, H, I, J, K, L, M, N, O*. This is called a *breadth-first* search and results in a flat frontier of newly examined nodes that progresses downward on the tree (figure 16.32). A different strategy is to have *C* select the deepest node on *ACTIVE*, preferring those on the left if there is a tie. This results in an order that goes to the bottom of the tree very quickly and then moves across the tree: *A, B, D, H, I, E, J, K, C, F, L, M, G, N, O*. This is called a *depth-first* search, and it gives a sideways movement for the frontier of new nodes (figure 16.33). Both strategies are common in applications because they exhaustively cover the whole tree. If a goal is to be found, they will find it. The only restriction is that for a depth-first search, the tree must be finite.

But a third strategy is often preferred over both. It assumes the system has some knowledge about how to find the goal, and node selections are made in the direction of the earliest possible achievement of the goal. For example, in the monkey and bananas problem, if there were many positions for the monkey to select, it might prefer to move to those near the bananas. If it were frustrated in its attempts to reach its goal, it might look for objects that could be used and bring them also near the bananas. Reexamining the example tree in figure 16.31, if *L* is a goal node, criterion *C* might select *A, C, F,* and *L* in sequence and immediately solve the problem. If the information were weaker, the algorithm might choose *A, B, C, F, G, M, L*, solving the problem quickly but with a small number of superfluous excursions. The design of the *C* function attempts to build in information that will enable the search to go as directly as possible toward the goal (figure 16.34).

Many times, when the *C* function is constructed, the designer is not sure whether the information being programmed will help. If it does help, the system will quickly converge to its solution. If not, the system will wander somewhat before finding the goal. In the

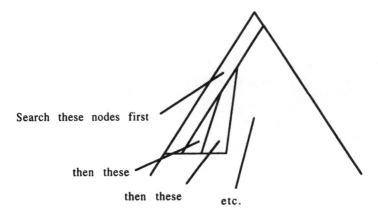

Search these nodes first

then these

then these   etc.

Figure 16.33

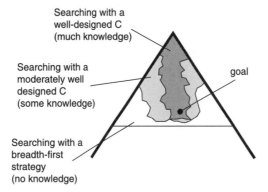

Searching with a
well-designed C
(much knowledge)

Searching with a
moderately well
designed C
(some knowledge)

goal

Searching with a
breadth-first
strategy
(no knowledge)

Figure 16.34

worst case, the system might never find the goal. When the *C* function is programmed with knowledge that may or may not help find the solution, it is called a *heuristic* function. Examples of heuristic functions are those that suggest that in a navigational situation going toward the goal is usually helpful, in a manipulative system trying a tool often helps if the task is not immediately solvable, in a building situation constructing the foundation is typically a good first step, and so forth. These heuristics often lead effectively toward solutions, but sometimes they fail, and a wider search is needed to solve a problem.

Exercise

1. Consider a grid of streets, with numbered streets going north and south (First Street, Second Street) and lettered avenues going east and west (Avenue A, Avenue B). Assume you are at the corner of Fifth Street and Avenue G and wish to go to the corner of Seventh Street and Avenue H. Further assume there are four operations E, W, N, S, meaning go east one block, go west one block, go north one block, and go south one block, respectively. Show the decision tree with the initial node at the top (the corner of Fifth Street and Avenue G). Show all possible decision sequences of length 3. Show the operation of the search algorithm of this section in the cases where

   (a) *C* chooses a breadth-first search.
   (b) *C* chooses a depth-first search limited to depth 3.
   (c) *C* selects the node closest to the direction of the goal.

Game Playing

We next consider reasoning processes when an adversary is trying to defeat our efforts. In a game-playing situation, one searches down the tree of alternative moves in a similar manner as in the previous section, but it is necessary to account for the opponent's actions. The nature of the search can be seen by examining the tree for the game of Nim with five squares (figure 16.35). This tree needs to be searched with the goal of finding a winning position. But the problem is made more difficult by the knowledge that the opponent will attempt to choose paths that avoid a win for the machine.

The tree has two kinds of nodes: those labeled M, where the machine is to move, and those labeled O, where the opponent is to move. Nodes are marked W if they are known, by one means or another, to lead to a win for the machine (figure 16.36a). If the machine is at a node where it sees a win for itself anywhere among the child nodes, it will move toward that child node. In fact, we can mark the parent node as a winning node because the machine is capable of making the move (figure 16.36b). But if the opponent is in the same situation, the move will usually be made away from the position W where the machine would win (figure 16.36c). For an O node, the position cannot be marked W as a win for the machine unless *all* the children nodes are marked W (figure 16.36d). That is, the opponent is not in a position where the machine is guaranteed to win unless all its choices are positions where the machine will win.

These observations lead to a method for analyzing a game. Begin at the bottom of the tree and mark with W all terminating positions where the machine will win. Then consider all nodes just above terminating positions. Nodes where the machine is to move that have at least one W-marked child are marked W. Nodes where the opponent is to move are marked W only if all their child nodes are marked W. This process is repeated for layer

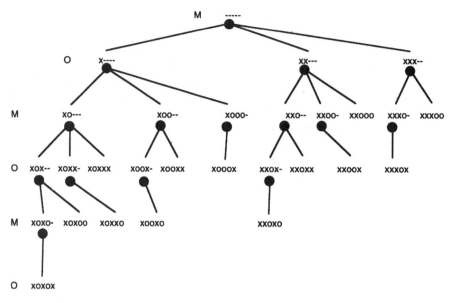

Figure 16.35

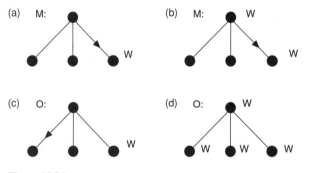

Figure 16.36

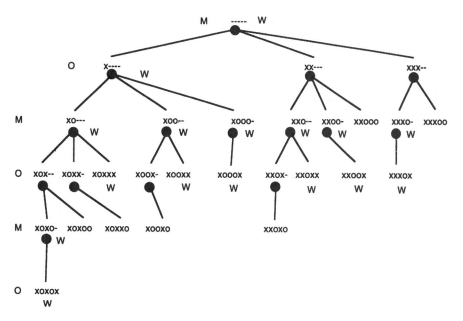

Figure 16.37

after layer of nodes up the tree until the top node is reached. If the top node is labeled W, the machine will be able to win the game, and its strategy is to move in the direction of the W at each decision point. If the top node is not labeled W, the machine will not win unless the opponent blunders.

Carrying out this procedure for the five-square Nim game tree, you can discover that the machine will win, and its first move should be a single X (figure 16.37). Regardless of what response the opponent gives, the machine will be able to win on the next move.

After some study, we realize that the Nim game of size 5 is not very interesting. The first player always wins, and the moves are obvious. As soon as we have decided who will play first, we know the winner even before the game begins.

We can then move on to larger Nim games, but they also can be solved in the same way. If we have a computer fast enough to build the tree and pass the W's to the top, those games will be solved as completely as 5-Nim. For those games also, it will be known before play begins who will win (although it will not always be the first player) assuming perfect play.

Generalizing even further, we can say that any game with the characteristics of Nim can be solved completely by building the tree and passing W's up from the bottom. But what are those characteristics? First, the game tree must be finite so that it can be completely searched. Second, it should be deterministic with no throw of the dice or other random process. It is not possible to analyze the tree so simply if the move outcomes are not known. Finally, the game must offer both players complete information about the state. If the opponent holds cards not known to the machine or if other state information is not available, the machine will not know where it is on the tree. *In summary, any deterministic, finite game of complete information can be solved by the procedure given here.* Before play begins, we can use the preceding procedure to determine the winner. (Some games allow for the possibility of a draw. This is easy to account for and is left as an exercise.)

Many common games fit the specification given. For example, chess and checkers are deterministic, finite games of complete information. If we had a machine fast enough to build their complete trees, we could determine who will be the winner of these games before the first move is played and how to make each move to achieve the guaranteed win. However, these game trees are so large that no one has been able to build them, so their solutions remain unknown. This is an example of a problem that cannot be solved because the execution time is too great. (These games might seem to be infinite because two players could simply alternate their pieces back and forth forever to achieve unending play. However, there is no need to analyze a game that loops back on its own previous states because such play results in neither a win nor a loss for the machine.)

The tree search methodology can still be used to play large games if a technique can be found to avoid following paths to the end of the game. The usual method is to have an *evaluation function* that can compute a number that estimates the value of a given game state. Then the decision procedure can attempt to reach states of high value. In the game of chess, for example, the procedure could add up the pieces on each side, giving greater weight to the stronger pieces such as the rooks and queens. The value of a position would be the weighted value of the machine's pieces minus the weighted value of the opponent's. The machine would then seek positions with greater piece advantages. Typical chess programs also allot points for positional advantage—such things as a castled king or a good pawn structure.

The search tree in this case would look more like the one in figure 16.38. The system has constructed move sequences to a constant depth—four in this case—instead of going to the game's end. The game state evaluation is given at each node reached along the bottom. Next you can compute a value for every other node of the tree. The value of the node at any machine move M is the maximum of the values of its children's values. This assumes it will always try to obtain the best position as scored by the evaluation function. The value of any node at an opponent's move is chosen to be the minimum of its children's values on the assumption that the opponent will harm the machine's position as much as possible. Using these two rules, the values can be passed up from the bottom to obtain a score at the initial node of the tree (figure 16.39). This is a process called *minimaxing*.

As before, the marker at the tree top shows the best achievable state reachable at the bottom of the tree. The nodes with this same value show the machine which move to make at each point to achieve this best value.

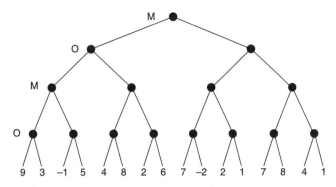

Figure 16.38

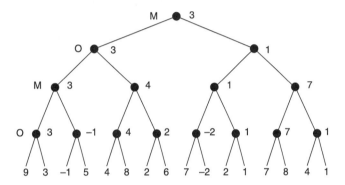

Figure 16.39

The tree search can be shortened by using *tree pruning* strategies that make it possible to omit parts of the calculation. The most powerful known technique is *alpha-beta* tree pruning, which uses partial results from the search to prove the uselessness of other portions of the search. An illustration of this is shown in figure 16.40, where the program has evaluated three board positions below the O nodes. The first O node has value 3, and the second O node has value 1 or less. Then the top node, which chooses the maximum of its children's values, will have value 3. Although one node (marked?) has not been evaluated, we know the value of the top node. So we can avoid the cost of generating that last node and evaluating its quality. This type of pruning can result in huge savings in realistic games.

Game-playing programs that use limited search with evaluation functions as described here completely depend on the accuracy of the evaluations for their quality of play. Precise accuracy will lead to excellent play, and moderate accuracy will lead to rambling play. Much recent research in game playing has been focused on improving board evaluations.

Figure 16.40

Exercises

1. At the beginning of this section, a method was described for backing W's up from the bottom of a game tree to determine whether the first player can force a win. Show how to modify this theory in the case where a game can have three outcomes: win W, loss L, or draw D.

2. Analyze the game of tic-tac-toe and determine whether it is a win, a draw, or a loss for the first player.

3. Assume that the minimax tree in figure 16.39 has the following values across its nodes at the bottom: $6, -10, 4, 7, 2, 19, -7, 4, 8, -2, -8, 3, 3, 11, 4, -4$. Do a minimax back up to determine the best value that the first player can achieve.

4. Repeat the minimax search but show that some of the values at the bottom of the tree are not needed to find the value at the tree root. The alpha-beta procedure enables a system to avoid computing some of these values.

*Game Playing: Historical Remarks

The history of game playing has gone through three rather interesting phases. The first came in the very early days of computing, during the 1940s. Many individuals at that time believed that computers would win as resoundingly at chess and checkers as they do at adding numbers. It was believed that computers could search and evaluate thousands of moves in these games whereas human beings looked at only a few dozen. With such a remarkable advantage, machines would clearly outsearch any human being and take over the world championships.

However, when the first programs began to work, their authors were shocked at their incredible incompetence. Even the most bumbling amateurs could beat them, and researchers scrambled to determine why. The answer lay in a combination of two factors, the first related to the nature of the game trees and the second related to the power of the human mind. Chess and checkers have average branching factors around 35 and 7,

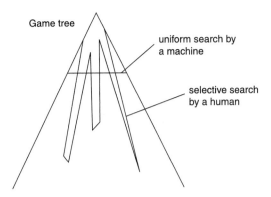

Game tree

uniform search by
a machine

selective search
by a human

Figure 16.41

respectively, so that the number of nodes at depth i is 35^i and 7^i. Even with substantial pruning, the programs could examine trees of depth no more than 3 or 4. Human beings, on the other hand, seem to have an instinct to look for the "right" moves, and they were examining lines of play far deeper than the machines (figure 16.41). The machines were wasting their computation time on evaluating huge numbers of positions that human beings ignore. The human beings were discovering the strong moves with their deeper, well-guided searches.

This led to the second phase of game-playing research—a period of about two decades when researchers attempted to capitalize on the early lessons learned. The common wisdom was that the combinatorics of the game tree made uniform search a ridiculous undertaking. Only selective search of the type that human beings do could succeed. Thus, a variety of heuristic tree search methods were developed, including ways to find "hot spots" on the board, play standard tricks on the opponent, and plan long sequences of offensive moves (figure 16.42). The resulting programs improved over the years and occasionally exhibited spectacular play. But against competent human players, they remained poor competitors. The programs were able to see many lines of play to a deep level, but they were not finding moves of the quality that human players can find. Human beings continued to have an instinct for the game that mystified the scholars.

About 1970 the community had another surprise. A group of researchers at Northwestern University rejected the accepted theory that selective search is the only reasonable approach to game playing. They brought a uniform search chess program to a national computer championship and defeated all other machines. And they continued to defeat all comers for some years after that. Their program also played better against human players than any previous program, achieving a good record against amateur but not master-level players. The analysis in this case was that for the best total game performance, conservative error-free tactical play is more important than occasional spectacular play. The faster

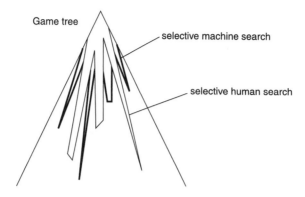

Figure 16.42

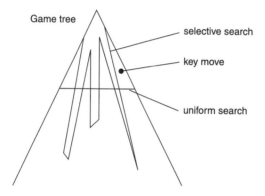

Figure 16.43

machines of the 1970s made search depths good enough, about 5 or 6 in chess, to achieve solid play, and within those depths the machines never made a mistake. If the opponent program ever missed even one key move during the game, the uniform search program would discover it and crush the opponent (figure 16.43).

The best chess programs have continued to use this same strategy. They examine millions of positions over a relatively uniform tree before each move and use a variety of methods to speed up search and improve evaluation. The most impressive of modern programs is Deep Blue of IBM Corporation, which defeated the chess world champion Gary Kasparov in 1997 in a widely reported and much discussed match. Deep Blue used a large parallel architecture (32 processors) for doing searches and examined approximately 200 million boards per second as it examined the game-playing tree. It deviated from purely uniform search in that it had a strategy for discovering critical lines of play, and it followed these to as many as 30 or 40 extra levels of depth. The program won two games, lost one, and drew three in the six-game match, thus achieving the greatest triumph for machines in the long history of human-machine chess. However, the program was later withdrawn from further play, leaving chess enthusiasts to wonder what would happen if a rematch were played or if other players were to challenge the program.

In checkers, much progress has been made but without the huge resources of IBM Corporation. In fact, a program called CHINOOK, written by Jonathan Schaeffer and several colleagues at the University of Alberta, played a very close match in August 1992 against Marion Tinsley, the reigning world champion in checkers. The program lost in a best-of-40-game match, winning 2 games, losing 4, and drawing 33. But in a follow-up match in August 1994 the program again played Tinsley, who withdrew for health reasons after drawing six games. This meant the program officially became the reigning world checkers champion. The program has since played and dominated other great checkers players. So it appears that machines have become better at this game than even the best human beings.

Computer game playing has provided a fascinating study in computer and human intelligence, giving insights on the nature of each. Computers continue to excel at doing simple activities millions of times, and their best performance is achieved when one is able to organize this activity to obtain useful results. Human beings continue to have astonishing, almost mystical abilities to recognize significant patterns and to use them effectively. In game playing, computers and people have achieved substantial levels of competence, but they use profoundly different methods.

Exercise

1. Assume the company you work for is proposing to build an automatic decision-making program for corporate decisions. It will receive information about economic conditions, the current corporate status, projected trends for the future, and so forth. The program is to search the tree of possible decisions for the coming years and decide which sequence of decisions will lead to the best long-term results for the firm. Is there any information that comes from the history of game playing that will affect your judgment on the current project?

Expert Systems

During the 1970s artificial intelligence researchers became interested in the reasoning processes of so-called experts. These people have worked at specialized jobs over many years and have developed apparently well-formulated routines for functioning effectively.

An expert begins a problem-solving task by looking for key factors and then selects some initial action, perhaps to gather some information. This may result in a decision and additional actions until the task is complete. At each stage, the expert seems to use an established formula for action: looking for certain facts, making appropriate conclusions, searching for other needed information, and so forth. The behaviors seem well formulated, predictable, rule based, and perhaps within the range of computer simulation.

Some examples of the kinds of experts that have been studied are doctors in the performance of routine diagnosis and prescription, repair people in the testing and diagnosis of equipment failures, geologists in the search for minerals, and agricultural experts in the task of giving advice on the care and nurture of crops. These people have been interviewed at length to discover their knowledge and how their decision-making processes work. They are led by the interviewer through innumerable typical scenarios and asked to explain in detail every thought that helps them reach their conclusions. Then the interviewer, sometimes called a *knowledge engineer*, attempts to construct a model of their expert knowledge and reasoning processes.

A common observation of many researchers in this field is that experts often express their knowledge in terms of if-then rules: "If I observe that X and Y are true, I know that condition Z is occurring. If condition Z occurs and A and B are true, I usually prescribe Q." In fact, the if-then form of knowledge representation is so common that it has become the basis for many computer programs that attempt to emulate expert behaviors. We now examine a portion of such a program to try to gain a feeling for this work.

Suppose the Internal Revenue Service of the U.S. government employs experts to decide when to audit income tax returns. Our task is to build a program to do this job automatically. We first interview an expert in this field and then attempt to code his or her knowledge in the form of if-then rules. Finally, we examine a processor of such rules, and observe its actions in mimicking the expert.

The following interview takes place:

Interviewer: When do you prescribe an audit?

Expert: I often look for something unusual either in the income declarations or in the deductions.

Interviewer: What kinds of peculiarities are likely to appear in income?

Expert: First, the income may be ridiculously low when you consider the person's profession. The other thing I look for is poorly documented income.

Interviewer: What do you expect in terms of income documentation?

Expert: The person should either have a W2 form or a systematic method for writing receipts for all funds received.

Interviewer: Let's go back to deductions. What do you look for there?

Expert: If I see the person claiming deductions that exceed 20 percent of their income, I become suspicious.

The interview may be complex and go on for many hours. However, we limit ourselves to analyzing only these few sentences.

Specifically, we wish to code the knowledge from the interview into a set of if-then rules. The first exchange between the interviewer and the expert yields this rule: "If the income is unusual or the deductions are unusual, then prescribe an audit." In abbreviated notation, this rule is written as

```
IncomeUnusual or DeductionsUnusual ==> Audit
```

The second interaction leads to another such rule, which can also be written in concise notation:

```
IncomeNotDoc or IncomeTooLow ==> IncomeUnusual
```

We assume that `IncomeTooLow` is easy to check. One notes the person's profession and then looks up in a table the minimum expected income for that profession. Let's assume that a function called `CheckData` exists to examine the income tax return and related tables. Then this rule is written as

```
IncomeNotDoc or CheckData(Income < MinIncome(Profession)) ==>
IncomeUnusual
```

The last part of the interview yields two more rules:

```
CheckData (No W2) and CheckData (No Receipts) ==> IncomeNotDoc
```

```
CheckData (Deduction > 0.2 * Income) ==> DeductionsUnusual
```

Next we need an algorithm to execute these rules like a kind of computer program. The algorithm resembles the preceding search algorithm in that it builds a tree beginning at the root node. The function of the computation, however, is not to find a goal at the bottom of the tree but rather to *achieve* a goal at the root of the tree.

The algorithm uses several ideas that need to be defined. We say a node is *achieved* if a rule leading to it is *satisfied* or if it is a `CheckData` call that yields "yes." The rules are of two kinds: those with left-side parts connected by and and those with left-side parts connected by or. If the left-side parts are connected by and, the rule is satisfied when all its left-side parts are achieved. If the left parts are connected by or, the rule is satisfied when at least one of its left parts is achieved. A node is said to be *fully explored* if it is a *CheckData* node and the check has been made or if there are no more rules with this node as a right side that have not been selected and added to the tree. The purpose of the search is to find enough facts to achieve the goal at the root. A list called *ACTIVE* is used as before to store the tree nodes that need to be examined:

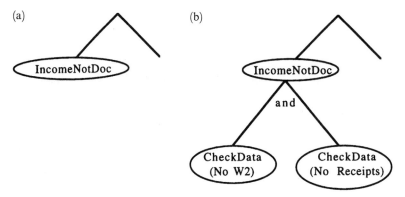

Figure 16.44

Put the goal node on the *ACTIVE* list (for the tax example, the goal node is *Audit*).
Begin building a tree by creating a root node that contains the goal.
While *ACTIVE* has nodes not fully explored do
  Select an unachieved node on *ACTIVE* that is not fully explored.
  If the node uses CheckData then
    Execute CheckData.
    If CheckData returns "yes" then mark this node as achieved and mark nodes above
      this node achieved if they are also achieved. If the root level goal is achieved then
      halt with success.
  Else
    Select a rule for achieving this node.
    Add it to the tree to give a new set of child nodes.
    Put the tokens on the left side of the rule on *ACTIVE*.
Halt with failure.

Each step of the tree-building process begins by selecting a node on the existing tree (from the *ACTIVE* list). For example, suppose *IncomeNotDoc* is chosen (figure 16.44a). Then a rule is selected that is capable of achieving that node:

```
CheckData (No W2) and CheckData(No Receipts) ==> IncomeNotDoc
```

The rule provides the basis for adding more nodes on the tree; each item on the left side of the rule becomes a new node (figure 16.44b). If the algorithm selects a node that is a *CheckData*, it does the data check rather than building more nodes on the tree.

This algorithm can now be illustrated by observing its actions on the income tax problem. Suppose the following simplified form has been submitted:

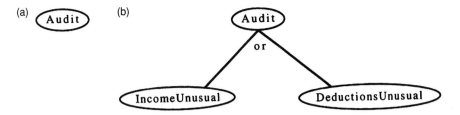

Figure 16.45

Name: John Smith
Profession: Professor
Income: $60,000 (no W2 or receipts)
Deductions: $10,000

The algorithm begins by placing *Audit* on the *ACTIVE* list:

```
ACTIVE = {Audit}
```

It initializes the tree by constructing the root node (figure 16.45a). It then enters the loop, selects a node on *ACTIVE*, and selects a rule for achieving this node:

```
IncomeUnusual or DeductionsUnusual => Audit
```

This rule is used as the basis for adding two child nodes to the tree (figure 16.45b). The *ACTIVE* list also receives these terms:

```
ACTIVE = {Audit, IncomeUnusual, DeductionsUnusual}
```

Repeating the loop, suppose the algorithm next chooses *IncomeUnusual* and finds a rule for achieving this node:

```
IncomeNotDoc or CheckData (Income < MinIncome (Profession)) ==>
                    IncomeUnusual
```

Then more nodes can be grown on the tree (figure 16.46) and the appropriate additions can be made to *ACTIVE*:

```
ACTIVE = {Audit, IncomeUnusual, DeductionsUnsual, IncomeNotDoc,
                 CheckData (Income < MinIncome (Profession))}
```

The third repetition of the loop results in the change shown in figure 16.47 if the *IncomeNotDoc* node is chosen. Additional repetitions will eventually result in the *CheckData* nodes at the tree bottom being selected. These each reference the income tax

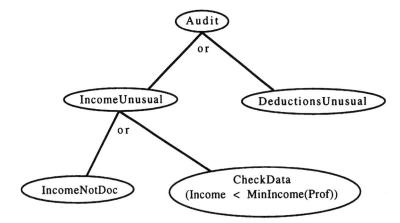

Figure 16.46

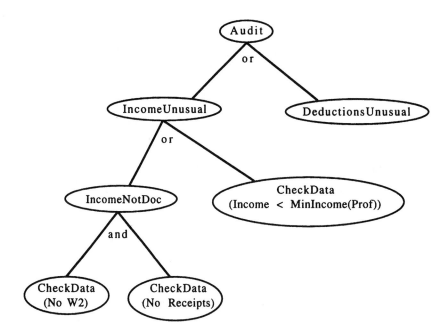

Figure 16.47

return and, for our example, return "yes." So they will be achieved. Their parent nodes will also be achieved; so also will each ancestor node to the top. In fact, the algorithm will halt with success; the *Audit* node has been achieved. The program recommends that this income tax return be audited.

The nodes on *ACTIVE* are not removed because there may be many rules that lead to any given conclusion. If one rule is not successful in achieving a node, perhaps some other one will be.

The tremendous value of such a program is clear. Instead of having a person perusing forms at whatever rate is comfortable, a machine can apply the same procedures to thousands of forms. If the knowledge engineer has correctly encoded the expert's methodology, the system will do the same job, and the effectiveness of the expert will be multiplied manyfold. Furthermore, the automatic system offers many other advantages. It can be studied for accuracy and improved possibly beyond the original expert's procedures, and it can be changed easily if the tax law changes. A new employee working in the area could also study the system and thereby learn the methodologies of the profession.

The type of system described here is called an *expert system*. Such systems usually have rules resembling those of our example and a similar execution algorithm. They often have complex node and rule selection heuristics of the kind described in the game-playing section. They also may enable the user to input facts with less than perfect confidence, and they may yield answers with less than perfect confidence, as a human being would do. Thus, a confidence factor with a value somewhere from 0 to 1 is associated with each fact, where 0 indicates no confidence, 1 indicates complete confidence, and fractions indicate intermediate levels. Finally, expert systems usually include an ability to print their own reasoning chain, the tree, so that the user can see what conclusion has been derived and what steps led to this conclusion.

Exercises

1. Show how the tax audit expert system would handle the following case:

Name:	John Smith
Profession:	Professor
Income:	$60,000 (W2 included)
Deductions:	$20,000

2. Show how the tax audit expert system would handle the following case:

Name:	John Smith
Profession:	Professor
Income:	$60,000 (W2 included)
Deductions:	$5,000

3. Design a set of rules that indicate the prerequisites for your favorite university-level course. The top-level goal should be *CourseRecommended*, and the rules should be designed to achieve this goal if a person meets the criteria that you specify. Demonstrate the use of these rules on typical cases by employing the algorithm for rule execution.

4. Interview an expert in some field, and design a set of rules to emulate the person's behavior when addressing some particular problem.

Perspective

We have studied how to store knowledge in a computer and how a computer can learn, reason, and understand. It would seem that the fundamental mechanisms are at hand and that it should be possible to build intelligent machines. If we want to build a machine to understand natural language, it would appear that we need only store sufficient knowledge and have some linguists compile a set of rules for the portion of the language of interest. If we wish to build an image-understanding system, apparently we need only build a knowledge base for that domain and construct the needed reasoning capabilities. If we want to build machines to invent jokes, compose music, analyze scientific data, interview job applicants, write stories, or create mathematics, we can hope that there will be knowledge bases large enough and reasoning systems powerful enough to do any of these jobs. Human beings are capable of all these behaviors, and we have reason to believe that they follow principled methodologies. Computers seem to have ample memory size and speed, so there does not appear to be a lack of computational power.

In fact, computer programs have been written that demonstrate almost every imaginable intelligent behavior. As an example, *Computers and Thought*, edited by Feigenbaum and Feldman, was published in 1963 (and republished in 1995) with 18 exciting papers describing such systems. Here is a brief description of some of the reported results:

"Some Studies in Machine Learning Using the Game of Checkers," A. L. Samuel. A checker-playing program is described that uses a tree search and board evaluation methodology similar to the one explained in this chapter. The board evaluation function has the form $f = C_1 X_1 + C_2 X_2 + \cdots + C_{16} X_{16}$, where the C_i are constants to be determined and the X_i are features of the board, such as the king advantage, number of pieces in the king row, or number of pieces in the board center squares. The C_i are numbers "learned" during actual play by slowly varying their values until best possible behaviors were achieved. The paper describes a game with "a former Connecticut checkers champion, and one of the nation's foremost players," which the program won by making "several star moves." (The quotations are from a journal that Samuel references.)

"Empirical Explorations of the Geometry Theorem Proving Machine," H. Gelernter, J. R. Hansen, and D. W. Loveland. A program is described for solving plane geometry problems typical of those taught at the high school level. It uses a diagram of the geometry problem to heuristically guide the search for long proofs. The use of the diagram reduces the number of child nodes below a typical node from about 1,000 to about 5 and thus greatly increases the program efficiency. This program found some proofs that would be difficult for high school students, some proofs having as many as 20 or more sequential steps.

"BASEBALL: An Automatic Question Answerer," B. F. Green, Jr., A. K. Wolf, C. Chomsky, and K. Laughery. A program is described that answers questions about baseball such as Who did the Red Sox lose to on July 5? or Did every team play at least once in each park in each month? The program stores data on baseball games in a tree structure, giving for each month a list of all places, for each place a list of all days, and for each day a list of all games. Answers are obtained by translating the question into a standardized form and then matching it to the tree of data.

"GPS, a Program That Simulates Human Thought," A. Newell and H. A. Simon. The General Problem Solver, GPS, is a general search program for finding goals using sequences of operators. It utilizes heuristic information to help choose the correct operator at each point, and it solves a variety of classical problems. The GPS system was studied both as an exercise in artificial intelligence and as a possible model for human intelligence.

With such impressive results in the early 1960s, one surely would expect profound machine intelligence within a decade or two of that time. In fact, in 1958, Herbert Simon and Allen Newell had already predicted that within ten years computer programs (1) would be able to win the world chess championship, (2) would find and prove some important new mathematical theorem, (3) would write music possessing aesthetic value, and (4) would be the models for most studies in psychology. The power of the new computers was clear, and the early results were encouraging. Many wise people were predicting a major revolution in the capabilities of machines. (Simon later received a Nobel Prize for his work in economics.)

Unfortunately, the original optimism proved unfounded. None of the early projects matured to astound the world. Forty years after the original period of great optimism, artificial intelligence remains a science in its infancy. All the systems described are examples of interesting laboratory studies, and many more of them have been undertaken in recent years. But researchers have had great difficulties expanding initial narrowly defined projects, which in principle demonstrate exciting behaviors, into large, practical systems evincing what people are willing to call intelligence.

The problem of building intelligent systems turned out to be much more difficult than the early researchers realized. People would begin projects, achieve a fraction of their goals in six months, and then predict that they could achieve all of their goals in a few years. They never dreamed that barely more than their original results would be achieved in their whole lifetimes. Again and again projects were begun in many fields of artificial intelligence with great early optimism but were never able to achieve more than limited success on small problems.

Why has the field of artificial intelligence had so much difficulty producing intelligent machines? We do not know, but we are finally aware that real intelligence involves far more complexity than was ever predicted. It involves vast amounts of knowledge that we do not yet know how to acquire, organize, or use. It involves complex reasoning of a kind that we cannot yet comprehend. It probably involves other mechanisms that we do not even realize are needed. We simply do not understand intelligence.

There have been advances, however, and one way to observe them is to trace progress on the Simon-Newell predictions. Chess turned out to be a very difficult challenge for computers, and certainly the expectation that they would defeat all humans by 1968 was optimistic. But several decades later, one machine has on one occasion defeated the best-known human player of the day. This is progress. Many critics refuse to accept this as the final victory of machines over humans in chess because there has not been an extended period of repeated victories of machines over humans. But it is progress, and it is hard to argue that any final victory that needs to be achieved is not within reach.

Concerning the other Simon-Newell predictions, a machine has found a proof of a theorem that had eluded mathematicians for decades. It involves what is known as the Robbins problem, and it was done in 1998 (McCune, 1998). A program has been created that simulates the composition style of some great composers, and on one occasion a music audience was fooled into believing that a computer-synthesized piece was written by J. S. Bach (Cope, 1996). A number of programs have been created to model psychological theories as exemplified by the neural net literature (chapter 14).

At the risk of oversimplifying a rather complex picture, we will include here a few comments that give a feeling for the state of the art in some of the well-known subfields of artificial intelligence.

Automatic Programming

This research area attempts to build systems that will automatically write programs. It assumes the user will give examples of the desired program behavior or will specify with a formal or natural language what the desired program is to do. The system will then write a program to satisfy the user's requirements. Automatic programming systems have been built that reliably create some small LISP programs, three or four lines long, from examples of the target behavior. Systems have also been created that enable a user to specify a program in an interactive session with a formal language, which then will create the target program. A few rather impressive programs have been developed using this approach. However, for serious general-purpose programming, such systems are usually not as convenient as traditional programming languages.

Expert Systems

Hundreds of these systems have been programmed for industrial and governmental applications. They usually have from a few hundred to a few thousand rules, and if they are properly designed, they can be depended upon to carry out their narrowly defined tasks with reliability.

Game Playing

Chess and checkers programs have been developed to the point described; they challenge or defeat the best human players. Many other games have been programmed with varying levels of success.

Image Understanding

Computer systems have been built that are aimed at specific domains, such as aerial photographs or pictures of human faces, and that correctly find and label the significant features a high percentage of the time.

Mathematical Theory Formation

At least one system (built by Douglas Lenat) can derive new mathematical concepts from more primitive ones. This system was demonstrated in a series of computations where it derived the rudiments of number theory from concepts of set theory. However, it is not clear that the approach is applicable to broader classes of problems.

Natural Language Understanding

A number of systems have been built that are aimed at specific domains, such as personnel databases or equipment repair tasks, and that deliver proper responses a high percentage of the time. Such systems usually have limited vocabularies and limited syntactic capabilities.

Natural Language Translation

If a system is constructed to understand natural language in a limited domain, it is within the state of the art to convert the system into a translator to some other natural language. Therefore, we can say that natural language translation can be achieved with high accuracy in limited domains where small vocabulary and narrow syntactic variety are needed. In an application where large vocabulary and wide syntactic variety are needed, completely automatic natural language translation is far beyond the state of the art. However, computers are still useful in these translation tasks by parsing input sentences, by displaying word alternatives in the object language that can be selected by a human translator, and by providing convenient editing.

Learning

The performance of a few systems has been improved by the use of learning mechanisms that optimize parameters, as described in the sections of chapter 14 on connectionist networks. The Arthur Samuel checkers program used this scheme. Also, concept-learning mechanisms have been applied to analyzing complex scientific data with the result, in a few cases, that trends or relationships in the data were automatically discovered.

Speech Recognition

Many systems have been built that enable a user to speak rather than type inputs to a machine. Vocabularies on these systems tend to be limited to possibly a few hundred words, although some systems with vocabulary capabilities up to several tens of thousands of words are becoming operative and moderately reliable. Currently these systems need to be specialized to a particular application in order to give robust behavior. This usually means gathering a large corpus of utterances from the application and building a probabilistic model of the actual word sequences that people tend to use. However, these systems can provide reliable performance in many current-day environments and can be expected to appear in many products in the next few years.

In summary, researchers have found that computers can be programmed to exhibit to a small extent almost any intelligent behavior—perception, learning, problem solving, language processing, and others. Numerous projects have demonstrated these kinds of behaviors. But to achieve any of these phenomena to a large extent or to integrate them to obtain moderately intelligent behavior is very difficult and in most cases far beyond the state of the art. The best results have occurred in the environment of narrow domains where only limited kinds of behaviors are needed and usually where there has been tolerance for error.

Some researchers believe that most artificial intelligence subfields face the same central problem of complex representation and reasoning and that if the problem could be solved in one field, it would be solved for all fields. For example, if one could solve properly the natural language problem to the point where a machine could process language as well as human beings do, then the methodology that makes this possible would be the key to solving many diverse problems, such as those related to vision, problem solving, theorem proving, automatic programming, and many others. Various researchers have called this hypothesis the *Thesis of AI Completeness*, and it is likely to remain a controversial idea for years to come.

In the commercial world, artificial intelligence has had some important successes. In the field of expert systems, large numbers of useful programs have been developed, and they are being operated regularly in many enterprises. In natural language processing, some commercial systems have become available, and thousands of people are now able to do some standard tasks, such as accessing databases with typed natural language input. Spoken language systems are beginning to enter the market and their success can be expected to increase. Game-playing programs have become commercially profitable and are widely available. Military strategists are using many programs for simulation and decision making that heavily employ artificial intelligence techniques. Perhaps a lesser noticed but extremely important product of artificial intelligence research has been the series of computer languages that have been created to do the research. These include LISP, which is widely used as a symbolic programming language; Prolog, which is becoming popular and has even served as a prototype language for the Japanese fifth-generation computer series; and a long list of languages for programming expert systems.

Finally, we have noticed that there are aspects of human intelligence that seem to be completely out of reach for the foreseeable future. First, there is the ability to understand the human condition—an ability that we propose is exclusive to human beings. Second, there is the astounding pattern recognition ability that people exhibit in game playing, for example. People are able to see in a single position things not visible to a machine in a search of a millions of positions. Last, there is the huge knowledge base that humans have and the incredible flexibility with which it is used in achieving intelligent behavior.

Exercises

1. Suppose you are asked to prepare the specifications for a robot vision and audio output system. The robot is to roam an area too dangerous for humans (because of radiation or other hazards) and report verbally its observations. The vision and audio output system will have three main subsystems: an image processor to find the important features in the scene, a problem-solving system to decide which features are significant enough to describe, and a language planning and output system to enunciate the needed utterances. Prepare specifications for each of the three subsystems that you believe are within the current state of the art.

2. Present arguments for and against the Thesis of AI Completeness.

Summary

Artificial intelligence is a field of study where researchers attempt to build or program machines with capabilities more complex than have been possible traditionally. These include the abilities to perceive and understand incoming data, to learn, to process natural language, and to reason. The fundamental paradigm for such studies includes the concepts of knowledge and reasoning, and these were examined in this chapter.

The knowledge of an object is the set of all information required to deal with it in related processing. Knowledge can be stored in various forms and is used in understanding perception or in reasoning processes. Knowledge can be input to a machine by being formatted and entered directly, or it can be acquired by the machine through learning.

Reasoning is the process of finding a sequence of linkages that will lead from one object in memory to another. Often, the goal of reasoning is to find a way to change the current state of the world into some desired state. Reasoning is done by selectively searching the tree of possible action sequences until the desired one is found. Many artificial intelligence systems have been built over the years using these ideas, and some of them were described here.

This section concludes this book, which is a study of what computers are, what they can do, and what they cannot do. The early chapters introduced programming and primarily studied what computers can do. A variety of example problems and their solutions were given, and the culmination was the Church-Markov-Turing Thesis, that any step-by-step process that we can describe precisely can be programmed on a machine.

The second part of the book examined what computers are, so that they might be understood in a deeper way. Specifically, they are simply boxes capable of repeatedly executing the fetch-execute cycle at very high speed. Their usefulness comes primarily from the fact that convenient languages can be translated into a form that is amenable to the fetch-execute style of computation. They are made up of millions of tiny switches etched into silicon crystals and organized to store information and compute.

The last part of the book examined advanced topics in computer science. These included the study of execution time and the division of computations into tractable and intractable classes. Then parallel computing was introduced as a means for reducing execution time, and some example problems were studied within this paradigm. One fascinating type of parallel machine is the connectionist network, which spreads information and computation across an array of tiny processors and programs itself through learning. Next we studied noncomputability and attempted to gain intuition for a class of functions that, as far as we know, cannot be programmed. Finally, we studied artificial intelligence and the attempts of researchers to build machines that can know, understand, learn, and reason in ways that are reminiscent of human thinking.

Appendix: The IntField and DoubleField Classes

The following Java code defines the two special classes used throughout this book, IntField and DoubleField. These classes enable the reader to read and write int and double numbers easily in applets without having to deal with additional Java syntax. You can put these into a directory labeled awb in your public_html directory and then use the import awb.* command at the top of each program. You can also just include this code in each program file and not reference an external directory.

This code is also available on the Web with other software and is reachable from Biermann's Web page.

```
/*Eric Jewart
11/13/97
*/
// mod 7/22/99 dr
package awb;
import java.awt.*;

public class IntField extends java.awt.Panel
{
    private TextField myField;
    private Label myLabel;

    public IntField()
    {
        myField = new TextField();
        setLayout(new BorderLayout());
        add("Center", myField);
    }
```

```
public IntField(int cols)
{
    myField = new TextField(cols);
    setLayout(new BorderLayout());
    add("Center", myField);
}

public IntField(int num, int cols)
{
    myField = new TextField("" + num, cols);
    setLayout(new BorderLayout());
    add("Center", myField);
}

public int getInt()
{
    try
    {
        int num = Integer.parseInt(myField.getText());
        return num;
    }
    catch (NumberFormatException ex)
    {
        return 0;
    }
}

public void setInt(int num)
{
    myField.setText(Integer.toString(num));
}

public void setInt()              // dr
{                                 // dr
    myField.setText("");          // dr
}                                 // dr

public void addLabel(String lab)
{
    if (myLabel == null)
    {
```

```
            myLabel = new Label(lab);
            remove(myField);
            add("West", myLabel);
            add("Center", myField);
        }
        else myLabel.setText(lab);
    }

    public void setLabel(String lab)
    {
        addLabel(lab);
    }

    public void setEditable(boolean b)
    {
        myField.setEditable(b);
    }

    public int getColumns()
    {
        return myField.getColumns();
    }

    public boolean handleEvent(Event e)
    {
        if ((e.id == Event.KEY_PRESS) && (e.target == myField))
        {
            int key = e.key;
            // numbers are always okay
            if ((key > 47) && (key < 58)) return myField.keyDown
                    (e,key);

            // minus sign okay if it's the first character
            if ((key == 45) && ((myField.getText().equals("")) ||
                    myField.getText().equals
                    (myField.getSelectedText()))))) return
                    myField.keyDown(e,key);

            // backspace and delete
            if ((key == 8) || (key == 127)) return myField.keyDown
                    (e,key);
```

```
                    // arrow keys, home, end, pgup, pgdown okay
                    if ((key > 999) && (key < 1008)) return myField.keyDown
                            (e,key);

                    // Enter--pass Action event up hierarchy
                    if (key == 10)
                    {
                        e.id = Event.ACTION_EVENT;
                        e.target = this;
                        return false;
                    }

                    // no other keys should do anything, so ignore them all
                    return true;
            }

            return super.handleEvent(e);
        }
}

/* Eric Jewart
11/13/97
*/

package awb;
import java.awt.*;

public class DoubleField extends java.awt.Panel
{
    private TextField myField;
    private Label myLabel;

    public DoubleField()
    {
        myField = new TextField();
        setLayout(new BorderLayout());
        add("Center", myField);
    }

    public DoubleField(int cols)
    {
```

```
    myField = new TextField(cols);
    setLayout(new BorderLayout());
    add("Center", myField);
}

public DoubleField(double num, int cols)
{
    myField = new TextField(Double.toString(num), cols);
    setLayout(new BorderLayout());
    add("Center", myField);
}

public double getDouble()
{
    try
    {
        double num = Double.valueOf(myField.getText()).
                doubleValue();
        return num;
    }
    catch (NumberFormatException ex)
    {
        return 0;
    }
}

public void setDouble(double num)
{
    myField.setText(Double.toString(num));
}

public void addLabel(String lab)
{
    if (myLabel == null)
    {
        myLabel = new Label(lab);
        remove(myField);
        add("West", myLabel);
        add("Center", myField);
```

```
        }
        else myLabel.setText(lab);
    }

    public void setLabel(String lab)
    {
        addLabel(lab);
    }

    public void setEditable(boolean b)
    {
        myField.setEditable(b);
    }

    public int getColumns()
    {
        return myField.getColumns();
    }

    public boolean keyDown(Event e, int key)
    {
        // System.out.println("typed: " + key);

        // numbers are always okay
        if ((key > 47) && (key < 58)) return super.keyDown(e,key);

        // one period is okay
        if ((key == 46) && (myField.getText().indexOf(".") < 0))
                return super.keyDown(e,key);

        // minus sign okay if it's the first character
        if ((key == 45) && ((myField.getText().equals("")) ||
                (myField.getText().equals(myField.
                getSelectedText()))))) return
                super.keyDown(e,key);

        // backspace and delete
        if ((key == 8) || (key == 127)) return super.keyDown(e,key);

        // arrow keys, home, end, pgup, pgdown okay
        if ((key > 999) && (key < 1008)) return super.keyDown(e,key);
```

```
        // enter key, for action events
        if (key == 10) return super.keyDown(e,key);

        // no other keys should do anything, so ignore them all
        return true;
    }
}
```

Readings

Astrachan, O. *A Computer Science Tapestry: Exploring Programming and Computer Science with C++*. 2d ed. New York: McGraw-Hill, 2000.

Atkinson, K. *Elementary Numerical Analysis*. 2d ed. New York: Wiley, 1992.

Boehm, B. *Software Engineering Economics*. Upper Saddle River, N.J.: Prentice Hall, 1981.

Brooks, F. P., Jr. *The Mythical Man-Month: Essays on Software Engineering*. Anniversary ed. Reading, Mass.: Addison-Wesley, 1995.

Cheney, W., and D. Kincaid. *Numerical Mathematics and Computing*. 3d ed. Pacific Grove, Calif.: Brooks/Cole, 1994.

Comer, D. E. *Internetworking with TCP/IP. Vol. 1: Principles, Protocols, and Architecture*. Upper Saddle River, N.J.: Prentice Hall, 1988.

Cope, D. *Experiments in Musical Intelligence*. The Computer Music and Digital Audio Series, No. 12. Madison, Wisc. A-R Editions, 1996.

Cormen, T. H., C. E. Leiserson, and R. L. Rivest. *Introduction to Algorithms*. Cambridge, Mass.: MIT Press, 1990.

Davie, B. S., L. L. Peterson, and D. Clark. *Computer Networks: A Systems Approach*. 2d ed. Morgan Kaufmann, 1999.

Davis, R. and D. B. Lenat. *Knowledge-based Systems in Artificial Intelligence*. New York: McGraw-Hill, 1982.

Decker, R., and S. Hirshfield. *Programming Java: An Introduction to Programming Using Java*. Boston: PWS, 1998.

Devaney, R. L. *Chaos, Fractals and Dynamics*. Reading, Mass.: Addison-Wesley, 1995.

Feigenbaum, E. A., and J. Feldman, eds. *Computers and Thought*. Cambridge, Mass.: AAAI/MIT Press, 1995.

Garey, M. R., and D. S. Johnson. *Computers and Intractability: A Guide to NP-Completeness*. San Francisco: W. H. Freeman, 1979.

Golub, G. H., and J. M. Ortega. *Scientific Computing: An Introduction with Parallel Computing*. San Diego: Academic Press, 1993.

Harel, D. *Algorithmics: The Spirit of Computing*. 2d ed. Reading, Mass.: Addison-Wesley, 1992.

Hopfield, J. J. "Neural Networks and Physical Systems with Emergent Collective Computational Capabilities." *Proceedings of the National Academy of Sciences* (USA) 79 (1982): 2554–2558.

Irvine, K. R. *Assembly Language for Intel-Based Computers*. 3d ed. Upper Saddle River, N.J.: Prentice Hall, 1999.

Kahn, D. *The Codebreakers: The Comprehensive History of Secret Communication from Ancient Times to the Internet*. New York: Scribner, 1996.

Luger, G. F., and W. A. Stubblefield. *Artificial Intelligence*. 3d ed. Reading, Mass.: Addison-Wesley Longman, 1998.

Marciniak, J., ed. *Encyclopedia of Software Engineering*. 2d ed. New York: Wiley, 2000.

McCune, W. "Solution of the Robbins Problem." *Journal of Automated Reasoning* 19 (1967): 263–276.

Miller, D. L., and J. F. Pekny. "Exact Solution of Large Asymmetric Traveling Salesman Problems." *Science* 251 (February 1991).

Nutt, G. *Operating Systems: A Modern Perspective*. 2d ed. Reading, Mass.: Addison-Wesley, 1997.

Peterson, L. L., and B. S. Davie. *Computer Networks: A Systems Approach*. 2d ed. San Francisco: Morgan Kaufmann, 1999.

Russell, S. J., and P. Norvig. *Artificial Intelligence: A Modern Approach*. Upper Saddle River, N.J.: Prentice Hall, 1995.

Schneier, B. *Applied Cryptography: Protocols, Algorithms, and Source Code in C*. 2d ed. New York Wiley, 1995.

Simon, H. A., and A. Newell. "Heuristic Problem Solving: The Next Advance in Operations Research." *Operations Research* (January–February 1958).

Singh, S. *The Code Book: The Evolution of Secrecy from Mary, Queen of Scots, to Quantum Cryptography*. New York: Doubleday, 1999.

Smith, R. W., and D. R. Hipp. *Spoken Natural Language Dialog Systems: A Practical Approach*. Oxford, U.K.: Oxford University Press, 1994.

Snyder, L., A. V. Aho, M. Linn, A. Packer, A. Tucker, J. Ullman, and A. Van Dam. *Being Fluent with Information Technology*. Washington: National Academy Press, 1999.

Stoll, C. *The Cuckoo's Egg: Tracking a Spy through the Maze of Computer Espionage*. New York: Pocket Books, 1995.

Tanenbaum, A. S. *Computer Networks*. 3d ed. Upper Saddle River, N.J.: Prentice Hall, 1996.

———. *Modern Operating Systems*. Upper Saddle River, N.J.: Prentice Hall, 1993.

Watkins, G. *Interception*. New York: Pinnacle Books, 1998.

Index